American Women and Flight since 1940

T-38A NO-30
SERIAL NO.60-551 A

SUITABLE FOR USE OF AROMATIC FUEL
SERVICE THIS AIRCRAFT WITH GRADE
JP-4 FUEL IF NOT AVAILABLE. T.O NO
42B1-1-14 WILL BE CONSULTED FOR
EMERGENCY ACTION

DANGER
EJECTION
SEAT
DANGER
DANGER

WARNING
THIS AIRPLANE CONTAINS A
CANOPY REMOVER CONTAINING
AN EXPLOSIVE CHARGE, SEE APPLICABLE
-2 AIRCRAFT T.O. FOR COMPLETE
INSTRUCTIONS

T-38

STEP

American Women and Flight since 1940

Deborah G. Douglas

*with the assistance of
Amy E. Foster, Alan D. Meyer,
and Lucy B. Young*

THE UNIVERSITY PRESS OF KENTUCKY

Publication of this volume was made possible in part
by a grant from the National Endowment for the Humanities.

Scholarly publisher for the Commonwealth,
serving Bellarmine University, Berea College, Centre
College of Kentucky, Eastern Kentucky University,
The Filson Historical Society, Georgetown College,
Kentucky Historical Society, Kentucky State University,
Morehead State University, Murray State University,
Northern Kentucky University, Transylvania University,
University of Kentucky, University of Louisville,
and Western Kentucky University.
All rights reserved.

Editorial and Sales Offices: The University Press of Kentucky
663 South Limestone Street, Lexington, Kentucky 40508-4008
http://www.kentuckypress.com

08 07 06 05 04   5 4 3 2 1

Frontispiece: Jacqueline Cochran. *Courtesy of Ann Wood Kelly.*

Library of Congress Cataloging-in-Publication Data

Douglas, Deborah G.
    American women and flight since 1940 / Deborah G. Douglas, with the
assistance of Amy E. Foster, Alan D. Meyer, and Lucy B. Young.
        p.   cm.
    Includes bibliographical references and index.
    ISBN 0-8131-9073-8 (Paperback : alk. paper)
    1. Women air pilots—United States—Biography. 2. Air pilots—
United States—Biography. I. Foster, Amy E. II. Title.
    TL539.D677 2003
    629.13'092'273—dc21   2003007976

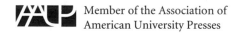 Member of the Association of
American University Presses

To my sisters, Laura and Heather

Contents

Acknowledgments

This book, now revised and updated, has provided some of the most satisfying experiences of my career. Resounding thanks to hundreds of women who have contributed to this adventure over the past two decades. You remain an inspiration. Among this group, I would like to express special appreciation to Pat Pateman, Marty Stanton, Ann Wood Kelly, Rosemary Mariner, Trish Beckman, Kelly Hamilton, Cindy Wilson, Patty Wagstaff, Susan House, Ann McGee, Peggy Carnahan, Ann Carl, Dora Strother, Dawn Seymour, Vi Cowden, Jean Ross Howard-Phelan, Diana Davis, Lynn Rippelmeyer, and Jeanne Holm.

Several organizations have been supportive over the years, and it is with pleasure that I acknowledge this help. Thanks to the Aerospace Industries Association and David Napier; Association of Flight Attendants, AFL-CIO and Carmen Mays; Defense Advisory Committee on Women in the Services; Federal Aviation Administration; International Women's Air and Space Museum; ISA+21 and Lori Griffith; the Minerva Center and Linda Grant DePauw; Ninety-Nines and its bibliographer extraordinaire, the late Dorothy Niekamp; Raytheon Aircraft and Tim Travis; Whirly-Girls, International Women Helicopter Pilots; Women Airforce Service Pilots; Women in Aviation International and Mary Ann and Gary Eiff; Women in Aviation Resource Center and Henry Holden; *Women in Aviation, The Publication* and Amy Carmein; Women In Military Service For America Memorial Foundation and Wilma Vaught; the Albatrosses and Women in Technological History, two interest groups of the Society for the History of Technology; Women's Research and Education Institute and Carolyn Becraft; and most especially to the Women Military Aviators.

My former colleagues at the National Air and Space Museum and the NASA Langley Research Center remain good friends and have contributed greatly to this effort. At NASM, I owe special thanks to Patti Williams, Melissa Keiser, Kate Igoe, Carolyn Russo, Dorothy Cochrane, Tom Crouch, Dom Pisano, Bob van der Linden, Carl Bobrow, and Alex Spencer. Likewise at NASA, much appreciation goes to Mike Finneran, Gary Price, Marny Skora, Cam Martin (now at NASA Dryden), and the staff of the Floyd L. Thompson Library, most especially the late Susan Adkins. Roger Launius is an inspiration and wonderful colleague and mentor. At the MIT Museum, I am grateful for the support of Sue Speisman, Kurt Hasselbalch, Gary Van Zante, Mary Leen, and our former director, Jane Pickering. I am also grateful for professional friendships with a number of historians, filmmakers, and writers. Thanks to Henry Holden for a copy of his first book; to Sarah Rickman for her passion (and her photo collection!); to Margaret Weitekamp for good conversation and for reviewing a piece of the manuscript; to Doris Rich for always knowing the facts and for her generosity; and most especially to Laurel Ladevich. I will always treasure our long conversations about the history of the WASP and I appreciate how much she taught me about filmmaking as a medium of history.

I was twenty-two when Tim Wooldridge and Claudia Oakes called me into Tim's office at the National Air and Space Museum and proposed I write a book about women in aviation. Words cannot describe my good fortune to have been given this opportunity so early in my career. Thus, when Zig Ziegler of the University Press of Kentucky and I began discussing the possibility of publishing a revised edition, I knew I wanted to involve young scholars in the process. It has been a very great privilege to work with two doctoral students who have just begun to make their mark in this field: Amy Foster of Auburn University and Alan Meyer of the University of Delaware. Amy researched, wrote the initial drafts for, and collaborated closely during the preparation of the final version of chapter 10. Alan completely revised and expanded the bibliography, checked all notes, and supplied general research assistance. I think they have produced some of the best work in print on this subject, and they have my gratitude for their contributions; I hope they found the experience as rewarding as I have.

Lucy Young's Navy nickname is "Juice," and one could hardly pick a better moniker to capture her tremendous enthusiasm for this new edition. Lucy is the type to light up a room; she makes things happen. Now retired from the Navy and a pilot for US Airways, she maintains one of the best collections of articles and information on women in naval aviation. She worked tirelessly to track down statistical information, opened doors at the airlines and to the military, supplied an airline "buddy pass" so I could attend a key conference, and updated all the appendices. It is wonderful to be able to recognize her collaboration, and equally wonderful to have her as a friend.

Finally, I have great friends and family. David and Pat Lewis, Dianne Deturris, Maura Hametz Webb and Todd Webb, Annette Finley-Croswhite and

Chip Croswhite, Nina Lerman, Molly Berger, Erik Conway, Deborah Fitzgerald, Arwen Mohun and Eric Rau, Shelley and Dave Petroy, Drew and Kate Landman, Danniella Muheim and Des Welch, Amy Garber, Steve and Amy Sandford, John Smith and Kim Carroll-Smith, and most especially Juan Cruz have made this a much better book for their friendship and caring. Books have a way of becoming a member of the author's immediate family, and this one is no exception. My parents Neiland and Priscilla Douglas, my sisters Heather Douglas and Laura Douglas, plus my brother-in-law Chris Donaghy and niece Cassidy Donaghy, have welcomed the effort and given all sorts of practical assistance as well as infinite understanding and love. From the bottom of my heart, thank you all.

Introduction

On Saturday, September 15, 2001, Cindy Wilson hovered seven hundred feet over hell. Wilson is a former Army helicopter pilot, tall, lean, and not the type to be fazed by much. Like most Americans, however, Wilson found what happened on the morning of September 11 shocking. "I thought the first news accounts were wrong. The first plane to crash into one of the Twin Towers . . . that was an accident. Then came the announcement of a second plane. I honestly thought, 'That can't be right. Pilots just don't intentionally fly aircraft into buildings.'" Of course, the terrible truth was apparent soon enough. Now a few days later, she was looking directly down over the wreckage and rubble that was once the World Trade Center. The fires were still intense, the smoke thick. Emotions among her passengers were running high because so many victims were still unaccounted for.

Wilson is the chief pilot of the rotor wing for Altria Corporate Services (then the Philip Morris Management Corporation). Years earlier, she had persuaded the management of Philip Morris to sign on as part of a disaster relief foundation that allowed New York City to call on corporate aviation units in times of emergency. No one had *ever* imagined this sort of emergency, but when the call came, her company CEO did not debate insurance liability issues or other risks that caused some signatory companies to break their agreements.

Helicopters, like all aircraft, have strict maintenance rules. The Federal Aviation Administration (and common sense) mandate checks, maintenance, and overhauls at very specific intervals. By Friday, the Port Authority of New York and New Jersey helicopters had reached those limits. So on Saturday, the white leather seats of the Sikorsky S76B helicopter were covered with canvas and helicopter N120PM became "Port 2." For two days, Wilson and her two crews ferried rescue workers from the Port Authority Emergency Services Police Unit, making eighteen trips to and from the Wall Street Heliport. Additionally, they

Cindy Wilson and her crew prepare to ferry Port Authority rescue workers on September 15, 2001. Philip Morris had a policy to make its corporate helicopter available in times of crisis. *Courtesy of Cindy Wilson.*

provided twenty-four-hour stand-by support for any other Port Authority helicopter needs.

Wilson, her crew, and her company would be the first to say they only played a very small part and that it was an honor to volunteer their services. People of all races and religions, young and old, rich and poor, male and female, would offer aid and become involved in the relief efforts in New York, at the Pentagon, and at the crash site in central Pennsylvania. For a short time anyway, people forgot about the things that normally divide us as a nation. The rescue workers riding in the helicopter piloted by Wilson barely even noticed her, let alone expressed any concern that she was female.

Wilson first told this story at the Women Military Aviators Conference, which I attended on September 21–23, 2001, in Arlington, Virginia. Carrying my suitcase on the "T" (the local mass transit system) to go to Boston's barely reopened Logan Airport, several strangers expressed their concern for my well-being. It only took minutes to check in because passengers were nonexistent at the US Airways Shuttle counter, and there were only twenty of us on the 6 P.M.

Cindy Wilson as a young Army helicopter pilot with the 56th Aviation Detachment in Germany in July 1982. *Courtesy of Cindy Wilson.*

Friday flight. Instead of landing at Reagan Washington National, which was still closed, the flight went to Dulles International Airport. I was the only passenger on the Washington Flyer shuttle bus and one of just a handful on the Metro's Orange Line train bound for Crystal City. It was nearly eleven o'clock when I finally checked into the hotel room, some eight hours after leaving my office at the MIT Museum. It is a trip that in the past had normally taken about three hours. Not surprisingly, my travel experience that weekend, coupled with Wilson's story, made me think about aviation history and this book in new ways.

This book began as the fourth volume in the Smithsonian Studies in Air and Space series United States Women in Aviation. The first three had been short monographs that took a decade-by-decade approach. They were unexpectedly popular. The illustrations were wonderful, and many readers were excited to discover the fact that women were involved with aviation. My former National Air and Space Museum colleagues Claudia Oakes and Kathleen Brooks had done a superlative job of "search-and-recovery" within the NASM archival files. These short works, though not intended to be comprehensive, had nonetheless proved pathbreaking and gave considerable inspiration to many future researchers.

The next logical addition to this series would have been a monograph on women in aviation during World War II. Circumstances changed at the National Air and Space Museum in the early 1980s and there was a new emphasis on scholarly research. Thus, while *United States Women in Aviation, 1940–1985* bore some resemblance to its predecessors, in other ways it was an entirely different work. The goal was to write "an introductory survey, highlighting the most critical events, organizations, and individuals in the war and postwar periods."[1] The extensive bibliography testified that research for the book extended far beyond the limits of the NASM library and archives. This research enabled a broader treatment and the possibility of situating the story within the larger currents of American history.

The response to the book has been gratifying. My hope had been that it would stimulate more detailed investigations of subjects that could only be hinted at in the text. While not a deluge, there have been some extremely important new studies, including Margaret Weitekamp's doctoral dissertation on the women who underwent the physiological tests given to the Mercury astronauts (and launched a campaign to put a woman in space) and Lee Kolm's work on flight attendants.

The challenge of issuing a new edition of a book is finding a way to incorporate (or at least acknowledge) the insights gained since the original manuscript was conceived and written. Many wonderful new works of scholarship have greatly influenced my thinking. Reading the writings of Judith McGaw, Ruth Schwartz Cowan, Judy Wajcman, Ruth Oldenziel, Arwen Mohun, and Nina Lerman, scholars specializing in the history of gender and technology, profoundly altered my understanding of this book. Originally framed as a study about women, I came to recognize how much it had to say about men in aviation as well.

On the subject of gender and citizenship, I can think of no more important book to me than Linda Kerber's *No Constitutional Right to Be Ladies: Women and the Obligations of Citizenship*. Judith Hicks Stiehm and Cynthia Enloe have authored several vital new works on women in the military, but in addition I have especially appreciated Leisa Meyer's *Creating GI Jane: Sexuality and Power in the Women's Army Corps During World War II*. This edition of *American Women and Flight* retains the original emphasis on the contributions of women. However, the two new chapters on the 1980s and 1990s plus the revised bibliography do reflect the influence of scholarly writing in the past fifteen years. As with the first edition, I hope this volume will encourage readers to think more broadly about femininity and masculinity in American society.

American women, like American men, have always been involved with the technology of flight. It is not hard to discover this fact, even if women's experiences are different from those of men. Especially since the advent of heavier-than-air vehicles at the start of the twentieth century, there is ample documentation of their participation. Open the pages of the earliest aviation publications and you will find pictures and stories. Many of these stories have been repeated several times over the past century—so often, in fact, the question we ought to ask ourselves is not "Were there any women in aviation?" but rather "Why do we keep forgetting?"

Amelia Earhart! listeners will always respond when you ask if they know much about the subject of American women in flight. Earhart is one of the most significant figures in modern history, so it is gratifying to hear her name mentioned even if what most people know about Earhart is that she disappeared during her attempt to fly around the world in 1937. But what about the others? What about such intrepid pioneers as Katherine Wright, Harriet Quimby, Blanche Scott, Matilde Moisant, Ruth Law, Katherine and Marjorie Stinson, Janet Waterford Bragg, Ruth Elder, Viola Gentry, Louise Thaden, Betty Gillies, and Pancho Barnes? What about Anne Morrow Lindbergh, wife of Charles, but also the first woman in the United States to earn a glider pilot's license? What about Bessie Coleman, the first black person—male or female—to earn a pilot's license?[2]

What *indeed?* It is not surprising that the names of the various women in aviation have been forgotten. Only specialists and devotees maintain such knowledge on the tip of their tongue. What is surprising is the assumption that, because the names have been forgotten, women must not have been involved at all, or only in such inconsequential ways as not to merit much attention of historians. This is a maddening fact for women in aviation today. They know that women are spectators, passengers, pilots, promoters, inventors, flight attendants, air traffic controllers, engineers, builders, mechanics, administrators, and investors in every aspect of the world of atmospheric flight. Whether a woman works in aviation or simply eats a kiwi fruit transported from the other side of the globe by an airplane, she is as much a participant as any man. Why, then, is her story told differently? Why is her experience different? And most importantly of all, does it matter?

To begin to answer these questions, it is useful to review the history of American women in aviation before the start of the Second World War. During the first four decades of the twentieth century, Americans transformed aviation from spectacle to system. Engineers trained in special university programs replaced "Try-and-Fly" experimenters. Uniformed pilots and flight attendants with nursing degrees serving passengers on regularly scheduled airlines gradually supplanted daredevil pilots who landed nearly anywhere and "stunted for cash." Cities transformed grass fields into permanent air transportation hubs. Entrepreneurs and workers at government bureaus and laboratories invented and installed systems for monitoring the weather, for flying at night or in bad weather, and for safely controlling the movement of large numbers of aircraft. Airworthiness standards regulated the design, construction, and maintenance of an aircraft and its engines. With plenty of government support, aviation became a viable business serving the transportation and defense needs of the nation.

At the start, the number of women involved as active participants was considerably smaller than the number of men. In American culture, machines had become a symbol of masculinity and modernity. This idea got expressed in myriad ways, both consciously and unconsciously. For example, in 1911 the *Mobile (Ala.) Register* published a feature titled: "Why a Woman Can Run an Airship Better Than a Man." The supposed proponent was an Austrian university professor who made countless unproved assertions such as: "because she has retained the primitive faculty of seeing with full retina; enforced modesty and flirting have caused this." The opponent was well-known British aviator Claude Grahame-White, who stated bluntly: "I have taught many women to fly and I regret it. The air is no place for women."[3]

Based on the experiences of the first women participants, Grahame-White's prejudices represented the norm. The first American woman to learn to fly an airplane was Blanche Stuart Scott. Her instructor was Glenn Curtiss, who reluctantly offered her lessons in 1910 after the promoter for his Curtiss Exhibition Company begged him to do so. Scott had gained considerable public attention when she became the first woman to make a transcontinental auto tour of the United States on behalf of the Willys-Overland Company. The promoter wanted Scott to join the Curtiss team, hoping "The Tomboy of the Air" would be an added draw for spectators. Glenn Curtiss was fearful that an accident involving a woman pilot might put him out of business, but he ultimately conceded and Scott would perform for six years.[4]

Scott did experience her share of accidents, but it was not broken bones that caused her to abandoned flying. "In aviation there seems to be no place for the woman engineer, mechanic or flier. Too often, people paid money to see me risk my neck, more as a freak—a woman freak pilot—than as a skilled flier. No more."[5] The idea that women represented the abnormal would both repel (mainly) and attract (some) women to the world of aviation. Gradually the word freak was replaced with more muted language, but the idea that women were biologically incapable of flight gained an even firmer hold on the American public's thinking.

Most women stayed away except as spectators and indirect consumers (e.g.

the sender or recipient of an air mail letter), although a determined few tried to demonstrate their exceptionalism. They were inspired in part by the passage and ratification of the Nineteenth Amendment. A better predictor was a college education, however. Affluent, well-educated white women sought adventure and admiration. Flying was far bolder than bobbing one's hair, smoking, or even driving a car. After Charles Lindbergh's trans-Atlantic solo crossing in 1927, there was a stunning burst of attention. Aviation became the glamorous high-tech industry of the day. The new mass-communication technologies of radio and movies transformed Lindbergh into a global figure. There were poems and songs, even Sunday sermons, not to mention inches and inches of newspaper columns about aviation and its place in modern American life.

The media was quick to sense public fascination with an aviation story that involved women. In 1928, a 20-hour, 40-minute flight transformed Amelia Earhart, a Boston social worker, into "Lady Lindy." Earhart, who was in fact a licensed pilot, was embarrassed by the attention given to a mere passenger. Though the press and the public did not care, Earhart did. She would fly the Atlantic again, but only as a pilot. She wanted to prove that she was more than "a sack of potatoes," that just because she was a woman did not mean she was incapable of flying. What would ultimately make Earhart significant to historians was her ambition to increase the opportunities for all women to take part in aviation, indeed in all of American society. She was part of a vanguard that believed it was prejudice—not biology—that had limited women's participation.[6]

Earhart had some very practical strategies for achieving her goals. While she gave plenty of speeches, she was an activist. In her autobiography, *High, Wide and Frightened*, Louise Thaden, also a prominent and accomplished pilot, would quote Earhart: "Each accomplishment, no matter how small, is important. Although it may be no direct contribution to the science of aeronautics nor to its technical development, it will encourage other women to fly. The more women who fly, the more who become pilots, the quicker we will be recognized as an important factor in aviation."[7] While participating in the National Women's Air Derby of 1929 (dubbed "The Powder Puff Derby" by humorist and aviation advocate Will Rogers), Earhart noticed the camaraderie that developed among all of the participants. The winner, Louise Thaden, remarked to the press: "I'm sorry we all couldn't come in first, because they all deserve it as much as I. They're all great flyers."[8] Within a few months, Clara Trenchman of the Curtiss Flying Service had found a way to reunite the Derby participants.

Trenchman was not a pilot, but she had started publishing a newsletter called *Women and Aviation* that documented every piece of news about her favorite subject. Curtiss employed four women as demonstration pilots, and

Trenchman thought Curtiss should sponsor a women pilots organization. Inspired by the recent race, she asked for corporate approval, and on November 2, 1929, the first meeting of what would become the Ninety-Nines was held. Earhart attended, and it was she who suggested the idea for the name: the total number of charter members. When the organization decided to adopt a more formal structure in 1932, Earhart was elected its first president.

Earhart used the post to promote women. In her book *The Fun of It*, Earhart offered a candid appraisal of the situation faced by women. The number of women was still very small, a fact she blamed on discriminatory attitudes. While some prejudice was blatant (e.g., military flying schools were closed to women and women got paid less than men for the same work), what Earhart focused on was the differing ways society educated boys and girls. Whether in school or the home, she observed, boys and girls were separated into "little feminine or masculine pigeonholes." Further, she noted, "as different as what they do are ways of doing it."[9]

While Earhart was exploring ways to prompt a revolution in American attitudes, many other men and women in aviation sensed a way to exploit the status quo as a means of promoting aviation. The stock market crash in 1929 did not fully impact aviation until the early 1930s. The Hoover administration had retained almost full-funding levels for aviation (most importantly for air mail contracts), making some in the business think theirs was a "depression-proof" industry. By the time the Roosevelt administration took office in March 1933, this fallacy had been shattered. The economic downturn prompted new thinking about "the selling of aviation." There was a particular receptiveness to the idea that women could be used in this effort.

In 1930, Ellen Church went to the San Francisco office of Boeing Air Transport wanting advice on how to become a commercial airline pilot. Not taking "no" for an answer, Church asked the Boeing officials' opinion on the idea of hiring women to perform the steward duties presently being handled by the copilot. Church was trying to find a way to fly, but Steve Stimpson, the San Francisco district manager, was taken with the idea of using women to show how safe air travel had become. In May 1930, the first eight stewardesses (as flight attendants were then called) began work on the Chicago–San Francisco route, a grueling twenty-hour trip that made thirteen stops. The idea appealed to passengers, if not initially to the male pilots, who perceived a loss of total authority over their aircraft. As soon as the other airlines noticed that United (Boeing's parent) was attracting more business, they swiftly began hiring women.[10]

The hiring of women flight attendants represented the first formal attempt to use women to "sell aviation." Far more controversial was the idea of women pilots. Some companies (e.g., Curtiss) but not all embraced the concept of employing women to attract men. Central Airlines hired Helen Richey in 1934 in hopes of securing some desperately needed publicity. Central was competing with Pennsylvania Airlines on a route between Washington and Detroit. When Central's president, James Condon, saw Richey's application to become a copilot, he asked the Department of Commerce for permission to hire her. Condon explained it was only for publicity purposes and that after two weeks, Richey would be transferred to another job. The Bureau of Aeronautics, headed by Eugene Vidal, a good friend and former business partner of Amelia Earhart's, gave its approval.[11]

Richey was ecstatic when Condon called. Condon did not tell Richey that it was just a temporary post, however. The news coverage proved greater than Condon's wildest expectations, but it meant that he could not reassign her as soon as he had planned without prompting a media backlash. Condon had another problem, too: almost universal hostility on the part of the men transport pilots. The Airline Pilots Association denied Richey's application for membership and even sent a letter of complaint to the Bureau of Aeronautics. Men pilots freely expressed their opinion that women did not have a place in the cockpit. After eight months, Richey understood what was happening and resigned her post.

Richey's good friend Amelia Earhart protested the situation loudly but to no avail. It was not a simple matter of men versus women either, as some of the harshest criticism came from other women. Ruth Haviland, also a transport pilot, declared: "In private flying or racing, women need not give ground to men but I've flown big transport planes and it's hard physical work. It takes strength and sometimes a great deal of it. A woman can't step in and fly at night readily either."[12] Haviland's assertion reminds us that most Americans believed there was an essential difference between men and women. In order to use women to sell aviation, the stereotype of women as weak, scatter-brained, and incapable of operating dangerous machinery had to be well established. The women who accepted these jobs had to decide between the causes of equality and aviation.[13]

The truth is that it did not feel like a choice for women. If you were "just plane crazy," as the pilot and aviation entrepreneur Evelyn "Bobbi" Trout once described herself, you took the job and hoped that Amelia Earhart was correct that any contribution, even under dubious circumstances, would advance the cause. The historical record reveals a more complicated situation. As the visibility of women in aviation increased during the 1930s, so too did the imperative to reassure the public that nothing had really changed. For example, the hotshot young pilot Jacqueline Cochran who learned to fly in 1932 took pains to emphasize her interest in cosmetics. Dorothy Lynn, the commander of the

Betsy Ross Corps, a volunteer group of women pilots who offered their services for humanitarian relief work, stated adamantly that "the requirements of the corps will never interfere with a member's first duty—her children and her home."[14] In order to fly, or have any involvement with aviation, women had to find ways to assure others (and themselves) that they were neither harming their identity as women nor the profession they aspired to practice.

It was impossible to reconcile these conflicting objectives as long as the view that there was a biological basis for limiting or excluding women's participation in aviation was widespread. This tension, broken only by a daring few, is what made women's experiences so different from men's and what ultimately so profoundly limited their participation in aviation until the Second World War. Women and men both used the word *freedom* to describe the experience of flight, but it did not—could not—mean the same thing for the two sexes. As Joseph Corn astutely observed: "The experience of flying, after all, opened to her a world of seeming power and freedom which belied the rhetoric of domesticity, the sacrifices on behalf of others, or the suffering of discrimination."[15]

Cataclysmic events often are accompanied by equally significant shifts in public opinion. The seismic jolts and upheavals of World War II profoundly altered the course of history for American women in aviation. Set apart and defined as a group because of their sex, the dramatic expansion in the scale and scope of women's involvement created a collective identification that had not previously existed. It is at this pivotal transition point that the story of this book begins. Part I: Can Women Fly? details the wartime experiences that caused American attitudes about women in aviation to be turned on their head. While in 1940 only a thousand women were involved in any aspect of aviation, five years later there were a half million. The biological argument for discrimination simply became untenable. While one could argue the exceptionalism of Amelia Earhart or Jacqueline Cochran, the thousands of Rosies, Air WACs, and WAVES came from more ordinary stock. However, this new recognition did not mean that women were treated equally or that prejudice vanished.

Instead, the debate about women's participation was reframed. Americans posed a new question: *Should* women be pilots, engineers, air traffic controllers, mechanics, assembly line workers, flight attendants, government officials, or executives? The answers—sometimes yes, mostly no—relied on stereotypes and group attributes. "Women for one reason or another have always come into each phase of aviation a little behind their brothers," wrote Jacqueline Cochran, one of the most famous and most important women in aviation. "They should, I believe, accept this delay," she continued in her 1962 pronouncement.[16] Nearly forty years later, the prominent sentiment is expressed in two words stitched on a baseball cap popular among the air show crowd: "Women

Fly." Yet, while today there is little interest or acceptance among women in aviation in the idea that women should wait for men to do things first, this remains the pattern.

The six chapters in Part II: Should Women Fly? explore why this is so. One of the issues that readers will notice is the emphasis among participants on the idea of increasing the numbers of women in aviation. Fifty years of evangelical-like efforts to change the socialization of girls and promote equal opportunity has not seen much success. Why? History offers some important insights. Most importantly, as long as women in aviation, like blacks in aviation, are defined as a group with specific attributes, it is easy to locate the problem there. Should women accommodate aviation or should aviation reshape itself to accommodate women?

When considering this last question, it will be wise to keep in mind the story of Cindy Wilson and the events of September 11, 2001. It is easy to become narrowly focused on matters such as the numbers of women airline pilots. Dramatic historical events can radically alter the terms of discussion. If the major airlines go into bankruptcy, will we even have airline pilots—as we understand the job today—in two decades? In the present War on Terror, do the terms "civilian," "soldier," and "combat" have the same meaning? Does it make sense to discriminate on the basis of gender in such a conflict? Will racial profiling and close scrutiny of flight schools make it impossible for non-white women to learn to fly? If the value of land around cities continues to skyrocket, will small airports become an unaffordable luxury? Should engineering programs train students to design a navigation system or mitigate engine noise rather than focus exclusively on the vehicle? How would changing the curriculum affect the demographics of the students choosing to become aerospace engineers?

The desire to fly may be a universal human experience, but every era redefines what that impulse means. The United States is a technological society; Americans both shape and are shaped by technology. The means of full citizenship are linked to an individual's ability to understand and manipulate the machines, processes, and systems that shape modern existence. This book explores this facet of history through the striking stories of women in aviation during the past half century. They are as interesting and important as ever; not only do they help us discover who we are, but also who we may become.

Part I

Can Women Fly?

American Women in Aviation during World War II

> We Can Do It!
>
> War Production Co-Ordinating Committee
> Poster designed by J. Howard Miller,
> Westinghouse Corporation, 1943
>
> It is on the record that women can fly as well as men.
>
> General Henry H. Arnold
> Commanding General, Army Air Forces
> "Address to Last W.A.S.P. Graduate Class," 7 December 1944

Students and Teachers, Clubs and Colleges

Women in Civilian Aviation Organizations

> O-o-o-oh, we flew through the air with the greatest of ease,
> The C-A-A's feminine C-P-Ts: But they tell us "Men Only,"
> they've kicked us right out. Now it's "Pay as you pilot, pu-lease."
>
> Pilette's Lament, author unknown

In the early morning hours of 7 December 1941, Cornelia Fort, a young flight instructor with Andrew Flying Service, was working with a student pilot near the John Rogers Airport in Honolulu, Hawaii. Her Sunday schedule included a busy teaching program in between giving a number of aerial sightseeing tours. That first lesson of the day was typical, filled with many practice take-offs and landings, and continuing work on the skills her student needed to qualify for his first solo flight. Suddenly, however, just before the two were about to land, Fort saw a military airplane speeding directly toward her. She grabbed the controls away from her student and managed to pull just above the oncoming airplane.[1] Fort described what she saw through the still-shaking plastic window:

> The painted red balls on the tops of the wings shone brightly in the sun. I looked again with complete and utter unbelief. Honolulu was familiar with the emblem of the Rising Sun on passenger ships but not on airplanes.
>
> I looked quickly at Pearl Harbor and my spine tingled when I saw billowing black smoke. Still I thought hollowly it might be some kind of coincidence or maneuvers—it might be, it must be. For surely, dear God. . . .
>
> Then I looked way up and saw the formations of silver bombers riding in. I saw something detach itself from a plane and come glistening down. My eyes followed it down, down and even with knowledge pounding in my mind, my heart turned convulsively when the bomb exploded in the middle of the Harbor.[2]

Fort continued her dramatic account, published in *Women's Home Companion* in 1943:

> Suddenly that little wedge of sky above Hickam Field and Pearl Harbor was the busiest, fullest piece of sky I ever saw.
>
> Most people wonder how they would react in a crisis; if the danger comes as suddenly as this did you don't have time to be frightened. I'm not brave, but I knew the air was not the place for my little baby airplane and I set about landing as quickly as ever I could. It was as if the attack was happening in a different time track, with no relation to me.
>
> A burst of machine gun fire rattled in my ear. I headed for the runway, landed and taxied the plane toward the hangars.
>
> That the attack did have relation to me was brought forcibly to my attention a few seconds later when I saw a shadow pass over me and simultaneously bullets spattering all around me.[3]

Cornelia Fort witnessed firsthand the Japanese attack on Pearl Harbor. The next day, 8 December, the United States declared war and formally entered the conflagration that had engulfed most of the rest of the world. The war would change the course of her life and the lives of all American women.

The United States had been sending huge convoys of arms and supplies to Britain and anxiously watching events in Europe and Asia, but it was not until the bombing of the American fleet at Pearl Harbor that World War II had a great impact on the daily lives of most Americans. The 1940s were a time of great change in American society. The war had the effect of unifying the American people to a great extent, bringing about a more cohesive community based on a broader and more inclusive definition of its citizenry. The necessities of war wrought greater social and economic justice but did not eliminate all of the barriers. Different groups progressed at varying rates depending on their status at the war's commencement. The mobilization of the nation's workforce and resources to meet the war's intense demands was such a force for change in American attitudes that there was much public debate about the necessity of working toward a more democratic and just society.

The demands, the mobilization, and the debate obviously had implications for everyone involved in aviation. For women pilots like Cornelia Fort, the attack on Pearl Harbor put a temporary end to certain kinds of flying activity; it also meant the creation of a whole range of other opportunities. Women's flying organizations, like the Women Flyers of America and the Ninety-Nines, altered their agendas to provide wartime service. Others, such as the disaster relief group Relief Wings, originated as a direct response to the war.

The government, at both federal and state levels, expanded the number of aviation programs open to women. Women were part of the Civilian Pilot Training Program (CPTP) almost from its inception, and later many participated in the Civil Air Patrol (CAP). Through the Civil Aeronautics Administration (CAA), women became Link Trainer instructors,[4] parachute riggers, and air traffic controllers—professions that demanded special aviation knowledge.

The demarcation lines between the civilian and military worlds were obviously much less distinct during World War II than during peacetime. Anyone with the ability to pilot an airplane had a valuable skill, but the avenues for wartime service were less open to women than to men. Barred from combat flying, women took advantage of many aviation occupations that were newly created (or newly open to women) but which did not involve any actual flying. This resulted in a more complete integration of women into all aspects of aviation, due not to planned development but to the greater abundance of nonflying jobs and the shortage of qualified people to fill them.

At the time the United States became involved in World War II, the Ninety-Nines, International Women Pilots Association, founded in 1929, was one of the aviation organizations working hard both to create new flying possibilities and to remove the restrictions imposed on women flyers. It had become a strong network by 1940, with more than four hundred women pilots, whose purpose was to provide "good fellowship, jobs, and a central office and files on women in aviation."[5] In general, these women tended to come from affluent or middle-class families and were well educated and white. Despite their position of economic and social privilege in American society, the leadership and inspiration these women provided for hundreds of other women in the field (and thousands who were spectators) was very important. They did not accept existing social norms concerning women in aviation; they flew in spite of them, abandoning prescriptions of proper feminine behavior without being overwhelmed by the combined disapproval of family and society for "inappropriate activity." These young women were described sympathetically by Juliet R. Arthur:

> What chance for a career is offered them in that most glamorous of pursuits, the business of flying? Everybody knows that the late Amelia Earhart swiftly followed on the heels of Lindbergh across the Atlantic; that Ruth Nichols took the altitude record from Colonel Chamberlain in the same ship that he had flown; that Phoebe Omelie bettered the record of men she competed with in cross-country and closed-course racing; and that Jacqueline Cochran, now America's foremost aviatrix, is winner of more awards than she has wall-space on which to hang them. But these are the stars, the top notchers, whose dazzling careers in relation to everyday jobs in aviation are on par with Metropolitan Opera singers, to whom the hopeful aspirants of the chorus look for inspiration.... A large number of women learn to fly for the same reason they enjoy driving a swift automobile, but after they have once learned, a number have found a hobby turning into a paying pursuit.[6]

In 1939, Betty Huyler Gillies, one of the charter members, was elected president of the Ninety-Nines. Like her predecessors, Gillies developed a strong program for the organization. She worked with Alma Harwood, who was a fellow member and the prime instigator for the creation of the Ninety-Nines' Amelia Earhart Memorial Scholarship Fund. Gillies led a battle against the Civil Aeronautics Authority (the CAA would shortly become the Civil Aeronautics Administration) over regulations concerning pregnancy. In March of 1940, it was reported that Gillies, as president of the Ninety-Nines, had submitted a petition challenging the CAA's right to ban pregnant women from flying. This immediately provoked a response from CAA officials saying that, while CAA medical experts disliked the practice, there was no official ban on pregnant women pilots, but there was a restriction for a short period during a woman's recovery. If a woman's license expired during this time of restriction, then she was required both to rewrite and refly the CAA examinations to win back her pilot's license. The Ninety-Nines under Gillies leadership were successful in having these regulations modified as well as in exposing the exaggerated view of the dangers to a pregnant woman in flying.[7]

In 1941 the famous pilot Jacqueline Cochran became president of the Ninety-Nines. Under Cochran's leadership the organization began to respond to the new climate for aeronautical activities. The United States' entry into the war curtailed civilian flying dramatically. In many coastal regions pleasure flying was prohibited. Despite the limitations, opportunities for women actually increased. Affluent women pilots with extensive flying experience, who once related chiefly to exclusive aviation country clubs, found ways to continue to fly that included service to their country. For the first time, learning to fly became an affordable possibility for women of a lower income level because of programs sponsored by the Women Flyers of America and the CAA.

The Women Flyers of America (WFA) was essentially a national flying club, open to any girl or woman involved in, or just interested in, aviation. The organization first invited members who wanted to learn to fly to take ground school classes (all courses offered were CAA approved). Upon completion of the course, a representative of the WFA would negotiate fees on behalf of all the women who wanted to continue with actual flying lessons. The large number of women involved meant that the representative had considerable bargaining power. The net result was to make flight lessons available at low rates. On average, WFA members paid $275 for ground instruction plus dual and solo training (from CAA licensed instructors), earning a private pilot's license in 35 to 50 hours. This was about 20 percent less than comparable fees (approximately $345) for a similar program taken by an individual. It was still a "pay-as-you-go" system, but the WFA acted as the guarantor for the airfields and their instructors.[8]

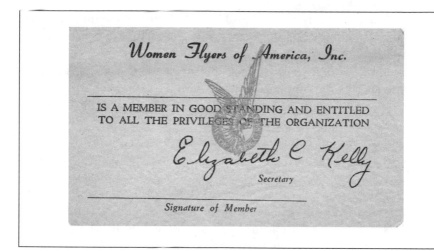

A membership card for the Women Flyers of America. The club obtained group rates for flying lessons. *Author's collection.*

The WFA's program was a remarkably popular concept. The organization, founded in April 1940 in New York, had a rocky start because the response to its modest announcement was so overwhelming. Nearly one thousand women wrote back, two-thirds of whom enclosed the $5 membership fee. The founders, Opal Kunz[9] and Chelle Janis, had initially intended to run a trial program of "installment plan" flying in the New York City area. But almost instantly it became a national organization, and the resultant mismanagement almost killed the fledgling group. Fortunately, in August 1940 one well-known WFA member, Vita Roth, a 1920s women's parachute jumping record holder, decided to assume the responsibility for organizing the group.

Roth found that most WFA members were young (averaging twenty to thirty-five years old), working (earning between $18 and $75 per week), adventurous, and concerned about national defense. Indeed, many WFA members voiced the wish to be available if America had an urgent need for ambulance and liaison flyers. One representative WFA class included individuals like Eleanor Scully, the fashion editor of *Vogue* magazine, and debutante Mary Steele, as well as several secretaries, file clerks, and nurses.[10]

WFA chapters were founded in Washington, D.C., Hartford, and Philadelphia. By the time of the attack on Pearl Harbor there were ten chapters in ten major cities. Pearl Harbor and the declaration of war created a surge of enthusiasm for flying, and many WFA trainees were particularly interested in having the WFA set up a joint application program with the Civil Air Patrol. Programs for teaching women to fly received positive reactions from another quarter: instructors of WFA students found them easier to teach than men because they were much more inclined to listen.[11]

Ironically, Director Roth was, at first, publicly opposed to women's involvement in the war, but she continued to lobby hard in Washington with defense agencies to provide opportunities for her fellow members.[12] At first she proclaimed: "We don't ever expect to be in combat: that's a job for men. It's all 'bunk' to say women are better pilots than men. We aren't. Most women don't have the mechanical talent or physical stamina of average men pilots; but we are qualified for secondary service behind the lines."[13] Immediately following the creation of the Women's Airforce Service Pilots (WASP) organization, however, Roth issued a more flattering statement, this time focusing on the abilities of leaders Nancy Love and Jacqueline Cochran: "We believe the choice of these two women is a particularly happy one and I speak for all members of Women Flyers of America when I say we stand behind them 100 percent. Mrs. Love is not only one of our best pilots in the air, she is an efficient and level-headed woman on the ground. Miss Cochran's qualifications need no elaboration."[14]

The WFA was not the only means for a woman to learn how to fly, but it was popular because of its lack of membership restrictions. Anyone could belong, whereas the Ninety-Nines was restricted to women pilots, and the Civilian Pilot Training Program took only college-age students, allotting only three percent of the slots to women. Furthermore, the WFA organization adapted well to the various demands and expectations of war. The WFA saw itself as the facilitator for women who wanted to get into the many facets of aviation, so it adopted training programs that would qualify graduates for Link Trainer schooling, air traffic control school, meteorology training, and parachute rigging. It also sponsored flying lessons and flight time for those who wanted to become ferry pilots or work with the Civil Air Patrol.[15]

Another significant nonfederal program was developed in 1941 by Stephens College in Columbia, Missouri.[16] "Air-mindedness" was the theme of the comprehensive curriculum, the first such program ever offered to women, according to the president, Dr. James M. Wood. It was a cooperative venture between this women's college, the Army Air Forces, the CAA, and twelve leading airlines, including Transcontinental and Western Air, Chicago and Southern, Mid-Continent, and Braniff. Stephens offered specific vocational training in many areas of aviation, always emphasizing safety and utility. There were courses for ticket clerks, reservations clerks, flight attendants, and other passenger service personnel. Stephens prepared drafting and blueprint readers and engineering draftsmen for the aircraft industry. Further, there were courses to prepare meteorologists and junior weather observers, Link Trainer operators, control tower

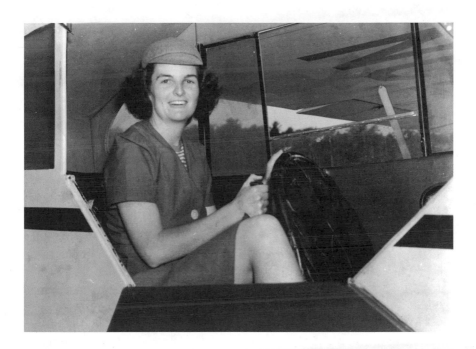

Ann Wood learned to fly through the Civilian Pilot Training Program (CPTP) at Bowdoin College. After earning her license, she became one of the program's instructors. *Courtesy of Ann Wood Kelly.*

operators, flight instructors, and mechanics. The goal of the college was to make it possible for each student to at least make a flight as a passenger whether or not she wanted to learn to fly. During the first years of the program in World War II, however, this "flight experience" was a requirement only in the elementary aeronautics courses and the airline job-preparation classes.

The program was experimental but very successful. Throughout the course of the war hundreds of Stephens graduates moved into a wide variety of aviation occupations. These women were the tangible results of the vision of the college officers who believed in a future aerial age accessible to all Americans.

Most college-age women (between the ages of eighteen and twenty-two) who learned to fly during World War II learned under the CAA's Civilian Pilot Training Program. The program was conceived by CAA administrator Robert H. Hinckley in 1938 as a way of introducing American youth to the air age. For the purpose of persuading Congress, which harbored strong isolationist sentiments, the CPTP was billed as a civilian program open to young men and women as a way of stimulating civilian aircraft sales in the faltering American aviation industry. Hinckley, however, viewed the program as an important way to increase the pool of qualified pilots available for national defense. This second reason was played down and, in December 1938, President Roosevelt announced the establishment of an experimental CPTP. One year later, the program had trained 9,350 men and women at 435 colleges. Arrangements were also made to open the program to unenrolled college-age youth through a competitive examination program.[17]

Women were generally admitted into the CPTP at the ratio of one woman to ten men. However, several women's colleges did take part in the CPTP, thereby increasing the total number of female participants. These schools included Lake Erie College, Adelphi College, Mills College, and Florida State College for Women. The CAA considered the inclusion of women to be experimental, a means for the agency to gain experience in encouraging women to become involved with general aviation. Its attitude was based on the premise that women made most of the important financial decisions in a household, and thus could have a substantial impact on the aviation sales market. For example, a woman who knew about aviation would be supportive of a pilot husband who wanted to buy an airplane.[18]

The CPTP was designed to be a cooperative program run by colleges in conjunction with local flying field operators. The colleges would provide ground school instruction (with CAA-approved teachers) in aerodynamics, meteorology, navigation, parachutes, air regulations, basic mechanics, and air history; the flight instructors would provide the elementary flying course, which included thirty-five to fifty hours of dual instruction and controlled solo flying. The federal government would set and maintain the standards of instruction, certifying both ground and flight personnel, and paying the expenses. By the end of the program's first year there were an estimated 980 new pilots.[19]

As war became imminent, the CPTP acquired a more military character. Early in 1941, trainees signed nonbinding agreements to serve in the military in case of war or national emergency. Even women had to fill out cards specifying the service they preferred. The pledge soon became a legal obligation for enlistment in the armed forces, and thus in June 1941 women were automatically excluded from the CPTP.[20] This action was protested by many women, each of whom received a letter signed by Robert Hinkley which stated: "If, or when, the time comes when trained girls are needed in non-combat work to release men for active duty, that will be a different situation. I believe that we may also assume that upon the cessation of the emergency, we would resume our former policy toward women."[21]

Eleanor Roosevelt, a strong supporter of women in aviation, publicly demanded an explanation. Though she received a personal letter from CAA officials, the essential message was the same: "It is generally recognized that male pilots have a wider and more varied potential usefulness to the armed forces than female pilots. We have had to make changes with this in mind, and during the past year our program has of necessity been closely integrated, with the needs of the Army and Navy aviation constantly in the foreground. To limit our training to young men is only another in a series of steps based on this philosophy."[22]

The CPTP officials did not want to abandon women altogether. The draft did not discriminate or differentiate in the slightest between the program's male flight instructors and their students. Both were equally likely to be drafted. This fact, combined with the rapid expansion of the CPTP, which trained 10,281 students in 1940 and 215,676 in 1944, meant there was a desperate need for flight instructors. The CPTP, and later the War Training Service (WTS), did use some women instructors, although records indicate that no more than fifty were ever employed and that their widespread use in this capacity was never seriously considered.[23]

Gertrude Meserve, for example, taught nine classes in Boston and Norwood, Massachusetts, as part of the CPTP 1939 test program. Later, when operations were moved inland to Orange, Massachusetts, because of coastal flying prohibitions, she taught students from the Massachusetts Institute of Technology, Harvard, Northeastern, and Tufts Universities. Meserve was a flying enthusiast. Her first airplane ride was in 1935 and her first lesson was at Boston Airport (now Logan International Airport) in East Boston in April 1938, just prior to her high school graduation. One year later she received her commercial and instructor's ratings, and in 1941 she was appointed flight inspector for private licenses by the CAA.[24]

Ironically, Meserve, immune from the draft by virtue of her gender, was nevertheless called up for the war effort. In September 1942 she received a telegram from Nancy Love asking her to join the Women's Auxiliary Ferry Squadron (WAFS). Meserve decided to become a member of the WAFS because the job sounded more exciting and more directly connected to the war effort than any other available opportunity to use her expertise.

The CAA made its first proposal at about this time for women flight instructors to train Army and Navy pilots. The CAA proposal was for a two-part program. They wanted to hire instructors such as Meserve immediately, and they wanted to start a training program specifically to prepare women to be flight instructors. This training program was directly inspired by the outstanding success of a state-run program in Tennessee developed by Phoebe Omelie.

Phoebe Omelie, one of America's top women pilots in the 1920s and 1930s, developed a program for training women flight instructors. In the summer of 1941, the Tennessee Bureau of Aeronautics opened a special school under

Omelie's supervision funded by revenues from the state's aviation gasoline tax. The original idea had been proposed by W. Percy McDonald, chairman of the Tennessee Bureau, but Omelie deserves full credit for its successful implementation.[25] She had been in Washington during the 1930s working with what was then the National Air Marking program of the Bureau of Air Commerce, but she decided to respond to McDonald's call to return to Tennessee and head up this new venture.[26] One of the motivating factors was the strong sentiment at the CAA that the best way for women to be involved in wartime aviation was to work as flight instructors. Omelie addressed that sentiment when she explained why it was that women in other positions, such as pilots or mechanics, got greater news attention: the novelty of women in those positions made good news copy in the minds of many men editors. The lack of publicity for women flight instructors did not, however, diminish the importance of their work; in fact, it indicated a higher degree of social acceptance.[27] "Naturally," stated Omelie, "the dashing uniformed woman pilot of a roaring warplane is going to get more attention (and photography) than her flight instructor sister, just as the uniformed volunteer gets more publicity than her coveralled sister at the factory work bench. Just as naturally, however, women are finding their proper places as instructors, the position women have filled better than men for generations."[28] The program Omelie created started out slowly. The first session involved training only ten women. If successful, the course would then expand as much as funding and interest allowed. An overwhelming one thousand applications arrived, and Omelie set up a special selection committee to choose the first ten candidates.

All of the applicants were required to have a private pilot's license, with 120 or more hours of flying time. The women had to be single or, if married, could not have dependents and their husbands had to be in active military service. Finally, they had to agree to instruct wherever and whenever the bureau decided to place them. The twelve-week program was a rigorous eight-hours-per-day, six-days-per-week course that provided uniforms, food, and housing. It offered considerable benefits to participants. With more than 60 hours of flying, 200 hours of ground school, and 160 hours of flight instructor's ground school, each woman was qualified for a CAA ground instructor's rating in meteorology, aircraft structure, aircraft engines, aerial navigation, and civil air regulations, in addition to becoming an "airborne" flight instructor.[29]

Graduates of the program were in very high demand. By August 1943, four months after the first class graduated, CAA officials were beseeching the Senate Appropriations Committee for $2.5 million to train five hundred more women in similar programs around the country. In addition to the five hundred prospective graduates, four hundred more women would have at least started training during that same six month period. The request was turned down, yet the CAA continued to support other efforts on behalf of women flight instructors.[30]

One such effort was to involve as many women flight instructors as possible in the re-rating process. Re-rating was a program instituted by the CAA just prior to World War II that required all instructors, regardless of experience, to turn in their old license and take an examination to requalify for a new instructor's rating. The purpose was to establish uniform standards for CAA flight instructors. Because there was no discrimination between men and women in regard to the examination, re-rating, by providing a tangible index of ability, helped raise the status of women within the flight instructor profession. In other words, now that there was a set of standardized test scores available for open comparison, it was quite difficult for an operator of a flying school to mask sex discrimination by claiming a woman who had participated in re-rating was not as qualified or well trained as male applicants.[31]

In the fall of 1941, forty-three women were listed as instructors in CAA-qualified flight-training schools around the United States. Eventually, many more women joined their ranks. Of the original forty-three, most exuded great personal confidence in their abilities. Yet, they very often used the traditional ploy of an earlier generation of women pilots—"If I can fly, certainly you, a man, ought to be able to"—in order to win over potential but skeptical male students.

At the same time, these women also tended to be a little more critical of women students, whom they viewed as more hesitant. Evelyn Kilgore, a flight instructor at Tri-City Airport in southern California, explained this attitude: "Girls make good flyers. They learn slower because they don't understand the mechanical end of flying the way men do. But they are smoother and more careful. Men like to 'kick a ship around.' Sometimes they get a little foolish. Women respect a plane more, feel their way into the business of flying better."[32] Interestingly enough, Kilgore, who was an outstanding pilot, contradicted her own stereotypes. She soloed after only eight hours of instruction and had a great personal commitment to aviation, which flew in the face of her comment that "Women don't get as far as men do because they fritter around. They have to spend money and time on clothes and cosmetics and things like that. They just about get started and they fall in love, too. . . . Men are different. When they start flying they stick to it. If they have a girl, they bring the girl to the field. Pretty soon she's flying, too sometimes." Most women instructors only rarely made generalizations about gender differences in learning to fly. Betty Martin, a CPTP graduate who got her instructor's rating and then taught in Texas, was quick to identify the real challenge of flight instruction, which was (and is) to find the right approach for each student. Many of the people involved with aviation during World War II were convinced that women made better instructors because they believed women were natural teachers with an "inherent ability to put themselves in the student's place."[33]

Flight instruction was not the only means of civilian participation in the war effort, but it was one of the few paying options for women. A small number of women operated aircraft service centers at small local airports. Called fixed-base operators, the women and men who owned these businesses provided such services as maintenance, fuel, and preflight preparation. Many also provided flight instruction or at least served as the contact point for students looking for teachers.

For women who did not require remuneration, there were several volunteer aviation organizations in which they could be involved: for example, a woman might serve as an air raid warden or aircraft spotter for the Office of Civilian Defense. One such volunteer group, founded just prior to the American declaration of war, was Relief Wings.[34] Conceived by Ruth Nichols, an outstanding pilot of the interwar years, Relief Wings was an air-rescue service comprised of private airplanes, volunteer medical professionals, and a network of medical facilities. Through careful organization of pilots, aircraft, doctors, nurses, airports, and hospitals, the organization was an additional component in a complex program of civilian defense, able to provide high-quality air-ambulance service. Thus its slogan was "Humanitarian Service by Air," and it received the active support of many airline executives.[35] Organized and run by women, all of its positions were also fully open to female participation. The creation of a well-organized group with a firm financial base took much of 1941, but when the Japanese attack shook the nation, Relief Wings was ready and able to function across the United States. In order to solve the problems of restricted private flying, Nichols went to Washington to confer with the appropriate military and aviation officials. The result of these meetings was to make Relief Wings an adjunct service of the Civil Air Patrol.

Organized by the Office of Civilian Defense just before the Pearl Harbor attack, the Civil Air Patrol (CAP) was another group that provided opportunities for women in aviation during the war. In the first months of 1942, the details of how the CAP would be structured were released. The stated purpose was to "weld civil airmen—and women—into a force for national defense by increasing knowledge and skill in every type of aviation activity."[36] The CAP would perform important courier services, coast and forest patrol, and ferrying operations within the United States, in order to release aviation personnel of the Army and Navy for active war service.[37]

The CAP was particularly receptive to teenagers and women. Women, however, were not permitted to fly coastal patrols, even though they often instructed the men who would. For example, Dorothy Heberding, a CAP flying instructor, taught anti-submarine patrol duty at a Florida base. She was a master sergeant, yet she herself was not permitted to join the aerial lookout for German submarines.[38] In an interview with *Flying* magazine, Heberding commented that her pet annoyance was "the reluctance of people generally to accept a woman whether as a pilot or a preflight inspector." She frequently would hear, "Hhh! A fee-male pilot to check us out! Nothing doing."[39]

Because the CAP desperately needed pilots, however, gender was frequently overlooked. Women and girls who wanted to get involved felt a certain pressure to do well. Georgette Chapelle put it like this when writing about the CAP:

> We women are trained to companionship, not generalship; to discussion, not discipline; to compromise rather than the "greatest good for the greatest number" policy by which a semi-military organization works.
>
> Put it this way: Women are accepted in the patrols as equals with men—in flying, in leadership, in the suppression of temperament. It's up to you to prove that this is the basis on which you want to remain, for every girl who accepts discipline cheerfully makes it easier for the next ten girls to follow her pioneering.[40]

Chapelle's statement underlines the lack of restrictions applied to participation in the Civil Air Patrol. Yet, given the volunteer status of the task coupled with the relatively large time demand, it is also obvious that participants needed to be free from such obligations as full-time childcare.

In addition to being open to women, the CAP did not discriminate on the basis of race. The well-known black aviator of the 1930s, Willa Brown, was active in the CAP. As a lieutenant and adjutant, she was the first black woman to be an officer in the organization. Based in her native Chicago, Brown taught aviation courses in the high schools and organized a CAP squadron. Her impact on aviation in World War II, however, went far beyond her CAP activities. She was the coordinator of war-training service for the CAA, and more importantly, was the director of the Coffey School of Aeronautics, the school selected by the Army and the CAA to "conduct the experiments" that resulted in the admission of blacks into the Army Air Forces. Later, Coffey became a feeder school for the Army Air Forces' program for black aviators at Tuskegee Institute.[41] Willa Brown's work as a teacher of aviation classes is a good example of the type of nonflying activities that were part of the Civil Air Patrol. Other tasks included maintenance, radio operations, weather forecasting, chauffeuring, and first-aid work.[42]

The U.S. Weather Bureau offered graduate scholarships in meteorology to both men and women who were college graduates (with a year of calculus and a year of physics) and holders of private pilot's licenses.[43] Training involved an eight-month course that resulted in the professional rating of junior meteorologist, earning about $2,000, plus overtime, per year. Very few women became meteorologists (by 1948 only eight women were professional meteorologists), but one important woman in this group was Lois Coots Tonkin, a graduate of Marietta College in Ohio, who learned to fly with that college's CPTP program. Inspired by her instructor, Lenore Harper McElroy, Tonkin advanced in the CPTP until she became a ground school instructor. A college physics professor heard of the CAA meteorology program and called Tonkin to see if she was interested. As a result, she became the only woman in a class of two hundred at New York University and eventually the first woman meteorologist at the Weather Bureau in Washington. Later Tonkin worked in Denver and then Detroit. In each place she encountered an initial resistance toward women, only to see that prejudice melt away as the men adapted to her presence.[44]

Women also worked for the Civil Aeronautics Administration. Like the Civilian Pilot Training Program, the CAA also experienced rapid depletion of its personnel ranks precisely when its need was increasing. One of its solutions was to develop intensive training courses for which the CAA encouraged inexperienced workers to apply. Another program was launched specifically to encourage women to apply for positions with the CAA. To enter at the more advanced level, one qualification that could be substituted for technical experience was a pilot's license. This allowed some women to begin their career with greater administrative responsibility and higher pay than was typical for women in the CAA at the time.

Most women interested in aviation, however, were encouraged by the CAA to start as aircraft communicators. These persons were responsible for taking and reporting weather observations and operating and maintaining radio telegraph, radio telephone, and teletype equipment. Applicants had to be between seventeen and forty years old and able to type forty words per minute to qualify for a trainee position. Once the orientation and training program was successfully completed, the trainees would become junior aircraft communicators. It was noted by a CAA personnel officer, Edward J. Gardner, that in 1942, 75 percent of the trainees were women.[45]

The CAA also trained supervisors in fields of aviation-related instruction that were controlled by the federal government. Maintenance supervisors oversaw the process of training and certifying aircraft and aircraft engine mechanics. Likewise, CAA ground school supervisors and flight supervisors were responsible for instruction, training, and certification in their respective fields.

In a different section of the CAA was the Air Marking Division, under the leadership of Blanche Noyes. Air marking involved making signs that would be clearly visible to pilots and would indicate location and compass orientation.

Started with a few women in 1935 under the Bureau of Air Commerce, it had been the first U.S. government program conceived, planned, and directed entirely by women. Owing to the war and the fear that air marking would aid enemy aircraft, the division reversed its task and began a program to remove all of the signs. At the war's end, it would revert back to its original function.[46]

The job for which the CAA was best known was air traffic control. This was still a relatively new and developing field. There were a multitude of openings because the CAA had recently taken over control of virtually all airport towers (many had previously been under local or state jurisdiction). To staff the towers the CAA developed an intensive training program, which was taught at seven centers located around the country. According to CAA estimates, about one-third of the controllers were women. It was specifically noted that their salaries were identical to those of men in equivalent posts. Together, these men and women would create the modern air traffic control system.[47]

The jobs within the CAA had identical counterparts in the military, and because of the war the distinction between military and civilian responsibilities and occupations was blurred. Organizations such as the CAP took on a military air while others, such as the Women's Airforce Service Pilots, though technically having civilian status, truly became in thought, word, and deed part of the military. Other aspects of aviation, such as air transportation and industry, had intimate ties to the military and the government and yet maintained a thoroughly civilian orientation. The next chapter explores these important segments of the aviation community, broadening the role of women in aviation from primarily avocational and unremunerated service roles to vocational (and therefore compensated) positions.

Many of the individual women and groups discussed in this chapter could never have been selected for an elite military program; they were disqualified because of marriage or children. Others did not choose to seek paid employment. The organizations such as the Civil Air Patrol and the Ninety-Nines, the college programs, and the Civilian Pilot Training Program provided these women with their only opportunities to begin or continue their involvement with aviation during the wartime years. Their contribution is an integral part of the larger history of women in aviation.

2

Coffee, Grease, Blueprints, and Rivets

Women at Work in the Aviation Industry

> We are beginning to find that there is no work dependent upon skill
> and dexterity that women cannot be taught to do very well.
>
> Fairchild Aircraft Company Official

The women who worked in the control towers or in other capacities for the Civil Aeronautics Administration remind us that women have been employed in a variety of positions in the air transportation business for a long time. From the earliest days of aviation, women had been involved with selling flight. During World War II the professional establishment of the flight attendants led airlines to experiment with women in other occupations, such as maintenance.

The demands of the war led to a huge expansion in the aircraft industry and enormously enlarged the opportunities in it for female employment. From engineer to riveter, women in the industry assumed new roles and consequently, like most women war workers, acquired a new view of their abilities and of their place in American society.

Prior to the war, the most prominent women in commercial aviation were those working with the airlines as flight attendants, ticket agents, reservations clerks, and other service personnel. Although two airlines continued to use male stewards (Eastern and Pan American), the draft promptly ensured women's virtual domination of the positions. Women did not have final authority over the processes of selection, training, and evaluation, although some flight attendants eventually became "chief hostesses," a position in which they exercised some managerial responsibility.

The ultimate airline position for women, the one that before the war personified women in aviation for most people, was the flight attendant, or stew-

Flight attendants from Challenger Airlines (a Frontier antecedent) are shown posing in full uniform for a public relations photograph. Until World War II all attendants had to be registered nurses. *Courtesy of the Association of Flight Attendants.*

ardess (or hostess as she was then called). In 1940 the standard requirements for each applicant for a hostess position were that she had to be between 21 and 26 years of age; between five feet, two inches, and five feet, six inches tall; between 100 and 125 pounds (weight had to be proportionate to height); a graduate registered nurse; a U.S. citizen; single or widowed; personable; intelligent; and attractive. These qualifications are apparent in Braniff Airlines' advertisement for their hostess positions: "Applicant must be of perfect physical condition, well proportioned, no disfigurations. Unquestionable family background. Irreproachable character. Poise, self-confidence, tact, diplomacy. Pleasant personality. Ability to deal with people."[1]

What these requirements mask is the discrimination against black and other minority women, which mirrored the character of the American aviation community in general. The airlines had a very specific concept to sell to the public, and neither the airlines nor the American public confronted the social dictates that limited the applicant pool to white middle-class women.

Airline managers believed that most of their patrons would be white middle-class men and that it would be "difficult for potential travelers [especially men] to admit fears of flying when young women routinely took to the air as part of an inflight crew."[2] The restricted nature of the pool of hostesses was not questioned or even noticed by most passengers or by the airline corporate executives. As Alice H. Cook puts it in her introduction to Georgia Panter Nielson's book on the history of the Association of Flight Attendants union: "From the beginning the flight attendants were treated like daughters of Victorian, middle-class families, girls who needed protection during the few months they would work. It was expected, of course, that they would not question the decisions of their employers or of the captains in the cockpits, and that they would just as unquestioningly stop work after they married."[3]

Marriage was a dilemma for the airline management. It was to their advantage to maintain a high turnover rate, because companies did not have to have elaborate wage increases, establish pension plans, or maintain expensive benefit programs. In fact, the base wage (approximately $125 per month) for attendants remained almost constant from the time they were first hired in 1930 through the end of World War II.[4] Further, the administrators liked to think of their "girls" as a highly desirable lot. For example, one Transcontinental and Western Air (later Trans World Airlines) instructor reportedly advised his class: "If you have not found a man to keep you by the time you're 28, TWA won't want you either!"[5]

The catch in this situation was that the airlines had made a financial investment in training the women for the job, an expensive proposition, when they might never work for the company. Hence the rule evolved that an attendant had to work at least a year before leaving, unless her future husband (or anyone else for that matter) was willing to "buy her freedom."[6]

World War II changed the flight attendant profession. By 1940 the Douglas DC-3 (the most widely used civilian aircraft) and the whole concept of air travel it helped establish had become fixtures in the minds of the air-conscious public. Carrying twenty-one passengers, the DC-3 expanded the airline passenger

population and made commercial airlines highly profitable. The new generation of air passengers had high expectations for their inflight service, including
meals as well as a multitude of other amenities. The DC-3, with its extended
range and larger passenger load, represented a substantive increase in the
workload for the hostess. The airlines could not offer these more sophisticated
services if, as had largely been the case until the DC-3, they depended exclusively on the copilot to interact with the passengers. This led to hiring substantially more women as hostesses.[7]

In the 1930s, to justify the resulting extra weight and reduction in revenue
passenger space occasioned by the addition of hostesses, the early promoters of
this female flight crew position had decided that the women should be registered nurses. They believed the nurse/hostess would provide psychological re-
assurance through the image of safety and caution. The nursing requirement
was dropped in the early 1940s as military and civilian hospitals began to experience a desperate shortage of nurses.

Although this change in qualifications opened the door for more applicants, it must be admitted that the nursing requirement had lent a degree of
prestige and status to the occupation. A trained nurse was a professional; work
as a stewardess represented an unusual adventure and a challenge. It might lead
to marriage, but if not, a woman's nursing training would enable her to provide for herself. Ellen Church, the first woman hired as a flight attendant, is an
excellent example. Church worked for United Airlines for a year and a half
until she injured her foot in a car accident (her tenure was a typical period of
service for attendants). She then returned to nursing and in 1942 entered the
Air Evacuation Service of the Army Nurse Corps. In September 1944 she became the first flying nurse to be awarded the Air Medal.[8]

Ellen Church, and many women like her, had a strong sense of self-esteem.
She was intelligent, well organized, and highly motivated; she was also extraordinarily well trained for the nature of the job that the airlines had in mind.
Hostesses were supposed to be "elite temporary workers [in a] . . . short-term
position for women to enjoy before being married to raise a family."[9]

The new women hired from 1940 to 1945 recognized the disparity between
the increased workload and the lack of a subsequent increase in pay. For example, at United Airlines the base pay in 1942 was $125 per month. If a woman
continued with United, after six months her pay would be increased to $140
per month. During a second year of employment her pay would be $150 per
month. Subsequently her wage would be increased annually by $5 per month
until a maximum of $170 was reached. Despite the white-collar status of the
flight attendant, the base salary was comparable to the wage of airframe production line workers (who earned about $0.96 per hour on average). However,

the stewardesses usually worked only 100 to 115 hours per month compared with the minimum of 160 hours for production line workers.[10]

During the war some stewardesses were required to work as many as 160 hours per month. This is not surprising, as the number of revenue passenger miles on U.S. domestic airlines increased approximately 220 percent, from 1,052 million in 1940 to 3,362 million, in 1945.[11] It was a difficult, if not impossible, time for the women to raise the issue of maximum hours and minimum wages with the airlines. Only twelve out of every two thousand applicants were selected for training and employment. The intense competition for positions meant that the airlines always had an adequate labor supply, despite the war. This, combined with the no-marriage rule, meant that the flight attendants did not initially develop any professional associations or unions, in contrast to the successful Airline Pilots Association.[12]

By 1944 the attendant's job had assumed a prestigious air. A United Airlines lawyer of that period later recalled: "The stewardess was an important part of our culture. This was not a working woman; this was a glamour job."[13] That attitude was reinforced by the media. It was also true that when compared with an assembly line position or secretarial work, the attendant's assignments were more diverse. However, as a result of their wartime experience, the women began to reexamine their occupation. They recognized that they were making a contribution to the war effort, and most stewardesses, unlike corporate airline officials, definitely perceived themselves as working women. It was in the mid-1940s that highly motivated individuals such as Ada Brown began to emerge from the ranks of the profession. She had become a stewardess with United in 1940, and in 1944 she began the movement that led to the unionization of the flight attendants.

Before boarding the airplane the passenger's first contact was with the "voice with a smile," or the "hello girl," as reservations clerks were commonly called. The job involved booking reservations and confirming tickets, a task made infinitely more complex in those days by the lack of computerization and by the particular demands of wartime. The war forged a special relationship between the federal government and the airlines. Seats were automatically given to the military and individuals traveling on war-related business. Further, the airlines assisted the military by providing air transportation around the globe.

The reservations clerk, as was typical of many other airline positions, was required to have qualifications at a level that far exceeded the actual demands of the job. A college graduate with experience in sales or secretarial work was preferred. In addition, it was stated by the airlines that women should be "unafraid of figures, for a 'consolidated timetable,' showing international air line, bus and train schedules, is the bible of their work. They [should be] alert and steady-nerved, accustomed to handling a multitude of details under pressure."[14]

Ada Brown worked as a flight attendant during the early 1940s. In 1944, she organized the first flight attendants union, the Air Line Stewardess Association (ALSA). *Courtesy of the Association of Flight Attendants.*

Both the "hello girls" and the women hired to work as ticket agents at public counters attended a six-week initial training course. The graduates often called this experience "personality training," but in addition to learning to alter their speech habits and understand customer psychology, they also studied timetables, airline routes, and common law as it applied to commercial transportation. Although these technical subjects represented the intellectual substance of the position, it was the cultivation and expression of feminine "charm and grace" that mattered to the companies and the clientele, as the "hello girl" image indicates.[15]

Not all women airline workers at this time were flight attendants or ticket handlers. Many became involved in the process of maintaining the airlines' fleets. Servicing the huge number of aircraft required the same degree of job specialization for mechanics as did the production line. New wartime mechanics were assigned to specific tasks rather than assuming responsibility for the entire aircraft. A small crew of specialists could service many more airplanes than the same number of individuals working alone. The other advantage of specialization was that it simplified the training process for new workers. Women who generally had had little or no experience in the field could be rapidly integrated into the hangar crews if they had to master only one facet of the occupation. Thus, the war produced teams of technicians, each masters of a small field, replacing the more traditional image of a multiskilled and masculine mechanic.

Transcontinental and Western Air started a program in conjunction with the War and Navy Departments called WAMS (Women Apprentice Mechanics). The program was developed to provide replacements for men called up for combat service. In 1943, 110 women were employed as "learners and helpers," but the estimates were that this could increase to the point where women filled almost 50 percent of the jobs. In general, 20 percent of TWA employees in 1942 were women, but by 1943 this grew to 35 percent.[16]

There were 814 women mechanics working for Pan American Airways in December 1942. An article in the company magazine described the dramatic expansion of the feminine presence: "Numbers did not tell the whole story, by any means. Equally important was the excellence of the work being turned in by feminine hands and brains. Many jobs were, in fact, proving more suitable to female than to male skills, eg. cleaning spark plugs."[17]

One of Pan Am's mechanic crews at La Guardia Field in New York was composed entirely of women. One was a former drugstore cashier, one was a sales girl, and three were housewives. In June 1943, this crew was considered by Pan Am to be the fastest and most capable on duty—male or "coed."[18]

Mechanic's Helper Betty Travis was the only woman in 1942 qualified to work directly on Clipper engines. Her previous experience in automobile engine repair indicates why she was able to assume this position so rapidly. Travis was clearly considered a model employee. The company reported that "four nights a week she is taking courses on motor transportation service, first aid and other subjects offered by the American Women's Voluntary Services, Inc. (AWVS), [and she] goes on duty as an air raid warden in her local district in Forest Hills one other night a week. She has also enrolled for the free courses in aviation mechanics soon to be sponsored in Pan American's La Guardia Field hangar by New York's Board of Education."[19]

The instructions to male employees at Pan American were clear—treat the women like men. False chivalry was not welcome, and for the first time there was a written policy on this matter. The most obvious manifestation of this order was that the men addressed the women only by their last names (the women spoke to the men in the same way). The company felt such changes in personnel policies (including the hiring of women) represented the "biggest opportunity air transport had offered women since the domestic airlines adopted flying stewardesses."[20]

Jobs for women in aviation were not limited to the air transportation industry. In fact, the vast majority of women were employed in some facet of aircraft manufacturing and production. Some of the positions traditionally held by women included work as public relations specialists. These women were expected to understand the industry thoroughly and to be able to answer both technical and nontechnical questions about aviation. An understanding of research skills and journalism was considered an important requirement for this job. Frances de Marquis, for example, worked for Fairchild Aviation Corporation. Her work was principally concerned with preparing press releases on the aircraft built by Fairchild, but she also responded to the large number of individual requests for information about the company.[21]

The industry became eager in the early 1940s to train and employ women engineers, reflecting an acute shortage of suitably skilled applicants. A 1942 article in *Independent Woman* by a woman engineer observed: "A year ago none of the plants wanted women. This year it's different and employment for women students who stick to their studies is virtually assured."[22]

Employment was "virtually assured" because in 1942 more than eighteen thousand new engineering jobs existed, but only twelve thousand qualified students graduated to fill them. Women engineers in any aviation specialty were practically nonexistent in 1940. Few schools of engineering admitted women; the principal ones that did were Pennsylvania State University, Massachusetts Institute of Technology, University of Tennessee, University of Colorado, Cornell University, and the Newark School of Engineering. In 1942 two of the three women members in the American Institute of Electrical Engineers were employed in aviation—Edith Clark at General Electric and Mabel Rockwell at Lockheed.[23]

It occurred to the manufacturers, however, that they could use women with a mathematics or physical science background if they were given an intensive (albeit highly abbreviated) course in engineering. The Chance Vought Aircraft Division of United Aircraft Corporation, for example, established scholarships for women in aeronautical engineering at New York University. The program recruited women who had completed their junior year in college for an eight-month program of specialized technical training at the Daniel Guggenheim School of Aeronautics of the College of Engineering at New York University. The women, about forty in each class, would receive their degrees from their original college through a transfer of credits from New York University. In order to receive the scholarship, the young women signed a formal contract with Chance Vought that included an option by the company on the student's services for one year after completing the training course.[24]

Rose Marie "Bonnie" Campbell (now Bender) of the second class of Chance Vought Scholars described the rigorous program. The first semester included mechanical drawing, calculus, and introduction to the three principle engineering fields: aeronautics, mechanics, and materials. In the second semester the women were taught aircraft design and drawing, aerodynamics, stress and weight analysis methods, and a survey of aircraft equipment and components. Those who successfully completed the course were taken on by Chance Vought in the Engineering Department. Their first six weeks were spent on rotation through each of the company's shops before receiving a permanent assignment. Bonnie Campbell, for example, worked on the stabilizer for the famous F4U-1 Corsair.[25]

Curtiss-Wright Corporation started an educational training program that was known as Curtiss-Wright Cadettes. Like Chance Vought, Curtiss-Wright also supplied tuition, living expenses, and a stipend for the women as they learned the profession. Curtiss-Wright, however, was much more ambitious. Its program involved eight hundred college sophomore-to-senior women who were sent to one of eight universities: Cornell, Northwestern, Purdue, Iowa State, Minnesota, Texas, Pennsylvania State, and Rensselaer Polytechnic Institute. Half were trained in the design of airframes, half in the design of airplane engines.[26]

Professors who had never taught women students before were surprised. At Rensselaer the faculty responded that the "Cadettes catch on in a hurry, ask more questions than do the boys, take the detail better, and therefore, learn their subjects more thoroughly."[27] After a ten-month course, the women were expected to work as professional engineers for Curtiss-Wright. These women were pioneers, seizing new occupational opportunities. They had a different status from that accorded to the trainees at Chance Vought and several other manufacturers that tended to see women as engineering aides and assistants.[28]

The aircraft industry was getting a bargain in its female engineering employees. The new subspecialties they filled made it possible to get by with fewer "full-fledged" engineers, and the overall production process was enhanced. The new aides or paraprofessionals performed routine engineering tasks, such as calculations, drafting, and illustration, which required less education and training.[29]

A few women in aeronautical engineering were prominently featured in the news media. Elsie Gardner was one of them. In 1942 she was the only female aeronautical engineer in the Navy. Gardner had previously worked for several companies, including Eclipse Aviation and the Wright Aeronautical Corporation. She had also spent five years with the Army Air Forces as the editor of *Technical Digest,* translating and condensing thousands of scientific articles on aviation topics from French, German, Italian, and English sources.[30]

Isabel Ebel was another engineering pioneer. She graduated from MIT in 1932, the only woman studying aeronautical engineering among a student body of thirty women and three thousand men. Unable to find work in any American aircraft factory, she went back to school at the Guggenheim School of Aero-

Like many wartime industries, the MIT Radiation Laboratory (which worked on radar) developed crash courses to train women with backgrounds in math and science in engineering fundamentals. Here the instructor is teaching a class about the radar system's signal generator. *Courtesy of the MIT Museum.*

nautics at NYU. No woman had ever been admitted previously, and only after the intervention of Amelia Earhart was Ebel accepted. Even with this additional academic work (she graduated in 1934), she was unable to find a company willing to hire her. Finally in 1939 she got her first opportunity, at Grumman Aircraft Corporation, where for two years she worked on several airplanes, concentrating primarily on the XF5F-1. She then worked for two smaller firms until 1942, when she took a position as a research engineer with United Airlines.[31]

Isabel Ebel summed up the reception given to these remarkable female aeronautical engineers: "The fact that I am a woman has never hindered me with any engineering work I have done, but I don't know that it has given me any particular advantage either. . . . I have found on the whole that once the original barrier is down, women are fairly well accepted."[32]

In the war years there were more women in engineering than ever before, yet, in both comparative and absolute terms, their numbers were very small. General Electric, for example, employed only 12 women as professional engineers and 206 women in paraprofessional jobs, such as computation or drafting.[33]

Although the female contributions to the war effort were generally recog-

Margaret Cook worked as a production test pilot for Convair's Stinson Aircraft from 1943 to 1946. *Courtesy of Margaret A. Cook.*

nized and appreciated by politicians, the public, and the press, it was commonly thought that the only possible motivation these women might have was patriotism and the desire to do something on behalf of a brother, father, or fiancé. That opinion was, in fact, largely justified. Many women engineers sought training and employment for exactly those reasons. Bonnie Campbell, the Chance Vought engineer, wanted to use her mathematical knowledge to help the war effort. She announced her engagement shortly after graduation from NYU, however, and left the company right after her year's obligation was complete in order to get married.[34] Both the women engineers and the corporations perceived female employees as temporary additions to the factory workforce. The experience of these women was therefore quite different from those who viewed themselves as a permanent part of the corporate world.

Three women who began work with the aircraft industry during the war and who did anticipate careers with their company were Cecil "Teddy" Kenyon, Barbara "Kibby" Jayne, and Elizabeth Hooker. They were hired to work ultimately as test pilots by Brewster A. "Bud" Gillies, a vice president of Grumman Aircraft Corporation (and husband of Ninety-Nines president and WAFS second-in-command Betty Gillies).[35]

Mildred Strelitz was the first woman engineering aide to participate in test flights at Wright Army Air Field, Ohio, on 9 November 1943. *Author's collection.*

He had become very concerned about the shortage of company test pilots, individuals who were critical to the manufacturing process. They flight-tested every airplane as it came off the assembly line. The first to fly the aircraft, these pilots were exposed to a fair degree of risk in order to certify the aircraft for delivery to the military. Gillies believed that hiring women pilots was a very good solution to the problem. He was shrewd in making his pitch to the company. The three women he selected were active professional pilots before the war, and they were well educated and very confident in their skills. Gillies allowed them to demonstrate their competence in a nonthreatening way to both the corporate officials and the male test pilots by first employing them as general pilots. Starting in late 1942, Kenyon, Jayne, and Hooker flew short ferry runs to pick up, transport, and drop off materials for Grumman. Then they learned to fly the amphibious twin-engined Widgeons as well as the twin-engined JRF. At that point, it seemed that any opportunity to fly the company's fighter aircraft was just a dream for these women.[36]

As soon as the three women had accumulated some experience with the company procedures, Gillies proposed to Grumman that they be allowed to work as production test pilots. His plan was a success. The company supported Gillies and had the women serve a trial period as test pilots on Grumman Hellcat fighter airplanes.

That decision had important repercussions. It reinforced the view that women pilots could operate combat aircraft safely and successfully. Further, it showed that women were as capable as men in the rigorous responsibilities of test piloting. Given the high media profile and visibility these women received, the three became vital role models to be cited by any advocate of women pilots. The three women's success was considered influential also in the decision to allow women to become air traffic controllers.

There was tension at Grumman despite the good work of Kenyon, Jayne, and Hooker. Margot Roberts described this problem in her 1944 article about the three in *Woman's Home Companion:* "As a class, men fliers are nobly [*sic*] conservative, masculine and inclined to think of a woman's place as being in the home. They rarely welcomed lady pilots in their midst. This is something that all the gal pioneers of flying have bumped into at times. As they have the normal feminine desire to get along with men, a problem is created at first—though a very short-lived one in most cases—and you can't always blame the men. There are several angles to this man-woman equality proposition. At Grumman, for example, there is the matter of sticky ships."[37]

"Sticky ships" were airplanes that were suspected of having serious problems that could not be found by mechanics on the ground. The women were not permitted to fly these aircraft, nor were they permitted to do experimental testing such as dives. The three were annoyed by the arbitrariness of the policy, which also complicated their acceptance by male colleagues. The men were ambivalent, resenting the unfair exclusion of the women, yet also still none too sure about the notion of women flying at all. Further, even other women fliers, such as the prominent pilot and director of the WASP, Jacqueline Cochran, were critical of the job the Grumman women were doing. They viewed it as a kind of "aerial dishwashing," yet within the restrictions imposed on them Kenyon, Jayne, and Hooker had ably demonstrated the competence of female test pilots. As Margot Roberts put it, "It isn't real dishwashing and [that is] one reason for the attraction."[38]

The vast majority of women in the aviation industry were production line workers. The employment of women in such jobs predated Pearl Harbor and the American declaration of war, after which the number of women involved increased enormously with the dramatic expansion of aircraft manufacturing.

Beginning in 1938 with Hitler's annexation of Austria, then the occupation of the Sudetenland, followed by the invasion of Poland, events in Europe had galvanized the attention of Americans. On Sunday, 3 September 1939, Great

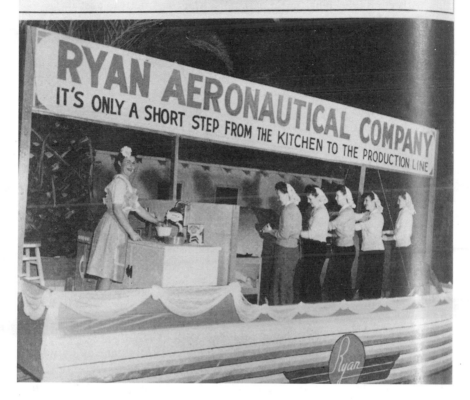

This parade float, sponsored by Ryan Aircraft in San Diego, California, was designed to encourage women to join the aircraft production line.

Britain, and then France, declared war on Germany. In turn, the slow and inexorable process of American mobilization for an oncoming war began to quicken.

The first major manifestation of change was in the aircraft industry. Demand increased radically as President Franklin D. Roosevelt and his administration became explicitly committed to the premise that air power would win the war. The effect of this on the military was the abolition of the Army's ban on the development and production of bomber aircraft such as the B-17 and the B-24. Military leaders in the Army Air Corps held a conference with the major aircraft manufacturers in order to establish plans for wartime production. That meeting was held in July 1939, and subsequently the manufacturers began to implement production of the two airplanes. The demand for aircraft already existed, and it was obvious that there would be a huge export market as the British and French became major consumers of American aircraft.[39]

Both the British and the French had identified the value of air power for offensive and defensive military programs. The disastrous experience with the German Luftwaffe in the Battle of Britain in the spring of 1940 reinforced the argument for bomber aircraft. Following the fall of France after the Dunkirk evacuation in June 1940, British prime minister Winston Churchill made an impassioned plea to the free world for assistance. It provoked an immediate response from President Roosevelt. Roosevelt persuaded Congress to provide the resources (political, economic, and military) in such measure that American industry would be capable of producing at least fifty thousand airplanes a year. Then, in January 1941, he worked to secure passage of the Lend-Lease Act, which would extend the military's ability to lend, lease, or transfer American military equipment to foreign countries whose defense was considered vital to the United States. One other congressional action stimulated by Roosevelt would particularly affect women in aviation: the establishment of the draft on 16 September 1940.[40]

These events meant that the aircraft industry was faced with the need for a phenomenal growth of volume output, which would be hampered by a serious labor shortage. The industry catapulted from forty-fourth (ranked by value of its output) in the United States in 1939 to first in 1944. Within the course of one year, from January 1942 to January 1943, total employment in all of the airframe, engine, and propeller plants of prime contractors changed from 460,356 to 1,027,914. These numbers do not include subcontractors and parts suppliers. There was a desperate need for workers, and as a result of the draft women became the single greatest labor source for the industry. In that same 1942 to 1943 period, the total number of women employed by prime contractors grew nearly 1,300 percent, from 23,137 to 321,788. Women represented 5 percent of the total general workforce in January 1942 and 31.3 percent in January 1943.[41]

In a wartime publication, *Education for Victory,* the lead article in June 1943 was on women in industry: "That old sign—'Men Only' no longer frowns unchallenged at the door of American Aviation. In many important spots of industry the ban on women workers has gone the way of the dodo bird. In others, it lingers feebly and outmoded, as untimely as last year's circus poster. And in numerous shop windows appears a new sign—fresh, realistic and inviting—with a new slogan—'Women are Welcome.'"[42]

In June 1943 women represented 35 percent of the total number of work-

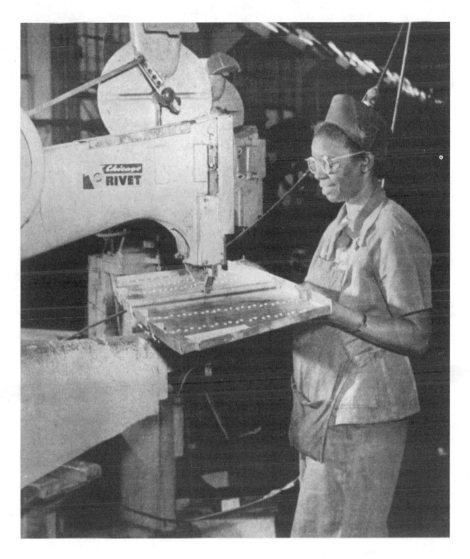

An unusual photograph of a black woman working on the aircraft assembly line at the Eastern Aircraft Division of General Motors. *Courtesy of General Motors Corporation.*

ers, a proportion that rose eventually as high as 36.9 percent (July 1944). At the peak of employment in aviation (November 1943) there were 486,073 women (36.7 percent) among 1,326,345 workers.[43]

The transition was not made quite as easily, however, as the statistics might imply. Manufacturers were initially hesitant to use women, partly because of

"Meet my wife and daughter—or vice-ver.
Drawn for Office c/ \   .formation

The novelty of women on the assembly line was the subject of many wartime cartoons. *U.S. Office of War Information.*

certain stereotypes regarding the kinds of work a woman could or should do, but mostly because of lack of experience with women in the workplace. High production demands temporarily suspended "philosophical" objections—women had to participate in the production lines if quotas were to be met.

It is noteworthy that much of this discussion refers to the experience of white women. Women of color found that they were faced with an almost impenetrable barrier of racism and sexism. They were often referred to the armed services if they wanted to work. Still, they responded strongly to the call for female labor, and most companies did hire women of color. Most often they were shunted into the least attractive and most dangerous jobs.[44]

Women were brought into three main areas as the factories tooled up for mass production. Most worked directly on the assembly line. A smaller group worked as clerks (both secretarial and production line). Slightly fewer were tool designers and makers. Male colleagues gradually had to concede that the women could do the job. Fairchild Aircraft Company issued a statement acknowledging that "they [women] have proved, on the whole, good workmen; though the same differences in skills and temperaments may be observed among them as among men."[45]

At the individual supervisory level, the comments of Ryan Aircraft Factory foreman Frank Walsh express a typical reaction toward women workers: "I was dubious at first. Many of the jobs in this department required machine shop experience. But most of these girls had never even seen a machine shop. Yet today some of them are operating mandrels, burring and cutting machines. Furthermore, they occasionally turn out records that beat all our previous standards."[46]

Despite such positive comments about the new women, however, many negative ones were also expressed. In the same Ryan factory where Frank Walsh worked, one official stated: "Hundreds of the girls we have are not yet disciplined to stand the noises and smells of a factory. They often don't have the right temperament for this sort of work. In some departments they don't work as fast nor as accurately as men. And some of our girls are serious offenders in absenteeism."[47]

There is no historical evidence that women were worse "offenders in absenteeism" than men, yet this was something that became identified as a feminine problem.[48] Leslie Neville, for example, wrote in his March 1943 *Aviation* editorial that while "invasion of the aviation manufacturing industry by members of the weaker sex has done much to solve the problem of meeting labor force requirements of our greatly expanded production program . . . it poses new and far reaching problems for management and government. . . . the most serious—and still unresolved—difficulty that has come about since the ladies took to aircraft building is absenteeism."[49]

Almost parenthetically, Neville added that this was not confined to women workers alone. The thrust of the article was that the workers, especially the women, were not fully aware of the serious nature of their work, that for some, working all-out for patriotic purposes was a novelty that "ebbs and flows with the headlines in their newspapers." Neville completely ignored the causes of absenteeism and argued that it was materialism that had consumed the new workers; in other words, the preoccupation of the workers was not victory but goods.[50]

Nothing could have been further from the truth. To participate in the aircraft factory life, women had to overcome several obstacles. First and foremost, they were not wanted. The most difficult prejudice for them to overcome was not the fact that feminine mechanical aptitude lacked social acceptance but rather the notion that women belonged in the home. The 15 April 1942 edition of the *Civil Aeronautics Journal* reported that "formerly custom, habit, the attitude of unions, the attitude of management, and the considerations of cost, all served to curtail the number and kind of openings available to women."[51]

When Elinor Collins became a mechanic's helper in the fall of 1942 in Pan American's Alaskan Carpentry Section, it was reported that "eyebrows raised, the men started pools on which thumb she would blacken first. After a week, neophyte Collins reported to Chief of the Carpenter Shop, C.W. Smith without even a chipped fingernail. Shortly she was hammering nails, finishing wood and operating a table saw with the smooth sureness of a masculine master craftsman. 'Yes, she's darn good,' admitted fellow workers. 'Mrs. Collins saws lumber the way my wife bakes a cake. She's brisk and efficient, never wastes a moment.'"[52]

The idea of a woman assembly line worker still grated on the American sensibilities, yet many women did manage to justify such activity in the name of patriotism and the war effort. The complexity of the definition and experience of patriotism made it a motivational tool of uncertain integrity. Propagandistic appeals to patriotism were frequently made in order to manipulate an individual, usually with the intent of producing some behavioral alteration based on a sense of guilt.[53] This tendency toward exploitation was recognized by several leaders, in particular by some connected with the employment of women in industry. Elinor Herrick, director of personnel and labor relations for the Todd Shipyards Corporation, wrote in the introduction to Laura Nelson Baker's *Wanted: Women in War Industry:* "But such an appeal to this patriotism must not be the preliminary to their exploitation. They must have decent working conditions, they must have safeguards for health, they must be given full recognition of their efforts in terms of proper pay, promotional opportunity and the rest."[54]

The huge influx of new workers meant a heightened awareness of the conditions of the factory workplace; the presence of women ensured media and public attention. Many managers, such as the Ryan factory official quoted earlier, implied that difficulties in adapting to the plant were a fault of gender.

The problem was not one of biology. Concurrently with the arrival of women—and other new workers—new labor laws developed. The Women's Bureau of the U.S. Department of Labor called for the promulgation of thirteen new labor laws, which applied to males and females alike. These included the eight-hour day, forty-eight-hour week, specified rest periods, a thirty-minute meal period, minimum wage guarantees, extension of workmen's compensation legislation, and compulsory health insurance.

The laws were progressive (and expensive for industry), and were designed to "extend our legal bulwarks to guarantee on all labor fronts protection against the foes of fatigue, illness, accidents—against the hazards of unemployment and old age."[55] These proposed regulations were not uniformly adopted, but their influence was felt. Foreman Gordon Shop at the Consolidated Vultee Plant in San Diego commented that women had made a difference in the plant. He was quick to point out that women themselves had not made the changes; it was the company that instituted new time- and strength-saving devices. However, it is equally obvious that without the presence of women, these changes—procedures and devices that benefited everyone—would not have been established as soon as they were (if at all).[56]

It is questionable whether the production line problems of the expanded aviation industry were actually the fault of women's gender. There was little contemporary recognition that the difficulties might be explained as a function of inexperience, different socialization, education, and background. Individual women were often praised in glowing terms. Foremen and corporations exhibited considerable pride in their *girls'* accomplishments.

Women collectively, however, were often blamed for larger problems experienced in the factories at this time. Perhaps this was part of the reason why women, in far greater numbers than men, did not choose to continue working at the plants at war's end.

All kinds of women worked on production lines, either full time or as occasional help. During summer vacation periods, for example, schoolteachers would come to work with the aircraft companies. Two California high school teachers, Constance Bowman and Clara Marie (C.M.) Allen, worked the swing shift at the Consolidated Aircraft Company building B-24 bombers. In the course of two months a significant transition was made. Bowman's book, *Slacks and Callouses,* reveals the moment that they first recognized the true value of their labor and their ability to make a substantive contribution. This occurred when they began to train their replacements, realizing that they were not "extras." "Our jobs were not going to be absorbed by other people in addition to their regular work. We had to be replaced, woman for woman, job for job."[57] This generated a feeling of pride that neither woman, despite her teaching career, had experienced prior to that point.

"You know, we really did do something this summer," said C.M.

"Don't I know we did," I said looking at the ships and then my hands, with callouses on the palms and cuts on the knuckles and not one fingernail that extended beyond the tip of the finger.[58]

Bowman and Allen were not alone in feeling pride in their accomplishments. A talented aviation writer, Georgette "Dickey" Chapelle wrote two books (under her maiden name, Dickey Meyer) during the war to encourage women to participate in aviation.[59] The key message of Chapelle's books and others like them was that women, while feeling proud about contributing to their country's war effort, also really enjoyed working in aviation. The latter feeling was what these authors believed would ensure a continued feminine presence in the industry. For example, Chapelle wrote:

> The aircraftswomen of today are proud of their skills, but they know that the system by which they work permits no primadonnas. The girls remember well the days when femininity and aviation met only in headlines and press pictures, and they do not propose to revive that unfortunate custom.
>
> They have begun a new tradition, and one which they believe will outlive the other by many generations. It is a tradition of accomplishment, of consistently getting things done. They are raising their standards ever higher each working day, and beneath their uniforms and coveralls their hearts have wings.[60]

What is especially notable about the period of World War II is that in the aircraft industry women were for the first time permitted to enter the higher-paying manufacturing jobs instead of being relegated exclusively to lower-paying nonmanufacturing jobs (usually secretarial work). Yet even as these changes were occurring, it is apparent that women were deliberately placed in specific occupations.[61] Starting out with skills equivalent to those of the men, women still found they were channeled into the dullest, most tedious occupations—all the while being praised for their wonderful ability to do inspection, sewing, small parts assembly, and rivet checking. A factory supervisor commented: "Men get tired of doing the same thing over and over again but some of the women will stick right by the job hour after hour. Jobs often have to be broken down and simplified for them, and extra-fine tooling is required—but once a simple job is set up for them they'll go to town on it without ever showing any signs of boredom."[62]

Women were assigned to jobs requiring fine, precise, detailed work such as inspection. Yet this work was considered to be of a lesser status in the factory than those jobs more commonly filled by men. Most factories rated their employees according to a specific code; the higher the rating, the more valuable the employee. Supposedly this was because the highest rating meant the greatest de-

Sorting rivets by size was the job of many female aircraft workers. *Courtesy of the General Motors Corporation.*

gree of versatility. In fact, in most companies it was usually physical strength, a quality that was neither an asset nor a requirement for many factory jobs, which received the priority code rating, and consequently the highest status.

Men still retained control of almost all the supervisory positions. Even when women worked in similar jobs, they often deferred to the men. Josephine R. Viall was the wife of a Marine Corps major as well as an editor of a Marine Corps magazine. When her husband was moved to the Pacific battle zone, she started working at the Ryan aircraft factory. She was bright, able, and capable of leadership. Yet, when she was placed in a new environment she attributed her successful orientation exclusively to the efforts made by others (in this case, men). Her comment was typical of the expressions made by many women:

Women were thought to have special skills that made them better suited to assemble small parts. This Raytheon Manufacturing Company employee is doing the final assembly of a cavity magnetron, the key component in aircraft radar systems. *Courtesy of the MIT Museum.*

"The men in the factory have been wonderfully patient in teaching me my job—even showing me around the factory so I'd see how my little operation fits in with the whole big picture."[63]

In terms of the big picture, most women on the production line were in dead-end jobs, and on average they were paid less. The average hourly earning of women in aircraft engine plants in August 1943 was $1.04, or 87 percent of the men's $1.19. In aircraft metal propeller plants the average hourly earnings for first shift workers in October 1942 were $0.81 for women and $1.05 for men. All women faced the possibility of eventually being fired because the men were guaranteed their jobs after the end of the war.[64]

A gradual shift in war propaganda began to occur in 1944. A hunger for "the good old days" had set in. Advertisements, which had at one time encouraged women to work in factories, began to promote their eventual return to the home and domesticity. Ambition was not encouraged. In aviation the situation was somewhat different. Many thought (naively) that war-level production rates would be sustained, even expanded, after the hostilities ceased. These individuals believed, therefore, that women would still be needed and desired for aviation work. Even among those who were not caught up in the visionary rhetoric of an impending "aerial age," there were many who argued that hardworking, capable women would not be fired. Although the view was a mistaken one, progress had been made and recognized.[65] "The war is teaching that many women have exceptional mechanical aptitude and can operate ponderous and complex machinery, sometimes more skillfully than men. . . . War teaches that nearly every man and woman can be used. And we are using many thousands of them. Many sociological thinkers believe that the social effects of these lessons that we are learning today may be more lasting than victory."[66]

"Rosie the Riveter," women mechanics, and their white-collar companions in air transportation and aviation manufacturing had a profound effect on American social history. The labors of these women were not part of any planned policy, such as the affirmative action programs of the 1970s and 1980s. Wartime mobilization had simply required a huge workforce. Most women entered the workforce through programs that were considered experimental and temporary. The voluntary participation of all citizens in the war effort was the goal of such programs, which is why working women in aviation became identified primarily as "volunteers" instead of as permanent workers or professionals. Despite these circumstances, women in the labor force exerted considerable influence on postwar America by removing many of the barriers against married working women.[67]

White women found there was a clear distinction between occupations that accepted (and often assisted) married women (such as work in aircraft factories) and those that did not (such as flight attendants). Black, Hispanic, and other minority women had an extremely difficult time trying to obtain war work, and for most Asian-American women the situation was impossible.

The military was slightly more tolerant. Almost every civilian occupation, except aircraft assembly, had a direct counterpart in the military. The story of military women in aviation during the war will be explained in the next two chapters and is critical to understanding the total wartime experience of women in aviation. However, by virtue of the sheer numbers of women in the aviation industry, it is the image of "Rosie the Riveter" that wrought the most change in American attitudes toward working women in the post–World War II age.

3

Daughters of Minerva

Military Women in Aviation

> For this is what the WACs declare to lads the world around: "You man the ships and guard the air and we will guard the ground."
>
> "Air WACs," author unknown

The development of air power in World War II encouraged many women in the belief that they could contribute to the defense of the United States. Female pilots were as eager as the men to put their flying talents into service. These women were not content to be shunted into peripheral roles; they wanted to be an integral part of the military. They wanted to be "daughters of Minerva," the Roman Goddess of War.

The idea of women in the military was actually not a novel one. American women had been serving the armed forces since the Revolutionary War, although often their service was either clandestine or auxiliary in nature. There are narrative accounts and documentary evidence dating back to the nation's first military struggles that confirm the service of women in combat, despite regulations officially prohibiting their recruitment. Little is known of these women because of the tendency of nineteenth- and early twentieth-century historians to assume that they must have been servants, camp followers, or prostitutes and therefore unworthy of mention in historical texts.[1]

Despite this meager historical record, it is a documented fact that women were asked to serve as enlisted personnel in World War I. The Navy, finding no explicit bar based on gender, recruited women as "Yeoman (F)" for the Naval Reserve. More than eleven thousand Yeomen (F) were in service (primarily as clerical workers) on Armistice Day, 11 November 1918.[2] The experience of that female Navy contingent was largely forgotten or ignored by later military planners and the public, although some of the leadership and many of the ideas for the various women's corps proposed during World War II came from these Navy women. But during the interwar years, the notion of women on active military duty was at least open to debate. Indeed, the degree of approval and acceptance the idea gained in the 1920s and 1930s was crucial in determining the extent of female participation in World War II.

Women had been exploring the potential avenues of military participation for some time. The well-known aviator Louise Thaden devoted an entire chapter in her 1938 autobiography, *High, Wide and Frightened,* to a fictitious story about two women flying combat missions. She wrote of women brought into the Army because of a severe shortage of trained, experienced male pilots. The story's two young protagonists are gradually drawn into increasingly danger-ous assignments, all the time worrying about personal failure lest it result in all women pilots being grounded. In the end, one of the women is severely wounded, losing a leg, but despite this personal tragedy the message conveyed is that one individual's injury should not affect women's participation in gen-eral, and that injury in the line of duty should be seen as a socially accepted hazard, regardless of sex.[3]

The use of women in aerial combat was not seriously considered before the United States entered the war. There were, however, serious proposals for employing women flyers in the military. It is hard to find accurate records of the many plans that emerged in the early days of World War II. There was con-siderable overlap and some duplication of programs being developed simulta-neously. Of greatest importance, the idea of women in military service received wide acceptance among individuals who, by virtue of their positions, could influence policy and effect change.[4]

In September 1939, the same month in which she had set a new women's international speed record, Jacqueline Cochran wrote to Eleanor Roosevelt about the use of women pilots in a national emergency.[5] The letter would have im-portant repercussions. Mrs. Roosevelt was very interested in women in avia-tion. Both she and the president had been good friends of Amelia Earhart, and Mrs. Roosevelt's personal desire to learn to fly was frustrated only by the Secret Service, which feared sabotage. Mrs. Roosevelt had written about aviation in her famous "My Day" columns, and later, during the war, she became a con-stant advocate for women pilots. Mrs. Roosevelt also knew of Jacqueline Cochran's background.[6]

Cochran was an indefatigable (and sometimes irascible) woman. Born into extreme poverty in northern Florida, Cochran's later triumphs remind one of a combination of Cinderella and Horatio Alger's Raggedy Dick. In her autobiog-raphy, Cochran describes her life in these terms: "It is a story of flights and fancies, of privations and places and perfumes and laces and of aces and kings and generals—all scrambled together."[7]

"Perfumes and laces" symbolize the first of her significant experiences, for Cochran began working in beauty shops at about the age of eleven. This was a violation of child labor laws, but her work was essential in helping to support her family. Soon after this, she left home and started working in another shop, where she eventually became a hairdresser. In the early 1930s she began working for Antoine's, a New York City beauty salon for the extremely wealthy. Later Cochran, still a hairdresser, worked at both the New York and Miami Beach locations of Saks Fifth Avenue, following the seasonal migration of her rich patrons.

Often invited to parties by her clients, she chanced to meet millionaire Floyd Odlum, a Wall Street financier who ran Atlas Utilities and Investors Company, Ltd. Cochran described to him her dream of starting her own cosmetics company. Her plan was so elaborate that Odlum suggested that in order to succeed she would need wings. Odlum's casual remark triggered Cochran's imagination, and in 1932 she spent a three-week vacation learning to fly at Roosevelt Field, Long Island.[8]

Cochran's fledgling cosmetics business proved a success, and her flying exploits were soon exceptional. Having entered her first major air race in 1934, she was soon breaking air record after air record. Then in 1938 she won the prestigious Bendix Trophy Race in a Seversky pursuit plane.[9] She was the Harmon Trophy recipient in 1938 and again in 1939, when she was also awarded the General William "Billy" Mitchell Award, which was given to the "American pilot who during the previous year had made the greatest contribution to aviation."

In 1936 Cochran had married Floyd Odlum. He was a friend of the Roosevelts (and many other prominent politicians) and a major contributor to Franklin Roosevelt's political campaigns. So it was that in September 1939 Cochran's letter to Mrs. Roosevelt was assured a warm reception.

Cochran wrote to the First Lady about using women pilots, asserting that "in the field of aviation, the real 'bottle neck' in the long run is likely to be trained pilots. Male pilots could be released for combat duty by assigning women to all sorts of helpful backlines work."[10] Later in the fall she made her pitch to the Ninety-Nines, but it was not until March 1941 that her ideas began to get serious attention. Cochran had served on the Collier Trophy Committee that year, and after the presentation made by President Roosevelt at the White House she went to lunch with General Henry H. "Hap" Arnold and Clayton Knight, the acting head of an American recruiting committee for the British Ferry Command. During lunch, Great Britain's dire need for pilots was discussed. Cochran was asked to help recruit pilots, but a greater opportunity soon presented itself

Jacqueline Cochran (left) won America's premier aviation competition, the Bendix Race, in 1938 and was awarded the Harmon Trophy, recognizing her as the nation's leading female aviator. The award brought Cochran into close contact with Eleanor Roosevelt. *Courtesy of Ann Wood Kelly.*

when General Arnold suggested that she actually do some of the flying. This, he thought, would be the best demonstration of Britain's genuine desperation.[11]

There is evidence that General Arnold and members of his staff were interested in the use of women pilots even before this encounter. Early in 1940, Lieutenant Colonel Robert Olds, then in the Plans Division of the Air Staff, had asked Nancy Harkness Love to list all the women pilots in the United States holding commercial ratings. Love complied, drawing from the Aero Chamber of Commerce lists. She also listed the women who had particularly outstanding records. There were forty-nine names on this latter list. Love requested that Olds take her name off, modestly stating she was only "obeying orders" by including it in the first place.

Nancy Harkness Love well deserved her place on that list. Having learned to fly in Houghton, Michigan, in 1930 at age sixteen, she exhibited a lifelong

Nancy Harkness Love learned to fly in 1930, earning a pilot's license at age sixteen. Working in aviation throughout the 1930s, she prepared a plan that would enable the Army Air Corps' Ferrying Command to use women pilots, enabling more men to serve as combat pilots. *Courtesy of Margaret C. Love.*

passion for aviation. She was well educated (Milton Academy and Vassar College), and her parents supported her varied interests. Her father (if not her mother) was enthusiastic about her learning to fly. She earned her commercial and transport ratings while in college and was dubbed "The Flying Freshman" in national news reports. Although she was forced to leave Vassar after her sophomore year in 1933 because of the Depression's effect on her family's finances, she continued to fly, and in 1935 she was one of three women hired by the Bureau of Air Commerce to work on its air-marking project.[12]

Married to Robert Love in 1936, she discovered on her West Coast honeymoon (flying, of course) that the Beechcraft Company had entered her in the Amelia Earhart Trophy Race at the National Air Races in Los Angeles. With no experience at pylon flying, she attempted to back out. Unsuccessful in her attempts to avoid the race, she managed to finish in fifth place.[13]

Back in Boston, the Gwinn Aircar Company hired Love to be a test pilot of a new light airplane with a tricycle landing gear. She and her husband had just started what was proving to be a very successful aircraft sales company called Inter-City Airlines when the war in Europe began to have an impact on her life.[14]

As a well-known pilot, Nancy Love, like Jacqueline Cochran, participated in ferry flights. In June 1940, she and other pilots from the Massachusetts Wing of the Civil Air Patrol were responsible for flying American airplanes to the Canadian border, literally pushing them across the international line, and then flying them to their Canadian destination, where the planes would await shipment to France. The airplanes were to have been used by France, which was under siege by the German Luftwaffe. Shortly thereafter, however, the German Army occupied France.[15]

The flights brought Nancy Love into contact with the operations of the Army Air Corps's Air Ferrying Command (which was known after 9 March 1942 as the Ferrying Division of the Air Transport Command). Her connection with this organization was later reinforced by her husband's duties. Robert Love was a reserve officer in the Army Air Corps and, in the spring of 1942, was recalled to duty in Washington as the Deputy Chief of Staff of the ATC.[16]

Robert Love's new job also brought his wife to Washington. She obtained a civilian post with the ATC Ferrying Division operations office in Baltimore, Maryland, commuting daily eighty miles round-trip by airplane. In the interim between 1940 and 1942, possibly at Colonel Olds's suggestion, Nancy Love had continued expanding on plans she had in mind for using highly qualified women pilots in a military effort. It is not clear, however, to what extent Love had promoted such a plan before her move to Washington. Because women had continued flying actively with the Civilian Pilot Training Program as instructors, even after they were banned as students in June 1941, the promotion of a military women's flying unit may not have seemed terribly urgent prior to early 1942.

American military leaders had turned their attention to the impending problems of full-scale mobilization as war clouds became ever more threatening over Europe in the late 1930s. Within this context there was planning for a women's army corps as early as October 1939. A memorandum prepared in conjunction with this effort recommended the use of women by the Army, but only in a quasi-military unit. "Women under no circumstances [would] be given full military status."[17]

With the passage of the Selective Service Act in September 1940, women's groups began to apply pressure on Congress and military leaders for permission to contribute. In March 1941, as Congresswoman Edith Nourse Rogers prepared to introduce legislation to provide for a women's corps, General George C. Marshall expressed the official military position toward women: "While the United States is not faced with an acute shortage of manpower such as has forced England to make such an extensive use of women, it is realized that we must plan for every possible contingency, and certainly must provide some outlet for the patriotic desires of our women."[18] The tone of Marshall's statement indicates a mellowing of official rhetoric, which had previously opposed any female participation, but it was obvious that until shortages of personnel became extreme, authorization would have a difficult passage through Congress.

The pivotal moment for women and military aviation occurred with the bombing of Pearl Harbor. The time lag between Pearl Harbor and the founding of the various wartime women's aviation groups resulted only from the need to pass enabling legislation and to set up the requisite organization structures. Military aviation jobs increased in large part because of factory output: the sudden appearance of a multitude of new aircraft resulted in pilot shortages for both ferry and combat missions. Women in the aviation industry were already "in action" well before the military would actually enlist female personnel.

At the same time that Nancy Love was working on the earliest plans for the Women's Airforce Service Pilots, Jacqueline Cochran was in the process of arranging a ferry flight for herself to England. The British Air Transport Auxiliary (ATA) was not quite as enthusiastic about the participation of Cochran and other American pilots as Clayton Knight had been. In fact they dragged their feet until Cochran appealed to the newly appointed British Minister of Procurement, Lord Beaverbrook, William Maxwell Aitken, who was a good friend of both Cochran and her husband. In early June 1941, the ATA invited her to their Montreal base for tests and check flights. Cochran passed the tests (which were extremely stringent) and was assigned to ferry a Lockheed Hudson bomber to Prestwick, Scotland.

Mass protests arose from the male ATA pilots, who did not want to be blamed if the Germans shot her airplane down. Further, it seemed they felt that the presence of a woman trans-Atlantic pilot would demean their position. Pride, prestige, and entrenched prejudice were really the issues. A compromise was worked out between the ATA and its objecting pilots: Cochran would pilot the airplane in flight, but her copilot would be responsible for takeoff and landing.

After she arrived in the United Kingdom, Cochran met with one of England's premier women pilots, Pauline Gower, who was the chief of the women fliers with the ATA. Gower asked Cochran if it would be possible to recruit American women pilots to augment the British group. The request triggered a responsive chord in Cochran.[19]

Immediately upon her return to the United States in July 1941, Cochran was invited to lunch by President and Mrs. Roosevelt. She spent two hours discussing with them the current state of Britain and the war in Europe. In particular, President Roosevelt was very interested in her assessment of the Royal Air Force. A few days later, Mrs. Roosevelt asked to speak with Cochran again. This time she wanted to discuss the use of women pilots, especially in the United States. President Roosevelt then requested that Cochran research this issue, and in support of this assignment he sent a letter of authorization to Robert A. Lovett, assistant secretary of war for air.

Lovett arranged for Cochran to be officially appointed (without pay) to

When U.S. military leaders turned down Cochran's initial offer to organize a women's pilot corps, she traveled to England to meet with Pauline Gower (left), chief of women pilots for the British Air Transport Auxiliary. Cochran agreed to organize an American contingent to support the British war effort. *Courtesy of Ann Wood Kelly.*

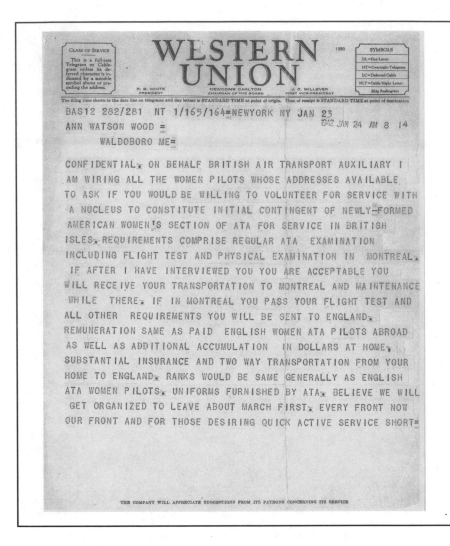

CLASS OF SERVICE

This is a full-rate
Telegram or Cable-
gram unless its de-
ferred character is in-
dicated by a suitable
symbol above or pre-
ceding the address.

WESTERN UNION

1220

SYMBOLS

DL=Day Letter
NT=Overnight Telegram
LC=Deferred Cable
NLT=Cable Night Letter
Ship Radiogram

R. B. WHITE
PRESIDENT

NEWCOMB CARLTON
CHAIRMAN OF THE BOARD

J. C. WILLEVER
FIRST VICE-PRESIDENT

The filing time shown in the date line on telegrams and day letters is STANDARD TIME at point of origin. Time of receipt is STANDARD TIME at point of destination

BAS12 282/281 NT 1/165/164=NEWYORK NY JAN 23

ANN WATSON WOOD =

1942 JAN 24 AM 8 14

WALDOBORO ME=

CONFIDENTIAL. ON BEHALF BRITISH AIR TRANSPORT AUXILIARY I
AM WIRING ALL THE WOMEN PILOTS WHOSE ADDRESSES AVAILABLE
TO ASK IF YOU WOULD BE WILLING TO VOLUNTEER FOR SERVICE WITH
A NUCLEUS TO CONSTITUTE INITIAL CONTINGENT OF NEWLY-FORMED
AMERICAN WOMEN'S SECTION OF ATA FOR SERVICE IN BRITISH
ISLES. REQUIREMENTS COMPRISE REGULAR ATA EXAMINATION
INCLUDING FLIGHT TEST AND PHYSICAL EXAMINATION IN MONTREAL.
IF AFTER I HAVE INTERVIEWED YOU YOU ARE ACCEPTABLE YOU
WILL RECEIVE YOUR TRANSPORTATION TO MONTREAL AND MAINTENANCE
WHILE THERE. IF IN MONTREAL YOU PASS YOUR FLIGHT TEST AND
ALL OTHER REQUIREMENTS YOU WILL BE SENT TO ENGLAND.
REMUNERATION SAME AS PAID ENGLISH WOMEN ATA PILOTS ABROAD
AS WELL AS ADDITIONAL ACCUMULATION IN DOLLARS AT HOME.
SUBSTANTIAL INSURANCE AND TWO WAY TRANSPORTATION FROM YOUR
HOME TO ENGLAND. RANKS WOULD BE SAME GENERALLY AS ENGLISH
ATA WOMEN PILOTS. UNIFORMS FURNISHED BY ATA. BELIEVE WE WILL
GET ORGANIZED TO LEAVE ABOUT MARCH FIRST. EVERY FRONT NOW
OUR FRONT AND FOR THOSE DESIRING QUICK ACTIVE SERVICE SHORT=

THE COMPANY WILL APPRECIATE SUGGESTIONS FROM ITS PATRONS CONCERNING ITS SERVICE

The telegram from Jacqueline Cochran to Ann Wood inviting her to join the contin-
Courtesy of Ann Wood Kelly.

work with General Arnold and General Olds (who had been promoted by this
time). General Olds was very interested in hiring a select group of highly qualified women pilots to ease his immediate shortage in the Air Ferrying Command, a plan that had gradually emerged from his requests for information
from Nancy Love more than a year before. Cochran worked furiously with CAA
records to identify all the commercially rated women pilots. Then she sent ques-

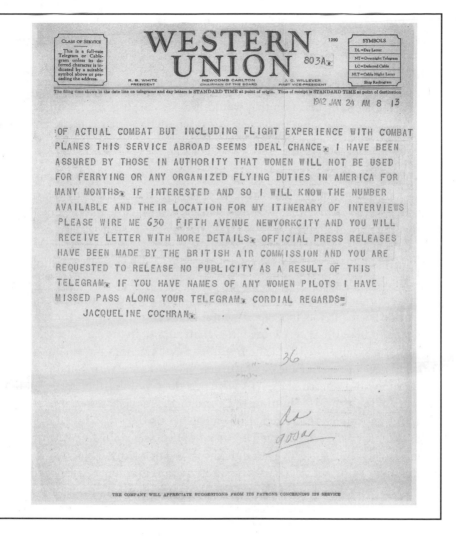

OF ACTUAL COMBAT BUT INCLUDING FLIGHT EXPERIENCE WITH COMBAT PLANES THIS SERVICE ABROAD SEEMS IDEAL CHANCE. I HAVE BEEN ASSURED BY THOSE IN AUTHORITY THAT WOMEN WILL NOT BE USED FOR FERRYING OR ANY ORGANIZED FLYING DUTIES IN AMERICA FOR MANY MONTHS. IF INTERESTED AND SO I WILL KNOW THE NUMBER AVAILABLE AND THEIR LOCATION FOR MY ITINERARY OF INTERVIEWS PLEASE WIRE ME 630 FIFTH AVENUE NEWYORKCITY AND YOU WILL RECEIVE LETTER WITH MORE DETAILS. OFFICIAL PRESS RELEASES HAVE BEEN MADE BY THE BRITISH AIR COMMISSION AND YOU ARE REQUESTED TO RELEASE NO PUBLICITY AS A RESULT OF THIS TELEGRAM. IF YOU HAVE NAMES OF ANY WOMEN PILOTS I HAVE MISSED PASS ALONG YOUR TELEGRAM. CORDIAL REGARDS=
        JACQUELINE COCHRAN.

gent of American women to fly with the Air Transport Auxiliary of Great Britain.

tionnaires to them, and 130 of the 150 on the list responded. All who responded were enthusiastic about the possibility of flying for the military. Finally, Cochran matched the respondents and their skill levels with aircraft due to be delivered to the military, in order to show that not only were women pilots available, but also that they had the requisite skills to fly the military aircraft in question. The resulting proposal package was submitted on 30 July 1941.[20]

A prototype group of crack women pilots was to be employed on a trial basis. If successful, a full-scale women's pilot division would be organized and commissioned in the Air Corps Specialists Reserve. Cochran naturally assumed that she would be retained as chief of that division. General Olds and Cochran disagreed, however, on one major point of this proposal. Cochran wanted to create a women's organization that would include an on-going training program. Otherwise, she said, "the female effort would be a flash in the pan."[21]

General Olds was not willing to recommend the creation of a significant new military subgroup, especially one composed of women. Cochran was resolutely committed to her idea. Unable to get her way, she resigned from her position, but not before she presented her case once more to General Arnold. Arnold verbally assured Cochran that he agreed with her in principle, but he convinced her that the present moment was not right for her program. He suggested that she continue to elaborate her plan, in the light of anticipated pilot shortages.[22]

Much as he may have personally liked and respected Cochran, Arnold in fact actually disagreed with her proposal. Like General Marshall, he was unconvinced that the shortage of personnel required the establishment of all-women divisions. It was too experimental, too controversial, and not really necessary because there were more pilots than aircraft in the Air Corps at that point in the summer of 1941. The result was that Cochran returned to New York and began to recruit a team of women pilots to serve with Britain's ATA.

The men and women of the ATA were described as doing the "grease monkey work of the airfields." Shuttling back and forth among bases, factories, and foreign countries, they delivered all the airplanes used by the Royal Air Force (RAF). Women had been admitted in early 1940 but were initially permitted to fly only small trainer aircraft. They quickly proved that female pilots were both capable and competent. All restrictions were removed, and the ATA began actively to recruit pilots, both male and female, from other nations.[23]

Jacqueline Cochran handpicked a group of twenty-four women to form an American contingent. She viewed this undertaking as an important means of demonstrating the viability of her proposals to the American military establishment as well as a way of keeping herself in the forefront of women in military aviation. The women she chose were not only highly skilled but also of upstanding character. Cochran did not want to risk failure because of personality problems or the appearance of less than exceptional moral behavior. Cochran had selected her group by late 1941, and the women began training. They received check flights in Canada first, before going to England to begin conversion training. One American, Virginia Farr, a young flight instructor before being recruited by Cochran to join the ATA, described her work to a friend in the States: "This work with the ATA—flying anything and everything

From left, Polly Potter, Ann Wood, Helen Harrison, a check pilot, and an ATA captain in April 1942. This trio formed the "3rd Group" of volunteer pilots recruited by Jacqueline Cochran to serve the ATA. *Courtesy of Ann Wood Kelly.*

of two motors or less, and trying desperately to keep them all in one piece is a real experience."[24] Farr continued with the ATA for three years even though she, like all the other American women, was only committed to eighteen months of service. The group was recognized as outstanding. All were good pilots, all were dedicated to helping Great Britain. Several American women were injured, and one, Mary Nicholson (Cochran's personal secretary), was killed when the propeller came off the aircraft she was ferrying.[25]

Some of the British pilots resented Cochran's ostentatious style. She accepted the rank of honorary Flight Captain even though she did very little flying, and she usually appeared at the field in a mink and a Rolls-Royce. She was, however, extremely effective in getting the job done, and in September 1942 she decided the time was right to make another pitch to General Arnold for an American women's air corps.

In the meantime, since Cochran's first proposal to Arnold in late July 1941, progress had been made in the creation of other women's corps to serve with the various branches of the military. The women's air corps idea did not develop in a legislative vacuum. The WASP, WAC, and WAVES groups developed simultaneously, and advocates for including women in the military used progress

Colonel Oveta Culp Hobby, director of the Women's Army Corps, talks to a group of officers before boarding an AAF aircraft. *Photo from U.S. National Archives and Records Administration, Still Pictures Branch (342-FH-4A-05045-29772AC).*

in one branch to promote advances in the others. There were elements of bluff, shrewd manipulation, and honest lobbying that engaged virtually all offices within the executive and legislative branches of government.

The crucial starting point is 28 May 1941, when Congresswoman Edith Nourse Rogers introduced H.R. 4906 to establish a Women's Army Auxiliary Corps (WAAC), a group not in the Army but rather with the Army. Hoping that this distinction would make the difference in gaining support, the bill's proponents carefully lobbied Congress. During the summer of 1941, even General Marshall became an enthusiastic supporter. He saw that women could be used effectively to counter future labor shortages; hence, he wanted in advance of any emergency to have the authority to recruit and train such a group. Still Congress balked, relegating the bill to the Bureau of the Budget. Here the measure sat until 11 December 1941, when all objections were withdrawn.[26]

Also in December 1941, the Army Air Forces began to exhibit considerable interest in creating an Air Force section within the proposed WAAC. Correspondence between General Headquarters, Air Forces, and the Chief of the Air Corps [*sic*] went so far as to state: "This headquarters would recommend a separate and distinct organization, except for the fact that there should be only one women's corps serving with the army."[27] In January 1942, the War Department indicated that an aircraft warning section would be a part of the proposed WAAC.

Congress finally passed the Rogers bill on 15 May 1942, and the next day Oveta Culp Hobby was sworn in as director of the new organization. From the time of the AAF Headquarters letter of December 1941 until the actual arrival of the first WAAC members on 20 September 1942, the Army Air Forces assumed the lead in developing plans for the use of female troops. The AAF leadership had a much broader view of employing women than restricting them to the roles of typists or telephone operators.

Nancy Love's and Jacqueline Cochran's early efforts made a significant impact on the AAF views, even though their proposals for using women pilots had not yet been implemented. The establishment of the Air WAACs (later Air WACs) and that of the WAFS/WASP were closely intertwined, although the female directors of these programs refused to acknowledge this reality. Each organization set precedents for the other, and this entwined relationship must be understood in order to appreciate the subsequent events of these organizations' histories.

As early as November 1942 the suggestion was made that the Air WAACs be used as Link Trainer instructors. The AAF was also very eager to have its women auxiliary members trained as aircraft mechanics and radio operators.[28] However, the first significant assignment of the Air WAACs was with the Aircraft Warning Service. The AWS was a vital defense component, constantly monitoring radios and other electronic devices for signs of enemy air attack. As this threat appeared to diminish, the AAF began, in early 1943, to phase out this use of the Air WAACs and to operate the stations exclusively with civilian staffs.[29]

This development should hardly be perceived as the AAF's lack of interest in its female staff. On the contrary, the WAAC strength limit had been raised the previous fall from the initial 25,000 to 150,000, and the AAF's quota of the total WAAC strength was 65,000, or about 43 percent. Long-range recommendations had been made to expand the Air WAACs to 1.5 million women by 1946.[30] This projection was based on the conclusions of a study by the adjutant general's office that 65 percent, or 406, of the 628 military occupation specialties could be performed by women.[31]

The impetus for this study was to be found in the efforts to convert the

A Women's Army Corps officer instructs a student in a Link Trainer. *Photo from U.S. National Archives and Records Administration, Still Pictures Branch (342-FH-4A-05175-27503AC).*

WAC corporal Lillian Levine reviews the flight plan of two AAF pilots. *Photo from U.S. National Archives and Records Administration, Still Pictures Branch (342-FH-4A-05025-31324AC).*

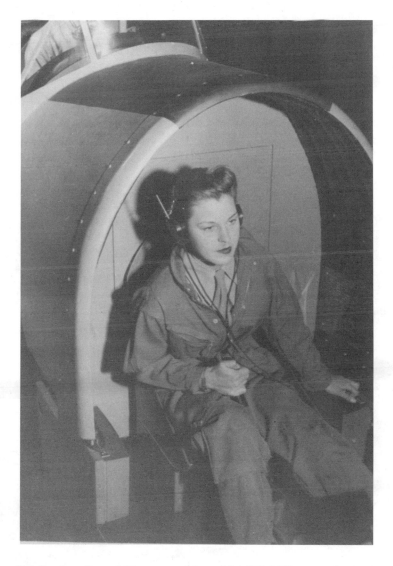

WAC private Betty S. Dayton working with a U.S. Military Academy cadet in the "Gunairinstructor." As the gunnery instructor, Private First Class Dayton would fly the enemy airplane on a projection screen and teach the cadet how to shoot down his target. *Photo from U.S. National Archives and Records Administration, Still Pictures Branch (342-FH-4A-05169-119416AC).*

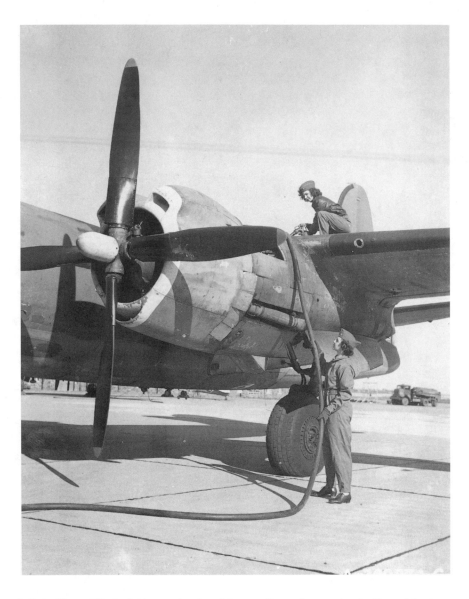

WAC officers Elizabeth Rogers (top) and Joanne Space (bottom) refueling a Martin B-26 Marauder on the flight line at Sioux Falls Army Air Field, South Dakota. *Photo from U.S. National Archives and Records Administration, Still Pictures Branch (342-FH-4A-05208-A36987AC).*

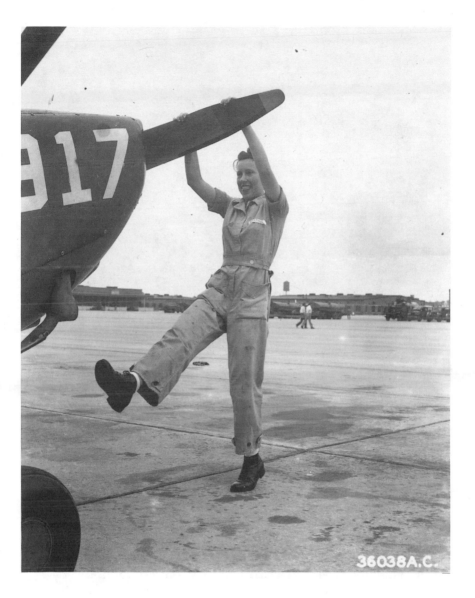

Private Doris Smith, WAC, worked on the flight line at Robins Field, Georgia. Here, Private First Class Smith is turning the propeller on a Stinson L-5 airplane. *Photo from U.S. National Archives and Records Administration, Still Pictures Branch (342-FH-4A05039-36038AC).*

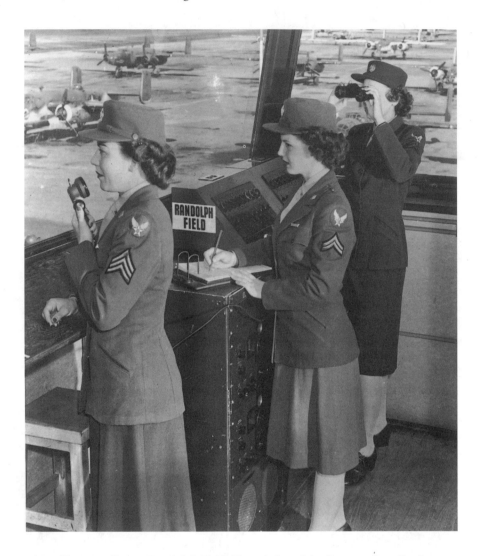

Air traffic controllers at Randolph Field, Texas: left to right, Sergeant Jean Daubert, Corporal Rose Chytal, and Corporal Lois White. *Photo from U.S. National Archives and Records Administration, Still Pictures Branch (342-FH-4A-05174-A-26421AC).*

women's auxiliary status into true military rank. The War Department decided it was desirable to integrate the WAAC into the Army to prevent further administrative and legal difficulties. Legislation was introduced in 1943 to set up the Women's Army Corps (WAC), and on 1 July 1943 the new group was officially established. All the women who had served as WAACs were offered positions in the WAC, but they had no legal obligation to enlist.

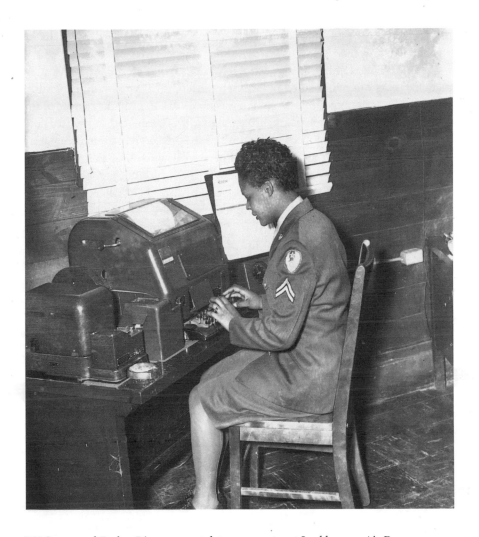

WAC corporal Evelyn Rivers was a teletype operator at Lockbourne Air Base, Columbus, Ohio. *Photo from U.S. National Archives and Records Administration, Still Pictures Branch (342-FH-4A-05000-34034AC).*

Regardless of the total strength goals, the War Department had, from the beginning of the WAAC program, made a firm commitment to ensuring the presence of black women among the ranks. The department, with full support from Director Oveta Hobby, proposed that up to 10 percent of the WAAC personnel be black. (This carried over for the WACs as well.)[32] They did not expect the criticism that came from several national black leaders; for example, Dr. Mary McLeod Bethune protested the WAAC's plan to follow the Army policy of segregated troops. The idea of integrated troops was hotly debated but in the end did not prevail.

Some black women did serve as Air WAACs (and later as Air WACs). In fact, 80 blacks out of a total of 440 women were part of the first officer-candidate class. Assignment of black women was made quite difficult because of the segregated troop policy. This often meant that more talented individuals did not receive the assignments or opportunities they deserved because they were forced to go to the same location as their black colleagues. For example, musicians would be assigned to work as cooks or postal clerks because that was where other black women were being assigned. In all cases, black women moved as a unit. Thus, black women were stationed at only ten AAF bases in the United States, and only at Douglas Army Airfield were there black women working as aircraft mechanics or on the flight line. The system in general excluded black women because of prejudice, so recruiters were never successful in attaining the 10 percent goal. At best, the peak strength was about four thousand, representing 4 percent of the corps.[33]

No other racial minority group enlisted in the corps in significant numbers either. Puerto Rican, Chinese, Japanese-American, Native American, and other women of color did serve, and for the most part they were not segregated. However, they were recruited only rarely. Language often represented a problem and could prevent a woman from being assigned to a technical aviation specialty.[34]

At the same time the WAAC was gearing up, the Navy developed its own women's group. Congresswoman Edith Nourse Rogers's interest in a women's corps was not limited to the Army. In December 1941, Rogers telephoned Rear Admiral Chester W. Nimitz to ask whether the Navy was interested in a bill similar to H.R. 4906 (the WAAC authorization introduced the previous May). Nimitz replied that clerical positions could potentially be held by women, but that she should ask the secretary of the Navy for an official view. Rogers did this, thereby stimulating the Navy bureaucracy to recognize that the formation of some sort of women's organization was probably inevitable. In that event, they preferred to devise their own plan rather than cope with "unworkable" congressional legislation.[35]

"Indifference and scant imagination" were the major problems within the Navy. Only the chief of naval operations and the Bureau of Aeronautics (BuAer) evidenced enthusiasm about the prospect of women serving. Of these two, it was the Bureau of Aeronautics that envisioned the use of women in a variety of technical and skilled positions. Consequently, the policy suggestions made by BuAer greatly influenced the major aspects of the organization and the structure of the eventual women's reserve section.[36]

Joy Bright Hancock had served as a Yeoman (F) in World War I. During that time she was the first woman to take the tests for chief yeoman, and despite opposition she earned her rating. She learned to fly in 1930. She also worked for many years as a civilian with the Bureau of Aeronautics, first at the Lakehurst Naval Air Station in New Jersey, and later as head of the bureau's editorial and research section. While working in the latter position, Hancock was given the responsibility in late December 1941 for outlining the ways that women could participate in the Bureau of Aeronautics. Based on these proposals as well as the introduction of the WAAC legislation the previous May, the Bureau of Personnel recommended on 2 January 1942 that the secretary of the Navy ask Congress for authorization to create a women's section in the Navy.[37]

The Navy officially proposed in early February to add a title to the Naval Reserve Act of 1938. Title V, Section 501, proposed a unit that was called a women's auxiliary, but in fact the group was to be fully integrated into the Naval Reserve. The Bureau of the Budget rejected the proposal out of hand, suggesting that the Navy reformulate its plan to follow the WAAC legislation.

Meanwhile the Bureau of Aeronautics was becoming so eager for legislation to pass that it initiated a lobbying effort of its own. Using political connections in both the House and the Senate, Title V, Section 501, was introduced. It passed through the House Naval Affairs Committee but met with opposition in the Senate. That opposition resulted in a revision that compromised several unique features of the bill that would have permitted women to fly naval aircraft. Even with the proposed changes, the legislation was opposed by Senate Naval Affairs Committee Chairman David I. Walsh. Walsh viewed the entire idea as a threat to femininity and motherhood.

This viewpoint did not prevail, however, and the Bureau of Aeronautics' lobby came to an understanding with the committee that it would report favorably on the legislation once it was rewritten along the lines of the WAAC model. The Navy (including BuAer) adapted the legislative proposal and grudgingly sent this new version to President Roosevelt on 25 May 1942. The president signaled his approval, mistakenly believing this to be the plan desired by the secretary of the Navy.

In a last-ditch effort to have the original plan (which proposed an integrated women's corps) approved instead, the Navy asked Roosevelt to reconsider. They outlined the problems with the Senate that had occasioned the compromise version, but it was not until the intervention of Eleanor Roosevelt that the president actually decided to investigate the differences between the two plans. About the same time the revised Navy legislation had been sent to the president, Harriet Elliot, dean of women at the State Normal and Industrial College (today, the University of North Carolina–Greensboro), had written to

Mrs. Roosevelt, outlining the details and rationale of the original Navy plan. Mrs. Roosevelt shared that letter with the president. Roosevelt, fully comprehending the situation, promptly informed Frank Knox, the secretary of the Navy, that the secretary had "carte blanche to go ahead and organize the Women's Reserve along the lines [he thought] best." The choice was made for a group fully integrated into the Naval Reserve. Congress acquiesced and the authorization bill, Public Law 689, was signed into law on 30 July 1942.[38]

The newly formed women's reserve program was called WAVES, which stood for "Women Appointed for Volunteer Emergency Service" (later "Appointed" was changed to "Accepted" because the former applied only to officers). From the start the Bureau of Aeronautics made them welcome. They asked for twenty thousand WAVES immediately, a number that staggered the imagination of the planners at the Bureau of Personnel, which had estimated the total need at only ten thousand women (and those primarily in the clerical field).[39]

The Navy exhibited considerably greater foresight than the other branches of the service. Drawing on the academic world, the Navy deliberately requested the assistance of faculty and administrators from several of the prominent women's colleges as well as noted female professionals from coeducational institutions. The members of this advisory council had a great deal of practical experience in dealing with women in institutional settings. They were particularly effective in setting up the basic administrative structure as well as in selecting the WAVES' first director, the dynamic and erudite Mildred McAfee, president of Wellesley College.

Holding first the rank of lieutenant commander and later captain, McAfee was acknowledged as an outstanding administrator throughout her tenure as director. Enthusiastic, intelligent, and gracious, McAfee was able to get along with everyone, from "Old Salts" and naval brass to young women enlistees. She was very interested in promoting "women in naval aviation," and one of her first decisions was to appoint Joy Bright Hancock as the Women's Representative to the Chief of the Bureau of Aeronautics. This meant that Hancock would also be in charge of all the WAVES assigned to BuAer.[40]

The women who served as WAVES came from many places, but they were a homogeneous group. A study published in *Naval Aviation News* in June 1943 characterized the majority of enlistees as twenty-two years old; five feet, five inches tall; 124 pounds; with brown hair. They were white, single, and most were high school graduates employed as office workers prior to enlisting. Many were motivated by a desire for a dramatic departure from their previous life, along with a patriotic enthusiasm for serving the war effort.[41]

WAVES in naval aviation served in many capacities. At the end of the war, the list of aviation officer billets (jobs are called billets in the Navy) for women included aerological engineering, aeronautical engineering, air combat information, air-navigation gunnery instructor, air transportation, assembly and repair vocational training, celestial navigation (air navigation), flight desk, flight records, Link training, photographic interpretation, recognition, recognition and gunnery, radio radar, schedules, and air traffic control. Enlisted women served as aerographer's mate, aviation machinist's mate (for both aircraft and instruments), aviation metalsmith, parachute rigger, radioman, aviation free gunnery instructor, navigational aids instructor, aviation electronic technician's mate, aviation ordnance man, control tower operator, and transport airman.[42]

WAVES did not fly aircraft as pilots. The women who served as noncombat crew members and the one hundred women officers trained as navigation instructors did receive fifty hours of flight time.[43] There were a few WAVES who had pilot's licenses, however, and who allegedly found ways to put their skills to use unofficially. For example, Irene N. Wirtschafter, an ensign with the Navy Supply Corps in 1944, had flying skills that did not go unused during the war. Wirtschafter (who continued with the Navy until her retirement as a captain in 1976) flew some unauthorized missions for the Supply Corps. Her comment was, "We had a job to do and war to win, either I flew or supplies didn't get transferred properly; besides, I loved to fly."[44] Wirtschafter and other women like her had a certain daring. They were willing to take risks if it meant doing something important for their country and the Navy that they loved, but there are no official records of such service, no mention of hours flown in these women's log books. Ultimately, that meant that their example and their courage would be officially forgotten.[45]

WAVES differed officially from male officers or enlisted men in that women originally were restricted to billets in the continental United States.[46] Other occupational discrepancies were also involved; for example, it was considered a critical test for all parachute riggers to make a jump with one of their own packs. However, at first, female parachute riggers did not have to do this. It was a source of considerable irritation among the men, until the women too were required to jump.

The inevitable tensions were there when the first WAVES entered service. *Time* magazine reported in June 1943 that "airmen had their fingers crossed when WAVES tower operators were proposed. They doubted they could master complex regulations, charts, procedures, meteorological and weather skills (The WAACs have shied away from assigning women to the occupation.), and were suspicious of how the women would bear up under control tower pressures."[47] The first class of twenty women did an outstanding job, and the Navy began actively recruiting women for the position. The only real difficulty these women encountered (apart from a certain chauvinism) was climbing the tower ladders in their uniform skirts, a problem remedied by making pants regulation wear.

The pay and training received by the WAVES was identical to the men's. Monthly base pay for an apprentice seaman was $50; seaman, 2nd class, $54; seaman, 1st class, $66; and so forth up to chief petty officer, $138.[48] The initial course was not coeducational. WAVE officers were trained at the Naval Reserve Midshipmen's School run at Smith College in Northampton, Massachusetts. Recruit training was held at the U.S. Naval Training School (Women's Reserve), which was run at Hunter College in New York City. All additional training, however, was coeducational. The opening to women of the five aviation specialist schools on 1 February 1943 was particularly important. It was this action that resulted in integrated classrooms throughout the Navy.

The WAVES had two sister organizations. The Marine Corps Women's Reserve (MCWR), the last of the military women's corps to be formed, was not started until 13 February 1943, nearly seven months after the program had been authorized by Congress. The MCWR depended upon the WAVES organization for help starting up. Nineteen WAVES officers transferred to the Marine Corps, and the first women Marines trained at WAVES schools. Initially half of the MCWR were put in aviation units, although later this number dropped to approximately one third. These women were principally aerographers, parachute riggers, control tower operators, and maintenance personnel. At the Cherry Point, North Carolina, Marine Corps Air Station, 90 percent of the parachute riggers and 80 percent of the control tower operators were women. Other billets with more limited enrollment were serial gunnery and Link Trainer instructors.[49]

One of the reasons Marine women were so active in aviation was that their director, Ruth Cheney Streeter, held a commercial pilot's license. Comfortable with the world of aviation, Streeter, like Joy Bright Hancock of the Navy, was a valuable role model and helped encourage Marine officials to allow women to work in these specialties. The MCWR was deliberately kept small. Initial recruiting goals were for five hundred officers and six thousand enlisted women, although this was eventually raised to one thousand and eighteen thousand, respectively. The actual total of women in Marine uniforms in October 1945 was eighty-five hundred.[50]

The second "sister" was the Coast Guard's SPARs, which was organized in November 1942. Their name came from the Coast Guard motto: "Semper Paratus—Always Ready." The corps mirrored the WAVES in everything from bureaucracy to uniform. Its goal was to release men for sea duty, so although its enlisted women performed the same sorts of tasks as WAVES, including aeronautical activities, there was not a great emphasis on women serving the Coast Guard in aviation roles. Like the WAVES and the MCWR, no SPARs were allowed to pilot aircraft. SPAR officers received billets in aviation ordnance, aerological engineering, navigation instruction, and aviation gunnery instruction. In terms of enrollment, SPAR leadership, including Director Dorothy Stratton, recognized that the Coast Guard was competing with all the other services (especially the Navy) for recruits, and thus they set very modest goals of one thousand officers and ten thousand enlisted women—goals that were achieved.[51]

On the first anniversary of the WAVES, 27,000 Navy women were on duty; on the second, 72,350; and by the third in July 1945, 86,000 women were serving in the United States and the territories of Alaska and Hawaii. More than one quarter of the WAVES, 23,000 women, were involved in some aspect of naval aviation. One month later, in August 1945, the Navy announced its demobilization plans for women. Demobilization was mandated by law, but in fact the Navy did not want to lose any of its female personnel. At the same time, it did need to achieve a more moderate peacetime level of operations. Although training for reserve personnel was temporarily discontinued, the women had been successfully integrated into the system, providing the historical evidence and justification for their continued presence in these "nontraditional" fields.[52]

From the beginning of the war effort, the Army Air Force leadership sought to incorporate women into its program in assignments that were not limited to the ground. General Arnold wanted to use women pilots as pilots, and thus in 1942 he became the critical factor in the efforts leading ultimately to the creation of a paramilitary organization called the Women's Airforce Service Pilots (WASP). By adopting the idea of hiring women as civilians, Arnold neatly sidestepped the limitations of the women's reserve legislation as articulated by Congress. He could not, of course, avoid confronting public sentiment, which generally was not favorably disposed toward allowing women to be military pilots. Notwithstanding this problem, he thought the use of women by the AAF would help to spur his troops to greater achievements and to dramatize the urgent need for the mobilization of other dedicated, highly motivated pilots.

Furthermore, in light of the fact that women had effectively been closed out of the CPTP in June 1941, he assumed there were female pilots who would be grateful simply to have permission to participate. By capitalizing on that gratitude, Arnold hoped he could recruit and deploy women to accomplish many of the essential but routine aviation tasks, such as ferrying. This, of course, would free additional men for the higher priority wartime tasks of combat flying. Arnold could see that the potential benefits—benefits that were being realized in countries such as Great Britain and the Soviet Union—were tantalizing.[53]

This type of program would also enable Arnold to take advantage of the leadership offered by such women as Jacqueline Cochran and Nancy Love. Further, it was an ingenious way of demonstrating that the AAF really deserved its own independent women's corps. If the existing legislation could be changed to permit this, then Arnold would have a well-established group ready for action. Unlike the Marine Corps or the Coast Guard, both of which depended on the WAVES, Arnold would not have to "steal" leadership from the WAC to implement his program, nor would he experience any great time delay because of transition procedures.

Arnold could not have expected—much less desired—the circumstances that resulted in the simultaneous creation of two groups of women pilots: the WAFS and the WFTD. The AAF leadership had been considering various plans starting in 1941, but no consensus existed as to what might be created, except that in the summer of 1942 Arnold had ordered General Olds of the Air Transport Command not to do anything with regard to women pilots until Jacqueline Cochran returned from England, where she was responsible for American women in the ATA. Olds had been the most eager to use women pilots, and Arnold probably suspected that Olds might try to go ahead and hire them. This would have put Arnold in a most difficult situation. Under pressure from the White House, he had promised Cochran that she would direct any women's program instituted by the AAF. Arnold knew that Olds disagreed with Cochran's plan for a training program—he also had some misgivings about it himself—but he did not want to risk snubbing Cochran and incurring the disfavor of both the White House and the War Department over a matter that represented only one small facet of the entire aviation effort in the war.[54]

With the establishment of the Air Transport Command on 9 March 1942, the Army Air Corps Air Ferrying Command was reconstituted as the Ferrying Division of the ATC. The new command consolidated a variety of programs serving the Army's transportation needs, and was firmly ensconced under General Arnold's authority. In addition to the Ferrying Division, the ATC included six foreign "wings." At the time of the reorganization, Brigadier General Harold George was in charge of the Air Ferrying Command, having replaced General Olds, who became head of the Second Air Force. With the reorganization, General George was placed in command of the entire ATC and Colonel William H. Tunner assumed responsibility for the Ferrying Division. This reorganization, which had also brought Nancy and Robert Love into the ATC, would be critical to the creation of a women pilots' program.[55]

Colonel Tunner had not been a part of the earlier discussions about women pilots, nor had he realized that their use by the military was a possibility. He was surprised to learn that the wife of his colleague Robert Love was an active pilot with a commercial rating; furthermore, Love indicated that she had more than a passing interest in the idea of using women pilots to ferry military aircraft. Truly hampered by a chronic shortage of qualified pilots, Colonel Tunner met with Nancy Love. Once again, Love presented her plan for an elite corps of women flyers, and at last she found an enthusiastic patron. Tunner conferred with General George, who immediately transferred Love to Washington to draft a proposal. A week later, on 18 June 1942, Tunner submitted a modified version of Nancy Love's plan to General George.

The proposal compromised some of Love's original ideas. Instead of choosing women on the basis of equal standards with the men of the Ferrying Division, female candidates would have to pass a more rigorous set of requirements.

	Men	Women
Age	19–45	21–35
Education	3 years high school	high school graduate
Required flight time	200 hours	500 hours[a]

[a] At least 50 hours flown in previous year.

Other more substantial changes were yet to come. Love's proposal assumed the women would follow the same path already established for the men of the Ferrying Division: they would be hired as civilians, and following a ninety-day trial period they would be commissioned into the AAF. Just before Tunner submitted Love's plan, the WAAC legislation was passed in Congress. Love and Tunner met with WAAC director Oveta Hobby to discuss the plan for women pilots. Hobby thought the program was an outstanding idea, but unfortunately the three did not immediately realize that the WAAC legislation did not allow for flying officers and flight pay in the women's corps: women pilots could not be legally commissioned in the AAF.[56]

When this problem became apparent, Love and Tunner recognized the great difficulties that would be encountered in any attempt to persuade Congress to amend the WAAC legislation. They were aware that the WAVES proposal, then before Congress, was experiencing substantial difficulties because it included a provision for women pilots. Gambling that legislation would eventually be passed to permit women pilots in the military, especially once women demonstrated their abilities, Love proposed they go ahead and hire the women as civilians. She stipulated, however, that the ATC had to make clear to the women that their status was temporary. She also asked that the ATC exert every effort to get these women commissioned.

Love recognized that her pilots would be scrutinized because of their uncertain future, so she further stiffened the requirements for women candidates. Now a female pilot had to have a CAA two hundred–horsepower rating and two letters of recommendation to be considered. Love wanted "blameless" types with exemplary personal conduct. Finally, she proposed that the women's salaries be set at $250 per month, $130 less than the men civilian pilots received. The reason for this was that the women would be flying only small trainer and liaison-type aircraft.[57]

The final written version of the plan for the Women's Auxiliary Ferry Squadron was sent to Arnold on 3 September 1942, along with current CAA statistics on women pilots, which Arnold had previously asked Love to update. Two days later, Eleanor Roosevelt restated the argument for women pilots in her "My Day" column. On 5 September 1942, General George decided to proceed with the program. According to Jacqueline Cochran, Arnold knew nothing of the further developments to the WAFS plan after seeing it on July 1. It seems preposterous to assume that Arnold did not know anything about George's decision to implement the WAFS program. The ATC had formally named Nancy Love to be director and it had sent telegrams to prospective female candidates to join the program. Finally, the date for the public announcement of the creation of the WAFS was set for 10 September; the announcement was to be made by Arnold from his office.[58]

Two things of interest occurred at this time. The first was the delayed departure of Jacqueline Cochran from England. As she was preparing to depart for the United States, General S.H. Frank of the Eighth Air Force had Cochran called from the airport, ostensibly on an urgent matter. The matter turned out to be a thank you dinner, but it held up Cochran for three days. She suggested that this might have been a deliberate ploy by the ATC or Nancy Love to keep her from interfering at the last minute in the events unfolding in Washington. It probably was not, but it did effectively prevent her playing any role in the week's scenario.[59]

The second odd turn of events was the absence of General Arnold on 10 September. When Love and George arrived at Arnold's office for the morning press conference, they were told that he had been called out of town; Secretary of War Henry L. Stimson would make the announcement. It is possible that Arnold foresaw that he would have great difficulty explaining to Cochran the following morning (he and Cochran had an appointment on 11 September 1942) why he had reneged on his commitment to make her the director of any women's flying program that the AAF might establish. If Stimson, on behalf of Roosevelt, made the announcement, it would deflect Cochran's irritation from Arnold onto George and Love. It would also prevent her going over Arnold's head to complain to the Roosevelts.[60]

Arnold's equivocation resulted in the creation of two women's flying groups. He conceded that he had not fulfilled his earlier promise to Cochran, and therefore he agreed to start the women's training program under her leadership.

This training program was known as the Women's Flying Training Detachment (WFTD, sometimes called "Woofteds"). Eventually it was fused with Love's Women's Auxiliary Ferry Squadron (WAFS) to become the Women's Airforce Service Pilots (WASP), with Cochran as overall director and Love as her subordinate running the WAFS.

The WAFS and the WFTD, as well as their successor organization, the WASP, comprise a vital component in the story of women in military aviation. While these women technically remained civilians and were drastically outnumbered by women in the regular military groups, their experiences present a paradigm for the service of World War II U.S. military women as a whole. Examples drawn from this elite organization vividly and accurately illustrate the scope of experience of their military sisters.

4

Nieces of Uncle Sam

The Women's Airforce Service Pilots

> On through the storm and the sun
> Fly on till our mission is done
> From factory to base,
> Let the WASPs set the pace.
>
> "WASP Song," Loes Monk, 43-W-8

Beginning in September 1942, a ten-month period of cautious and superficial calm existed between the leaders of the Women's Auxiliary Ferry Squadron (WAFS) and the Women's Flying Training Detachment (WFTD). Nancy Love, director of the WAFS, and Jacqueline Cochran, director of the WFTD, represented two very different personal styles. Each drew partisan support from interested individuals who were in sympathy with the vision or character of one or the other of the two leaders. Love evoked loyalty and respect from her small group of women pilots. A leader by example, she was an active participant in her cadre of talented flyers. Cochran was, by contrast, a born administrator, skilled in achieving her ends by personal influence and negotiation.

There were those within the Pentagon and on Capitol Hill who were inspired by Cochran's political skills, and others who saw Love as the most gifted leader of women in the field. Out of the conflicting attitudes emerged a power struggle. This battle was initiated by Cochran, who, some thought, aspired to a position of complete control over all women's military flying programs.

The first evidence of this is an angry memorandum sent to Colonel William Tunner from Captain James Teague of the Air Corps on 22 September 1942. Teague wrote: "she [Cochran] made it quite clear that she considered herself the only person who could efficiently be in charge of the Women Ferry

Pilots. This was all done by innuendo, and at no time did she actually express this thought in words of one syllable."[1]

Teague voiced further complaints about Cochran because she apparently wanted her own opinions to supercede Nancy Love's authority in determining the final selection of WAFS members. He concluded his memorandum: "We are in this position: Miss Cochran, as far as the public is concerned, is coming to us and bringing us women who have been trained, and we should be appreciative. I, on the other hand, fear the Greeks bearing gifts. I have discussed this with Capt. Tucker and he agrees with me that some method should be found by which those people who are in authority above us should be told exactly what our attitude is, and a clear line of demarkation [*sic*] drawn now. I am afraid that if we let this thing go too long, Miss Cochran will take inch by inch and try to move in on us. I don't believe I am exaggerating the extent to which she will go."[2] Captain Teague's memorandum was only the earliest piece of written evidence for the conflict that surrounded the emerging Love-Cochran rivalry. Other documentation confirms that various military leaders took sides on this issue, generally supporting one woman or the other. It is likely, however, that these partisan opinions were influenced as much by personal attitudes regarding women's participation in the military as by any assessment of the programs or leadership style associated with either of the two women. There was little high-level support in the military for a female pilots program, but also little public opposition. Many of those with strong views believed the issue was so controversial that to vocalize their objections would have a negative impact on their job.[3]

For a variety of reasons, Tunner, George, Olds, and Arnold all wanted women in their programs. Countering this enthusiasm, however, was the constant scrutiny of every activity that women pilots engaged in. For example, in July 1943 the two paramilitary programs for women pilots came under Senate investigation by the Truman Committee. Confidential memoranda between Julius Amberg (special assistant to the secretary of War), Lieutenant Colonel Miles H. Knowles, Colonel G.A. Brownell, Major General Barton Yount, and General Arnold during this month went back and forth raising charges, complaints, and allegations about "Cochran's program." Some of the military support for "Love's program" may have been derived from the fact that it was perceived as the lesser of two evils.

Whatever the internal problems, the ATC and the AAF did not publicly discuss the issue; however, stories such as the July 1943 *Newsweek* article entitled "Coup for Cochran" occasionally did become public, in spite of the ban on press coverage of the WAFS imposed by the War Department in October

Gertrude Meserve was one of the "Original 27" recruits for the Women's Auxiliary Ferry Squadron. Before she got the call to join the WAFS, Meserve was a flight instructor for the Civilian Pilot Training Program in Boston, teaching students from the Massachusetts Institute of Technology, Harvard, Northeastern, and Tufts Universities. *Courtesy of Gertrude Meserve LaValley.*

1942. All parties directly involved were eager to treat the women as if they were in the military, with the expectation that this would soon be a reality. The women pilots for their part were just as eager to participate in flying for the war effort. Applications came flooding in, making the WAFS and the WFTD the only women's groups affiliated with the military to have a surplus of recruits.

The "Original 27" WAFS were handpicked, but the invitation to apply did not guarantee a position. If the woman accepted, she would report to an AAF base (at her own expense) for a physical. If the results were satisfactory, the woman would then be asked (again, at her own expense) to report to the New Castle Air Base in Wilmington, Delaware, to undergo flight checks, examinations, and a personal interview with Nancy Love. Finally, the candidate would appear before a review board of three ATC officers who would examine her dossier (Nancy Love was permitted to sit in as an ex officio member). In order to become a WAFS member, a woman had to receive the board's approval, just like any male Air Force candidate.[4]

The original WAFS were an elite corps. Among the most experienced women pilots in the nation, they were articulate, bright, and enthusiastic. They exuded an aura of athleticism, good humor, and self-confidence. They are remembered as talented individualists from a variety of different backgrounds, not as "society dames," as Cochran once called them. It is important to remember that some of the WAFS were as talented at flying as Cochran herself. It would take more than flight experience for Cochran to earn respect and the right to leadership among these women.

The ATC needed convincing that women could really fly, so they subjected them to all manner of tests and ground school classes, even when the women had more experience then their military instructors. They also introduced the women to military procedures. Finally, on 20 October 1942, forty days after the invitations to apply had gone out, WAFS began to ferry aircraft.

Piper L-4 Grasshoppers and Fairchild PT-19s were the first craft assigned. Stoically the WAFS performed the physically, if not intellectually, arduous task of transporting these trainers from the factory to the various air fields around the United States. They did extremely well during the first months, with a delivery record of 100 percent. Their performance was noticed by the ATC commanding officers, and in December 1942 General George commented, "If they can fly four-engine bombers safely after proper periods of training and preliminary work, I see no reason now why they may not get the chance."[5]

Cornelia Fort, one of the original WAFS, best expressed her colleagues' desire for acceptance: "Because there were and are so many disbelievers in women pilots, especially in their place in the army, officials wanted the best possible qualifications to go with the first experimental group. All of us realized what a spot we were on. We had to deliver the goods or else. Or else there wouldn't ever be another chance for women pilots in any part of the service."[6]

A new era had begun. For the first time, American women were flying military aircraft. To the surprise of many, they did a good job, and they provided significant service. The WAFS were proud of this, but most of their satisfaction came from the knowledge that they were able to combine an activity they loved with a challenge and a service. They also enjoyed working for Nancy Love, who was considered a model of the ideals many WAFS held. She was regarded as a great leader because she was a pilot first and an administrator second. Her willingness to fly tough missions, to surprise the group by arranging for the provision of their own grey-green uniforms, and to tirelessly act as their advocate were among the many reasons accounting for her popularity. Her personal conduct was always gracious and civil. Most important, she conveyed her pride in the organization without appearing to seek personal recognition.[7]

The WAFS expanded their base of operations after the first trial months, and Love named several WAFS to serve as commanding officers (COs) at these new facilities. When Love was transferred to ATC headquarters in Cincinnati,

Nancy Harkness Love, WAFS director, caught during a busy moment while on a visit to the 4th Fighter Operational Training Unit, Brownsville Municipal Airport, Texas. *Courtesy of Margaret C. Love.*

Betty Gillies became CO at New Castle. Delphine Bohn headed a WAFS flight squadron at Love Field, Dallas, Texas; Barbara Donahue (Ross) at Romulus, Michigan; and Barbara Erickson (London) at Long Beach, California. Farmingdale, Long Island (at the Republic Plant), and some other locations were added later. All of these COs performed well, but Barbara Erickson, later WASP commander at Long Beach, California, deserves special notice. In March 1944, Erickson, who had flown tirelessly, was awarded the Air Force Medal by General Arnold and given a citation signed by President Roosevelt. The marathon mission for which she earned this honor involved making four 2,000-mile flights in three different aircraft within a five-day period.

The WAFS began to grow larger once Jacqueline Cochran's training program was under way. On 24 April 1943 the first WFTD class graduated, and all twenty-three members reported to the WAFS. They were followed by forty-three graduates in May and thirty-eight in early July. The fourth graduating class, with its 112 women pilots, reported to ATC bases in August 1943, and the WAFS were on the way to operating as a full-strength ferrying squadron. Ap-

The 6th Ferrying Group at the Vultee Factory in Long Beach, California. Left to right, Barbara Towne, Cornelia Fort, Evelyn Sharp, B.J. Erickson, and Bernice Batten. *Courtesy of The Woman's Collection, Texas Woman's University.*

proximately 150 more graduates would be assigned to the WAFS before the end of 1943.

By this time Cochran had convinced the AAF to assign women pilots to various other flying duties throughout the training commands and numbered air forces. In August 1943 the AAF reorganized the command structure of the women pilots. The WAFS, who before August were a separate entity under the Ferrying Division of the ATC, were placed under the control of the Director of Women Pilots. Cochran was appointed to this new post, and although Love remained in charge of the women pilots from the Ferrying Division, she now reported directly to Cochran in the Pentagon on matters relating to assignment and disposition of personnel. Cochran was still in charge of training operations, although the WFTD name was dropped. The new organization was named the Women's Airforce Service Pilots, or WASP. This was still a civilian

Betty Gillies before ferrying a P-47, one of the fastest WWII fighter aircraft. Gillies, who was barely five feet tall, used special blocks to help her reach the rudder pedals. *Courtesy of the International Women's Air and Space Museum.*

group, but the AAF had created a single hierarchical unit through which it could experiment with the deployment of women pilots.

By June 1944—D-Day in Europe—the AAF began to retrench, closing down most of the pilot-training bases. This brought about a major ferrying job, which required the services of hundreds of pilots to move surplus training aircraft from these bases to storage and disposition areas throughout the country. The decision was made to transfer to the training command all WASPs assigned to the WAFS section except for those pilots who were qualified to fly pursuit aircraft. (The WAFS were thus subsumed under the WASPs; only the "Original 27" maintained their WAFS identification—despite the reorganization.) There were 123 women who qualified as Class 3 pilots, capable of flying combat aircraft such as the P-47 Thunderbolt fighter, to ports of embarkation in support of the invasion of Europe. All of these women possessed instrument ratings (i.e., they were able to fly on instruments alone); 98 percent had twin-engine ratings; and 80 percent had both single- and twin-engine fighter aircraft ratings. Five of them, Nancy Love, Betty Gillies, Barbara Erickson, Dora Dougherty, and Dorothea Johnson, were qualified at the highest level, Class 5. Dougherty and Johnson later qualified to fly the B-29 bomber aircraft.

Many of the original WAFS were not interested in being a part of "Cochran's program," and despite the name and program change they never considered themselves WASPs. Even today, some of these women identify themselves as WAFS, express preference for their original uniform, and proclaim loyalty to Love rather than to Cochran. The young women who learned to fly the "Army Way" through Cochran's training program were less affected by such tensions. Jacqueline Cochran was their hero, and many hoped to emulate her remarkable personal achievements.

In the spring of 1943, Cochran told the first class of trainees that this was "the greatest opportunity ever offered women pilots anywhere in the world."[8] The Women's Flying Training Detachment (WFTD) was first based at the Houston, Texas, Municipal Airport. (The other designation for the Houston phase of the program was the 319th Army Air Forces Flying Training Detachment [AAFFTD].) It was inactivated when operations shifted to Sweetwater. There was a deluge of applications for this program (in the end, Cochran reported that she received more than twenty-five thousand), but the requirements were stiff. Like the WAFS, applicants had to be American citizens between twenty-one and thirty-five years old. The women had to be at least five feet tall (later five feet, four inches) and pass the flight surgeon's physical. The difference between the WFTD and the WAFS was in the extent and level of previous flight time required for admission. The WAFS demanded five hundred hours, a two hundred–horsepower rating, and a commercial license. The training program initially required two hundred hours without regard to horsepower. Following the outbreak of the war, obtaining a license became quite difficult because of the ban on flying within one hundred miles of the U.S. border, the extra security clearance requirements on cross-country flying, and the shortage of civilian aircraft and instructors. For these reasons, the requirement of a valid license was dropped before the first class was filled. The required hours were subsequently reduced to seventy-five by January 1943, and ended up with a minimum requirement of only thirty-five hours.[9]

The other important aspect of the selection process was the personal interview with Cochran or one of her representatives. The interview was used to assess the candidate's personality, her stability, and various aspects of her background that might be indicative of her future performance under stress. Given the physiological requirements and the limited number of women who were pilots, the women who were finally selected tended to be fairly similar. They were certainly kindred souls when it came to flying. This was manifest in the feeling that the recognition of their sister pilots was more important than the approval of their male flight instructors. The entire WASP experience gave them a unique self-confidence, resulting in the ability to persevere through all kinds of difficult and unusual situations during the war and, naturally, later on in their lives.

The personal interview also allowed Cochran to determine the race of the applicants. The program had only limited minority participation: two Chinese Americans, one Native American, and a few Jewish women. There were no black women, although several applied. Cochran was remarkably candid in her autobiography about her treatment of these applicants. She hoped that they would fail the preliminary examination, so she could always claim fair treatment.[10]

The first black woman (unidentified by Cochran but most likely Janet Harmon Bragg) to successfully reach the final stages of selection had a rather unusual reception. Cochran made a special point of interviewing her. At that meeting Cochran says that she made a strong case for the problems of integration in military life; further, she stressed the program's experimental status. According to Cochran the young woman understood the situation and withdrew her application. The barriers a black woman (and all minority women) faced were threefold—race, class, and sex—and each militated against her participation. Given the climate of the day, Cochran probably was correct in assessing how difficult it would have been to get both the military bureaucracy and Congress to overcome their bias against blacks as well as against women. She believed that to interject the race question into the project might well have spelled its demise.[11]

The discrimination and the profound difficulties, even dangers, that would have had to be faced by a lone black woman pilot ferrying aircraft to isolated bases all over the country were very real. Cochran sensed the true sentiment of the military toward the participation of blacks. Just by acknowledging the issue of racism, Cochran was more conscious of it than the majority of white Americans. However, her actions continued to reflect the majority sentiment.[12]

When the WFTD candidates who had been selected arrived at Houston (at their own expense) in October 1942, they entered a program that was still being created. The women boarded in hotels and started classes run by a contractor, Aviation Enterprises. The goal was to teach the women to fly Army trainer aircraft. The first approved curriculum had 115 hours of flight time, 20 hours in a Link Trainer, and 180 hours of ground school. The trainees first flew in liaison aircraft, such as Piper Cubs and Taylorcrafts. In the second phase they flew in military training planes, such as the PT-19 and the BT-13. The last 15 hours were spent in advanced trainer aircraft, such as the AT-6 and the AT-17. The trainees wore large coveralls designed for men (affectionately called Zoot suits) and fleece-lined leather flying jackets. No provisions for meals and formal uniforms were made, which meant that often the women did without. In other ways the group was expected to be just like the military, and their curriculum included physical training, calisthenics, and marching.[13]

The women of this first crew had initially expected their training to last only a few weeks. It turned out to be a demanding five-month course, but the spirit of these women was indomitable. On the long bus rides between Houston and the airport, they sang and they laughed. Bound together by a spirit of camaraderie, this class is best characterized by their altered rendition of George M. Cohan's "Yankee Doodle Dandy":

> We are Yankee Doodle Pilots
> Yankee Doodle, do or die
> Real live nieces of our Uncle Sam,
> Born with a yearning to fly.
> Keep in step to all our classes
> March to flight line with our pals
> Yankee Doodle came to Texas
> Just to fly the PTs
> We are those Yankee Doodle Gals!

Gradually, conditions improved and the program became more organized. The second class arrived in December 1942. They were still located in Houston, but at least the contractor had opened a mess hall, to which the women were expected to march, Army style. During their tenure, housing was consolidated to a few large blocks of cottages and motel rooms. The curriculum underwent revision and extension, until it was much like the AAF program for male cadets and lasted twenty-two and a half weeks. The table below indicates the training schedule.

PRIMARY (50 hours)
Fundamentals of Flying	46
Navigation	4

BASIC (70 hours)
Transition (to BTs)	30
Instruments	20
Navigation (Day 18, Night 2)	20

ADVANCED (60 hours)
Transition to AT-6	10
Transition to twin engine (AT-17 or AT-10)	20
Navigation (Day 18, Night 2)	20
Instruments	10

The first three intakes and half of the new fourth class were based at Howard Hughes Field, Houston Municipal Airport. There were just twenty-two various civilian and military training aircraft available to them there, but that did not at first affect the capability of the school. More serious was the winter weather along the Gulf Coast, especially the fog, which resulted in a perpetual scramble for the women to log the specified number of hours needed to complete the course. This required constant rescheduling and flying on Sunday, the only free day. Despite the difficulties, the women were doing exceedingly well, and the decision was made to increase dramatically the number of students. The original plan for 396 students was increased first to 700 and then to 1,000 in 1944.[14]

This decision made it imperative to seek new facilities. From the start, Cochran worked to align the WFTD (and later the WASP) completely with the Army training program. Although following procedure and method was relatively easy, using military facilities was not. Cochran was successful in getting an entire military base for the training of women pilots. The new base, Avenger Field in Sweetwater, Texas, was being used to train Canadian cadets, and Mrs. Leni Leah Deaton, Cochran's chief administrative officer, found them still on the field when she arrived to prepare for the WFTD move. Deaton, who had set up the operation in Houston, managed the enormous task of moving half of the existing unit to Sweetwater, while also preparing for the integration of a new class every month through 1944. Deaton had been a Red Cross swimming administrator for many years and brought with her a broad knowledge of how to manage large programs. By April 1943 the WFTD had the field to them-

Mary Ann Wetherby (left) and Yvonne "Pat" Pateman, members of
WASP Class 43-5 at Avenger Field in Sweetwater, Texas. *Courtesy of
Yvonne C. Pateman.*

selves. With the move to Sweetwater, they finally had adequate room for the
training program run the Army way.

Not everyone cared about the Army way. A few went so far as to say that
the military aspects of the program were something to be endured. Toby Felker
of the 44-W-2 (i.e., the second class of women pilots in 1944) proclaimed that,
to her, what really mattered was the opportunity to fly. "All sorts of very inter-

(Top) On the flight line at Avenger Field, Sweetwater, Texas. *Courtesy of Yvonne C. Pateman.*

(Left) Flight Commander John O'Keefe was an instructor for the Primary Training Phase at Avenger Field, Sweetwater, Texas. *Courtesy of Yvonne C. Pateman.*

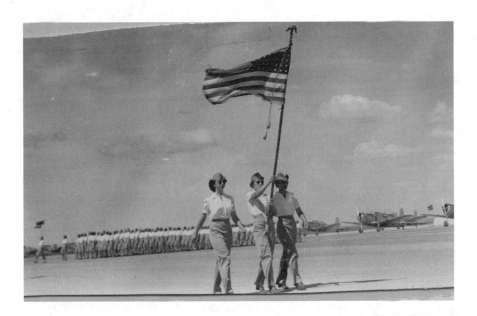

Graduation Day for Class 43-2 featured military parades and a memorable ceremony in which the graduates received their WASP wings. *Courtesy of Yvonne C. Pateman.*

esting things happened because these women who liked to fly—who wanted to fly—were going to do so, using any means they could. I really felt that was an exciting part of it. None of us really cared very much for the military regiment [*sic*] . . . but that was just one of the things you had to do."[15]

Flying was, of course, the main activity during training, "their single-minded consuming passion," as Doris Brinker Tanner described it. Life at Sweetwater marked the change to Army-style living with barracks, footlockers, and shared bathroom facilities. The flying curriculum was gradually expanded, partly in response to the applicants' diminishing flight experience (two hundred hours had been lowered to one hundred, to seventy-five, and finally to thirty-five hours) and age (from twenty-one to eighteen and a half). The final program was a thirty-week course of flight training and ground school classes. The flight training consisted of 210 hours of aerial instruction. Ground school involved 560 hours divided among various programs in military training, academic studies, aircraft equipment maintenance, physical education, and medical training. Academic work included mathematics, physics, navigation, the principles of flight, engines and propellers, code, instrument training, and communication. Examinations were inevitable and tensions were high for both ground and aerial tests.

Contrary to expectations, the elimination rate for the women proved to be about the same as for AAF male cadets. Of the 1,830 women applicants accepted (out of 25,000 inquiries), 30.7 percent were eliminated due to flying deficiencies and 2.2 percent for other reasons. Eight percent passed but resigned before assignment. This resulted in the final tally of 1,074 graduates, or 58.7 percent of the total who had been accepted.[16] Most of the "wash outs" occurred in the primary phase (although it was not unusual for candidates to experience difficulty when making the transition from light aircraft to the PT-17 or PT-19). When comparing the success of male and female student pilots, it is important to note that the AAF sometimes deliberately failed candidates (by altering requirements) in a particular class if there were fewer pilot combat casualties than anticipated.[17]

Some women did not complete the training program because of accidents. Of the thirty-eight fatalities in the overall WAFS/WFTD/WASP program, eleven occurred during training.[18] Aside from the obvious aspects of the loss, the hidden tragedy of these accidents was that there was no insurance, no death benefits—in short, no official recognition of service. As civilians, the women began their training aware of the risks as well as the benefits, but gradually, through the training program, they became thoroughly indoctrinated with the concept of service for their country, just as the male cadets were. When a woman died, the other women felt betrayed that the government was incapable of expressing condolence through some formal gesture of recognition to the survivors. Their expectation that this gesture should be made, in terms of some sort of financial assistance or insurance, was in accord with the values of President Roosevelt, the New Deal, and, increasingly, American society at large. In being treated and trained as equals with men, they had come to expect, at the least, equal recognition in the form of comparable death benefits.

Graduation brought a number of options for the women who succeeded. At first, there was only one task—that of ferrying trainer and liaison aircraft. Following the August 1943 power shake-up between Love and Cochran, each successive graduating class gradually expanded their range of tasks and responsibilities. The next major duty to be undertaken was target towing at Camp Davis, North Carolina. This meant flying with a long strip of fabric attached to the airplane by a long tow line, in order to provide anti-aircraft gunnery practice. At first the women were not welcome. Twenty-five were assigned to test fly Piper Cubs, doing work incongruous with their training, until Cochran visited the base. Finally, the women were put on the target-towing project.

The condition of the aircraft at Camp Davis was considered to be quite poor. Priority for parts and supplies, not to mention new airplanes, was held by AAF units in combat. One woman in the Camp Davis program was killed in an accident caused by contaminated fuel, an incident that was strongly rumored to have been the result of sabotage. Cochran denied this, and investigations resulted in a plausible alternative explanation of equipment failure. Years later, however, Cochran admitted that sugar had been found in fuel tanks and that other women had died because of sabotaged aircraft. This information had been suppressed for fear that adverse publicity would end the entire women's program.[19]

Gradually, the base commander, admittedly prejudiced against women, came to accept the group and acknowledge their skills. They were used for searchlight tracking practice and mock strafing missions. Soon thereafter, classes were sent to many bases to fly radar missions and remote-control drone airplanes.[20]

A few WASPs were sent to advanced schools after graduation. Seventeen of them from classes 43-W-5 and 43-W-6 went to Lockbourne Army Air Field in Ohio to learn to fly B-17s. When they had successfully completed the course, thirteen of them reported to operational assignments, flying gunnery and tow targets for aerial and ground gunnery practice. A second group from these two classes transferred to Dodge City, Kansas, to train on the B-26 bomber, known to be a difficult craft to handle. In the case of the B-26 and the B-29, WASPs were deliberately used to counter the undeserved discredit then given these aircraft by the men. The theory that "if a woman flies it, it must be safe" proved effective, and it only took a few flights (along with an extended wingspan) to have the image of these airplanes transformed into "safe" and "good" aircraft according to the male pilot grapevine.[21]

WASPs also worked as administrative pilots, assigned to different groups such as the weather wing, which worked with the Air Weather Service. They flew cargo runs and often flight-tested newly delivered aircraft. One WASP, Ann Carl, became the first woman (and one of the first pilots in general) to test fly the Bell YP-59, America's first jet fighter.[22] When the WASP program ended in December 1944, the 916 WASPs on active duty were assigned primarily to the training command and the air transport command. Eighty women worked with the Second Air Force, with the remainder scattered among various bases and commands.[23]

Despite the variety of their assignments, most WASPs exhibited little awareness of other women in the military. Few recall having much contact with other women apart from the nurses. Periodically, however, hints of a bit of interservice rivalry would surface. For example, the verse of a favorite WASP song asks facetiously if the listener would rather be a WAC:

> A WAC may be an officer
> With bright bars that shine,
> Her olive green and everything looks fine.
> She's very proud of the name she bears,
> As for you, you don't want her cares;
> Her olive green was never meant for you,
> You want the Santiago Blue.

Santiago Blue referred to the attractive new uniforms that arrived in April 1944. In 1943, the AAF quartermaster general had proposed to Cochran that the women pilots wear uniforms based on surplus WAC and Army nurse uniform supplies. She summarily rejected this idea and arranged for a New York designer to create a new outfit, which was finally approved by General of the Army George C. Marshall.

The women were glad finally to have something to replace the awkward, ill-fitting, and very unofficial-looking outfits of men's trousers and shirts because, at least in part, it was another step toward professional recognition. The uniforms were an important symbol of the WASP program and they helped the wearers to feel more a part of the military and of the AAF. The response was also favorable from base commanders, military police, and other personnel, who found it desirable to have the women suited up in clearly recognizable uniforms. Cochran had demonstrated her authority once more: by keeping her group visibly distinguishable from the WACs, she had made it more difficult for the WASPs to be subsumed under Oveta Hobby's control.[24]

New symbols do not always lead to the establishment of the particular new reality that is desired. For the WASPs, transformation into formal military status was the critical step to be taken, but Congress was not as easily persuaded of this change as General Marshall had been in the matter of a new uniform. By the summer of 1944, Arnold was absolutely convinced that the WASP program should be continued. It was accomplishing everything he had originally hoped for, and thus he began to submit proposals to Congress for legislation authorizing the incorporation of the WASP program into the AAF. Congress, on the other hand, did not envision an expanding role for women pilots in the AAF, but rather a postwar return to normalcy—an AAF without women pilots. The emotional side of the issue was further influenced by a series of editorials and letters protesting the AAF's failure to utilize the abilities of recently discharged CAA flight instructors.

A congressional investigation, chaired by Robert Ramspeck, was formed. Preliminary report comments were not positive: "To recruit teenaged school girls, stenographers, clerks, beauticians, housewives and factory workers to pilot the military planes of this government is as startling as it is invalid. The militarization of Cochran's WASPs is not necessary or desirable; the present program should be immediately and sharply curtailed."[25] The committee was acting on House Resolution 4219 proposed by Congressman John Costello of Los Angeles. The resolution was designed to commission the WASP in the AAF with full benefits. In response to questions put during the inquiry, Nancy Love and General Tunner compiled extensive statistics and reports from commanding officers and other personnel who had worked with the WASP. This study showed that the stereotypes about women pilots were incorrect and unfair. WASPs were not accorded preferential treatment in assignments, and if resentment existed among male pilots, it was confined to a limited (but vocal) minority whose primary interest appeared not to be the most efficient operation of the Ferrying Division, but rather the preservation of an all-male environment.[26]

These facts were supported by the testimony of numerous individuals, most importantly General Arnold. In executive session Arnold explained that, in the matter of training, he preferred the WASPs over the regular civilian instructors for reasons of ability and attitude. Ultimately, however, the AAF could, according to Arnold, absorb both the WASPs and the CAA flight instructors, although the men might be used in different capacities.[27]

Cochran complicated the situation by refusing to compromise certain aspects of her program. Even though there was a favorable response in Congress toward keeping the WASPs who were already trained, there was no support for continuing the training program. It was on this point that Cochran balked. She insisted on a continuing program and on an organization separate from the WACs, because of her unwillingness to become subordinate to Oveta Hobby. Most observers at the time suggest that had Cochran been willing to attach the WASPs to the WAC, the program likely would have been militarized. Her refusal to compromise on this issue generated a high level of publicity and assured that the status of women in the military would remain controversial. Some men who had been civilian instructors were quick to highlight every criticism, including the erroneous assumption that women pilots were grounded each month for their menstrual period, thus having fewer hours of flight time than a man. The press openly criticized the women, calling the WASPs "glamour girls" who weren't legitimate pilots.[28]

Arnold's position supported Cochran: he had previously stated that the women pilots should not be incorporated into the WAC because of the "need for undivided and administrative and functional control which would not be possible if the WAAF [sic] was serving two masters, i.e., the WAC and the AAF."[29] It should be remembered that Arnold was involved in breaking the ground to separate the AAF from the Army, and further, that he had originally proposed a separate corps of Air-WACs. For Arnold, what counted was the fact that the women were performing their jobs well. But Arnold's attempts at using the women as a means of motivating his male pilots had backfired. The men were angry over attempts to make them feel guilty and to shame them into performing aspects of their jobs they thought were risky.[30] This irritation was compounded when the women earned praise and publicity for their performance of a job that went unnoticed when performed by a man. To a certain extent the men were justified in their reactions. For instance, men who had flown tow targets did not attract national media attention; this job became newsworthy only when some women replaced men in its performance. Sometimes in their eagerness, the women ignored the validity of protests made by men about equipment or procedures.

The debate raged on, with conservative congressmen lashing out at the military for conducting social experiments. The efforts of 1,074 women flying more than 60 million miles in almost every airplane in the AAF inventory did not, in the end, matter to Congress. The bill did not pass, and orders were given to demobilize the WASPs on 20 December 1944. During the fall, rumors percolated through the ranks about ex-WASPs being rehired. On 5 October 1944 Arnold adamantly stated: "There will be no—repeat—no women pilots in any capacity in the Air Force after December 20 except Jacqueline Cochran."[31]

Many of the women were bitter. Barbara Poole wrote a scorching piece for *Flying* magazine's December 1944 edition entitled "Requiem for the WASP":

> We have spent large sums to train the WASP. Now we are throwing this money away at the demand of a few thousand male pilots who were employed, until recently, in a civilian capacity on government flight programs. The curtailment of the program has thrown these pilots out of work. And now they are to get the WASPs' jobs.
> The demands of the unemployed male pilots have been a little far-fetched.
> "Throw the women out," they cried—meaning "and make room for us." They say, "The women can't be drafted, but we can and will be."
> But that's the very reason the women should have stayed where they were. What our Army needs most, our generals tell us, is men to fight on the ground. This is a sorry state of affairs for our pilots but after all we're running a war, not an employment bureau for disgruntled flyers.[32]

While the WASPs were prevented from joining the military, the WACs, the WAVES, and the MCWR all managed to convince the legislators of their worth. The women who packed parachutes or served as flight nurses would continue to operate in the military beyond World War II, keeping alive the consciousness of women in military aviation.[33]

Before the war the aviation organizations and events in which women were involved were small, characterized by an economically, and often intellectually, elite membership. World War II changed that by institutionalizing female participation in two major centers of power in American society—industry and the military. Women pilots were a special case. It took their desire to participate and the advocacy of several key individuals, Eleanor Roosevelt in particular, to bring men to acknowledge the inherent usefulness of a talented woman pilot (especially one willing to do virtually any kind of flying). Previously, the planning of military leaders had not automatically included women pilots, but by

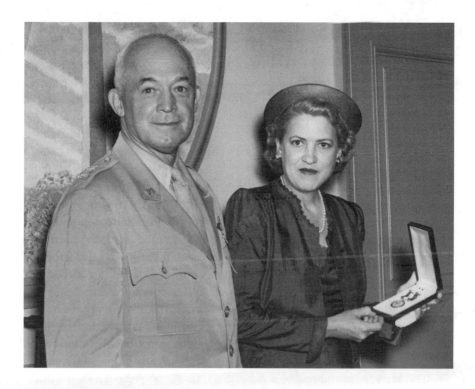

General H.H. Arnold presents Jacqueline Cochran with the Distinguished Service Medal for her work as director of the WASP. *Courtesy of Ann Wood Kelly.*

war's end this had changed. General Arnold's letter to each WASP announcing demobilization reiterated the statement he made to the last class of WASP to graduate: "It is on the record," he said, "that women can fly as well as men. . . . We will not again look upon a woman's flying organization as experimental."[34] Arnold believed that women pilots would be used in future military actions.

The women in military aviation were proud of their accomplishments. They wanted recognition and publicly acknowledged status in conjunction with their work, which is why they were so concerned about military status. Most WASPs felt that being in the military was peripheral to the act of flying military aircraft; to them, demobilization was devastating. Even though these women could continue to fly civilian aircraft, there was a keen sense of loss at not being able to fly military airplanes. It took thirty years for the controversy to cool sufficiently for women to petition Congress seriously again on this subject. Nevertheless, when the war ended, women in civilian and military aviation joined in the general relief and happiness that it was finally over.

Like other Americans they looked forward to the "return to normal" that peace-time was supposed to bring.

Their participation at every level of society, whether university or factory, Civil Air Patrol or Ninety-Nines, WAC, WAVE, or WASP, had established the foundation for a new age in aviation for women. The exceptional leadership offered by such women as Cochran, Love, Hobby, and Hancock marked the first appearance of women in such responsible roles. They were successful, competent women who became integrated into the existing power structure by adopting the norms and expectations of the male leadership. Their acceptance into the top echelons was generally contingent upon their not challenging the existing power structure.[35]

Establishing a permanent presence for women in this arena was a difficult task because, in the eyes of American society, all of the programs for women in military aviation were experimental. Leaders who sought to overcome existing prejudices insisted on exceptional job performance from the women in their programs. The quality of a woman's work had to equal or exceed that of a man's if unreasonable biases were to be dispelled.

Although discrimination in the armed forces based on gender had lessened somewhat by the end of the war, racial segregation still prevailed. There had been little real progress in the integration of women of color into military aviation. Here, as in the rest of society, integration was viewed as too controversial for serious consideration; attempting to put it into practice was still believed to jeopardize the already tenuous status of any program for women. A change would not come until 1948 with the Integration Act.

During the war, American women demonstrated to themselves and to all U.S. citizens that women were capable of working in aviation occupations. A significant period of time would have to elapse before this knowledge would have its full effect. Building on their wartime experience, women would expand their aviation opportunities enormously over the next half century. It was no longer a question of biology, as it was clear that women could design, build, test, repair, direct, and pilot aircraft. This is the legacy of World War II.

Should Women Fly?

*American Women in Aviation
during the Second Half of the
Twentieth Century*

Two things were learned in the gulf situation: first, that it is very hard to delineate where a combat area is and where a safe area is: and the other thing we learned was that to fly an F-15 or any other sophisticated plane, the overriding issue is not physical strength. You have to be bright, you have to be quick, and you have to be well-trained, and we have men and women pilots that fit that description.

Barbara B. Kennelley, Representative, First District, Connecticut
"Address to the House of Representatives," 9 May 1991

Escape, evasion, capture, and the eventual molestation and brutalization of U.S. women aviators, when a plentiful supply of males is available to run those risks, is contrary to the American value system as I know it. Therefore, after serious deliberation, I conclude that placing women in combatant aircrews, where they may be subjected to capture by nations which do not share Western values and have shown disregard for the Geneva Conventions, is wrong national policy.

General Maxwell R. Thurman, U.S. Army (Ret.)
Member of the Presidential Commission on the
Assignment of Women in the Armed Forces,
From his "Commissioner's Statement," 1992.

5

Demobilization and the Postwar Transition

1945–1949

> They were girls who could not sit beside
> The hearth and let go by
> All the joy and pride and thrills that ride
> With rovers of the sky
>
> "To the Ninety-Nine," Louis De Jean

Women's participation in aviation, institutionalized during World War II, was somewhat tenuous during the immediate postwar period. Wartime expectations of what the return to peace would mean for America were quite different from what actually happened. The war seemed to have fostered an optimistic expectation that peace would usher in the dawn of an aerial age in which women would have a significant part. This image ultimately collided with the economic reality of diminished demand for the production of airplanes. Certain social expectations had a negative impact also. Definitions of postwar normalcy were based on prewar stereotypes. For example, as VE-Day (8 May 1945) drew nearer, in contrast to earlier advertisements that had exhorted women to work in the factory, the popular press, at the government's instigation, began to encourage women to return to the home and family. Home was where most of the WASPs, WACs, and WAVES went, though somewhat less eagerly than the women working in the aircraft factories.[1]

Those women who remained in aviation jobs began creating the legal framework necessary to reinforce and encourage continued change in American attitudes concerning gender roles for men and women. Society became accustomed to, although not fully accepting of, women in nontraditional occupations, such as on the assembly line or in the military. Military women did not want to relinquish their newly gained positions. It was during the late 1940s that the military women's corps became permanent components of the services, partly as a result of the Women's Armed Services Act. The various women's aeronautical associations began to reorganize themselves after a wartime hiatus in activity. The aviation industry, after retrenching somewhat, began reorganizing for peacetime production.

It was the era of the nuclear bomb, the Marshall Plan, and the advent of Cold War relations between the United States and the Soviet Union. This climate of international affairs influenced all aspects of American life, from politics to technology. Aeronautical technology was intimately involved in these disparate spheres of activity, and it also became a positive factor in the American image and national pride. Certainly aeronautics represented the key factor in the nation's defense program. "The Bomb" may have been the ultimate weapon, but it was the airplane that delivered it.

At the time of demobilization, women in each of the different aviation areas were in the process of both challenging and adapting to the institutions that, in the past, had been organized and run primarily by men and which had frequently barred the participation of women altogether. The process involved a gradual but persistent questioning of the narrow expectations concerning the appropriate role of women. The resulting changes would set the pattern for subsequent generations.

Most women in the aircraft industry left the factory. Women were encouraged to do this for reasons other than the drop in production. A well-known Madison Avenue advertising firm, Batten, Barton, Durstine & Osborn, put out a pamphlet entitled "Women and Wrenches" explaining what they viewed as the chief effects of women's production line labors. "Women may have acquired a passion for machinery, although laying a wrench on a certain nut, or spot-welding identical spots several hundred times a day, is hardly a comprehensive course in engineering, metallurgy, and inorganic chemistry. We venture the cautious prediction that when dungarees and lunch-boxes are put aside, the girls will continue to be more interested in what a thing will do for them then in how or why it works. However, one good may result from women's adventure in industry. They can hardly fail to appreciate the integrity of American production."[2]

The pamphlet described a postwar world filled with all sorts of technological wonders that would require considerable adjustment. However, the company noted that they thought it very unlikely that it would have to hire engineers and scientists to create advertising copy to "cater to machine-mad women."

Women working in factories did not continue to attract the media attention they had during the war. The jobs had lost the glamorous aura of wartime patriotism, and further, company executives could see no advantage in attracting women to the plants. It was generally expected in this postwar period that young men and women could finally resume their lives, establishing the households and families that had been delayed for several years.

The aircraft industry was thrust into a period of extreme instability as the Army Air Forces and Navy demobilized and the government began selling surplus warplanes. The commercial airlines failed to flood the market with new orders. In addition to the drop in demand, the composition of the labor force was also being altered. During the war most workers were involved in production, but the ratio of engineers to line workers began to change in favor of the professional staff. This trend had particular influence on the employment of women.[3]

The AAF became thoroughly committed to a program of research and development for jet fighter and bomber aircraft. In all, fifteen new programs were started, but this work had little immediate impact on production. The Navy ordered a few aircraft that had been developed late in the war, but on the whole, government business was quite small. This had been expected. What had not been anticipated was the sluggish nature of the commercial airline and general aviation segments of the business. The first year after the war had witnessed the opening of many new small airports and an increase in the numbers of students. This proved a short-lived phenomenon, however, as aircraft operation costs overtook salaries and disposable incomes. The market for new planes bottomed out after a brief flash of intense activity, and hundreds of thousands of workers were laid off.

In October 1947, only 272,000 workers remained in the aircraft manufacturing industry, half the number employed in 1941. Interestingly, the percentage of women employees did not drop to 1941 levels. In October 1947, 28,500 women were employed in the industry, representing 11.8 percent of the total. Yet five years earlier they had composed, at 23,000, a mere 5 percent of the industry's workforce. The 11.8 percent mark was as low as it would ever get after World War II, but it was typical of the demobilization period.[4]

The year 1948 was a very bad year for the aircraft industry. Ironically, its sales were nearly twice prewar levels, but a much greater overhead precipitated heavy losses. The industry eventually sank from its first-place rank among American businesses in 1944 to forty-fourth, based on dollar value of production output. It was at this point that the aircraft industry turned to the federal government for assistance—an action that would affect both the financial condition of the industry and the composition of the workforce.

Initially, federal aid triggered a small rise in the number of women employed. Out of a total of 266,000 workers in September 1949, 12.5 percent, or 33,000, were women. They were limited almost exclusively to production workers or clerks, although a few women worked in the white-collar occupations of engineering or management.[5]

Betty Gillies was an example of a woman working in one of these white-collar positions. She was hired for a brief period to work as a test pilot for Ryan Aeronautical Corporation. This unusual opportunity was made possible by the fact that her husband was in charge of the test program for BT-13s and FR-1s.[6]

Olive Ann Beech, who had founded Beech Aircraft Company in 1932 with her husband, Walter, was one of the rare women in aviation management. A chief executive of the company, she often promoted other women involved in aviation. She was behind the donations of Beech airplanes to Louise Thaden for the 1936 Bendix Race (won by Thaden) and to Ruth Nichols for her Relief Wings organization. Walter and Olive Ann Beech's partnership in running the corporation strengthened during World War II. In the postwar period, Olive Ann was responsible for preserving the company's economic viability, as well as for developing a program of diversification to extend services beyond the general aviation market. She also continued her interest in women's advancement and was credited with forming the liberal labor policies at Beech. These included special attention to situations affecting women in the training and personnel programs. She created a special center for women to increase their knowledge of business and industry. Her work was recognized (as happened many times later in her life) just one year after she formally assumed the Beech presidency, in 1951, when she was named "Woman of the Year in Aviation" by the Women's National Aeronautical Association.[7]

Other women combined technical talents with more traditional feminine roles. The postwar period marked the advent of the "flying secretary." Jeanne Coffey, who had been educated at Stephens College, worked for the Aeronca Company. She was a secretary, officially, but she spent her afternoons instructing potential customers, test flying new aircraft, or ferrying Aeronca airplanes from the factory to the buyers' local fields.[8] Elizabeth Gardner, who worked for Piper Aircraft before the war, then served as a WASP, returned to Piper in 1945. She worked in the public relations office and was often called on to use her flying skills. Soon she was writing all of William Piper's speeches; later she was entrusted to deliver them to audiences in the Defense Department and to other companies involved in aviation.[9]

Gardner was not the only WASP who wanted to stay in the aviation business. Many of the former WASPs desperately sought jobs in the field. Most had to settle for roles peripheral to piloting, construction, or design, and only rarely did they fill supervisory positions. Former WASP Yvonne C. "Pat" Pateman worked at a California airport. She pumped gas, ran an airport café, and delivered airplanes. She became assistant manager after about a year. There were so

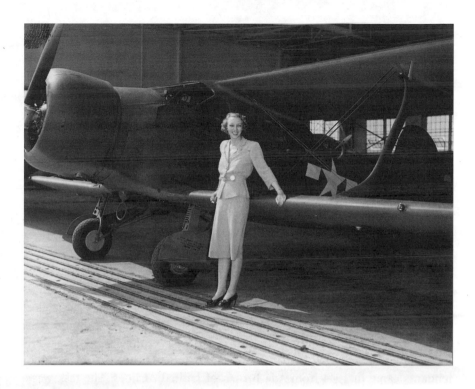

Olive Ann Beech cofounded Beech Aircraft Corporation with her husband, Walter, in 1932. In 1950, following Walter's death, she assumed the presidency. She remains the only woman to have headed a major American aircraft company. *Courtesy of Raytheon Aircraft.*

many used aircraft for sale that Pateman had many opportunities to ferry small airplanes between the distributor and the local field.[10]

In the spring of 1945, jobs ferrying surplus warplanes became available. The Defense Plant Corporation and Reconstruction Finance Corporation contractors had to supply their own pilots to fly the airplanes to the eight sales centers across the United States where the government sold its surplus warplanes.[11] Delphine Bohn, a former WASP member and one of the "Original 27" WAFS, served as a ferry pilot with the Defense Plant Corporation before going to work at the Pacific Aircraft Sales Company. Pacific was a Beech dealership based in Los Angeles which serviced California, Oregon, Washington, and Nevada. A "Girl Friday," as Bohn described her job, she served as office manager, secretary, test pilot, charter pilot, salesman, demonstration pilot, and ferry pilot. Bohn, who often demonstrated aircraft to famous actors and actresses from Hollywood, appeared to have a glamorous job. She worked very hard, but often her mink jacket and stylish clothing belied the high caliber of her experience and ability. In only a few years she was able to start her own aircraft dealership.[12]

Despite the diverse work of individual women in various phases of aviation's private sector, the largest group was still the flight attendants. These women, as well as their coworkers in ground occupations (like ticket sales and reservations), were caught in an unusual situation: an expanding job market offered tantalizing possibilities for raising their status and pay, but these opportunities proved beyond the individual's grasp.

Airlines executives shared the overly optimistic estimations of the aircraft manufacturers concerning postwar air travel. Both assumed that the civil aircraft market would replace the military demand, and they hoped to sustain their wartime revenue levels. Based on a doubling of passenger miles between 1945 and 1946 and the advent of transatlantic service, the companies placed hundreds of new orders in 1945 and 1946.[13]

As a result of the expansion of airline passenger service, increasing numbers of women were hired to work as flight attendants. The profession had become firmly established during the war, but now the women began collectively to desire an improvement in status, pay, and working conditions. One stimulus for this situation was that other airline personnel had successfully lobbied for such changes. Leadership of a movement to organize the flight attendants came in 1944 from Ada Brown of United Airlines. The task was a formidable one. Most women approved of the goals that Brown and others suggested, but the idea of a "union" was practically anathema. Unions, which then served mostly blue-collar laborers, were outside the experience of most of the flight attendants, whose upbringing was hostile to the overtones of radical activism from the 1920s and 1930s, which unions still had. Ultimately, they wanted to have their job viewed as a professional career, and to call any association of flight attendants a "union" seemed to downgrade their status and job prestige. For this reason, Brown always referred publicly to the proposed organization as an "Association."[14]

Appearance was still considered particularly important, as was being unmarried. Instead of a nursing degree, applicants were now expected to have at least one year of college education. The job training had not changed as a result of the war, except that the women no longer had to concern themselves with wartime photography restrictions and baggage searches. For example, the course conducted by Transcontinental and Western Air (TWA) lasted six weeks and concentrated on "the principles of aerodynamics, aircraft meal service, baby care, first aid, and the social amenities."[15] In that era of piston-engine aircraft, the attendants had time to spend with passengers, and were expected to point out significant geographic features and answer questions about how the aircraft operated.

The women, who were required to be at least twenty-one, were usually called "girls" and were treated as if they were minors. During training, they were housed in dormitory buildings under constant supervision of a headmistress (*in loco parentis*), who was the director of the training program and dormitory housemother. (This practice was also typical of many colleges in their treatment of their female students). The directors of many flight attendant divisions in the various airlines were women. While many of these women did not have great influence on airline policy, it is important not to underestimate their value as mentors to the younger women. They were competent, well-educated professional women who had decided against marriage in favor of their career. They served as vivid examples of the options women had apart from raising a family.

Most of the women they supervised chose not to follow their example. Even before the war was over, eight attendants a month, on average, were leaving TWA to marry. Yet apart from the year's service requirement initiated during the war, little attempt was made to retain their services. The reason for inaction stemmed from the management's conception of the job and why women were suited to do it. Before the war, women were used to help convince passengers to fly, but as public air travel increased, the rationale changed. An article about Braniff flight attendants noted that "for certain positions it has been found that women are better adapted than men—for example, the air hostess. Since the early thirties, when the first young girl flew as the third member of the air crew, no substitute has been found for her position. Just as a woman is best suited to receive guests in her home, so she is employed by the airlines to make guests feel at home aloft in a plane."[16]

The name change from "stewardess" to "hostess" in the popular postwar press is significant because it placed the profession in the context of accepted roles for white, middle-class women. It was acceptable for women to work in this job because it was perceived as a short interlude of adventure granting polish, grace, and professional charm to bright young women. When people described the occupation, it was always in terms of the benefits. Travel, shopping, and dining were seen as major aspects of the job description and not as perquisites of a demanding profession.

Some of the women in the profession had begun to see their work from a different perspective. Brown resigned her job as chief stewardess for United Airlines in December 1944 to become a full-time attendant again and to organize a union under the provisions of the Railway Labor Act of 1926. Her reason for doing this stemmed from her frustration at being unable to negotiate better wages and greater job protection while serving as chief stewardess. She began to organize the San Francisco region, while her colleagues Sally Thometz and Frances Hall assumed responsibility for the Denver and Chicago bases respectively.

United Airlines was very responsive to this work. William Patterson, president of United, believed that unions served important functions in industry and society. He also recognized that, since the flight attendants held, in effect, short-term positions, it would be much easier to work with a single established agent such as a union negotiation team rather than try to bargain with each individual. Within two months, 75 percent of the United attendants had signed "authorization-to-act" cards, and elections were held. Ada Brown became president; Frances Hall, vice president; Sally Watt, secretary; Edith Lauterbach, treasurer; and Sally Thometz, conferee. A constitution and bylaws were written, which officially established the group as the Air Line Stewardess Association (ALSA) on 22 August 1945. The women had also begun to prepare a contract to present to United.

The group initially was entirely within United, but its goal was to represent flight attendants on all airlines. Hence, the women maintained close contact with the Air Line Pilot's Association (ALPA), which had just such a broad-based membership. ALPA wanted to organize all of the airline workers but also wanted control, especially of any organization of flight attendants. For this reason, ALPA president David Behncke saw the autonomous ALSA as a threat. He was annoyed when ALSA failed to cooperate with his plans. Although ALSA had originally asked ALPA for advice in organizing, it was not at all interested in being subordinated to ALPA. Brown did not hesitate to tell Behncke this.

Without the support of the pilots, ALSA had to face the difficult task of negotiations without the resources of experience and money. ALSA leaders were always hampered by the turnover of membership, and constant vigilance was needed to keep the membership rolls current. Undaunted, Brown submitted ALSA's first request for conference dates in August 1945 in order to negotiate a new contract for the United flight attendants. That first meeting was a long struggle to find a common ground. The major point of discord between ALSA and United was over the reduction of the number of hours flown each month. United at first failed to take the women's demands seriously. Each group stood firm, and the situation was tense, with the company seeming almost to be avoiding progress.

The company lawyers eventually agreed to arrange meeting times around the flying schedules of the union team members (who could not afford not to work), and United always provided free transportation. In March 1946, after a seven-month effort, ALSA decided to consult the National Mediation Board.

This resulted in a mediation process that lasted over a month. The time was well spent, for in the end ALSA received a positive ruling. On 25 April 1946, Brown, Thometz, and Hall signed the first contractual agreement with United. In addition to gaining a contract, ALSA forced United to recognize the Association as a union—the first formal recognition of any flight attendant organization.[17]

That first contract served to legitimize the profession, increase wages, and improve working conditions. It also established a grievance procedure and legal protection from harassment and unfair labor practices. The starting salary was raised from $125 to $155 per month, the first such increase since 1930. A uniform allowance was provided, and mandatory rest periods were created. Flight time was limited to 85 hours per month, with a maximum of 255 hours "within any three consecutive calendar months." Further, a stewardess could fly only eight hours a day and was entitled to a rest period of two hours for every flight hour.

The successive agreements of 1947, 1948, and 1949 were based on the 1946 contract. One unusual provision added in 1948 was a graded pay scale based on the type of aircraft flown. As the airlines adopted better equipment, flight times were being dramatically reduced. However, the aircraft inventory of the airlines was still quite varied, and thus attendants flying identical routes could end up with different flight times. The goal of the contract was to guarantee that attendants on the swifter airplanes would not be penalized with a reduced paycheck.

ALSA was beset with financial difficulties from the start. As a small union its greatest liability was its inability to administer and process the grievances of its membership. United was effectively free to violate contractual provisions because it knew that ALSA was financially unable to defend its interests. In 1947 the company reinvoked the requirement that attendants be registered nurses on its Hawaiian route. ALSA protested the move but failed to file a grievance officially until 1948. When the case finally reached arbitration, it was ruled that ALSA had followed improper procedures and could therefore no longer protest United's requirement.

Other challenges were brought to the union in 1947. Ada Brown married, thus becoming a "no marriage" rule casualty. Further, other groups were beginning to form all around ALSA to compete for the participation of flight attendants. In particular, ALPA had created a rival group known as the Air Line Stewards and Stewardesses Association (ALSSA) to compete directly with the "recalcitrant" ALSA. ALSSA, founded in August 1946, began a campaign to incorporate ALSA into the fold.

It was not until 2 December 1949 that ALSSA was successful in its attempt. The merger had been proposed by Irene Eastin, ALSA's third president. Follow-

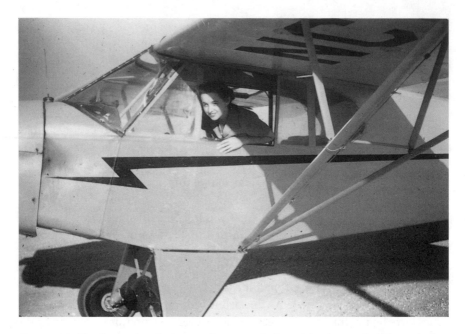

Eleanor Tarpley learned to fly in 1947 because of a bet with a beau. She'd learn to fly if he'd learn to dance. When she earned her license, the local papers called her Danville, Virginia's "Flying Bookkeeper." *Courtesy of Eleanor Tarpley.*

ing the unsuccessful protest of the reinstatement of the nursing requirement, it was readily apparent to her that, without a broader economic base and a larger membership, the union would fail altogether. The decision was made to join ALSSA in order to prevent losing all ground, but there were serious doubts. The United flight attendants were not convinced that ALPA, ALSSA's parent, really cared about them at all. Further, they did not want to lose their right of self-determination. Nonetheless, ALSA reluctantly agreed to come under ALPA's umbrella.[18]

Nonprofessional organizations also experienced much change during demobilization. The women's flying organizations spent this time getting themselves back into regular general aviation activities—especially flying. Like the flight attendants, middle-class women who wanted to fly had to prove that it would not affect their housekeeping abilities. In March 1945, *Woman's Home Companion* sent staff writer Mary Merryfield to Parks Air College on what Merryfield described as "the not too flattering assumption, I suspect, that if I could [learn to fly], any of their readers could."[19]

Merryfield made several important observations about her experience. First,

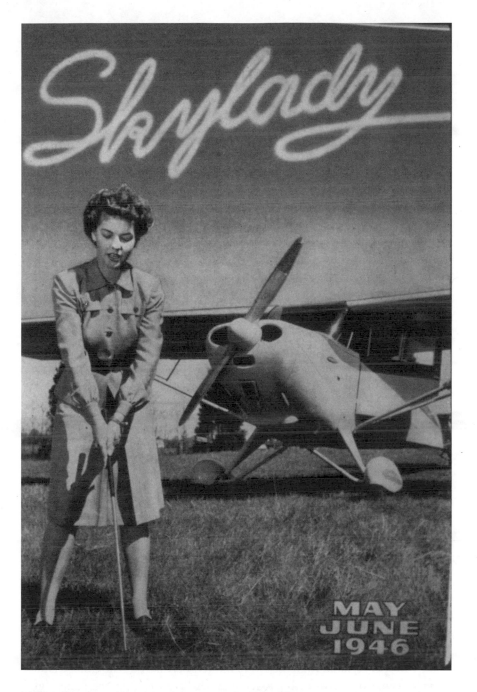

Skylady was the publication of the Women's National Aeronautical Association. The WNAA helped promote the idea of a postwar "Aerial Age" in which women used airplanes like family cars to shop and pursue leisure activities.

both the school and her fellow students (mostly men) expected she would fail because she displayed the "normal" feminine interests in home and husband. Second, she discovered that only by her determination to succeed could she demonstrate that these interests were not mutually exclusive: "I hope I proved to a lot of husbands who were in my flying class that we housewives can love our homes and still get up the momentum to fly a plane. My own husband for one, is pretty pleased that his wife can keep up with modern things and still darn his socks properly."[20]

Merryfield, in fact, was asked to talk to many of the wives of her fellow students in the hope that she could convince them to obtain their pilot's license. The men realized that it was not impossible for a woman to fly and that it might be enjoyable to share certain aspects of general aviation flying.

Many groups made formal attempts to convince women of their part in a postwar air age. The Women's National Aeronautical Association (WNAA) had been founded in 1928 to provide both a forum and an educational opportunity for women associated with men who were involved in aeronautics. During the postwar years, WNAA became more prominent, giving awards and even publishing a bimonthly magazine, *Skylady.* The WNAA national president, Gladys Dallimore, summarized the organization's goals as furthering aeronautical education of the public, stressing the safety of flying, and promoting the achievements of the airlines. When asked what the significance of the WNAA was, she responded, "What does all this mean—membership increased—students stimulated—women conscious of the air ocean—men gradually acknowledging that there is a place for women in aviation? . . . It is for the WNAA to do a good job, to fulfill its mission of putting forth a combined effort to promote, develop and stimulate the aviation industry, if wings are to have their rightful destiny."[21]

The WNAA tended to project a supporting role for women, rather than encouraging women to assume leadership roles such as pilot, business executive, or military officer. The WNAA defined itself as an organization for the wives, daughters, mothers, and sisters—any women associated with men in aeronautics—which would enhance their enthusiasm about aviation. As the notion of an air age gradually disappeared, the group, which had focused so closely on this faddish image, lost its purpose.

Changing times also overtook the two major wartime flying groups for women, the Ninety-Nines and the Women Flyers of America. The Ninety-Nines, alone, was able to survive, owing to its members' concentration on meaningful activities and issues centered around their interests as established pilots. The WFA eventually disbanded in 1954, in large part because they had concentrated on boosting opportunities for new people to take flying lessons at a time when the number of interested potential students was dwindling.

The postwar period was a turning point in the history of the Ninety-Nines. As a result of the WASP, CAP, and CPTP programs, a large number of new women pilots had been trained. For the first time it was possible for the Ninety-Nines to have a significant number of members who were professional, not avocational, flyers. Prior to the war, the club had always been defined in terms of the needs of recreational flying. The Ninety-Nines were proud of their members who had become WASPs, but despite debate on how best to expand the membership, genuine efforts to assimilate the wider focus of this pool of potential members failed to materialize.

In general, the interest was in reinstituting the same purposes and activities they had supported before the war, such as general education programs, air shows, and air races. Air marking was the public service activity most frequently promoted. It was an easy activity to organize and implement with a volunteer labor force, it was not very expensive, and yet it was an invaluable aid to the general aviation pilot.

The organization was concerned about the increasing costs connected with flying small aircraft, but it did not really seek to exert any influence on fixed base operators to lower costs, nor did it inaugurate any scholarship program to aid less well-off individuals. There was a direct correlation between the expense of flying and the kind of membership attracted to the Ninety-Nines.[22]

The Ninety-Nines' approach was to appeal to new members through personal recruiting and air shows. It was a grassroots program that emphasized the fellowship aspects of the organization. Unconsciously, the Ninety-Nines opted not to become a professional or business organization. If WASPs and other women who had worked in aviation in a professional capacity wanted to join, they were heartily welcomed, but it was the new members who adapted to the social club format instead of the group changing to meet the needs of prospective members.

Under the leadership of new president Jeanette Lempke, who was elected immediately after the war, the focus of the group became the rejuvenation of the women's air races. In November 1946, the first discussions were held about a Ninety-Nines-sponsored event at the Miami Air Races. Within six months plans were underway to participate in the National Air Races. During this time membership was expanding, from seven hundred members in September 1945 to just over one thousand in 1946.[23]

In February 1947, the Texas chapter of the Ninety-Nines sponsored a women's aviation convention. It was held in San Antonio, and over one hundred women flyers attended the two-day affair that included speeches by Hazel Raines of the Royal Air Force women's section, Edna Gardner Whyte, Blanche Noyes, and Dorothy Lemon. The event served to boost preparations for the first All-Women Air Show, which followed one month later in Tampa, Florida. An estimated thirteen thousand spectators watched the program of records, races, and aerobatic contests, encouraging the Florida chapter to plan a second event one year later. The event was held to raise money for the Amelia Earhart Scholarship Fund (a program to help members acquire advanced ratings) and to promote public relations.[24] An editorial in the *99s Newsletter* stated: "The show will be presented in such a manner as to cause the Mrs. Average American Housewife to become more air-conscious and realize the importance of the aviation industry to our national economy and security and that they have a place in the air world."[25]

The event prompted air derbies and air-marking parties throughout the United States, but in Miami viewers were treated to parades, precision-flying competitions, sailplane demonstrations, parachute jumps, races for all categories of aircraft, and aerobatic flying.

A tradition of annual women's air races was begun. Organized by Mardo Crane, a former WASP, on behalf of the Ninety-Nines, the first race was held in 1947. That event, which ran 2,242 statute miles from Palm Springs, California, to Tampa, Florida, only had two entries, but the following year the field expanded as six aircraft and seven pilots competed for $1,500 in prize money. This race, like the one that followed in 1949, was called the Jacqueline Cochran All-Woman Trophy Race. (Cochran had graciously donated the prize monies.)

The 1949 race marked the formal beginning of the All-Woman Transcontinental Air Race (AWTAR). Crane, Dee Thurmond, and Irma Story of the Los Angeles chapter drafted the first real set of rules and regulations and developed an official timekeeping system (an honor system had been used previously), which firmly established the race as an annual event.[26]

These standards were based on the experiences of the second All-Women Air Show in 1948, which included that year's Cochran All-Woman Trophy Race. This show had resulted in a tremendous swell of pride in accomplishment, a sense that, for the first time since before World War II, there was more to prove than flying skill. Blanche Noyes, one of the most prominent women in aviation, wrote this about the show: "At a national aviation meeting a year ago, I heard a woman make a speech about women fliers looking like bums at airports. I wish that woman could have been present to see these charming, well-groomed girls and women who were at the air show. Any one of them could have taken the prize for the best dressed woman in America."[27]

Noyes, who was the president of the Ninety-Nines from 1948 to 1949, had captured the essence of the unique experience of women pilots. This was maintaining a feminine appearance, planning activities independent of the major "male" shows and races, and always behaving like "ladies." In spite of the seemingly unfeminine activity of its membership, the Ninety-Nines chose to follow the social dictates of American society in determining its organizational activities and priorities. It was a women's club that politely broke with convention, an attitude that affected the diversity of its membership, such that there were few members from minorities.

Postwar female flying activities were not limited to adult women. The Girl Scouts started a program known as Wing Scouts to encourage young girls to get involved in aviation. The heyday of this Scout group was from 1945 through the early 1950s, a time when young people were especially enthusiastic about flight. Exposed to the CAA's education series and excited by the exploits of wartime aviators, many children—both boys and girls—wanted to learn to fly. To enter the Wing Scouts, girls had to fulfill preliminary requirements, such as learning first-aid and identifying at least twenty-five parts of an airplane. Once the prerequisites were accomplished, the girls were to specialize in one of four fields. Wing Scout "Cadets" had a scientific orientation and concentrated on learning the principles of aerodynamics. Wing Scout "Workers" focused on learning all about aviation careers with the airlines. Wing Scout "Builders" explored careers with aircraft manufacturers, studying production line techniques and learning about stitching, welding, inspecting, and other construction jobs. Finally, Wing Scout "Flyers" prepared themselves for the day when they would be able to become student pilots and learn to fly. Local chapters of the Ninety-Nines, the WFA, and the WNAA all helped sponsor Wing Scout troops. William Piper donated a Piper J-3 trainer craft to be used for giving the girls rides (no actual lessons were given).[28]

One activity that the Wing Scouts participated in was air marking. From its earliest days this endeavor had grown to become the cause célèbre of women in aviation. Women across the nation were painting signs to guide pilots, as part of a campaign for aerial safety and community service. Blanche Noyes was still in charge of that division for the CAA (and was the only woman who had permission to fly government airplanes). She never missed a chance to promote the cause of air marking. Now that the war was over and there seemed to be a surge in the number of general aviation pilots, Noyes believed it was critical not only to replace the signs removed during the war but also to add even more of these navigational aids. An active pilot and charter member of the Ninety-Nines, Noyes had instant rapport with all of the women's organizations. Her ability to win their support in this effort is an early illustration of the power of what might be called an "Old Girl" network: women pilots who had joined together in common interest and ability. No one else, male or female, seems to have ever tapped this network in the way Noyes did when she wanted to achieve a goal, such as her air-marking campaign, or to have taken seriously

Blanche Noyes headed the Air Marking Division of the Civil Aeronautics Authority (CAA). Noyes served as president of the Ninety-Nines from 1948 to 1949 and later was a member of the Women's Advisory Committee on Aeronautics in the 1960s. *Courtesy of the National Air and Space Museum, Smithsonian Institution (SI 86-12151).*

the potential of this small and, therefore, supposedly insignificant band of women.[29]

Women in military aviation would eventually form similar networks within the ranks of their respective services. Until 1948, they were involved in the confusion of demobilization, and as members of small corps, the women were often situated in critical positions. Personnel officers and military leaders had the dilemma of wanting to release all the women immediately (the desire of each of the wartime women's corps' directors) and, at the same time, needing to keep many of the women in their wartime occupations to ensure the smooth functioning of a particular base or operation.

Only the Coast Guard SPARs were completely demobilized by June 1946 (the Coast Guard reverted to civilian control at the end of the war). The other services (the Air Force was soon established as a separate branch) found the dilemma complicated by internal debate over the question of whether women ought to have a role in the peacetime organization. Ironically, some of the very individuals who might have been expected to be most supportive—Oveta Culp Hobby, Mildred McAfee, Ruth Cheney Streeter, and Dorothy Stratton—all opposed the permanent retention of women. They never expressed their views publicly, however, and refused to testify before Congress in order to avoid the suggestion that they were criticizing the efforts made by women during the war.[30]

The military leadership ultimately decided that women should stay, and they prepared to lobby Congress for authorizing legislation. The services would certainly have missed the female support staff, whose roles had become essential but were considered unsuitable for the returning male personnel. Each service tried a different method of handling the crises of personnel shortages. The Navy asked that at least 5,500 WAVES volunteers remain on active duty until July 1947. Further, the Navy had a drive to re-enlist 2,000 former WAVES in a newly created reserve group. Of the fourteen major occupations available during this time, nine were in aviation. There were approximately 1,500 enlisted women and 170 women officers serving naval aviation.[31]

The Army followed the Navy's example and also proposed a reserve organization. This proposal did not take into consideration that most of the WACs had already been demobilized. Also, the WAC leaders opposed the reserve plan, not because they felt there was no role for women in the Army, but rather because they believed the reserve plan as proposed could not be properly administered. In response to these objections, the Army decided to create a plan that would incorporate women directly into the regular service, instead of limiting women to only a reserve option.

The underlying question was still whether it was appropriate for women to become established professionally within the permanent military organization.

Peace allowed the recurrence of the old nagging doubts as to feminine suitability in this tradition-bound male environment. Vocal and often virulent opposition to the presence of women in the military was voiced from many diverse sectors of American society. Individuals in positions of power, influence, and authority, however, did weigh in on the other side of this debate.

Eleanor Roosevelt was one of the most important advocates of women in aviation. Her insistence and persistence in this area often proved to be the key to altering the debate from *whether* to *how* women could participate. Secretary of Defense James V. Forrestal, Generals Dwight D. Eisenhower and Omar N. Bradley (Army), General Hoyt S. Vandenberg, and Brigadier General Dean C. Strother (Air Force), Admiral Louis E. Denfield and Vice Admiral Arthur W. Radford (Navy) all testified before the Armed Services Committees of Congress on behalf of legislation to keep women in the peacetime military. The view most effective in ultimately convincing Congress was not the philosophical argument on a woman's right to serve, but rather the shortage of "man-power."[32]

The Women's Armed Services Act of 1948 was passed on 2 June 1948, 206 to 133, and signed into law on 12 June by President Truman. Major General Jeanne Holm, USAF (Ret.), described this event in her book on women in the military:

> The act was many things to many people: to feminists, a leap forward for women's rights; to most women veterans, recognition of their contribution and vindication of their service; and to the military women who worked for its passage, sweet victory.
>
> To the generals and admirals who actively supported it, the law was a vehicle for mobilizing women's skills in the event of a future national emergency and for meeting the military's more immediate requirements for volunteers, especially for those needed to fill clerical and other so-called women's jobs.[33]

Despite the occupational emphasis on clerks and typists, there were some opportunities for women in aeronautical fields. The Army dramatically curtailed the number of aviation specialties available to women. (This was the situation until the advent of women helicopter pilots in the 1970s.) However, both the Navy and the Air Force did have many openings for women in aviation, though all were nonpilot positions.

On 7 July 1948, six new WAVES were sworn into regular service with the Navy. John Sullivan, the secretary of the Navy, remarked to those present at the ceremony: "Although you have been reduced to 2,000, it is my understanding that within the next two years you hope to induct 6,000 enlisted women into the WAVES, and I assure you the Navy will welcome them. In such highly specialized fields as communications, aerology, aviation training and many other fascinating and interesting fields they are better than any men we have ever had and we are proud to have them."[34]

In addition to the technical specialties, WAVES also worked with the Naval Air Transport Service. Women served as flight orderlies, the military counterpart to the civilian flight attendant. Other women served as air transport officers (ATOs). The ATOs were responsible for all aircraft moving through their stations. They planned the loads, met the airplanes, and supervised the fueling, cargo and mail loading, and passenger boarding. They took care of all flight papers and were responsible for seeing that each flight was dispatched according to schedule. WAVES also continued to serve as tower operators, aerographers, and flight instructors (on training equipment only). Finally, Navy flight nurses and WAVES flight orderlies often worked together on air ambulance crews.[35]

One feature of the postwar WAVES program was the integration of black women. The WAVES had not permitted blacks to enlist until December 1944. They did not then establish any mechanisms for segregation since it was anticipated that very few black women would enlist, and thus it would not be necessary to expend administrative energy to separate them from the other women. At the war's end, there were sixty-eight black enlisted women and six officers. In 1946 there were five black WAVES and one nurse. In February 1948, there were still only six black women in the Navy. Limited attempts had been made to recruit black women, but to no avail. The Marine Corps Women's Reserve did not have any black women until March 1949. When the Marine commandant was asked specifically if black women could join the Corps, he replied, "if qualified for enlistment, Negro women will be accepted on the same basis as other applicants." The number of black women Marines was too small in this postwar period to find records of their job assignments or where they were stationed.[36]

The WAF (as Women in the Air Force were identified) was born with the Women's Armed Services Act, 12 June 1948, but it was essentially a reconstitution of the Air WAC. WAFs could occupy almost every occupation in the Air Force, from airborne radio operators on B-17 training flights to aircraft mechanics. The WAF did not have the WAC's rigidly prescribed structure, and in theory the new program was intended to accomplish a full and complete integration of women into the Air Force. In practice, the WAF acronym helped to create an unofficial, but very real, distinct corps. Unfortunately, the "director" of this body had no power other than to serve as advisor, when consulted, on matters concerning women.[37]

By the end of June 1948, only 168 officers and 1,433 enlisted women formerly with the Air WACs had signed on with the WAF program. There were communication problems between the WAF and the demobilized Air WACs.

WAC corporal "Torchy" West was the only woman checked out as flight engineer on a transoceanic trip. Corporal West was assigned to the West Coast wing of the Air Transport Command and flew on Douglas C-54 aircraft. Here she is making the final preflight inspection of the airplane. *Photo from U.S. National Archives and Records Administration, Still Pictures Branch (342-FH-4A-05027-31568AC).*

After World War II, some women who had served as air traffic controllers for the military were able to find positions with the Civil Aeronautics Administration. This woman is working at the Kansas City Air Traffic Control Center in 1945. *Courtesy of the Federal Aviation Administration.*

Reenlistment procedures were not clear and many women did not fully understand their options. These factors obviously contributed to the poor initial showing. The goal of the WAF was to be an elite group of women modeled after, but superior to, the WAVES. Because it wanted to open opportunities to women without college degrees, the Air Force did not have the same recruiting requirements as the Navy. The recruiting results were disappointing: inadequate numbers were compounded by the poor quality of recruits that did enlist. Air Force leaders, especially General Hoyt Vandenberg, were surprised by this. Instead of choosing to work from within the service alongside Director Geraldine May, Vandenberg would soon decide to try to solve the problem by seeking the advice of Jacqueline Cochran.[38]

The five years following the end of World War II were exhilarating and exasperating for women in aviation. The air age anticipated by aviation enthusiasts seemed to have been illusory, yet American women were more air minded than ever before. Women were participating in nearly every phase of aviation. They continued even in the nontraditional fields of production and maintenance, where they had first gained entry during the war. Peace and a new economic environment produced more pressure for women to demonstrate that they were fully "feminine," an image that was, to many people, at odds with female involvement in aviation.

The various branches of the military were more progressive, at least on paper, than the civilian aviation world of the late 1940s. Regulations can only mandate standards of behavior, but the postwar rules for women in the military did mark the beginning of a change in American attitude. Women in military aviation offered valuable services and helped each of the different branches to meet personnel requirements. Still, the postwar period is characterized by the protracted debate over whether this was any place for a woman. The protests of enlisted men may have had some effect during this period, but they did not hold much ground once the Korean War began.

The small number of women and the lack of actual integration with men resulted in the women being grouped in small, isolated corps structures. These women were convinced of the value of their service and excited by the unusual opportunities offered by military aviation, but they could not count on support from the public. It was an unusual and individualistic woman who chose a career in military aviation during the late 1940s, just as the women who joined the Ninety-Nines or continued to work in the plants were also unusual. At least by 1950 their corps, organizations, and networks were functioning well, so that those remarkable women were no longer alone in the aviation world.

6

"The Feminine Mystique" and Aviation

The 1950s

> Have you tired of office job, or school, or nursing—
>   Yet thrilled to the flash of silver in the skies;
> If you can realize all aviation's problems
>   But aid the vision of its future plans
> Then you will know this miracle of flying,
>   The comradeship, the progress, and what's more
> You'll feel the very pulse beat of our country!
>   Welcome to the Stewardess Corps.
>
> "The Goal," Alma Frank

There were some remarkable women flying during the 1950s, women who broke out of "The Feminine Mystique," a concept that would soon be exploded by Betty Friedan's landmark book of the same title. These women were not bound by the mythic glorification of housekeeping and childcare in their quest for personal fulfillment and serious careers.

Most of the women in aviation were considered unusual in any circle, but there were some notable individuals who attempted specifically to extend the threshold of technological possibilities and perform new feats of adventure. Jackie Cochran crashed the sound barrier, Marion Hart flew the Atlantic (symbolizing a revival of challenging flights for light aircraft), and a major new organization for women in aviation was founded—the Whirly-Girls, the International Women Helicopter Pilots Association. Women, in small numbers, tenaciously hung on to positions in industry although its orientation had been transformed from the aircraft production line to new aerospace ventures that required a dramatic increase in the numbers and roles of engineers. That change, of course, had major effects on the lives of women in military aviation, also. There was enough adventure and change, both technological and social, to ensure the vitality of most of the existing organizations for women in aviation. Clearly, the sustained presence of women in aviation during the 1950s was strong evidence of their collective influence and staying power, although their numbers were still small.

Among this group were women such as Ruth Butler. Growing up in Maine, Butler had learned to be an aviation mechanic during her high school years in the early 1940s. Her first flight, in 1944, was in a commercial airliner. Two years later, in 1946, she first put her hands on the controls of a Stinson. When asked, after soloing on 13 June 1952, what her ambition was, she replied: "To own an airplane and fly and service it myself and prove that there is a place for women in aviation. Nothing glamorous. Nothing sensational."[1] A year later she was part of an expedition to fly over both the North and South Poles (the first woman scheduled to do so), serving as a flight technician. Still, she claimed: "I don't want the glamour of stunt flying or racing or flying jets. I think it would be wonderful to be an airline pilot, but women haven't broken into the field yet. I think the ideal job for a woman flyer would be as secretary-pilot to a business executive, flying his private plane and accompanying him on his trips."[2]

Other women proved to have as broad an imagination with regard to personal adventure and flying as Butler did. Marion Hart had always been a pioneering woman professional. In 1913, she was the first woman to earn a B.S. degree in chemical engineering from the Massachusetts Institute of Technology. Later she earned a graduate degree in geology from Columbia University. She also sailed around the world in a seventy-foot boat. For her, "distance and course" always represented the ultimate challenge. She did not learn to fly until 1946, when she was fifty-four years old. Eight years later, she enlarged the list of her many accomplishments by flying the Atlantic and breaking what she termed a "psychological barrier."[3] Yet, praised her friend Robert Buck (in a *Reader's Digest* feature, "The Most Unforgettable Character I've Met"), Marion Hart was not a feminist activist. "I've been amused more than once to watch her at an aviation gathering, where talk is rampant and male pilots tell tall tales. She takes it all in and then, during a lull, will ask a question so quietly and humbly that a repeat may be requested. The question is invariably phrased to inflate the male ego; but if you know Marion you realize she already knows the answer, a lot better, frequently, than the man she asks."[4]

Jacqueline Cochran maintained her reputation as the most adventurous and influential of all women in aviation. During the 1950s, Cochran parlayed her considerable influence with the Air Force leadership into opportunities to break numerous aviation records. Eagerly, she became one of the first women to fly jet aircraft. Cochran did not want to set *women's* records; she worked to

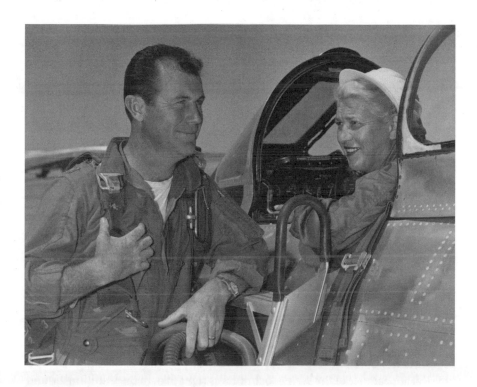

Jacqueline Cochran collected numerous speed records during the 1950s. In 1953, she became the first woman to break the sound barrier. That year and during a set of 1962 record-breaking flights (shown here), Cochran was coached by Chuck Yeager, one of the nation's top test pilots and the first person to fly faster than the speed of sound. *Courtesy of Ann Wood Kelly.*

set *absolute* records. By June 1953, she held all but one of the principal world airplane speed records for straightaway and closed-course flight. Of particular note was her May 1953 flight at Edwards Air Force Base, California, when she became the first woman to break the sound barrier, in a Canadian-owned Canadair F-86 Sabre jet.[5]

These were the kinds of personal challenges that interested Cochran most. She preferred competing with men rather than participating in events such as the All-Woman Transcontinental Air Race. To Cochran there was no status associated with the women's events. A "woman's record" to her was second best. By competing with men she felt she earned the right to be part of the flying elite. She cherished her relationships with individuals such as Chuck Yeager, Fred Ascani, President Eisenhower, and the majority of Air Force generals. She had worked hard to be a part of their club and was usually associated with "women's groups or events" only in the role of benefactor. Her considerable wealth accorded her access to the highest echelons in politics, military affairs, and society, but her records brought her honors and public adulation. Among them was the Harmon Trophy, awarded annually to the outstanding woman aviator in the United States, which she won a number of times. These awards also extended her credibility as advisor on all things related to women in aviation. In many cases, however, her advice was detrimental to the existing programs and the participation of women. The worst example was her report on the women serving in the Air Force.[6]

During the fall of 1950, Air Force Chief of Staff General Hoyt Vandenberg requested that Cochran examine the WAF (Women in the Air Force). As a special consultant, she was to determine if the existing program represented the best and most effective use of women during peacetime. In the background of this question was the fact that America had become involved in the Korean War.

On 6 December 1950, Cochran submitted a report to General Vandenberg that railed against the existing program. Cochran opposed the concept of integration (of gender; race was not considered). If there had to be women in the military, and Cochran was ambivalent about that, then they must be the "best" women. The "best" was not defined according to the substantive issues of job performance. Cochran's report was extremely disparaging of the uniforms and physical appearance of the WAF. Cochran was right that, in the tradition-bound world of the armed services, if women wanted to become a part of the system, they were going to have to adopt all of the trappings of military decorum. Cochran's report, however, went further. According to Jeanne Holm, she equated good work with a particular standard of physical attractiveness, a criterion that must have caused offense even in 1950.[7]

Cochran certainly knew how to produce action among male Air Force leaders. She accurately sensed their attitudes toward women and capitalized on these biases, but it should be noted that at the same time she also engendered considerable animosity among the enlisted women and officers. They resented her ability, as they interpreted it, to "cavort" with generals and give advice on matters of which she really knew little. When the WAF was being established and the directors were working out the plethora of bureaucratic details, Cochran was traveling around the world enjoying privileges bestowed by General Arnold. According to WAF director Colonel Geraldine May, Cochran had gambled away the future of the WASPs, and now it appeared she wanted to run the WAF. Her report proposed a civilian position of special assistant to Vandenberg; it was strikingly similar to her previous post as director of the WASP.[8]

The Air Force was not willing to go along with Cochran's recommendation of a civilian corps director for fear it would stimulate other minority groups

First Lieutenant Yvonne Pateman was the only woman stationed at Clark Air Base in the Philippine Islands in 1953. Pateman returned to the Air Force when the military "recalled" former WASPs to active duty during the Korean War. *Courtesy of Yvonne C. Pateman.*

(in particular, blacks) to demand similar representation. Cochran's advice did result in a reevaluation of the integration of women into the Air Force. She had proposed a separate women's group, and although Director Geraldine May stood firmly opposed to this, she could not match Cochran in her ability to influence Air Force generals. The Air Force retrenched and made attempts to redesign its WAF program by imitating many aspects of the WAVES program.

May was replaced by Mary J. Shelley, who had to face the challenge of making the new program a functional one—despite the Air Force's inability to decide what it wanted. With the outbreak of the Korean War, the need for personnel increased, and the Air Force naturally wanted and needed to employ its female components. Air Force leaders also thought they could recruit women in the same manner and numbers as they had in World War II. They failed to realize that most Americans were not as eager to participate in this seemingly lesser conflict. Enthusiastic patriotism did not surface to help diminish society's anxieties about women in the military. The "no marriage" rule was a great handicap; weddings became an easy way to break a service contract. These factors combined to make the recruiting goal—a leap from eighty-two hundred to fifty thousand—not only unbelievable, but also ridiculous. It was impossible to persuade that many women to volunteer (indeed, when the need to recruit an equivalent number of men had been discussed, the Air Force leaders stated that it would only be possible if there was a draft). The Air Force did not understand their recruiting failure and began to fault the women who were already in the program.[9]

The women who served offer a different perspective on the situation. Obviously, they wanted to be an integral part of the Air Force. To civilian women, WAF officers seemed to have made major advances in gaining equality. The key to success, however, was to be able to accomplish a military job while maintaining the external trappings of feminine behavior. This was a tricky balancing act, and it subjected women to the additional burden of scrutiny for reasons of their sex. For example, Lieutenant Colonel Marion Lee Watt, chief of the Classification and Evaluation Branch, Military Personnel Division, who was considered a successful WAF officer, received this complimentary assessment: "Tact, firmness, farsightedness and progressiveness mark her thought and action. It has been said, 'She thinks like a man, yet is flatteringly feminine.' What's more, she gets the job done."[10]

One thing that the Korean War did achieve was an end to the exclusion of women from nontraditional specialties. WAFs could be found in almost every aviation specialty, including airplane dispatchers, weather observers, blind-flying instructors, air traffic analysts, mechanics, and parachute riggers. Many Air Force women served as flight attendants. These women were full-fledged members of the Air Transport Service, although their jobs were similar to the civilian occupation. The difference lay in the fact that WAFs were part of the military and had to submit to the discipline and rigor of the organization."[11]

The essential requirements for a woman's enlistment in the WAF were that she be eighteen to thirty-four years old (women over thirty-five were eligible if they had served in the WAC during World War II and their number of years in service equaled or exceeded the number of years over age thirty-five), a high school graduate, single, and have parental consent if under twenty-one years of age. To be eligible for Officer Candidate School, a woman had to be between twenty and a half and twenty-six and a half years old and have at least two years of college education, unless she already had enlisted status.

Basic training for both officers and enlisted personnel was held at Lackland Air Force Base in Texas and lasted between eight and eleven weeks. The six major elements of basic training were general orientation, lessons in military correspondence, inspection and parade training, aircraft spotting, Air Force operations basics, and aptitude tests. After basic training, the women were sent to specialty schools for additional training.[12]

Utilization of women by the Air Force was not limited to the WAF. Some civilian instructors and employees in the aviation field were also women. Gottie Schroeder taught in the Department of Engine and Technician Training at Sheppard Air Force Base. Her specialty was reciprocating engines, and she was qualified to work on anything from the sixty-five-hp Continental to the Air Force's largest reciprocating engine, the Pratt & Whitney R-4360.[13]

Women had been in naval aviation for ten years by 30 July 1952. They were working in almost every department at naval air stations and taught everything from the physiological aspects and use of ejection seats to parachute rigging. In 1952 about 13 percent of WAVES recruits were selected for airman training. As was true in the WAF (paralleling the role in civilian life), one of the coveted jobs was serving as a flight orderly with a transport squadron. Training and job assignments were, in general, integrated with the men. Other jobs for WAVES included air controlman, aerographer's mate, aviation electronics technician, aviation store keepers, and trademan.[14]

Women Marines often worked side by side with WAVES, and in one experiment three female Marines and one WAVE volunteered to try their hands at firefighting techniques used at airfields. The women who performed these tasks often had experience in other nontraditional jobs. For example, when the Navy lifted its ban on WAVE mechanics in late 1953, Ann Alger quickly abandoned her yeomen's job to join the flight line. Having tinkered with engines since the age of fourteen, she was a natural with airplanes, particularly the Corsair engines with which she worked most frequently.[15]

The only WAVE entitled to wear air-navigation wings was Commander Frances Biadosz. She served on the staff of the Air Navigation School during World War II, and after the war she became involved with the Navy's Public Relations Department. In 1959 she was assigned to NATO's Advisory Group for Aerospace Research and Development, where she served as a special assistant to the famous aerodynamicist Dr. Theodore Von Kármán. Biadosz's attraction to aviation was shared by many other WAVES. Jacqueline Donnelly gave up her job as a New York telephone switchboard operator to become an aerial photographer for the Navy. "I have always enjoyed flying and being near planes," explained Donnelly, "and now I can do both. I've been on many assignments taking photographs and the training is exciting. I'll sign up again the instant my four-year enlistment ends. I like being a WAVE."[16]

That attitude was produced by an environment of good organization. Joy

Bright Hancock had continued in command of the WAVES program until her retirement in 1953. Her experience in two world wars and the demobilization period stood her well. The Navy leadership listened to her plans for recruitment, training, and deployment of women because they were consistent with the Navy's goals and philosophy. She knew how to work within the organization and make her presentations and proposals attractive to her superior officers (all male). Further, she had an understanding of women in the military that could be matched by few. For example, during the Korean War, she only proposed a 75 percent increase in female personnel, from 6,300 to 11,000 WAVES. Similarly, the Marine Corps only raised its ceiling from 2,250 to 3,000. When recruiting campaigns could only manage to acquire 8,000 WAVES and 2,400 Marines, the programs did not suffer the disastrous consequences that the Air Force's overzealous attitude toward recruitment and serious overestimation produced in the WAF.[17]

A notable characteristic of women in the military was their ability at the administrative level to work together, regardless of branch affiliation. The directors often met with each other to discuss mutual problems and propose solutions. Another example of cooperation is seen in the joint training of Navy and Air Force flight nurses at Gunther Air Force Base, Alabama. The coordinated curriculum taught subjects like aeronautics, air evacuation, physics of atmosphere, and the effects of high altitude. Together they practiced water "ditching" (abandoning an aircraft over—or in—water) and other survival techniques.[18] This joint training program was a model the Department of Defense found useful, because it avoided the costly duplication of almost identical training courses. The development of other such joint service programs was part of the stimulus for the creation of a special citizens' advisory group, known as the Defense Advisory Committee on Women in the Services (DACOWITS).

DACOWITS was the brainchild of General George C. Marshall, then secretary of defense. In September 1951, he invited fifty women recognized as outstanding leaders in a variety of professions and civic enterprises to meet in Washington and advise on the subject of women in the Armed Forces. The problem of greatest urgency was recruitment, and to that end DACOWITS helped set up a unified recruiting campaign. DACOWITS became part of the defense establishment virtually overnight. By the end of the September ad hoc conference, a formal committee to work directly with the assistant secretary of defense for manpower, personnel, and reserve had been created. Working groups were established in several areas: training and education; housing, welfare and recreation; utilization and career planning; health and nutrition; recruiting and public information; professional services (for nurses); and standards (recruitment).[19]

The new group was a vital advocate for women in the services, but it also provided an essential and progressive forum for consideration of any question even tangentially related to women in military aviation. It consistently supported the right of women to participate in nontraditional fields. During the 1950s, DACOWITS's concerns centered first on recruitment, and then on issues such as housing and public acceptance of military service and military careers for women. In 1955, members made the first of their many recommendations to the Air Force to include women in their Reserve Officer Training Corps (ROTC) program, but it took until 1969 for the Air Force to comply. The committee was unique in the view it took of the direct connection between occupation and the quality of life enjoyed by an individual; from the start it asked the military to replace conventional definitions and stereotypes of women with a creative vision as to how to make the most of everyone's talents in service to the nation. Their advice was listened to and taken seriously (if not always acted upon immediately). Later the group would examine critical questions about the role of women in military aviation, including the training and use of female pilots.[20]

The military was not the only avenue for a young woman to enter the field of aviation. The Wing Scout program was still in existence, and several colleges were promoting aviation activities. Stephens College maintained its aviation studies program into the fifties, although the tone of its stated purpose had the clear ring of Cold War pressures: "Today the purpose of aviation studies at Stephens is to develop attitudes based on the realities of the Air Age since students will be participants in a society using airplanes as the dominating force for world unity." Many college women learned to fly at Stephens, and more than a thousand had completed the airline traffic course when an article about the school appeared in *Flying*. One interesting statistic in this article is the fact that while in 1953, 90 percent of all students had parental permission to fly, ten years earlier less than a third of the women's parents had responded favorably to the college's standard request for this approval.[21]

Other colleges had aviation programs for women. The National Intercollegiate Flying Association (NIFA) also sponsored clubs and flying contests. Jane Baker was a senior at Oklahoma Agricultural and Mechanical College when she won a major NIFA contest and was named NIFA College Woman Pilot of the Year. Baker had soloed in March 1953 and was a member not only of NIFA but also the Civil Air Patrol and the Ninety-Nines.[22]

The Civil Air Patrol had continued to grow after World War II to ninety-one thousand members in 1956, fourteen thousand of whom were women or girls (teenage girls participated in the youth wing called the CAP Cadets). CAP pilots and observers flew more than 50 percent of all hours flown for aerial search and rescue missions in the United States. Harriet Robertus, the wife of an Air Force officer, was a typical CAP pilot. She first came into contact with the CAP when her husband became the CAP liaison officer for the Air Force. Always connected with airplanes (she worked for an Army Air Corps contract flying school and often flew with her husband), Robertus became an aerial observer for the CAP. When questioned about her priorities, she responded that "next to my two children, Frances and William, the Civil Air Patrol comes first."[23]

Nona Quarles was also active in the CAP. She became a victim of instant notoriety when she decided to try for her pilot's license. As the wife of the secretary of the Air Force, she had flown many miles as a passenger but had delayed taking flying lessons until 1957. Because of her husband's position, there were many obstacles to her ambition to fly jets. One article in *U.S. Lady* described the situation:

> Her husband, Secretary Quarles, has interposed no objections to her becoming a pilot. He even indicated his willingness to be her passenger on occasion. But so far he has nixed her every chance to become jet borne.
>
> She almost made it though, during the Air Force Convention in Washington last summer, Jacqueline Cochran invited her to crash the sound barrier [as her copilot] and Mrs. Quarles lost no time in collecting her flying gear and making her way out to Andrews Air Force Base. To her dismay someone had tipped off the Secretary, and Air Force officials at the field firmly but politely told her there would be no jet ride for her that day.[24]

Quarles wanted to participate in the CAP because of its service to the public. Accepting the fact that much of the media attention focused on her resulted from her husband's position, she was able to use this situation to bring positive attention to the CAP. By way of reinforcement, she also demonstrated that her husband supported her aviation interests and activities.

Ruth Nichols was another famous female flyer with the CAP. A lieutenant colonel in the program, Nichols maintained a strong focus on youth, as typified by her frequent work with the CAP Cadet program. Apart from the CAP, Nichols made a global aviation tour to focus attention on the United Nations International Children's Emergency Fund (UNICEF). It was planned that she would be the copilot of the Douglas DC-4 on this trip, but unfortunately she did not have enough hours of multi-engine flight time to qualify as a transport pilot on the DC-4. She did serve as a "courtesy" or extra pilot, which allowed her to assist in operation of the craft. After this tour, Nichols continued her work with the CAP. She led the effort to standardize the aeronautical rescue procedures of the CAP, which included coordinating pilots and aircraft for air evacuation, air rescue, and air ambulances.[25]

The Ninety-Nines continued to be the principal women's aeronautical organization. In 1950 the Florida chapter sponsored their fourth and last All-Women Air Maneuver. The Amelia Earhart Scholarship Fund was a principal interest of the organization, but it aroused less zeal in the Ninety-Nines than the All-Woman Transcontinental Air Races (or Powder Puff Derby, as it was called by the press). Gill Robb Wilson, founder of the Civil Air Patrol and president of the Air Force Association, called it "the best single showcase of dependability of the light airplane and its equipment."[26]

In 1951 and 1952, in response to the Korean War, however, the race was called "Operation TAR" (Transcontinental Air Race) and was operated as a training mission to "provide stimulation as a refresher course in cross-country flying for women whose services as pilots might once again be needed by their country."[27] After the war, the event became an official race open to all women pilots (not just the Ninety-Nines); it adopted knots and nautical miles as standard measurement and acquired a new leader, Betty Gillies.

Under Gillies's leadership the pilot requirements were stiffened. An FAI (Federation Aeronautique Internationale) sporting license was needed, and all pilots were required to have a minimum of one hundred hours of solo time, including twenty-five hours of cross-country flying. Further, a ten-year age limit was put on aircraft in order to allow for two-way radio communication and proper handicapping. The race was flown by a multitude of aircraft with vastly different airspeed capabilities. A "handicap," or par speed, was assigned to each aircraft in order to equalize the competition. The ten-year age limitation on aircraft eliminated highly modified World War II military planes from the event in order to assure the fairness of the competition. It was next to impossible to determine what the "handicap" of such a one-of-a-kind craft should be because there was no point of reference, such as other similar airplanes, by which to judge. Safety was always a major concern, and FAA inspections were required.

The AWTAR became a major event with its own office and a permanent executive secretary, former WASP Barbara Erickson London, who was hired in 1956. Run by a nine-woman board of directors, each AWTAR required a full year of preparation. The plans had to be coordinated with dozens of federal agencies, aviation associations, and other civic bodies.[28]

The race was becoming a cherished experience for its participants. The women eagerly donned coordinated outfits for their flights and post-race social events, but more importantly they delighted in each other's company and the challenge of flying their aircraft over a difficult course.[29] Fran Bera was a regular AWTAR contestant. Flying in nineteen consecutive races beginning in 1951, she placed in the top ten seventeen times, with seven first place finishes to her credit. Her reflections on the race expressed a common sentiment held by participants:

I was very competitive and winning seemed everything. The AWTAR meant many other things to me, such as making friendships with other women pilots that have lasted a lifetime. These were women from all parts of our country and the world. They understood the pure joy of flight and the beauty of seeing our country unfold from coast to coast under our wings, while we tested our skills to the utmost. It meant the excitement of competing, while we took off into the rising sun on a still morning, and at day's end the fun and companionship we shared while telling our stories of frustrating minutes lost, the humorous things, the bad breaks, the good tailwinds and making it over the finish line just in the nick of time to miss the thunderstorm that would close the field. It was wonderful to communicate all of this to other women and know they understood.[30]

Over the decade, hundreds of thousands of miles were flown by contestants traversing the continent, as 499 aircraft and 905 pilots participated in this extravaganza of general aviation. General Hoyt Vandenberg, chief of staff for the Air Force, wrote to race chairwoman Mardo Crane, sending his regards to the 1952 contestants. He recalled the contribution of the WASPs during World War II as background to this forecast: "In flying the Sixth Annual All-Woman Transcontinental Air Race the fact will once more be demonstrated that American women pilots can undertake exacting flights and complete them with safety and efficiency."[31]

Safety was always understood as a priority in the AWTAR, and gradually, after years of extraordinarily well-run events, the message could hardly have been made any clearer to the public—women were good pilots. Women were earning a collective reputation for safety consciousness within aviation circles that distinguished them from archetypal male pilots. Women were believed to avoid stupid and unnecessary risks. Still, there was often a hint of sarcasm when people talked about women pilots, traceable to the popular image of a pilot as hero, bold adventurer, and daredevil that had emerged during aviation's golden years of the 1920s and 1930s.[32]

Women in aviation during the 1950s did not fit that image. Most women pilots held only a private license and flew recreationally. For the first time since the government began collecting aviation statistics, it stopped reporting separate totals for the number of male and female pilots (and for holders of various types of certificates as well). Thus it is difficult to document whether significant changes in women's participation in aviation occurred during the decade. Nonetheless, the anecdotal evidence is fairly abundant and suggests a steady, if moderate, growth in the number of women flyers. A good example of such anecdotes is to be found in Jo Eddleman's charming book, *Cows on the Runway*. Eddleman achieved a certain notoriety in 1957 when she promised to reward any of her junior high school math students with an airplane ride if they main-

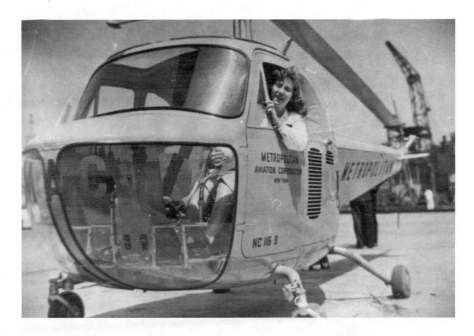

Ann Shaw Carter was the first American woman to become licensed specifically as a helicopter pilot. She received her commercial license in 1947 and began working for New York's Metropolitan Aviation Corporation, flying sightseeing trips around Manhattan. *Courtesy of the National Air and Space Museum, Smithsonian Institution (SI 81-1256).*

tained a 95 percent average. Thirty-six students did, warranting a notice in Elsie Hix's "Strange as It Seems" nationally syndicated news feature.[33]

Jean Ross Howard thought she was breaking a tradition, earning her helicopter rating in 1954 with the cooperation of the Bell Aircraft Corporation in Fort Worth, Texas. She had convinced company president Lawrence Bell that she ought to learn to fly a helicopter because it would enable her to do a better job as assistant to the director of the Helicopter Council at Aircraft Industries Association. Once she passed the CAA examination, Howard began to wonder exactly how many other women also had a helicopter rating. She discovered there were twelve others (excluding the possibility of some women pilots in the Soviet Union, who did not respond to inquiries), each of whom responded affirmatively to her suggestion that they form a club.

The Whirly-Girls, International Women Helicopter Pilots, came into being on 28 April 1955. It was a very informal group at first, and Howard was chosen to serve as coordinator to handle correspondence and news announce-

The Whirly-Girls, International Women Helicopter Pilots, was established in 1955. The first meeting, or "Hovering" as gatherings of Whirly-Girls are known, was attended by, from left to right, Ethel Sheffler, Jean Ross Howard, Edna Gardner Whyte, Ann Shaw Carter, and Marilynn Riviere. *Courtesy of The Whirly-Girls, Inc.*

ments. The organization's initial goals were to "promote interest among all women in rotary wing craft, to establish scholarships to help other girls learn to fly helicopters and to provide a standby women's helicopter reserve for Civil Defense and other national emergencies."[34] Later, this last goal was replaced with the more broadly based aim of promoting heliports and landing facilities for hospitals.

The Whirly-Girls, like the helicopter, firmly established themselves in the aviation world, and by the close of the decade membership had expanded to about thirty-five. The helicopter played a role in the professional lives of many of the members. Dr. Dora J. Dougherty (later Strother) was a Whirly-Girl. A human factors engineer with Bell Aircraft and a former WASP, whom Paul Tibbetts had trained to fly the B-29, she had been assigned by Bell to design helicopter cockpits. Bell decided that, like Jean Howard, she too should know how to fly helicopters. Dougherty, a highly skilled fixed-wing pilot, found the rotorcraft not only challenging but also fun to fly. With only thirty-four hours of helicopter flight time, Dougherty set two world records for altitude (19,406 feet) and distance (straight line, 404.36 miles).[35]

Dr. Dougherty was in a profession that certainly could have used women. Aeronautical engineers were in great demand, as government contracts required ever-increasing levels of research and development. The industry was undergoing a major transition from aircraft production to aerospace engineering. The successful Soviet launch of the Sputnik satellite in 1957 marked a significant turning point. Only two years later, Aircraft Industries Association changed its name to Aerospace Industries Association (AIA). In its annual *Facts and Figures,* AIA noted: "Due to increasing pressures of the technological race in which the aerospace industry is involved, a wide range of measures are being taken by the industry to motivate, encourage, and in many cases finance young people of talent in pursuing higher education in engineering and the sciences. . . . Paradoxically along with the two-year recession in general aerospace manufacturing employment needs, there has been a continual recruiting plea for highly trained engineers and scientists."[36] The pleas of industry were obviously being heard, because between 1954 and 1957 the number of engineers and scientists rose 75 percent, from 48,500 to 84,900.[37]

Few qualified women could be found despite the demand. Industry did little to develop this "largest single source of new engineering talent," according to a U.S. Air Services article on women in aviation engineering. The problem was not entirely the fault of the companies, however. Estelle Elliot, an associate aircraft engineer with Lockheed Marietta, noted at a Wing Scout dinner that "most parents and teachers never think of suggesting engineering as a career for a girl, even though she may have shown mathematical, scientific or mechanical aptitudes." She noted that in 1955 only ten thousand engineers would graduate from college, yet there would be thirty thousand new engineering jobs created that same year. To help dispel myths, Elliot told her audience of girls: "Let's face it. A certain amount of glamour exists because you crawl over, under and through an airplane and come out still being a woman! Many engineering jobs consist solely of desk work. . . . The course of study is not difficult, if you are mechanically or technically inclined . . . and if you are willing to work."[38]

Women did not enter aeronautical engineering except in very small numbers. At Boeing, for example, there were forty-seven women engineers employed in 1955, accounting for less than one percent of the company's engineering staff.[39] Many engineering schools did not admit women students. Those that did nonetheless failed to actively recruit women. In general, women were not demonstrating any great eagerness to seize the opportunities in aeronautical engineering. College enrollments for women students were declining and societal pressures dictated that the prime function of the collegiate experience was not education but matrimony. Further, engineering was perceived as a career; in the fifties middle- and upper-class white men pursued careers, but most white women (regardless of class) did not.

Elaine Gething, a junior engineer in the aerodynamics section of Boeing's pilotless aircraft division, is an example of the rare female aeronautical engineer of the time. Gething had majored in mechanical engineering with a concentration in aeronautics at Oregon State University, but her first job, typical for most women, even college graduates, was as a secretary in her hometown. She hated it and quickly transferred to Boeing in Seattle, Washington, in 1950. Even so, an article describing her background stated: "One of these days she expects to marry and settle down to being a housewife, but in the meantime her work and year round schedule of outdoor recreation are a happy combination."[40] Gething's self-assessment illustrated the difference between men's and women's life and career expectations.

Significant numbers of women did continue to work in less technical positions in the industry, however. Throughout this period they averaged about 16 percent of the aerospace labor force, with the lowest percentage (12.4) occurring in September 1950 and the highest (18.0) in September 1952.[41] The fluctuations of the actual numbers of women employed followed those of the total employment curve. As production line techniques came to require more sophisticated skills, women seemed to keep up with the trends. One benefit of working for this newly revitalized industry during the Sputnik era was good wages. Average weekly salaries in the aviation industry in 1959 were $107, based on hourly earnings of $2.68. This was about $5,500 annually, compared with a median female annual salary of just over $1,200; 45 percent of women working in 1959 earned less than $1,000 per year.[42]

The women in aviation who worked for the government were scattered in several occupations. Air traffic control was one of the more important fields. In 1959, sixty women were certified as controllers out of a total of twelve thousand. The new Federal Aviation Agency (created in 1958) sought to overcome its shortage of controllers by allowing trainees to substitute certain educational qualifications for the pilot's license requirement. Most of the women who entered the special training class in Oklahoma City had become involved with aviation during World War II. Male air traffic controllers were respectful of the women but always reminded them of the controller's guiding axiom: "You have to be right, or you don't work tomorrow."[43]

The business connections between government and industries were often made by women. This gave rise in the late 1950s to a group known as the Topside Aviation Club. Located in Washington, D.C., the club had about fifty members,

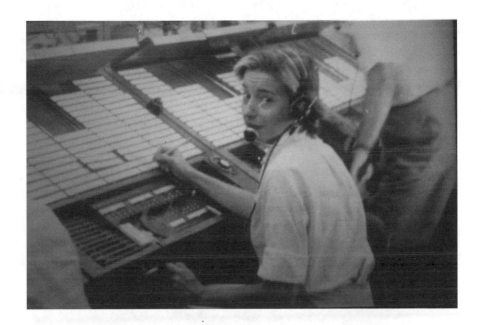

In 1958, Marian Olmsted became the first woman controller at the St. Louis Center. She was one of a few dozen women controllers working for the Civil Aeronautics Authority when Congress passed legislation creating the new Federal Aviation Agency. Several tragic accidents prompted changes in air traffic control practices and increased job opportunities for women. *Courtesy of the Federal Aviation Administration.*

all of whom were women in key positions in the aviation world. "Key position" was broadly construed to include women who were administrative assistants to top men in the airlines, government, the armed forces, and other aviation industries or associations. For example, group president Anne Meljunek was the administrative secretary for FAA administrator E.R. "Pete" Quesada. Essentially a social organization, the work of Topside Aviation Club members was described by the *Air Force Times* as "often smoothing the way in lining up appointments for their bosses, coming up with hard information or merely 'oiling the machinery of mutual business.'"[44]

A world apart from the Washington aides in the Topside Club were the women who worked as aircraft mechanics. In the early 1950s, just before dissolving, the Women Flyers of America sponsored the first All-Women's Aircraft and Engine Mechanics class at the Teterboro School of Aeronautics in New Jersey. The course was open to twenty women and provided two scholarships.[45] Despite the fact that being a mechanic was an unusual job for females, women with sufficient aptitude and interest found ways to work on airplanes

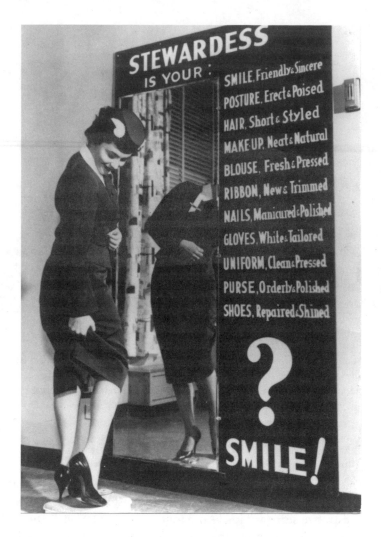

The most important function of a flight attendant in the 1950s was to present a particular image of youth, vitality, and feminine charm. As illustrated by this Frontier Airlines flight attendant, who is undergoing a "preflight check," matters of grooming were of prime importance. *Courtesy of the Association of Flight Attendants.*

and engines all across the United States. In many cases women ran their own maintenance companies or aviation service businesses for pilots at small community airports.

Often escaping from those same small towns were women who became airline flight attendants. It was a job that one attendant, Lucille Chase, described as a combination of "hat check girl, nurse, babysitter, mother, cook, waitress, diplomat, psychiatrist, confidante and companion." The most important qualifications for an applicant were good physical appearance and the ability to get along with others. Whether a young woman underwent training at a company center or at a private school, classes taught inflight procedure, airline routes and codes, company history and policy (if a company school), stewardess regulations, and geography. Women also had to pass a CAA course in regulations and procedures (primarily safety procedures). Chase's descriptions in her book *Skirts Aloft* reveal that male chauvinism in the cockpits was a problem. Airline pilots and flight engineers often mistreated the attendants, making the women's jobs more difficult. She also noted that many passengers during this period were "first-time" passengers and consequently required a considerable amount of attention from the flight attendants.[46]

The attendants had been unified in 1949 under the Airline Pilots Association's Air Line Stewards and Stewardesses Association (ALSSA). One advantage of this merger was that ALPA performed the arduous work of bringing together the women on a majority of the commercial airlines. This had been one of the original goals of Ada Brown's ALSA. In 1953 there were thirty-five hundred members, but the assets only amounted to $32,000—not enough to provide adequate services for members. The women, who constituted the vast majority of ALSSA's membership, still perceived themselves as an independent unit, and they attempted to function as such by electing officers and reorganizing their administrative offices. This naturally conflicted with ALPA's intentions to retain control over the flight attendant organization. ALPA had to contend with the women who were actively seeking their own charter with the AFL-CIO and both the Teamster's and Transport Workers unions, which had been expressing interest in having the flight attendants join their respective organizations. The antagonism between ALPA and ALSSA only intensified.[47]

During the decade, the advent of the jet had increased both the number of flights and the responsibilities of the flight attendants. The women wanted the 1959 contract to reduce the number of required monthly flight hours. ALPA, preoccupied with conflicts within its own ranks between pilots and flight engineers, wanted the flight attendants to drop their demands, claiming that the question of pilot salary was more important. It was an issue of health versus money, and the battle caused upheavals in union leadership and the loss of some attendants to the Transport Workers Union. It was the start of a struggle that would lead eventually to the re-creation of an independent flight attendants organization.[48]

The "air hostess," "stewardess," or "flight attendant" still retained her primacy as "woman in aviation," but female engineers, pilots, and executives were increasingly important. The end of the 1950s saw women in aviation on the threshold of a turbulent decade in the struggle for an even greater role. At the moment of transition, Gill Robb Wilson reflected on the presence of women aloft. His remarks are strikingly similar in tone to those of General "Hap" Arnold's, spoken fifteen years earlier to the last graduating class of WASPs.

> The presence of women at the controls aloft, stunting in airshows, sometimes winning races in open competition, and spanning the continents and oceans in solo projects was a vast leavening in the dour opinion held by the public concerning the ultimate utility of flight.
>
> And it must be remembered that the women did not easily come by their skills in the cockpits. There is always that element of pseudo masculinity that sustains its own ego by isolation of competition it cannot face. This the ladies met head on and overcame with the logic of tophand performance. In due course the bond of common experience became the criterion of pilot fraternity for men and women alike— and there it stands today. But it was a point that had to be settled if aviation was to be something more than a parade of muscles and myopia.[49]

Wilson's words were part reflection, part optimism. In the less prominent areas of aviation, such as light plane flying and production line assembly, greater equality had been achieved. The doors of power—the airline cockpit, the military flight schools, and the industry boardroom—were still closed to women. These were the places that women in aviation in the 1960s would attempt to integrate; they were ready for more than general aviation.

7

The Impact of the Women's Rights Movement

The 1960s

> An employer may not discriminate in his employment practices
> on the basis of sex.
>
> Civil Rights Act of 1964

Toward the end of the 1950s, highly confidential experiments were conducted by the Air Force on the physiological characteristics and suitability of women for space flight. Ruth Nichols, founder of Relief Wings, participated in a set of these "astronaut" tests at Wright-Patterson Air Force Base in Dayton, Ohio, during which time she suggested that aerospace medical researchers ought to compile data on women as well as men.[1]

Then in September 1959, Geraldine "Jerrie" Cobb, a young, talented pilot, was introduced to two of the nation's most distinguished aerospace medical researchers, Brigadier General Donald D. Flickinger of the Air Force and Dr. W. Randolph Lovelace, head of the Lovelace Foundation for Medical Education and Research. The Lovelace Foundation was a private organization, but it had government contracts to conduct some of the most unusual and often top-secret investigations for the military and the Atomic Energy Commission. It was Randy Lovelace who was overseeing the astronaut candidates' physiological testing for the National Aeronautics and Space Administration (NASA).[2]

Cobb was twenty-eight years old, with seven thousand hours of flight time, three world records, and the FAI (Federation Aeronautique Internationale) gold wings of achievement. She was a pilot and manager for Aero Design and Engineering Company, which manufactured the Aero Commander aircraft, and was one of the few women executives in aviation. Lovelace and Flickinger had already discussed the idea of having women undergo the same battery of physiological tests as NASA's male astronauts. "Was Cobb willing to try," they asked? There would be no reward and Cobb would have to take unpaid leave, but she was more than willing to head out to Lovelace's facility in New Mexico.[3]

Cobb successfully completed all three stages of the grueling physical and psychological tests that were used to select the original seven Mercury astronauts. Her performance led to further tests for women. Invitations to twenty-five women, all of whom were selected because they were outstanding aviators, were issued; eighteen agreed to participate.[4]

Cobb's scores also led to the proposal that the United States be the first nation to put a woman in space. Various individuals, including a few in the military and NASA, supported the idea, but keenest of all was Cobb. Her enthusiasm was closely matched by the other twelve women who passed the first round of tests at the Lovelace Foundation. It was Cobb who went back to the U.S. Navy to see if Lovelace could continue to test the women at the Naval Aviation School of Medicine in Pensacola, Florida. Using connections to obtain the necessary approvals, Lovelace had tested Cobb there in May 1961. This time, however, the Navy could not accommodate Lovelace without official approval.[5]

The twelve women were supposed to go to Florida in July 1961, but the test was rescheduled for September. Some of the women quit their jobs in anticipation of joining "America's Space Race." There had been a flurry of media attention, including features in *Life, McCalls,* and *Parade.* Cobb had been named a NASA consultant. The "Fellow Lady Astronaut Trainees," or FLATs as Cobb decided to call this group of thirteen, seemed bound to form the nucleus of an official NASA program to train women as astronauts. Unfortunately, Cobb and the other women were deeply mistaken. NASA not only refused to authorize the Pensacola tests, the agency firmly and unequivocally said "no" to the idea.[6]

The decision to cancel the tests caused deep disappointment (almost inconsolable in the case of Cobb) and anger toward the NASA administrators. The resulting controversy involving NASA, Congress, the vice president, and a handful of determined young women set the stage for a decade of furious debate on the role of women in aviation.[7]

Jacqueline Cochran was once again in the fray. Cochran paid all of the test program expenses for the women "astronauts," but then testified during special congressional hearings against the idea of including them in the space program. She believed that the only way to include women was through a trained corps of specialists, strongly reminiscent of her vision for the WASP and WAF; but, she stated, the nation could not afford the time or money to conduct such a program. She spoke of women's lack of commitment and high attrition rates due to marriage and pregnancy.[8] In a personal letter to Cobb she wrote: "Women for one reason or another have always come into each phase of aviation a little

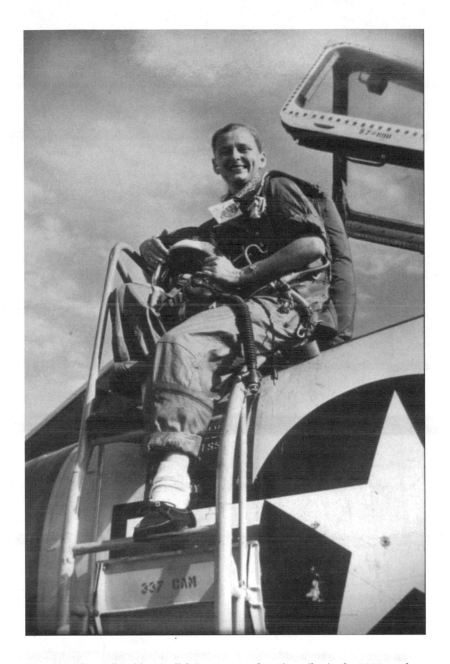

Geraldine "Jerrie" Cobb, a well-known, record-setting pilot in the 1950s and early 1960s, was invited by the Lovelace Clinic to take the same physiological tests given to the Mercury astronauts. Her surprising performance led to the testing of additional women and a questioning of NASA's exclusion of women from the astronaut program. *Courtesy of the National Air and Space Museum, Smithsonian Institution (SI 79-6359).*

behind their brothers. They should, I believe, accept this delay and not get into the hair of the public authority about it. Their time will come and pushing too hard just now could possibly retard rather than speed that date."[9]

This letter, which was secretly circulated among top Air Force and NASA officials, earned Cochran praise for her "statesmanlike" understanding of the situation.[10] Cobb and Jane Hart, wife of Michigan senator Philip Hart and one of the successful test candidates, refused to take Cochran's advice and, instead, insisted on their right to participate. They lobbied Congress, Vice President Lyndon Johnson, and NASA administrator James Webb for inclusion of women in the astronaut program.

NASA reacted by noting that the most important of the requirements for selection was that a candidate must have had experience as a military test pilot. President Eisenhower had mandated that all candidates come from the pool of experimental test pilots in the military and every individual subsequently involved in the process had concurred. Experimental test pilots were trained to communicate with engineers. Following a decade's experience developing jet aircraft for the military (from the Century Series to the famous X-planes), this was deemed the most critical skill to the success of the Mercury mission. But as human space flight was a new endeavor, the list of "requirements," indeed the entire selection procedure, had not been fully codified. In pressing the case for women astronauts, the proponents forced NASA's hand. It was now on the record that only jet test pilots would be considered.[11]

This development negated the chances of selection for almost every woman in the United States. Ann Carl, who had tested the first American jet, the Bell YP-59, was not current. Only Jacqueline Cochran had this experience. Cochran, using her inside connections (mainly through her husband Floyd Odlum), had continued to fly jets after breaking the sound barrier. She served as an occasional test pilot for two manufacturers of jet aircraft and had continued to remain visible in the aviation world by setting new speed records, such as the 100 km closed-circuit record on 1 May 1963 in a Lockheed TF-104G Starfighter and the speed record over the 15/25 km course on 11 May 1964, also in a Lockheed TF-104G. Cochran's connection with civilian contractors that built military jet planes was very unusual even if she had been male; there were not many civilian jet test pilots. In general, the only way an applicant could acquire the requisite jet test-piloting experience was through affiliation with the military, and women were not allowed to fly for the military.[12]

When the Soviet Union launched Valentina Tereshkova into space in 1963, Claire Booth Luce wrote an editorial in *Life* magazine condemning NASA officials: "Why did the Soviet Union launch a woman cosmonaut into space? Failure of American men to give the right answer to this question may yet prove the costliest Cold War blunder."[13] Of course, the motivation of the space program was public relations, Luce argued, and NASA was being hypocritical to deny that propaganda and public relations were important components. Luce's comments were indicative of a larger struggle that was occurring in American society.

The question of civil rights had been much in the forefront of American consciousness for some time. Two laws were passed in quick succession that would prove to be particularly important to women in all professions, not just aviation. The first was the Equal Pay Act of 1963, which required equal pay for equal work. The second important law was Title VII of the 1964 Civil Rights Act. Title VII prohibited all discrimination on the basis of sex for any reason in determining employee compensation.[14] The laws empowered the government and individuals to take legal action against discrimination; and yet no significant change seemed to happen. The President's Commission on the Status of Women produced a lengthy report in 1965 that once again detailed wage discrimination and the declining number of women in professional and executive jobs but failed to offer any genuine prescriptions for change. In June 1965, the National Organization for Women (NOW) was created. It became, among other things, an important advocate for women's rights in the cockpit.[15]

Women in the aerospace industry found that the debate about women's rights initially had little effect on them. Most of these women were clustered in specific unskilled occupations, and within these fields "equal pay" generally was the norm even if equal advancement or career potential was not. One interesting note is that in 1962, Aerospace Industries Association stopped reporting the employment figures for women in aerospace. Some researchers, such as Cynthia Enloe, argue that this was a continuation of the sociological trend toward a diminished and less visible female presence in the aerospace industry.[16] The actual number of female employees, however, remained relatively stable. Women represented between 14 and 17 percent of the aerospace industry workforce throughout the decade. Fluctuations occurred as production responded to escalation of the conflict in Southeast Asia.

The disappearance of the statistics does indicate two facts. First is the lack of attention by the industry to the contributions of women. This is not surprising, as the aerospace community had almost completely switched its emphasis to research, science, and engineering and away from production, where its women employees were concentrated. It was the leading employer in manufacturing in the United States, yet there was little status or prestige attached to the production end of the business, where no one, male or female, was receiving much recognition.

The second fact is the relatively small number of women in the aerospace engineering field. The lack of encouragement for young girls to take mathematics and science courses in the 1950s militated against the presence of women engineers in the 1960s. Only one percent of the doctoral degrees awarded in engineering were earned by women during this decade. Likewise, women represented about the same percentage (one percent) of the undergraduate enrollment in engineering.[17]

Nancy Fitzroy was one of the few women in the 1960s engaged in an engineering career. She began working as a heat-transfer engineer for General Electric in 1953. During the 1960s she worked on the thermal design of the afterburners for General Electric's J79 jet engine. To her knowledge there were only four or five other women engineers working for General Electric at that time, and while they did not seek each other out, she felt there was a certain unspoken bond born out of the common experience of being female in a male-dominated environment.[18]

Fitzroy was a pilot with both fixed-wing and helicopter ratings. Her work on a multitude of General Electric projects at various work sites provided her with the opportunity to commute by air (using her own airplane). This provided her the added benefits of increasing her piloting proficiency as well as cutting travel times to a fraction of what ground transportation would require.

In the late 1960s, she wrote a short pamphlet on her job as an engineer. It was part of a career-education series and contained information on her job and her lifestyle. In it she noted some of the difficulties she had when she was first hired. It took a major effort to convince the company that she was a serious career woman. The company's contrary stereotype resulted in her being passed over for job promotions or being paid a slightly lower salary than her male colleagues. The 1960s civil rights actions seemed to have lessened some of these discriminatory practices, but they did not succeed in removing them altogether.[19]

Fitzroy was a member of the Society of Women Engineers, which had been founded in 1952. The 1960s were a lean period for the society's membership; numbers were so small that it was difficult for them to be effective in realizing common aims—including their desire to see a greater number of female engineers. Women in aerospace engineering are rarely discussed for the decade of the 1960s because there were so few of them.

Another area that was hardly even considered was the hiring of women pilots by commercial airlines. Women did work as professional pilots: small airports, local flight schools, and light plane dealerships all hired women to fly for them. Jan and Marion Dietrich were two of these professional pilots; the twins had qualified in the Mercury astronaut tests. Jan was an FAA flight examiner, and Marion an aviation writer. Jan Dietrich described her reaction the first time she was hired to work as a pilot (she gave rides to potential customers of an airplane dealer at a small airport): "Commercial women pilots were about

Sheila Widnall earned all three of her aeronautical engineering degrees from the Massachusetts Institute of Technology (B.S./M.S. in 1961 and Sc.D. in 1964). She was the first alumna to be a professor in the School of Engineering at MIT, the first woman chair of the faculty, and, in 1992, the first woman secretary of the Air Force. *Courtesy of the MIT Museum.*

Throughout the 1960s, women participated in most aspects of aviation. The most typical positions remained the flight attendant and the secretary. At the NASA Langley Research Center, photographers frequently asked attractive secretaries to pose in the wind tunnels. *Courtesy of the NASA Langley Research Center.*

as acceptable as female ship captains. I had never heard of anyone deliberately wanting to hire a woman pilot. This seemed amazing if not downright charitable."[20] Slowly the real reason for her selection would become apparent: "I demonstrated the planes, working hard making the tires whisper onto the runway. A passenger remarked, 'Why the airplane practically lands itself,' and Larry [her boss] beamed at me. Like breaking through the overcast, suddenly I realized the reason for having a lady pilot. If a girl does something well especially a small one who dresses and looks like a girl—it seems easy, as if anyone could do it. And I hurried off to change the stocking that had just run."[21]

It was the old ploy of using women's apparent limitations to sell an aviation product, but change was on the horizon. In the 1960s, people were becoming considerably more aware of the hollowness of stereotypes associated with specific occupations. For example, an article on aviation careers described the desirable characteristics for an airline pilot: "The preferred applicant is married (this gives some assurance of stability and motivation) and although no one will say so, has completed his military obligations. He has a good achievement record in college with some interest in athletics and has a stable work history. In general he is an extrovert and has assumed leadership roles in his activities. He is outgoing, stable, mature, "outdoorsy," dominant (but not cocky) and shows judgment."[22] Soon after this description appeared in *Flying* magazine, however, there were numerous objections from readers about the blatantly biased language. These protests demonstrated the slowly evolving trend of the time toward less gender-specific terms.

Spurred on by debates and public consciousness, highly visible organizations such as the aviation magazines were hiring women as writers and editors. *Flying* magazine inaugurated a regular column on women called "Skirts Flying." Month after month, author Sally Buegeleisen, herself a pilot, followed the progress of women in aviation. Through her articles she developed an open debate and public understanding of the subject of women in aviation that had never really existed before. From this vantage point she could see the connections between the women's rights movement and women flyers. Though not herself a radical, she could not help posing the questions that encouraged the male-dominated aviation community to think differently about women.

This was one reason why *Flying* encouraged its new editor, Patricia Demarest, to learn to fly helicopters. The magazine wanted to make her a successful editor, and at an aviation publication knowing how to fly was practically a professional credential. Without it, Demarest could hardly hope to be taken seriously and could expect to encounter barriers to her career advancement. Demarest had been an airplane enthusiast since childhood, but she had never taken any flying lessons. She described the trials and tribulations of learning to fly a helicopter in an article that appeared in *Flying*'s special August 1965 "Women in Aviation" issue.

Demarest made an important observation on the differences between men and women student pilots: "It's probably true that it takes a woman longer to learn to fly than it does a man. While a male student pilot is reviewing his last lesson and imagining his next, his student pilot wife is more likely to be cooking dinner and deciding if the ironing can wait until Wednesday."[23]

Demarest had identified an important social phenomenon. She and other contemporary journalists contributed to the late 1960s sharpening of the parochial debate within the aerospace world on the role of women in aviation. Robert Parke wrote an editorial stating forthrightly that:

> of course the presence of hordes of women in an activity does revolutionize the activity. . . . The hardy airplane salesman has known since the dawn of aviation that airplane sales would truly zoom—not if prices were cut, not if airplanes

Marge Gorman was among the first one hundred women to earn a helicopter rating. She is shown here in 1965 with her first passenger (and daughter), Gayle Gorman Freeman. Gayle, who is also a helicopter pilot, is president of Manairco, airport and heliport lighting specialists. *Courtesy of Gayle Gorman Freeman.*

were prettier, not if the National Safety Council endorsed the airplane—but if women took to them.

To some the feminization of flying will be akin to holding a woman's bridge party in a monastery. And it's true the day of rowdiness of the Quiet Birdmen and the all-night hangar session may pass. But for many men this is a small price to pay when the approval of a spouse can mean the difference between flying and not flying.

And for those to whom flying is an escape from the cares of the ground—something to be savored best when solo—the beauty of the sky is that it is big enough for both of us.[24]

Evidence of the change in attitude toward women in aviation came in the quantity and scorn of the letters to the editor in response to Milton Horowitz's article, "For Men Only?" Horowitz claimed it was impossible for a real woman to fly because it violated her normal feminine sensibilities. Flying was the last bastion of masculinity, and the presence of women diluted the experience, according to Horowitz. His remarks provoked a wave of protest from both men and women, who totally disagreed with the sweeping generalizations made in the article.[25] "Why are men so afraid of flying women? Don't you know we're out to join you, not beat you?" wrote one woman in a letter to the editors of *Flying* in November 1965. That was precisely the message newly organized feminists were preaching.

One group in the aviation industry that was dramatically and immediately affected by Title VII of the Civil Rights Act was the flight attendants. The saying among airline executives had been, "Use them 'til their smiles wear out; then get a new bunch."[26] The airlines seemed oblivious to the discrimination involved in requiring attendants to resign when they married or reached the age limit (thirty-two to thirty-five, depending on the airline). The airlines claimed that the hostess was the personal representative of the company. They felt they had the right to project an image of youth, freshness, eagerness of service, and seeming tirelessness. The same airline executives complained about the expense of having to train so many women. They neglected to mention that training was significantly less costly than funding pay raises, pension plans, and health insurance. They never discussed the airlines' fear of a flight attendant who was married and a part of a two-income household. Such a woman would be in an extremely advantageous position in contract negotiations because she could afford to go on strike. Hence, a powerful reason for wanting to continue the "no marriage/out by 32" rule was the fear that these women would exert considerable influence over the company management and alter the status quo.[27]

These fears surfaced in the first suits brought against the airlines. In *Cooper v Delta Airlines, Inc.,* the court ruled against Eulalie E. Cooper, who had filed the 1967 case protesting that her termination with Delta was discrimination on

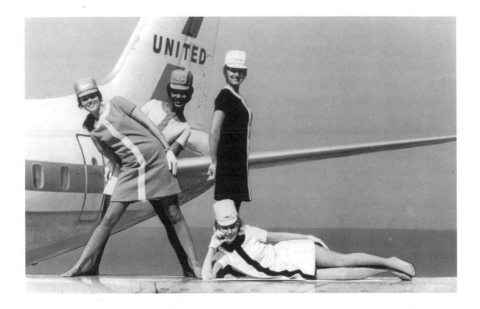

Flight attendants for United Airlines pose for a corporate public relations photograph showing off the uniforms designed by Jean Louis. *From the Association of Flight Attendants Collection, courtesy of United Airlines, Inc.*

the basis of sex. Delta only employed female stewardesses, and thus the court ruled the discrimination was between married and unmarried women, not between men and women. The case prompted the new Equal Employment Opportunity Commission to examine the question of whether discrimination based on marital status, when applied only to one sex, could be considered sex-based discrimination. Both the attendants and the airlines were eager to have a ruling.[28]

NOW played an important part in the hearings, actively supporting the attendants by helping with legal assistance, garnering legislative support, and drawing media attention to the issues being raised by the union. NOW's president, Betty Friedan, even testified at one set of proceedings.[29] The commission issued its opinion that marital restrictions did in fact violate Title VII. The opinion was nonbinding, but most airlines began to change their policies anyway. United Airlines, the largest carrier with the greatest number of flight attendants, refused to change the rule. Finally in 1968, United, still the last holdout on "no marriage," agreed to discuss the issue with ALPA and its Stewards and Stewardess Division (which had replaced ALSSA in 1960). The union wanted to win reinstatement and back pay for flight attendants who, in their opinion, had been unjustly fired. United resisted each of the many proposals, although the company was financially capable of making such a restitution, though obviously at the loss of some profit. In 1969, a limited and marginally acceptable agreement was reached on reinstatement, but the question of back pay would not be resolved until the early 1970s.[30]

The women who worked as flight attendants during the 1960s were still young, attractive, and mostly single. Salaries had improved, with base pay starting at $345 per month. Wages had built-in incremental increases for the subsequent ten years of employment. Thus, top pay for an attendant with a decade of experience would be $520 per month. Another issue of great import concerned flight attendants. Most of them were white, college-educated, middle-class women. Asian, Native American, and Hispanic women had been hired in limited numbers and primarily to service special routes in areas such as Hawaii, Latin America, or the Southwest. Virtually no black women were hired until the Civil Rights Act of 1964 was passed. Prejudice continued to operate against any large influx of minority women. Further, there is no evidence that the union leaders made any significant effort to alter the situation by encouraging the companies and their membership to increase minority representation. Nevertheless, the legal protection of the Civil Rights Act made it much harder to willfully exclude blacks and other minorities.[31]

The vast majority of the women pilots in the 1960s were involved in general aviation. Their numbers more than doubled from 1960, when there were 12,471 licensed women pilots in the United States (3.6 percent of the 348,062 total), to the end of the decade, when there were nearly 30,000 women pilots (still only 4.3 percent of the total number of aviators, which had grown to 683,097).[32]

There were many organizations in the 1960s that focused on women in aviation, but the general public usually only gave its attention to remarkable individuals, such as Geraldine "Jerrie" Mock and Joan Merriam Smith. Both of these women flew around the world in 1964, unintentional rivals in this, the first (and finally successful) two attempts of the feat by a woman since the disappearance of Amelia Earhart in 1937. Smith's route was a re-creation of Earhart's famous but ill-fated flight. "I had had the dream for years, first to fly an airplane, then to fly one as she [Earhart] did. When I was in high school, I would tell my friends and classmates that someday I was going to fly around the world just like Amelia Earhart. Everybody just laughed. They knew I was a baseball-playing tomboy, and this was a tomboy fantasy. But I knew that since Amelia disappeared in 1937, no other woman had attempted to fly around the world. This only heightened my ambition to be the first one."[33]

Smith realized her dream, but she was not the first woman to fly around the world. Jerrie Mock in a single-engine Cessna 180 called the *Spirit of Columbus* earned that honor. Mock had applied for and received official sanction

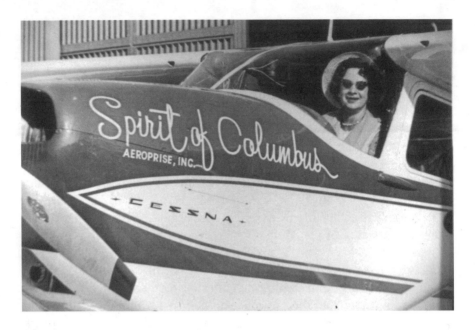

Geraldine "Jerrie" Mock became in 1964 the first woman to pilot an airplane around the world. This photo was taken just prior to her March takeoff. *Reprinted, with permission, from the Columbus Dispatch.*

from the National Aeronautic Association (NAA) for a world record before Smith did. Because only one attempt at a time on this sort of world record can be made, Joan Smith's belated application for a virtually simultaneous try cost her the right of official sanction. She decided to make the flight anyway, and since both she and Mock were departing about the same time during the spring of 1964, the press immediately presupposed a "race." It was hardly a race, because the two aircraft and the routes were very different, but the situation engendered a bit of competitive spirit and drew public attention to the participation of women in aviation.[34]

The Ninety-Nines were, of course, very interested in these flights. They also helped Ann Pellegreno with her round-the-world flight in 1967, a thirtieth-anniversary celebration of Earhart's attempt. However, the prime interest and major commitment of the Ninety-Nines during the 1960s was air racing. In addition to the AWTAR, they embraced the All Women's International Air Race, or "Angel Derby," as it came to be known. The race was open to any woman pilot, but the Ninety-Nines provided help in organization and management, not to mention forming the largest core of enthusiastic contestants.[35]

Doubts about the value of the events, especially the big race, the AWTAR, were smoldering in the minds of some observers. Sally Buegeleisen wrote: "There is also a growing skepticism among the racers about whether anyone with limited income has any chance of winning. 'The present system,' one of the women said, 'rules out any possibility that any but a select few will ever be on top in this race.' There is a growing resignation among the women who are racing that 'people with average incomes . . . cannot afford to have their planes prepared' and so don't stand a chance."[36]

Buegeleisen's criticism may have reflected a concern of participants, but it failed to convey one of the most distinctive features of this "race." People external to the event assumed that competition was the sole purpose of the race. There were occasional suggestions that all of the work needed to put on this event was not being adequately compensated or recognized. Recognition, to such observers, was usually understood in terms of male sporting events, where column inches on a sports page, sponsorship by aviation corporations, or a large purse was perceived as the standard. The intangible rewards, however, were of greatest value to the organizers and participants in this event. Pride was a big factor. The event, like the Ninety-Nines in many ways, was a self-contained entity and the participants did not measure success strictly by commercial or masculine standards. Although the women always viewed public recognition through the media positively, they valued chiefly the fact that every year there was a celebration of women in aviation, and anyone connected with flight was a winner in this event.

Women were attempting to share the values of the race with the larger aviation community. The Ninety-Nines, like its sister organization, the Whirly-Girls (which had expanded to 140 members in 1969), were exploring different ways of communication. They first turned to their men's auxiliaries. By encouraging the presence of men at their functions, the women pilots hoped to open a positive dialogue about the role of women in aviation, both as individuals and as a group. They wanted it to be taken for granted that they were serious and accomplished aviators.

The organizations, however, were not all talk and philosophy. They were also interested in making real contributions to aviation, and they felt no compunction about seizing the appropriate moment. That is what the Whirly-Girls did when at a tea with President Kennedy: their representatives actively lobbied for an increase in the number of heliports in metropolitan areas, especially Washington.[37]

One of the most promising means of communication was created by the federal government. On 4 May 1964, President Lyndon Johnson announced the formation of the Women's Advisory Committee on Aviation (WACOA)

The Whirly-Girls celebrated their tenth anniversary in May 1965 on the steps of the U.S. Capitol. *Courtesy of The Whirly-Girls, Inc.*

After WWII, Ann Wood Kelly rose through the airline ranks to become a senior executive in the field. She was the first woman to become a vice president at Pan American World Airways and was among the founding members of the Women's Advisory Committee on Aviation (WACOA), established to advise the FAA administrator on matters of concern to women. *Courtesy of Ann Wood Kelly.*

within the Federal Aviation Administration. The idea for such a group had been proposed by FAA administrator Najeeb Halaby, and its purpose was to provide recommendations about public relations and education programs on flying as well as to encourage greater family participation in aviation. There were thirty-two members (twenty-seven public appointees and five from government, serving ex officio), all women with outstanding reputations in aviation and community service. Of the original thirty-two, all but two were or had been active pilots. The two who were not were the director of stewardess services at American Airlines, the top female executive in that company, and a contract manager at Hiller Helicopter.[38]

WACOA was organized along the same lines as the Defense Advisory Committee on Women in the Services (DACOWITS) had been, and in fact met with their military counterpart during their preliminary planning meetings. Thus, they divided into five subcommittees, each representing an area of major concern—airports and heliports, airmen, aircraft, flight standards and procedures, and education and public relations.

Based on the subcommittee reports, the group made many recommendations to the FAA. For the most part, WACOA's suggestions were not new, and this seemed to surprise outside observers. It was as if these individuals believed the feminine experience in aviation to be so different from that of men that women's ideas for change and reform would likewise be different. Concentrating on the basics, WACOA proposed parallel runways, suggested that there be a required cleanup of aircraft accident wreckage at airports, and argued for better cockpit design. The women knew that their proposals had been voiced before but believed they could take advantage of their unique position to stimulate the FAA into taking action on some of the most basic goals of aviation. The media was quick to promote the committee's more "feminine" proposal of airport beautification. The idea was in keeping with the Johnson administration's (and specifically, in this instance, Lady Bird Johnson's) programs on highway cleanup, but it was not a major preoccupation of the committee.[39]

The degree of influence wielded by the committee varied. As an advisory group to the FAA administrator, the women could potentially affect policy. Even if the committee did not take any major actions, their very presence served as a constant reminder that women were involved in all capacities within aviation. The problem with the group was that it lacked the resources to do anything other than make suggestions. Though WACOA existed until President Carter dissolved it in January 1977, it became clear within a few years that WACOA's value was somewhat limited. It did create another means for top-level women to communicate with each other, and their collective voice did help encourage the FAA to make further advances in certain areas of general aviation. Its greatest weakness was that it tended to concern itself with changing programs without considering the dynamic social changes that were occurring. In other words, cleaning up runways was important, but doing so was not going to encourage more women to take flying lessons.

Major social upheavals occurred throughout the 1960s, and the decade saw a protracted reexamination of public ideals. The changing attitudes of Americans about work, pay, and what constitutes discrimination began to be reflected in a demand for these changes to take place within the military. These debates helped open up the field of military aviation to women.

It was not an easy process. Enthusiasm for women and men in uniform was at an all-time low in the early sixties. Many studies from within the mili-

Lieutenant Colonel Ann Johnson (left) and Lieutenant Colonel Yvonne Pateman, both of the USAF, at Tan Son Nuht, Vietnam, in October 1967. Johnson and Pateman were among the many women who served on active duty in Vietnam during the war. *Courtesy of Yvonne C. Pateman.*

tary suggested that no women should be involved in any facet of the armed forces. From the mid-1950s on, women had been gradually phased out of participation in many aviation functions, including serving as flight orderlies. Nevertheless, there were certain aviation specialties for which enlisted women in the Air Force were still preferred over men, including work in air intelligence and defense combat control centers and in passenger air-transport operations. These preferences were soon eliminated, as the leadership decided that women's military occupations ought, in their words, to be "in conformance with the 'present cultural pattern of utilizing women's services in this country.'"[40] This meant that in the Air Force enlisted women were no longer permitted to work in intelligence, information, or weather forecasting, or as flight attendants, or in equipment maintenance and control tower positions. Only thirty-six of sixty-one noncombat specialties remained open (70 percent of those left were in clerical work, and another 23 percent were in medicine). In general, women were being slowly but systematically removed until, in 1965, only 30,600 women remained on active duty. Feminist groups took no action about this situation, partly due to the pacifist tone of their rhetoric and their general ambivalence toward the military.[41]

The key to the shift in attitudes was the escalation of the Vietnam War. The manpower problem was exacerbated by the increasing unwillingness of Americans to serve in a war they did not believe to be just. The draft was reinstituted in 1967. Concurrent with that announcement, plans were made to increase the number of women in the military.

The impetus for this action had come from the Defense Advisory Committee on Women in the Services in the spring of 1966. DACOWITS discovered that thousands of women had volunteered for service in Vietnam but had been turned away because of the recruitment ceilings. DACOWITS urged the military to define a more rational policy that would, at the very least, allow the recruiters to achieve the full 2 percent quota of women that was permitted by law. DACOWITS did not stop there, however. With persistent and effective lobbying it helped to bring about the passage of Public Law 90-130, signed on 8 November 1967. The law accomplished two things. First, it removed all restrictions on the promotion of female officers. Previously women could achieve no rank higher than colonel in the Army, Air Force, and Marines, or captain in the Navy. Second, it removed all limitations on the number of female personnel who could be employed in the armed forces. Although the law was intended to bring greater equity to the career development of women in the military, it failed to resolve several issues. Two of particular concern to women in military aviation were the barring of women from the service academies and the statutory restrictions on women serving aboard aircraft engaged in combat missions and on ships of the Navy (except hospital ships and transports).[42]

The law did mean, however, that women were once again being utilized in "nontraditional" career specialties. In 1967, 1,223 WAVES, or about 20 percent of all women in the Navy, were assigned to naval aviation. At least seven of the twenty ratings open to women enlistees were directly connected with aviation. These included aerographers' mates, radiomen, aviation electronics technicians, tradesmen, air controlmen, aviation store keepers, and aviation maintenance administrators. Officers were also assigned to these fields. Ensign Sharon Fernando was the first WAVES officer assigned to work with a fighter squadron. She assumed the public affairs and educational services functions for VF-126, an instrument training squadron for Pacific Fleet fighter pilots. Training for this job included experience with the pressure chamber and ejection seat.[43] Another officer, Ensign Gale Ann Gordan of the Medical Services Corps, was the first woman in the history of the Naval Air Basic Training Command to fly solo in a Navy training plane. She received the flight training as part of the 111th Flight Surgeon Class in order to become an aviation experimental psychologist. The only woman among one thousand male students, she studied the same course they did, noting that her biggest problem was not the training but the flying clothing—all much too large.[44]

Marine Corps women were also involved in aviation medicine. This meant that women were routinely asked to complete the ejection-seat training program. During the 1960s women in naval aviation often underwent survival training, but in 1967 Airman Virginia Rookhaysen was the first woman to complete both the land and sea phases of the survival school at Pensacola Naval Air Station.[45]

Minority participation was slowly increasing. In 1945 there had been two black women Navy officers; in 1968 there were thirty-one, although this was still less than 0.5 percent of the total number of female Navy officers. By contrast, the Air Force had approximately 218 black women officers during the years between 1966 and 1970, which amounted to about 4.6 percent of the total number of female AF officers.[46]

Between five hundred and six hundred Air Force women served in Southeast Asia during the Vietnam War. Operations officer Major Norma Archer gave the daily briefings on air strikes for the senior staff of the 7th Air Force. Air Force Intelligence was one of the most important functions performed by the women who served in Vietnam. In terms of numbers, the flight nurses were the largest group of military women in aviation to serve in Vietnam. In fact, nurses represented the majority of American women in this location. One of the larger contingents was the 9th Aeromedical Evacuation Group, which arrived in Saigon in 1965. Many of the "ground" nurses were included in flying missions as part of air-evacuation teams to rescue casualties from active combat sites. Nobody seemed to object to the nurses' involvement in combat action. An important, though rarely acknowledged, part of the nurses' function was to boost the morale of the injured. Many women officers could not understand why it was acceptable for nurses to serve in the midst of the battle action, yet unacceptable for women in any other function.[47]

A turning point occurred when the Air Force began to make public its discussions on the potential use of women as pilots. Although the motivation was not completely apparent, part of the stimulus came from the public sector and part from internal pilot shortages. In August 1967, the *Air Force Times* published an article by Bruce Callander entitled "Why Can't a Woman Be a Military Pilot?" In the article he wrote: "The Air Force has never seriously considered training women as military pilots. Its main reason is that all pilots are potentially eligible for combat assignments, and the Vietnam War has underscored this philosophy. AF has so far rejected even the idea of accepting female pilots for limited, non-combat duty although the approach has been offered as one possible solution to the pilot shortage."[48] Callander made the case that historically women had proven capable as pilots. As we have seen, they flew Air Force aircraft to set records and participated in special tests. For example, Wally Funk, Jerrie Cobb, Jean Hixson, Ruth Nichols, Jacqueline Cochran, and many others all flew military jets during the 1950s and 1960s. Callander proposed that, while Congress might restrict combat flying, a compelling case could be made to use women for noncombat missions. Finally Callander suggested:

> The ultimate question, however, may have little to do with any of the more practical factors of physical differences, mechanical aptitude, or emotional stability. For all their stress on equality of the sexes, Americans have perhaps the world's most over developed sense of what kinds of work are proper for women.
> The "front offices" of both military and commercial aircraft are likely to remain off limits to women for the foreseeable future. Still, male pilots should listen closely for an unfamiliar sound in the cockpit. This could be a feminine knuckle knocking ever so gently on the cabin door.[49]

The article was unusually progressive. During the 1960s, most women in aviation struggled to gain acceptance, let alone equality. Manifestations of the flying housewife still existed; programs were still sponsored for women because, as one *Flying* magazine article put it, "as mothers they would be able to influence their children."[50] However, greater numbers of women, both nonpilots as well as pilots, were beginning to recognize the role of aerospace technology and achievement in American society. Increased participation by women in aviation also resulted in empowerment—the possession of professional skills to accomplish a job and an awareness that these qualifications entitled them to a place in the aviation world. Examples of women who were conscious of this experience during the 1960s were the members of the Women's Advisory Committee on Aviation and the Defense Advisory Committee on Women in the Services. The influence of these women extended further as they came to represent the first frequent and persuasive images of accomplished women in the field. Yet even these women were quick to recognize that this was just the beginning; they had yet to assume most of the real positions of influence on an equal basis with men.

During the 1960s, women in aviation were equipped with the legal tools of the Civil Rights Act of 1964, the Equal Pay Act, and Public Law 90-130, which removed career and manpower restrictions on women in the military. There was also a newfound sensibility with regard to the feminine potential. The concept of equal rights did strike a responsive chord in most Americans. Doors had been opened, and a new generation of pioneers was about to enter.

8

Women with the "Right Stuff"

The 1970s

> There is an implied promise, today, of equal opportunity for everyone in the Armed Forces. It is part of a new environment to recognize women as persons today, as well as pilots.
>
> Antonia Handler Chayes, Assistant Secretary of the Air Force for Manpower, Reserve Affairs, and Installations

The title of Tom Wolfe's book *The Right Stuff* has become a popular description of the combination of ability, instinct, personality, and fitness that is supposed to characterize the supreme all-American male. Originally applied to the seven astronauts of the Mercury space program during the early 1960s, the expression also describes many of the women who were involved in aviation a decade later.

The 1970s encompassed a number of major international crises that caused domestic shock waves in American society. These ranged from the last years of the Vietnam War, to the Camp David Peace Accords, to the American hostage crisis in Iran. The Watergate scandal rocked the nation and challenged America's faith in government. It was a decade when there was a shift from the 1960s' style of effecting change through confrontation, to a new emphasis on seeking change through legislation and litigation.

Women in aviation in the 1970s, reflecting this pattern, often relied on the law and the American legal system to reinforce their claims to full and equal participation. In general, the presence of a woman in a nontraditional field no longer produced universal feelings of hostility. Americans, especially women, soon became enamored with the coverage of "female firsts." In aviation, that meant airline and military pilots, engineers, and corporate executives. The women were sometimes only token female employees, but never in any period since World War II had so many new fields opened up simultaneously, nor had so much attention been paid to women. In this respect women in aviation were very much like their counterparts of the 1920s and 1930s; their exceptional status attracted attention in itself and was also seen as a feminist statement. The women of the 1970s were the new pioneers. They were brave in the face of ceaseless media spotlights that sought to document the impact of female achievement (or perversely, failure) on America. Like the women flyers of the 1920s and 1930s, they were scrutinized and made involuntary role models for a movement toward equal rights.

In 1972, approximately 156,000 women were employed in aerospace industries. They represented 17.2 percent of the total aerospace employment of 912,300. Gradually, both the number and percentage of women increased during the 1970s. In spite of industry stagnation and the slight decline of total aerospace employment figures, women made substantial gains. In 1979, 21.3 percent of the total industry employment (1,099,200), or 234,500, were women. This was a 50 percent jump in the total number of women in aviation in seven years.[1]

In manufacturing, women predominated in microelectronics assembly, which involved putting together the computer and electrical components that form the "nerve" system of modern aerospace equipment. This was the fastest growing area of aerospace manufacture. The first reason for the attraction of greater and greater numbers of female workers into aerospace electronics was that it was a light industry, and physical strength was not needed to participate. Light industries, such as electronics, food processing, textiles, and garment making, traditionally have had higher concentrations of women employees than heavy industries.[2]

The second reason for the increasing number of women in aerospace was related to the changes in college enrollment patterns. More women were attending college or other schools of higher education. Further, more women were majoring in the sciences and engineering. The number of women receiving bachelor's degrees in engineering tripled during the decade; even from 1967 to 1972 the number more than doubled, from 2,350 to 5,317.[3]

Women were being encouraged from all sides. Any industry dealing with the government was required to have an affirmative action plan to increase the presence of women and minorities and promote equal opportunity for all. Universities began actively recruiting female students. In 1973, the Massachusetts Institute of Technology sponsored a symposium on "Women in Science and Technology," first to develop an understanding of why women had not enrolled in large numbers in the past, and second, based on that knowledge, to find ways of altering the pattern. The most important conclusion to come out of this conference, and many others like it, was the realization that in order to increase the number of women in science and engineering, proper primary and secondary school preparation in mathematics followed by similar training in college had to be provided.[4]

This message was echoed by women engineers. Kiki Fleck, a thermodynamics engineer at Lockheed who worked on the cooling of advanced avionics systems for the P-3 Orion and the S-3A Viking aircraft; Phyllis Veit, who worked at Aerojet Solid Propulsion in the Propellant Development Section; and Dr. Dora Dougherty Strother, chief of the Human Factors Group at Bell Helicopter, all emphasized the importance of education. Each felt an obligation to take vociferous exception to the idea that women could not understand mathematics or become engineers; for example, Dr. Strother was a frequent speaker for Girl Scout troops, which she felt was a good way of communicating her thoughts to young girls.[5]

Olive Ann Beech still ranked as the preeminent woman executive in aviation management. In 1973 and again in 1978, *Fortune* magazine recognized her as one of the "Ten Highest Ranking Women in Big Business."[6] Beech was also a role model for other women in the aviation business, such as Athley Gamber, who ran one of the six largest small-aircraft service and sales companies in the southeastern United States. Gamber, who founded Red Aircraft (later part of Cigma Investments) in Fort Lauderdale, Florida, with her husband in 1954, took over operations in 1968. When asked if she experienced any difficulties because of her sex, she replied, "The few women who are running businesses are highly capable. They've worked in the aviation game for a long time. And the biggest company in the United States, Beech Aircraft, is run by a woman. In a way, that sets the criterion for the whole industry."[7]

New laws and regulations that mandated affirmative action programs brought an influx of women employed by the federal government into aviation professions. In 1971 there were two important "firsts" for women working at the Federal Aviation Administration. On 4 April 1971, Ruth Dennis became the chief of the FAA's San Diego Flight Service Station, and on 16 May, Gene Sims became the tower chief of the Cuyahoga County Airport in Ohio. Both were the first women ever to hold such positions.[8]

At the end of the decade the FAA rewrote its Aviation Career Services pamphlets to include only gender-neutral terms; for example, ramp serviceman became serviceperson, and "he" and "she" were used jointly throughout the text. In addition, the FAA also reprinted for public distribution a series of magazine articles about women. The four reprints included information on women in Navy and Air Force aviation, as well as more general surveys. Yet, for all the official "equality," numbers and attitudes changed slowly. During the late 1970s women accounted for only about five percent of the total number of air traffic

Olive Ann Beech was twice recognized by *Fortune* magazine as the top woman executive in aviation management during the 1970s. *Courtesy of Raytheon Aircraft.*

controllers. Lynne DeGillio, who was an air traffic controller at John F. Kennedy International Airport in New York, described the tower as retaining its "locker room ambience" despite the addition of women. "Throwing insults or teasing, sometimes on the most juvenile level, is a release for them—a time when they're not thinking about airplanes—and they do it at every chance they get. Everyone's personality is magnified in that tower, and you can't let it get to you. You have to become one of the guys to get along in what appears to be their world. At the same time, you have to hang on to your femininity."[9]

DeGillio resented the outmoded attitude of her colleagues, and felt tension between being part of the group and just being herself. That additional stress was a common experience for women in aviation, although it was not limited to the airport tower. For example, other FAA women who worked as accident inspectors, flight examiners, or engineers all reported similar feelings. However, the government was better than much of private industry, in that at least there had been a sustained, if small, presence of women in most fields of federal employment for some time.[10]

U.S. airlines, on the other hand, had experienced a long hiatus between the first woman commercial airline pilot (Helen Richey in the mid-1930s) and the next in the 1970s. Around the time U.S. airlines began to hire women pilots, the Soviet Union reported that its first female commercial airline pilot had been hired in the 1950s. The first confirmed report was of Durba Banerjee hired by Indian Airlines in 1966. Fiorenza DeBernardi started with Aeralpi in 1967, and in 1969 Scandinavian Airlines System hired Turi Wideroe. In the early 1970s, women pilots were flying for many foreign airlines, including Sabena, Mexicana, El Al, and Air Inter of France. It was not until 1973, however, that the first American woman was hired to fly for a major airline. In January of that year, Emily Warner became first officer on a Convair 580 for Frontier Airlines, opening up for American women one of the last sex-segregated aviation occupations in the nonmilitary side of the aviation industry.[11]

Warner was thirty-three when Frontier finally hired her in 1973. Flying since the age of seventeen, she had held jobs as diverse as flying traffic reporter, FAA examiner, and flight school manager. She was the chief pilot for the Clinton Aviation Company in Denver when she first applied to Frontier in 1968. The employment opportunities for pilots were limited, but when Frontier decided to recruit a new group in 1972, Warner was there with application in hand. She was very persistent, and when she was finally hired, a spokesperson for the airlines said: "We couldn't think of any reason not to."[12] In 1978, there were about fifty women out of a total of thirty-eight thousand pilots flying for U.S. airlines. Except on very small feeder lines, most were flight engineers or second officers, if for no other reason than they had not accumulated sufficient hours and seniority to become captains.[13]

The women wanted to be pilots for the same reasons as men. First, they loved flying, but they also loved using their talents in respected, well-compensated work and they loved the feeling of belonging that the airlines try to create. Many also had strong family connections with flying. Often they had relatives who flew or worked for the airlines.

The obvious question that was being asked in the late 1970s was "why weren't women hired before 1973?" The airlines claimed that qualified women had not expressed interest or applied. Economic and marketing priorities were more decisive factors, however. Highly regulated by the federal government and unable to manipulate either routes or fares, the airlines competed for passengers through service. Image was extremely important. In the early 1970s, there were still significant numbers of Americans who had never traveled, or had traveled only once, on an airliner. Even for trips over two hundred miles, most Americans still drove their cars. Consequently, the airlines were still very much wedded to a public relations program of safety and convenience. They deliberately cultivated the image of the pilot as "father" and were uncertain as to whether or not putting women in the cockpit might instill new fears in passengers' minds.[14]

The airlines had little experience with women as career professionals and did not see them as primary wage earners: men needed to support families, women did not. The airlines argued that women would soon quit to start a family, thus supposedly validating the notion that hiring women would not be cost effective. The jokes about "women drivers" were rife in the back rooms of executive suites and behind the closed cockpit door.[15]

The airlines were dependent on the Civil Aeronautics Board for subsidies and protection from competition. In the 1970s, the airlines had to become "Equal Opportunity Employers" if they were to receive federal money. Further, the equal rights movement constantly lobbied the companies. The movement had much to gain if women were hired. Airline pilots were highly visible and well regarded. The National Organization for Women wanted visible role models of women in nontraditional careers to demonstrate the legitimacy of its philosophy and goals.

Regulations and enthusiasm aside, the airlines did not have hordes of women pounding on their doors. The requirements for application were stiff. An applicant had to be at least twenty-five years old, have four years of college, and possess the following credentials: a commercial license; an instrument rating; an airline transport rating; fifteen hundred hours flying time, including both night and cross-country flying experience; and a first-class medical certificate. In addition, applicants had to be familiar with navigation, FAA regulations, and the principles of safe flight. They were required to have exceptional hearing and sight and meet physical requirements, such as minimum height (five feet, six inches for American; five feet, eight inches for Delta). Fifteen hundred hours was a considerable amount of flight time. Outside of the armed services, preparation for a career as a pilot meant a substantial financial investment. Women had just begun to fly in the military; a number of years would have to pass before this could be used as an avenue of career preparation.[16] In addition, it should be noted that these requirements resulted in an even smaller presence of minority women working to attain employment with the commercial airlines. There were only 110 black pilots working for the airlines in 1978, when Jill Brown was hired by Texas International Air. At the time, news articles celebrated Brown as the first black woman to qualify for a major U.S. commercial airline. She had also attracted attention when she became the first black woman to enter the Navy's flight school (in 1974), though she left the military after six months of training. Brown resigned from Texas International Air after two years on the job.[17]

The airlines did not have a consistent policy to encourage the presence of women; nor did they have one that might alter the ratio of white women to women of color. The female pilots who advanced in their careers did so in spite of the existing conditions. Likewise, women who sought to work in management and other executive positions at the airlines experienced a similar inconsistency in the airlines' reactions to their career potential. Nevertheless, there were some highly successful female airline executives.

United Airlines had several women serving in high-level management positions. Julia McMurray was named manager of the women's market in 1972. Because the airlines were so conscious of their market image, McMurray's job was to plan and direct programs geared for women travelers. Barbara Allen headed the section that included computer and data processing systems. Marge Segal worked as an account executive, handling United's convention sales. Peggy Ann Moore was an assistant flight dispatcher based in San Francisco. Most women at United who worked in management positions during the 1970s were in the public relations department. No women had become chief executives, but they were slowly beginning to advance in the corporate hierarchy.

A good illustration of this evolution can be seen in the career of Ann Wood. Wood learned to fly through the Civilian Pilot Training Program and was immediately hired as an instructor for the same Bowdoin College program. Jacqueline Cochran handpicked her to be one of the twenty-four women to fly with the Air Transport Auxiliary in the United Kingdom during World War II. During the postwar period, she worked for America's first civil air attaché of the U.S. embassy in London. In the 1950s she was director of public relations for Northeast Airlines in Boston. In the early 1960s, Wood served as the project officer in a Massachusetts Mass Transportation Demonstration Project. Between 1966 and 1977 she worked at Pan American World Airways in public relations. She left the company as staff vice president to begin a new position as assistant to the president of Air New England, where she continued her work as liaison between the New England community and the federal government.[18]

The other principal group of women connected with the airlines was still the flight attendants. The single most important development in the 1970s was a shift in corporate and public opinion, so that the attendant was now seen as a career professional, not simply part of the service personnel. This change paralleled the increase in the average tenure of a flight attendant from two years to seven. There were indications, such as a high level of job satisfaction, that this average would continue to rise during the 1980s. Even with this change, flight attendants were still perceived as "attractive, mature personalities with glamorous jobs." True as this perception was, the image had changed over the years. Class and age requirements became less rigid. Applicants were still expected to be attractive and congenial, but it was a "clean and wholesome rather than glamorous appearance [that was] desired."[19] By 1979, starting salaries ranged from $8,000 to $17,000 annually, plus a variety of benefits, such as reduced travel costs, insurance, annual leave, and retirement plans.

Salary, benefits, and working conditions were negotiated by union representatives at contract meetings. The three main unions were the Association of Flight Attendants (AFA), the Teamsters, and the Air Transport Division of the Transport Workers Union of America (TWU). The largest of the company unions was the Independent Union of Flight Attendants (IUFA), which represented attendants with Pan American. Total combined membership of the independent unions was nineteen thousand. In contrast the AFA, the largest of the multi-carrier unions, had about twenty-two thousand members. The Teamsters had roughly fifty-one hundred flight attendant members, and the TWU about seventy-one hundred.

The AFA was the new autonomous union of flight attendants that had grown out of ALPA's Stewards and Stewardesses Division (S & S Division). It was the largest union and represented approximately half of the unionized flight attendants in the United States. Under the original S & S Division arrangement, it had been possible for a flight attendant to be elected as president of ALPA. When the ranks of attendants began to swell in the early seventies, it was anticipated that the S & S Division's membership would surpass that of the pilots. Fearful that the women (S & S was predominantly female) might elect one of their members as president and that they would lose control of "their" union, many pilots, in conjunction with the ALPA leadership, began to encourage the formation of an independent union. The attendants had mixed views on the situation. Some wanted total independence, others wanted to preserve the status quo. In October 1973, J.J. O'Donnell, president of ALPA (head of the pilots), and Kelly Rueck, vice president of ALPA (head of the S & S Division), met to discuss the creation of a new organization. The proposal created separate but affiliated pilot and flight attendant organizations, which would continue to share administrative offices, supplies, and legal counsel.[20]

Kelly Rueck was elected vice president of the Air Line Pilots
Association for the Stewards and Stewardesses Division in
1970. She later became one of the chief architects of the new
Association of Flight Attendants, serving as AFA's first
president until January 1976. *Courtesy of the Association of
Flight Attendants.*

The agreement was ratified in November 1973, and preparations were made
to seek the National Mediation Board's recognition of the newly created Association of Flight Attendants (AFA). The board ruled in December 1974 that a
"simple majority of one vote more than 50 percent" by the attendants of each
separate airline that had formerly been a part of the S & S Division would serve
to legally transfer bargaining representation from ALPA to AFA. Over the next
five years attendants at each of the sixteen carriers voted their approval to give
AFA bargaining rights in contract proceedings.[21]

Contract negotiation took on a new air as the women reorganized their methods and became as professional as possible. They took classes on negotiation techniques and took the time to research the history of past negotiation efforts. This involved interviewing all of the participants and rereading all of the previous contracts and the supporting documentation. For the first time the flight attendants truly had an understanding of the attendant's place within the corporate structure. The first test came with United Airlines. Initially the company had agreed to the requests of the negotiation team, but problems quickly developed. Essentially, the flight attendant team wanted to be recognized and treated professionally and as equals. Using the strategies of ALPA and the other airline unions, the United flight attendants submitted typewritten proposals, insisted on regularly scheduled meetings, and asked to be treated as equals by company negotiators. United was completely surprised by the flight attendants' new tactics (more than by the actual contract demands), but instead of offering acceptance they branded the women as radicals. Company officers claimed that members of the team were out of touch with the United flight attendants, that the negotiators were not like the other "normal" attendants. This was an attempt to explain the company's failure to completely control the proceedings.[22]

The women ultimately succeeded both in winning contractual gains and in unifying the members by a process of intensive education. The flight attendant leaders and the United bargaining team improved communications in order to make sure all understood the goals as well as the means that would be necessary to accomplish those ends. The women learned not to place artificial restrictions on themselves based on societal expectations and unquestioned stereotypes.

The airlines experienced considerable growing pains as they began to relinquish the old notions of what the job of a flight attendant really represented. It was no longer primarily an adventure, but was essentially work. As personnel turnover rates dropped during the 1970s, the airlines slowly recognized that they would have to regard the attendants as more than short-term employees, and accord them a new and greater status within their corporate hierarchies.

The military, in contrast, was on the verge of a public relations campaign to convince young women that they should join up precisely because participation would mean "adventure" and "not just a job." The creation of an all-volunteer force in 1973 filled recruitment officers with anxiety. They were uncertain about their ability to meet the strength requirements being set forth by the Department of Defense. Concurrent with this dilemma was the congressional debate on the Equal Rights Amendment. One of the central issues in those discussions was the role of women in the armed forces. This triggered a

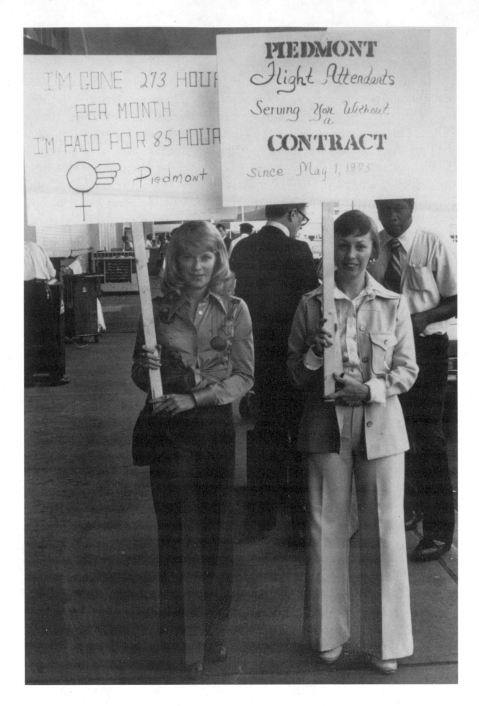

Piedmont flight attendants participate in a strike caused by stalled contract negotiations. Strikes were part of the new negotiating tactics used by the unions to force a company to make concessions. *Courtesy of the Association of Flight Attendants.*

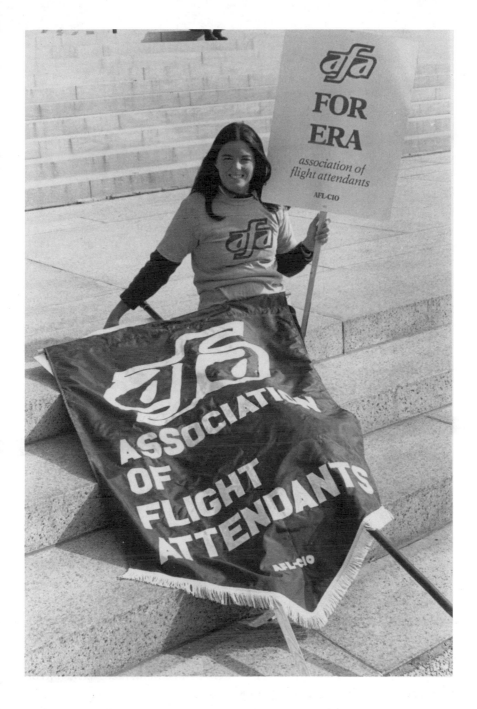

During the 1970s and 1980s, the Association of Flight Attendants actively worked in support of the proposed Equal Rights Amendment. *Courtesy of the Association of Flight Attendants.*

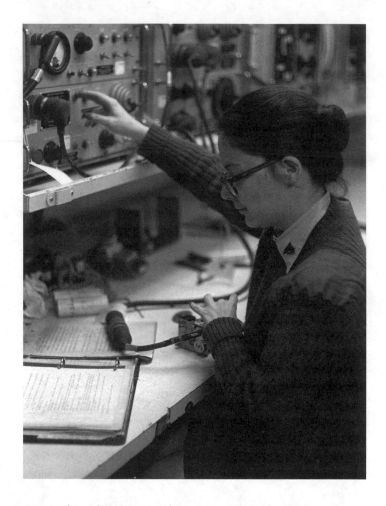

Corporal Smith, USMC, working as an avionic electronics technician at the Marine Corps air station at Cherry Point, North Carolina, in 1979. *Courtesy of the U.S. Defense Visual Information Center.*

renewed awareness among the manpower strategy experts at the Defense Department as to the potential value of women. In any event, there seemed to be a good possibility that the military would soon be required by law to use women without restriction. Numerous special studies on the deployment of women cropped up, each coming to the conclusion that there ought to be an increase in the number of female personnel. George A. Daoust, Jr., deputy assistant secretary of defense (manpower research and utilization), asked each service to

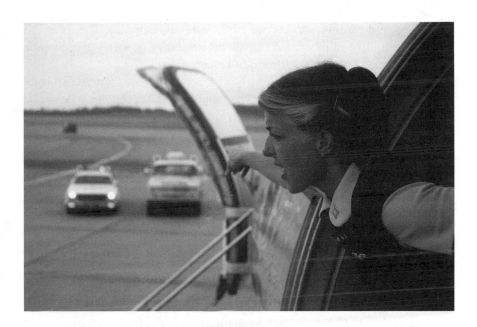

Flight nurse Captain Cathy Young, USAF, was a member of the 375th Aeromedical Airlift Wing. Here she directs an aeromedical unit to move emergency vehicles from the path of the C-9 Nightingale aircraft, which is about to take off. *Courtesy of the U.S. Defense Visual Information Center.*

develop contingency plans for the increase in the number and use of women in anticipation of a law such as the Equal Rights Amendment being passed. Daoust also indicated that each branch, except the Marine Corps, should plan to double its female ranks by 1977. The Marines were only asked to produce a 40 percent increase.[23]

Once the individual services began to examine the issue seriously, their contingency preparations became effective plans of action. Throughout 1976 there was a 20 percent growth rate for women in the military. After that year the rate slowed to five percent, as the armed services sought to determine the impact this enlarged percentage of women would have on operations and effectiveness.

The women who had signed on found there were a multitude of new opportunities in aviation: Reserve Officer Training Corps programs were opened to women, restrictions because of sex were removed from many military occupations, the academies became coeducational, the first women were promoted to the rank of general or admiral, and most significantly the first women were being trained as pilots. What was so important about this last change was that flying was, and continues to be, one of the essential activities of military air service. Even if the numbers were small, the advent of women's participation was symbolic of a movement toward full integration.[24]

In January 1973, Secretary of the Navy John Warner announced that eight women had been selected to enter the Navy flight-training program at Pensacola (officer training for women would be held at Newport, Rhode Island). Their course would be identical to the men's, because the goal was to determine the "feasibility of using women in non-combat flying billets in helicopter and transport squadrons."[25] Eighteen months later, in 1974, six of the eight had earned their official Navy Wings of Gold: Jane M. Skiles O'Dea, Barbara Allen Rainey, Judith A. Neuffer, Ana Marie Fuqua, Joellen Drag, and Rosemary Conaster Mariner. Rainey (then Allen), who was the first woman to receive Navy wings, commented on the experience: "Everybody goes through a stage of being depressed. The hours are long and the work is hard. You sometimes think, 'What's the use? There's so much to learn. I can never do it.' I think all students go through that."[26] The women faced the additional pressure of questions, spoken and unspoken: "Can they adjust? Can they do it?" The first class demonstrated that women could learn to be good military pilots. The personality traits and skills needed to complete Navy flight training were shared by women and men alike. Based on that knowledge and the good experience with the first group of women, a second class was authorized in 1975.

The authorization did not come without controversy. Many in the Navy felt there simply was not a place for women pilots. Their objections were voiced in influential quarters and in sophisticated rhetoric. The excerpt below is taken from an essay in the *U.S. Naval Institute Proceedings:* "Until such a time as women are legally and physically able to occupy any job in any location under the same conditions as men, a most unfair and discriminatory practice exists and the Navy must stop it. Let's chalk up the initial input of female aviators to an interesting experiment in equal opportunity that didn't really provide equal opportunity and stop at that."[27] Women in aviation have usually found that participation has hinged on proof of ability. The military leadership was convinced the passage of the Equal Rights Amendment was imminent; hence it wanted to determine the potential of women in various roles previously closed to them. Many still defined women in terms of their limitations, however. This created an environment of tension for women, although with each successive (and successful) class of women, a portion of the conflict abated.

The third class followed quickly on the heels of the second. It was also the first to have the Aviation Officer Candidate School phase conducted at Pensacola. (The previous two had held this phase in Newport before transferring the women to the Florida air station for flight training.)[28]

In 1973, shortly before the flight programs for Navy women began, 12 percent, or 713, of the enlisted women in the Navy worked in aviation specialties. That same year the WAVES corps was abolished, and women were brought into the regular Navy. Instead of being WAVES or WAVES officers they were simply officers and enlisted women in the Navy. By mid-1977 there were four thousand enlisted women involved in Naval aviation in twenty-four separate ratings. In addition, more than one hundred officers and a thousand enlisted women worked in aviation as part of the Naval Reserves. This growth, matched by the successful adaptation of women, has obviously meant many changes for the Navy.[29]

Yet the key question regarding women in combat remained. When asked why she wanted to participate in combat, Lieutenant Junior Grade Rosemary Conaster (now Mariner) replied:

> Why do I want to go to a tactical squadron, to fly off a boat, and perhaps be shot at?
>   My reasons are the same as those that have always attracted men to Naval Air. It is because I have experienced the satisfaction of the first step—winning Gold Wings and I want to continue to succeed at what is the most demanding form of aviation. I want to become a full professional in my chosen vocation.[30]

To be a fully accepted member of the Navy, women recognized they would need to share in the risks and responsibilities.

The Army began to include women in flight-training programs at almost the same time as the Navy. Lieutenant Sally Murphy received her wings in 1974, becoming the first woman aviator in the Army's history. Unlike the Navy, which had a separate class of women, Murphy was simply one of twenty-five members of Officer Rotary-Wing Class 7414 at the Army Aviation Center based at Fort Rucker, Alabama. Like many other women pioneers in military aviation, Murphy stressed that, in spite of being the first and only woman, her colleagues were very accepting of her. "I was allowed to maintain my femininity, but the men did not pamper me nor give me special treatment—they maintained a perfect balance in our relationship."[31] Women were trained in many of the Army aviation specialties, including maintenance. They attended "Jump School," learning the skills of an Army parachutist. Several women encountered difficulties in learning certain specialties because of their lack of experience with tools and machinery prior to attending Army technical schools. The Army had not anticipated this situation and did not make any curriculum adjustments to compensate, despite explicit congressional instruction to do so. The attitude was that women would have to adjust to the existing standards the same way men did, whatever the consequences. This did affect the participation of women, as some dropped out of the specialty, and others were discouraged from even trying.

This was true in the other services as well. Navy airplane captain Ellen

Mahoney stated: "On my first plane I was plenty nervous. For the first couple of weeks I became a hermit. I was so tired when I got home, I just died. I'd ask the guys if they felt the same way and they would say 'no.' They always seemed to feel great. Now I've found out that it takes a lot of getting used to."[32] Mahoney really liked her job. She was quick to praise her colleagues and officers, although she still had to prove herself to the men. Her boss commented, "When I heard I was getting a girl on my line, all I could think was 'Why me?' But she sure has turned my attitude around."[33] The combined pressures of learning a new job as well as having to prove oneself were overwhelming for some women.

The Coast Guard, which during peacetime was considered a civilian agency under the control of the Department of Transportation (it is now under the Department of Homeland Security), also trained its first woman helicopter pilot in the seventies. Janna Lambine applied for flight training while attending the Coast Guard's officer candidate school in Yorktown, Virginia. On 4 March 1977, she earned her wings and was designated a naval aviator at Whiting Field Naval Air Station. Lambine was definitely a token woman, as the Coast Guard had shown only a limited commitment to training women aviators. The organization was sensitive to the public pressures that demanded at least the appearance of integration. Lambine experienced an isolation that was typical for the first representative of a particular minority when entering the profession of military aviation.[34]

The Air Force took longer than either the Navy or the Army to incorporate women into its flight-training programs. It maintained that even though women had completed their programs in the other services, the reason for exclusion was not that the Air Force did not believe women could be pilots, but rather that the legal restrictions on women in combat made it difficult for them to justify an extensive program to bring in women. The Air Force claimed that all pilots were combat pilots, though many pilots might "spend their entire careers as instructors, transport pilots and other assignments without drawing a combat tour."[35]

Eventually the Air Force began to include women in other aviation programs that included flying experience. For example, in July 1975 Captain Jane Holley graduated as the first women flight test engineer. Coincidentally her class was also the first held at Edwards Air Force Base. She went to school side by side with the Air Force test pilots. In the forty-four-week course she had over one hundred hours of flight time. Her one comment upon graduation was: "I only hope I have done well enough so that other women will be welcome at the school."[36]

In November 1975, there was a major change in Air Force policy on this question. During his farewell address at Andrews Air Force Base, Secretary of the Air Force John McLucas, to the surprise of many in the audience, announced that women would soon begin training as pilots. McLucas noted that the Air Force was considering the development of a two-track pilot program, combat and noncombat, but was not convinced this was the only way to train women.[37]

The first official reports on the plan came on 10 December 1975. The *Air Force Times* noted that representatives from the Air Training Command and Military Personnel Center in Texas had met with Air Force legal, logistics, personnel, and medical staff to discuss anticipated problems and coordinate the entire operation. One result of the meeting was the decision to permit women who would be entering the Air Force Academy the following fall to take the T-41 training program, if the general program was successful.[38]

In January 1976, the Air Force announced its program goals. These were to determine (1) how women pilots could be used within the Air Force outside of combat missions, and (2) what curriculum modifications would be needed if a permanent course for women were added. The Air Force wanted to determine potential career paths for women that included a list of positions for which they would be eligible.[39] At the same time, the Air Force called for applications. By April the committee had decided which airplanes the women could fly and where the training would be held—Williams Air Force Base, Arizona. The Air Force also decided to eliminate the helicopter components of the experiment, because they felt the Navy and Army had fully demonstrated that it was possible to train women to fly rotary-wing craft without any problems.

Following the initial decisions on the course structure, the Air Force turned to the logistical details of the plan. The first major problems they confronted were related to physiological and medical issues. Probably the second greatest barrier to women pilots in the military was the physical dimensions of the cockpit and the complete failure of aircraft designers to apply knowledge about female physiological characteristics, such as average height, sitting position, reach, and eye height. The design of a cockpit could make the difference between safe and unsafe operation of an aircraft. The average stature of pilots, a determining factor in safe cockpit design, would be reduced if the female physique were taken into account. Ignoring this change would introduce an element of danger with regard to existing aircraft. It was recognized that the permanent inclusion of women would necessitate changes in everything from cockpit configuration to uniform design and supply. That recognition triggered the surfacing of latent resentment toward women for upsetting the system. Finally, there was the debate over whether women pilots would be allowed to take birth control pills, as up to that point pilots could not be on medication of any kind.[40]

In August 1976, members of the first two women's classes were named. During the press announcement an official commented that "although the AF

The first ten women officers to graduate from the Air Force Undergraduate Pilot Training Program pose for a group photo in front of a T-38 training aircraft. *Courtesy of the U.S. Defense Visual Information Center.*

refers to the female pilot training program as a 'test program,' some AF officials see no reason why they should not be successful. Women have been flying for almost as long as men."[41]

Before the first half of the first group had even finished training, the Air Force decided to continue the program. Another nine women would begin training in February 1978. The reason for this was the positive reactions of the instructors at Williams. Lieutenant Colonel C.T. Davis, operations officer for the 96th Flying Training Squadron, reported that "a lot of people had a lot of ideas that women wouldn't be able to hack it because of their lack of physical strength, because of inadaptability to stress, because of this, because of that. So far our experience has been that it hasn't changed things at all. The women are going through exactly the same training as the men and are hacking it just as well."[42]

When the women were asked in public about how well the men accepted them, they always replied positively. Privately, many expressed a fear that any criticism on their part might end the program.[43] There were difficulties, often created by the extra attention given to the women, yet it was that attention which helped women bear the additional pressures of success. Captain Kathy La Sauce commented: "When you step out of the airplane and take off your helmet, the transient maintenance guy almost falls over backwards. That sort of keeps us going."[44] There was a great deal of pressure to be good, to succeed lest the door be shut for other women.

Women pilots faced a very uncertain future. They were doing what they loved best, yet their career options were rather limited. The Air Force was subtly letting women know that it was not "women's lib," but rather a shortage of qualified men that had led to the decision to train them. The implication was that if more men had been available, the women would not have been pilots. In light of their continued progress, however, the Air Force began to want to remove some of the combat restrictions placed on women so that more of them could be used. It strongly supported requests to Congress in 1977 and 1978 from the Department of Defense that would have allowed the secretaries of each service to establish duty assignment policies. The proposed amendment to Title 10, Sections 6015 and 8549 of the United States Code, would have specifically allowed the assignment of women to noncombat ships and aircraft. The wording of the amendment was such, however, that the possibility for ending any and all restrictions on women in combat would also have existed. This amendment was not successful and the original policy remained unchanged in 1985.[45]

The other major flying career newly opened to women in the Air Force was navigation. The first class of six women entered school at Mather Air Force Base in March 1976. The course lasted thirty-three weeks, and the women who graduated were to have the opportunity of flying in KC-135, WC-130, C-141, and WC-135 aircraft. Captain Bettye Payne, who graduated with this first class, said she applied after receiving encouragement from OV-10 aircraft pilots in Korea. She wrote a brief article in which she said, "The best thing about being a navigator [was] the challenge of flight. No two flights [were] alike and I liked that element of surprise."[46]

Two other major congressional battles dealt with women in military aviation. The first was the decision to open the service academies to women. Unlike the Navy and the Army, the Air Force did not express unanimous opposition to the idea of admitting women. WAF director Jeanne Holm went on the record as supporting the idea (her counterparts in the other services did not agree), and Secretary of the Air Force Robert Seamans also indicated his approval when he said the Air Force would accept women nominated by Congress if funds for new facilities (housing, bathrooms, locker rooms, etc.) were provided. In general, however, the Department of Defense opposed the idea and made every effort to lobby against the bill. Jacqueline Cochran took this occasion to testify forcefully against admitting women to the academies, because she felt the proper and primary role for women in American society was mother and housewife.[47] Despite her own experiences and those of the Women Airforce Service Pilots, she felt there was no role for women in the military during peacetime. It is alleged by several of Cochran's colleagues that individual members of the Air Force prevailed upon her to take the stand she did. Congress refused to listen to such arguments, and in the spring of 1975 the mandate was issued. Public Law 94-106 decreed that as of September 1976 the academies would admit women. The Air Force took the most active role in encouraging women to apply, and after the first summer of training the Air Force had the lowest attrition rate for women of any academy.[48]

The importance of the decision to open up the academies is that it provided another avenue for women to obtain leadership positions. The academies' goal had been to prepare men to be combat officers. They also provided an elite corps, many graduates of which would ultimately attain the highest ranks in their respective services. The inclusion of women naturally altered the educational process, but it also opened up another set of options for a young woman who wanted to be a career military officer. The women graduates would be well placed to influence the participation of women in military aviation. Their mere presence had a liberalizing and liberating effect on their male colleagues. Further, academy graduates (especially in the Air Force) who became pilots stood the greatest chance of one day being promoted to general.

The second important congressional battle of the seventies regarding women pilots dealt with individuals at the other end of the chronological spectrum. This was the newly reopened lobby for the provision of official recognition and veterans' benefits for the WASPs. The first attempt was a bill introduced by Representative Patsy Mink in May 1972. It failed even to be considered by the House Veterans' Affairs Committee, largely due to the opposition of the Veterans Administration (VA). On 26 March 1975, Senator Barry Goldwater introduced another bill on behalf of the WASPs. Like Mink's bill, Goldwater's also died in committee, again blocked by the VA. In May 1975, Representative Mink made yet another attempt. The bill was killed in committee a third time. Then in September 1976 a bill came before Congress to award veteran status to Polish and Czechoslovakian citizens who fought with the Allies and who later became U.S. citizens. Senator Goldwater added an amendment to the bill that provided like recognition for the WASPs. The Senate passed the bill with this amendment, but the House steadfastly refused. With the removal of the amendment the WASPs lost yet again.[49]

The following year, 1977, was declared the "Year of the WASP" in hopes of winning recognition through an intensive program of lobbying. Representative Lindy Boggs of Louisiana and Senator Barry Goldwater sponsored bills in the House and the Senate respectively. It was the only bill (up until that time)

In 1977 Congress passed legislation that granted veteran's status to the women who had served in the WASP during WWII. Though the military had resisted this development, once President Carter signed the law the Pentagon showed its support by installing a permanent historical display honoring the WASP. *Courtesy of Yvonne C. Pateman.*

ever to be cosponsored by every woman member of Congress. The WASP received the support of the military news weekly *Stars and Stripes,* along with that of Antonia Handler Chayes, assistant secretary of the Air Force for manpower, reserve affairs, and installations. The Carter administration, however, following the recommendation of the Veterans Administration, did not support the bill at all. The Veterans Administration argued that if status were granted to the WASPs, then precedent would be set for innumerable civilian wartime organizations to make the same request. Like its predecessors, the 1977 House bill would have died in committee but for the inclusion of one small item in a packet of documents forwarded to Representative Olin Teague. Teague staunchly opposed the bill, but when he saw that the copy of Helen Porter's WASP discharge was identical to the official World War II Army honorable discharge certificate, he changed his mind. Teague acknowledged, for the first time, that the women had been de facto military personnel. With his support the bill passed easily on November 3. The next day the Senate also passed the resolution. On 23 November 1977, President Jimmy Carter signed the bill into law.[50]

The support of Secretary Chayes had been critical to the successful passage of the law. Chayes believed that the WASPs were an important part of Air Force history. Their recognition, she believed, would be significant in the ultimate integration of women pilots in the Air Force. Defeat of the bill would have sent the wrong message to women who had just started pilot training in the Air Force and would have fueled opposition by military leaders who did not want women fliers.[51]

The media concentration on so many women pilots from a previous generation did inspire many young women military pilots. Through newspapers and television programs, the WASP issue brought attention to all women in aviation. In 1970 there were 29,832 licensed women pilots. Nine years later there were 52,392, an increase of nearly 80 percent, in contrast to an 11 percent increase in the number of male pilots.[52] The vast majority of the 52,392 were general aviation pilots.

In the early seventies, two scientists began to conduct studies to determine the personality characteristics of general aviation pilots. It was the first such research effort to include women. The first hypothesis the scientists formed was that female pilots possessed a personality distinct from the standard U.S. female adult population. The second was that there was a "pilot's personality" that transcended sex differences. The research strongly supported both hypotheses. The personality of female pilots was called active-feminine (in men active-masculine) and was described as a woman who was "courageous and adventuresome, one who is oriented toward demonstrating competency, skill, and achievement; one who finds pleasure in mastering complex tasks; and one whose sexual orientation is decidedly heterosexual."[53]

The purpose of the study was to collect data on women in aviation as part of a program of increased aviation safety through human factors research. It was demonstrated that there was no scientific evidence of "dramatic" differences between men and women pilots. In fact, according to the study, they were very similar in character. Critical factors that the test failed to explore were whether race, ethnicity, or economic status made any difference in pilot personality traits. It was impossible to tell whether or not the subject pool reflected the general U.S. population. Because of the considerable expense involved in flying, the economic status of the subjects would have been illuminating. Had public policy or engineering decisions been made on the basis of this data exclusively, the net effect might have been to perpetuate the status quo, which would have meant the continuation of general aviation as the sport of wealthy white men.

Returning to the original theory about a "pilot personality," none fit the profile better than Mary Gaffaney, who was the subject of a feature article in *Sports Illustrated* in March 1973. A native of Miami, Gaffaney had been a professional pilot and aerobatic champion for twenty-six years. A five-time U.S. National Women's Aerobatic Champion, she also won the Women's World Aerobatic Championship in 1972 at Salon-de-Provence, France. Fellow contestants uniformly praised her abilities. "The consensus among Mary's past and present peers is that she has succeeded in aerobatics because she works hard at it, and since she is in the flying business, she can afford the game."[54]

Aerobatic flying skill took countless hours to perfect. It required constant access to an aircraft and the financial resources to pay for the costs connected with flying. Gaffaney was the co-owner of a flying school. She was also a skywriter (the first woman to enter this elite form of precision piloting), which gave her additional practice time.

Gaffaney's flying skill was not limited to fixed-wing craft. She was also a helicopter instructor, a Whirly-Girl, and the third pilot for the U.S. team at the Second World Helicopter Championships held in July 1973 at Middle Wallop, England.

The Whirly-Girls were well represented at the World Championships, which were open to teams of men and women (both mixed and single sex) from all nations. Whirly-Girls from several countries served as individual pilots. Amidst all of the Army, Air Force, and Navy teams from around the world, only the United States fielded an all-woman team, made up of Ilovene Potter, Betty Pfister, Betty Miller, Charlotte Graham (now Kelley), Mary Gaffaney, and Jean Tinsley. The team delegate and judge for the United States was Jean Ross Howard.[55] All of the women were exceptional pilots, and although the team did not win any of the competitions, their participation was a strong tribute to the Whirly-Girls, who had provided the leadership needed to organize a team and who had secured full sponsorship from Bell Helicopter. The team illustrated the new level of acceptance and respect being accorded to women in aviation—both nationally and internationally.

The Ninety-Nines likewise achieved wider recognition during the decade. The scope of their activities and membership broadened considerably. During the 1970s, the Ninety-Nines became very involved in the National Intercollegiate Flying Association, contributing money and time (for example, by judging competitions) to encourage young women (and men) in aviation. Further, there was a strong emphasis on humanitarian work. The Ninety-Nines worked with groups like Happy Flyers, Flying Samaritans, Blood Flights, and the Civil Air Patrol. The Ninety-Nines often featured articles in its magazine about members' contributions, public service, and relief efforts. For example, Jerrie Cobb, whose advocacy of women astronauts in the early sixties failed, found a new cause in the Amazon River area of South America. Over the decade she helped fly doctors, missionaries, anthropologists, and supplies to the Indian tribes, as well as providing an air ambulance service.[56]

The changing composition of the membership transformed the Ninety-Nines. The advent of female military pilots, commercial airline pilots, and an increase in the number of women professionally involved with aviation gave the organization a new vitality. Growth and development were inevitable.

The last All-Woman Transcontinental Air Race was held in 1977. The demise of the race was caused by rising costs, diminished corporate sponsorship, and new levels of air traffic congestion.[57] Competition in the air was still important, as the continued existence of other races, including the Angel Derby, proved. Women's air races were described as "joyous aviation community effort. . . . Everybody in this adventure must win, whatever winning is, and the afterglow spreads through the entire aviation community."[58]

Other activities absorbed the energies of the organization in place of the AWTAR. In particular, the Ninety-Nines became committed to a program of aviation education. The international officers of the organization wanted to make people everywhere, especially the young, interested in aviation. They appealed to a broad base, because it was important to the Ninety-Nines to demonstrate that every woman was welcome to participate. Realizing the value of example, they rarely missed a chance to publicize the outstanding accomplishments of their members.

During the 1970s, the Ninety-Nines transformed their organization into a network of both professional and nonprofessional women in aviation.[59] They provided support and enthusiasm for each other, but their greatest contribution was to encourage women to move beyond the glow of being first to do this or that in aviation and to establish themselves with confidence in their chosen profession or avocation. This attitude, they believed, would pave the way for increased participation of women in aviation at a more equitable level. In fact, women's accomplishments in the 1970s did establish the broad base needed for the expanding presence of women in aviation that has subsequently unfolded.

9

Captains of Industry, Airlines, and the Military

1980–1992

> I believe all individuals should have the choice to pursue their talents and desires without limits. And I look forward to the day when there aren't any restrictions on what women can and cannot do.
>
> Lieutenant Colleen Nevius, USN

The Reagan Revolution began in the fall of 1980 when voters rejected President Jimmy Carter and turned to former California governor Ronald Reagan to bring about "Morning in America." Political, economic, and social conservatives were united in the hope that Reagan's election would mean rolling back changes wrought by two decades of progressive political activism. Antiwar activism, civil rights, women's rights, gay rights, abortion rights, welfare, Medicaid, Earth Day, and concern for the environment were all anathema to the coalition that brought Reagan to power. Wherever one fell on the political spectrum—attracted or repelled by the new president—it was an electric moment in American history.

Over the decade of the 1980s, through the presidency of George H.W. Bush, amidst what was often called the "Culture Wars" (over the aforementioned issues and ideals), there was a steady shift in American attitudes to more conservative political, economic, and social views. In particular, there was an acceptance of Reagan's philosophy that "government was the problem" and therefore that special vigilance was required to limit the scale and scope of government. While this shift would suggest that women in aviation should have seen diminished opportunity during this period, just the opposite occurred. Opportunities for women, especially professional women and women serving in the military, increased greatly. In fact, by the time Iraq invaded Kuwait in the fall of 1990 the groundwork had been laid that would culminate in one of the more significant legal changes in the second half of the twentieth century: the repeal of the combat exclusion law for women military pilots.

Professionally and socially, women in aviation in the 1980s were for the most part less isolated because of their gradually increasing numbers. With expanded participation and documented success came greater confidence. There was a clear sense that women had the necessary legal tools to reinforce their rights of participation. It was not utopia and there was not unanimity of public opinion, but there was progressively diminishing need to define women in aviation as novelty (even if they would not quite achieve "normal" status in this period).

In the mid-eighties, Shirley H. Woodie became president of the Alabama Aviation and Technical College (AATC), a two-year public technical college that enrolled five hundred students. Women college presidents were quite rare, and Woodie was one of the first to lead a technical school. Not surprisingly, she was very eager to encourage more women to choose aviation as a career. Her strategy to was to go directly to parents and educators of middle and high school-aged children. Woodie also hoped to extend her reach beyond the state of Alabama, as she perceived a broader mission. She proved an effective spokesperson and soon organized a project to write a booklet to encourage girls' interest in aviation and space careers. The project was funded by several Alabama state education organizations and was distributed nationally with the support of the Federal Aviation Administration.

Woodie named Sandra H. Flowers, AATC's director of institutional development, to direct the project and write the text for *Women in Aviation and Space*. Flowers, like many advocates for women's rights, believed the key to reversing sex-role stereotyping was to provide ample role models, historical perspective, and sources for additional information. This approach did not explore the underlying causes of women's invisibility, it only sought to remedy inequity by disseminating information. Thus, the emphasis was on contemporary examples. Twenty women prominent in aviation in the 1980s were featured. Flowers mainly allowed these women to speak for themselves, inserting additional biographical information and career suggestions so that readers could see the various pathways into an aviation career.[1]

However, the FAA and the Alabama Aviation and Technical College were not the only enterprises engaged in such efforts. After eighteen years of tireless effort, the International Women's Air and Space Museum dedicated its new quarters and opened to the public for the first time in the restored Asahel Wright House in Centerville, Ohio, on 6 March 1986. (Today the museum is located in Cleveland, Ohio.) The Smithsonian Institution's National Air and Space Museum undertook a multi-year commitment to publish a set of monographs on the history of U.S. women in aviation (of which this book was originally the fourth volume in the series). Companies began to support special education programs. For example, in 1989 TRW announced the company's intent to make a $1 million donation (over ten years) to support the new California Academy of Mathematics and Science. In particular TRW wanted to encourage the Academy's goal of increasing the enrollment of young girls and minorities. There was an evangelical quality to such projects, in part because extreme conservatives within the dominant political party tended to express outspoken disdain toward the participation of women in the workforce, especially in technology-related disciplines.[2]

The question was: Would such efforts work? Both proponents and opponents were uncertain. Factors beyond the "Culture Wars" would prove critical, including recessions and economic expansion, the extensive military buildup, and military actions in Grenada, Panama, and most especially the Persian Gulf. In short, this era—the final decade of the Cold War—would prove a critical eleven-year period in the history of American women in aviation.

The numbers of women workers in the aircraft industry (including aircraft parts manufacture) increased slowly over the decade. In 1980, women comprised 18.4 percent of the workforce (115,500 women out of a total 633,100). A decade later the industry employed 161,100 women, 23 percent of its 712,300 workers. The space side of the business was more mercurial, with a sudden climb from 24,400 women workers in 1980 to a high of 54,900 in 1987, and then a decline to 48,200 in 1990.[3]

Budget increases and cutbacks caused expansions and contractions in the industry. The early eighties saw record growth. Not only did Congress approve numerous military projects, but in 1983 it approved NASA's plan to build a space station. Sales increased dramatically, and while the country as a whole was experiencing record trade deficits, the aerospace industry reported a backlog of orders, producing a trade surplus. Nonetheless, it was a complicated period. Knowledgeable observers, such as the editors of *Jane's*, characterized the general trend in the American industry as "a struggle to reconcile the need for rationalisation with the demand for competition."[4] Uncle Sam could not afford the level of competition required by regulation, creating a brutal business atmosphere.

In general, however, news accounts of the aerospace industry simply took note of the hirings and firings that followed corporate consolidations as well as the success or failure to win new contracts. For example, in 1986 the *Los Angeles Times* reported that several hundred men and women waited up to three hours in line for an interview and a chance at one of fifteen hundred new positions. Lockheed had just won a big defense contract to build a prototype of the new Advanced Tactical Fighter. By contrast, two days earlier Rockwell International had just laid off ten thousand workers. Between 1986 and 1988, Grumman made two major cutbacks, eliminating eighteen hundred positions. Then in 1988 Fairchild Republic closed its Farmingdale plant, laying off three thousand workers and virtually wiping out the Long Island aerospace industry. But on the West Coast it was just the opposite: business boomed.[5]

Among the engineers and scientists, the number of women was very small. In 1985, only 14.4 percent of all engineering graduates were women.[6] In 1986 Northrop reported that 10–12 percent of its ninety-four hundred college-graduate engineers were women. Of its four hundred new hires that year, eighty-eight (22 percent) were women.[7] Most women engineers went to work in industry. Nelda Lee, a prominent woman engineer today, graduated with a degree in aerospace engineering from Auburn University in 1969, one of only a handful of women in the entire engineering program. She took a job with the newly merged McDonnell Douglas company and by the late 1980s had risen through the ranks to became a senior manager for the F-15 Flight Test Engineering group.

The 1980s also saw a slight increase in the number of women aerospace engineers and scientists hired by universities. For example, Ann Karagozian earned her Ph.D. in 1982 in mechanical engineering from the California Institute of Technology for her study of the fluid mechanics of combustion systems. The number of women earning doctoral degrees in aerospace engineering was infinitesimal. Karagozian, who was considered one of the brightest students in the country, was immediately hired by the Department of Mechanical and Aerospace Engineering at the University of California–Los Angeles, thus beginning a stellar career in research and teaching.[8]

Women engineers did attract attention. It was a demanding profession requiring considerable abilities in mathematics, science, and technology. While women were less likely to be told they should not become engineers because women "cannot do math and science," there were still many who wondered why a woman would want to work in a male-dominated profession regardless of her intellectual abilities. Still, when it came time for special honors or news stories, it was the women engineers who were often singled out. For example, in 1986 Nancy Fitzroy (whose career is described earlier) got considerable press coverage when she became the first (and, as of 2003, *only*) woman president of the American Society of Mechanical Engineers. Not all the stories were positive. LuAnne Beckley's first job assignment at Rockwell International was to an all-male laboratory with no women's restroom. She would ultimately leave the company after being passed over for its management training program.[9]

One of the more dramatic stories came in 1988 when six Democratic members of Congress ordered a General Accounting Office investigation of employment discrimination in the southern California aerospace industry. An article about this investigation in the *Los Angeles Times* quoted James Foster, a volunteer attorney for the Los Angeles chapter of the National Association for the Advancement of Colored People, saying: "They will hire minority people. The problem is advancement and promotion—and it's particularly relevant to black women, because very rarely will an (aerospace) employer have black women supervise white males." While industry representatives argued that the labor pool of highly-skilled women and minority workers was extremely limited, members of the House Subcommittee on Employment Opportunities opined that little progress had been made despite federal mandates on record for more than a decade. "There's no reason why, in all this time, they haven't been able to bring people up to the upper management levels," stated the committee chair, Representative Matthew Martinez.[10]

Martinez and his colleagues hoped to get Hughes Aircraft, TRW, McDonnell Douglas, Rockwell International, General Dynamics, Northrop, Lockheed, and Litton Industries to embrace federal affirmative action requirements more seriously. Combined, these eight firms received 21 percent of *all* federal contract dollars, hence the threat of being barred from obtaining new federal contracts was a serious one (albeit one that companies were hoping would not be quickly or fully enforced if George H.W. Bush succeeded Ronald Reagan as president).[11]

Affirmative action laws did have a profound impact on employment patterns. Even after the Supreme Court suspended affirmative action requirements for contracting in 1989, many government agencies called for voluntary compliance. The Metropolitan Washington Airports Authority noted that even though contractors were no longer legally required to give one-quarter of their business to businesses owned by women and minorities, they expected similar levels of participation in all future bids.[12]

This attitude had been cultivated through the eighties, as federal agencies, even more than contractors, gave significant attention to hiring and promotion of women. The number of women in aviation who worked at government agencies such as the Federal Aviation Administration and the National Aeronautics and Space Administration did increase. Elizabeth Dole was appointed U.S. secretary of transportation in 1983, becoming one of the most influential individuals in American aviation. She had overall responsibility for federal civil aviation programs as well as those in the Coast Guard.

Apart from Dole, astronauts such as Sally Ride, Kathleen Sullivan, Anna Fisher, Rhea Seddon, and Judith Resnik were the most visible women federal employees associated with aerospace. Ride became the first American woman to fly in space in 1983. Trained as a physicist, Ride had a Ph.D. from Stanford. She was a mission specialist, one of a new breed of scientist-astronauts no longer required to be test pilots. However, many of the women astronauts were also pilots. Further, all had the opportunity to fly trainer aircraft. (Later, women who were military pilots would be recruited for "flying" astronaut jobs of pilot and shuttle commander.) The history of the women in the space program is really a story apart from this volume; nonetheless, they have had a major impact upon the motivation and participation of women in aviation. In this way, these first women astronauts served as powerful role models for those women (and especially young girls) who wanted to pursue a career in aviation- or aerospace-related fields.[13]

Women air traffic controllers comprised the single largest group of female federal employees in aviation. The 1980s would prove a pivotal and tumultuous decade for air traffic controllers. Airline deregulation in 1978 had a profound impact on commercial air transportation. Competition was cutthroat as new upstart companies forced the old established airlines to slash fares. Passenger traffic jumped in 1979 from 254 million to 293 million emplanements. Though the numbers would decline to 273 million the following year, the nation's air traffic controllers were very worried about the system's capacity. To draw attention to the problems of old equipment and heavy workloads, controllers orchestrated a series of "slowdowns" that snarled traffic and created hundreds of flight delays in the summer of 1980.[14]

In 1981, the air traffic controllers' union, the Professional Air Traffic Controllers Organization (PATCO), decided to go on strike. PATCO was unusual among labor unions in that it had vigorously supported Ronald Reagan's bid for the presidency and a significant portion of its membership identified itself as Republican. Union leaders had assumed that the administration would be supportive of their efforts to reduce the workload and increase the pay of controllers. It was a grave mistake. Instead of bargaining, the administration decided to initiate its larger political strategy of union busting. When PATCO called for action in August, President Reagan ordered the firing of all striking controllers. Almost 11,400 union members lost their jobs that year. Shocking to most of the controllers was the fact that the American public was not sympathetic to their cause.[15]

The impact of the strike on women was enormous. The firing of almost 70 percent of the air traffic control workforce essentially meant a blank slate. The pressing need to hire new controllers meant that any prejudices against hiring women had to be set aside.[16] Thus, the early eighties were an especially hopeful period for advocates of women in technical positions. None were more hopeful than Jacqueline Smith and Sue Mostert, who had founded the Professional Women Controllers (PWC) in 1979.

PWC originated as a dream of Smith and Mostert when they met at the

FAA Academy in 1968. There were many problems faced by women in this profession, principally because of their isolation. There were so few women that typically a female controller found herself to be either the first or the only woman at a given location. Smith and Mostert wanted to create an organization for women air traffic controllers that could break down the barriers of isolation by serving as a network of communication. PWC was not a union and was never intended to compete with the union functions of PATCO. (As a result, while PWC's membership was affected by the 1981 strike—which had led to the disbanding of PATCO—the federal government did not force PWC to break up.) The goal of PWC was to help women realize their full potential in the profession through education, communication, and support. PWC supported both the FAA and the new air traffic controllers union in efforts to recruit women and, in turn, received the endorsement of these organizations.[17]

The necessity for PWC was underscored by the case of Deborah Katz. Katz passed the air traffic controller test in 1972 and was assigned to the FAA's center in Leesburg, Virginia, to begin her apprenticeship. From 1977 to 1980, she was the only woman at the Leesburg facility. Subjected to daily verbal abuse, she appealed to her supervisor. Instead of support, her supervisor, John J. Sullivan, suggested she have sex with another male controller who she had rebuffed when approached for a date. Katz lost her case because the judge ruled that she had failed to prove the harassment was intentional. In 1983, the federal appeals court overturned the ruling. The 4th Circuit Court of Appeals ruled that an employer had an obligation to stop harassment; beyond having a written policy, employers had to enforce it. Katz suffered both personal and professional losses as a consequence of pursuing legal action (and she was among those who lost their jobs in the 1981 strike), but she felt the struggle was worthwhile. Her lawyer told reporters that *Katz v Dole* would become a landmark case, helping improve the workplace environment for women and men.[18]

Over the course of the decade, there were some signs of improvement. The system of training controllers came under scrutiny. Critics felt that the requirement that all future controllers attend the FAA Academy in Oklahoma City was one reason the FAA had difficulties recruiting women and minorities. The entering class in the fall of 1991 was 30 percent women and 16.5 percent minorities (of 673 students), but the nationwide force of controllers was still 92 percent male and 88 percent white. A new decentralized training system was proposed and the FAA began to certify a handful of schools around the country to begin training programs. While the main reason for this initiative was to save the government money (students now had to pay for their training), it was reported that one of the FAA's objectives was "to produce a diverse population of controllers."[19]

On the surface, it appeared that attitudes toward women in aviation had changed. In addition to new recruiting efforts, public relations officers reconfigured their practices over the decade. Corporate publications and news releases demonstrated new sensitivity toward the inclusion of women and minorities. The women pictured were tokens. In some instances the images did help women become more permanently integrated and accepted in a predominantly male workforce; in others (especially within the military) it exacerbated tensions. American news reporters viewed "women" as a "good" story—a "new" angle—and voraciously gobbled up the story "ops" (opportunities) given to them by the public-relations types.

Particularly attractive were stories about women in the military. The attraction was the inherent controversy these accounts engendered. Few groups had cheered more loudly after the election of Ronald Reagan than the members of the U.S. military. In was common knowledge that most military leaders despised Jimmy Carter. They claimed that the Carter administration's policies had been ruinous, leaving the nation with a "hollow force." Though women accounted for less than 10 percent of the armed forces in 1980, particular venom was reserved for policies that had expanded the opportunities for women in the military. There was a widespread perception that the military was becoming feminized, in part because of the high profile of a small number of women who were just graduating from the service academies and women military pilots. Military planners and strategists were concerned that women would adversely affect troop cohesion and thereby diminish combat effectiveness.[20]

The laws and policies prohibiting women from flying aircraft in combat remained in effect throughout the decade. What constituted "combat flying" was a subject of continuous debate, as was the scale and scope of women's participation in military aviation. Shaping this debate was a conflict faced by military leaders who wanted to expand the military force but knew such growth would be impossible without resorting to a draft. Experience since the 1973 creation of the All Volunteer Force (AVF) had proven that only by recruiting women could any of the services meet their enlistment goals. Even those who were not enthusiastic about women soldiers balked at the high number of male high school dropouts (50 percent for the Army in 1980) that had to be accepted in order to maintain (let alone expand) the size of the military. In the end, even those who had been most opposed conceded that women were both necessary and useful. Critical to that change were the efforts of a few hundred women military pilots.[21]

From the strident tone of the debate it would be easy to assume that the numbers of women military pilots were substantial. In 1985, the Marines had no women pilots (4,132 men); the Navy had 10 women pilots (1,120 men); the

Lieutenant Mary Jorgenson, a pilot with Fighter Squadron 126 (VF-126) points out some of the rear seat cockpit controls to Midshipman Cindy Mason. Naval ROTC students taking a one-week aviation training program got to take a demonstration ride in a TA-4. *Courtesy of the U.S. Defense Visual Information Center.*

Air Force had 274 women pilots (18,131 men); and the Army had 314 women pilots (14,582 men). The 598 women constituted 1.55 percent of all military pilots. In 1990, there were 779 women pilots (1.8 percent) and 42,502 men pilots.[22] It was often asserted that national defense was being compromised because less-qualified women displaced more competent men from pilot jobs. The claims were specious for, even if true in some instances, the number of women pilots was statistically insignificant.

Because the prejudice was so virulent, advocates for women military aviators kept close tabs on their performance and were quick to highlight an initial ("first") meritorious accomplishment. The Women's Research and Education Institute (WREI) became one of the most influential public policy organizations to study women in the military. Under the leadership of Carolyn Becraft and with the support of the George Gund Foundation, the Ford Foundation, and du Pont de Nemours and Company, WREI's "Women in the Military" project carefully documented the progress and problems faced by women in the service. Likewise, Professor Linda Grant De Pauw, a noted military historian and feminist scholar at George Washington University, expanded her schol-

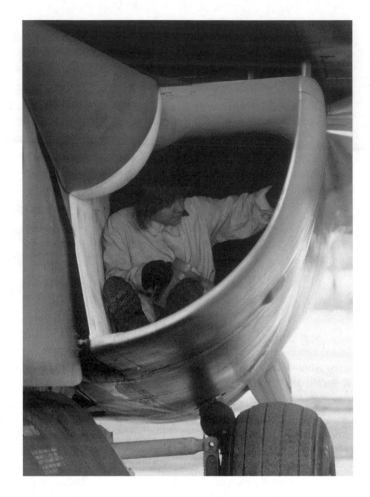

A ground crew chief inspects the intake of an F-111A aircraft.
Courtesy of the U.S. Defense Visual Information Center.

arly and publishing efforts in this field to form the Minerva Center. Together
with the Defense Advisory Committee on Women in the Services (DACOWITS),
WREI and the Minerva Center would become the key data repositories and
important loci of advocacy for women in military aviation.

At first, the flying jobs open to women in the military were quite restricted.
The Coast Guard, which was under the Department of Transportation in peace-
time, allowed women to pursue any aviation career path without restriction.
All of the other services established quotas. However, there was no consistency

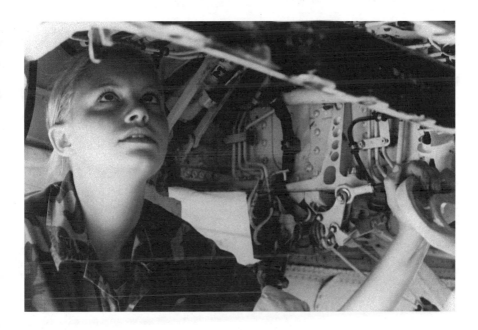

Lance Corporal Regina Martin checks the condition of her aircraft. Martin is a plane captain with the Marine Light Attack Squadron 223 (VMA-223). *Courtesy of the U.S. Defense Visual Information Center.*

among the different branches. Identical aircraft or jobs could be open to women in one branch of the service and closed in another. Study after study was commissioned. Outright prejudice was often disguised with the language of troop cohesion. Everyone agreed that men and women were different physically and socially; there was no agreement as to what (if any) implications those differences should have on national defense preparations and practices. This created a particularly challenging environment for women military aviators, but it did not squelch their determination.

Over the decade, women military aviators fought for more numerous and varied flying assignments. There were a number of important milestones. One was the Navy's 1982 decision to allow women pilots in the jet pipeline to become "carrier qualified" (trained to land on an aircraft carrier). Another milestone was Colleen Nevius's 1983 graduation from the Navy's test pilot school at Patuxent River, Maryland. When Nevius graduated from high school ten years earlier in 1973, the Navy had just admitted its first women pilots. She knew this was the career for her. Nevius received a full Navy ROTC scholarship at Purdue. After graduation she started Aviation Officer Candidate School in Pensacola,

The first Air Force all-female crew to fly an overseas mission. From left to right: Captain Giuliana Sangiorgio, aircraft commander; Captain Barbara Akins, first pilot; First Lieutenant Terri Ollinger, copilot; Technical Sergeant Donna Wertz, flight engineer; Staff Sergeant Denise Meunier, flight engineer; Sergeant Mary Eiche, loadmaster; and Airman First Class Bernadette Botti. They made the flight in May 1983. *Courtesy of the U.S. Defense Visual Information Center.*

Florida, in 1977. Women were still not allowed to fly jets in the Navy, so she entered the helicopter pipeline. Nevius earned her Wings of Gold and began flying. Ambitious and talented, Nevius soon set her sights on Pax River.[23]

The work of a test pilot is especially demanding, and graduates are considered among the most elite. The NASA requirement that the Mercury astronauts be test pilots had added special luster to the profession. Nevius did not experience any setbacks (other than the normal frustrations shared by all trainees) and was well respected among her peers. She gave considerable credit to the officers on the selection board. From her perspective, they took as much of a risk as she did.[24]

Though no one stated it explicitly, it was clearly understood that Nevius's success would not only open the doors at Pax River to women but also the doors to many other aviation specialties. Just prior to Nevius's graduation in June, the *New York Times* ran an article headlined "Women See Gain as Pilots." In the early eighties, each branch of the service sought public attention for

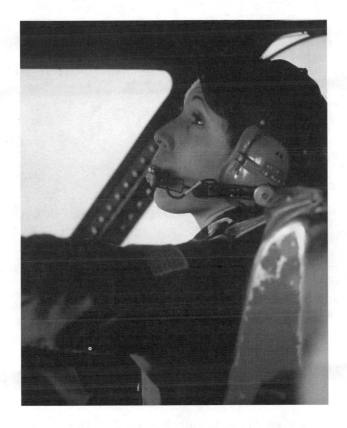

Captain Barbara Akins served as copilot during the landing of a C-141 medevac aircraft at Lajes Field, Azores. She was part of the first all-female flight crew to fly an overseas mission of a C-141 from McGuire Air Force Base, New Jersey, to Rhein-Main Air Base, West Germany. *Courtesy of the U.S. Defense Visual Information Center.*

flights made with all-women crews, and the *Times* was reporting on the first transatlantic military cargo flight with its seven member female crew. Both Captain Giuliana Sangiorgio and her copilot, First Lieutenant Terri Ollinger, expressed optimism that both the number of opportunities for women and their total numbers would continue to increase, although neither woman thought the process would be easy.[25]

Peacetime publicity/recruitment missions proved much easier to orchestrate than combat operations. In the 1980s and early 1990s, the United States took military action in Lebanon, Grenada, Nicaragua, Libya, Panama, and the Persian Gulf. Each successive action tested the military's deployment strategies

Captain Mary Collier is an aircraft structural engineer for the Air Force. She is listening for stress cracks in the wings of an F-111 aircraft. *Courtesy of the U.S. Defense Visual Information Center.*

with regard to women. Not every military job included the possibility of direct hostile contact with an enemy. The Army, for example, introduced the Direct Combat Probability Coding System in 1983. A job coded P1 had the highest probability of engaging in combat, whereas P7 had the lowest. Women were not allowed to serve in jobs rated P1.

In theory, the purpose of these systems was to maximize the opportunities for women. In practice, the process of creating and implementing them sometimes codified and reinforced discriminatory practices and attitudes. Almost everyone in the military found these systems complex and sometimes cumbersome. They were also *new*. A tradition-bound institution, the military found that adjustment to new practices and policies did not come easily. Among the lower ranks, the changes felt "imposed," and under these circumstances it is not surprising that women became the targets of blame. The U.S. military is most inclusive when the risk to life and limb is greatest and the career benefits of service lowest; and it is most exclusive when the circumstances are reversed, observed the political scientist Judith Hicks Stiehm.[26]

According to all the laws, policies, and regulations, women pilots were not allowed to fly missions to Grenada (Operation Urgent Fury) until U.S. control of the island had been achieved. Nonetheless, women were involved. Susan Cunningham flew six C-141 supply missions for the Air Force. Celeste Hayes, also a C-141 pilot, delivered troops from the Army's 82nd Airborne in South Carolina to Salinas Airfield on Grenada. As Cunningham described it: "women are going to be launched before they realize the women are launched."[27] In Panama, three women Army helicopter pilots would be nominated for the Air Medal because of their performance when their craft came under fire. Lieutenant Lisa Kutschera, Warrant Officer Debra Mann, and Warrant Officer Caryl Newberry had not been assigned to combat missions, but in the course of their duties each experienced enemy fire while operating their helicopters.[28]

The medals provoked some controversy. Ribbons and medals matter in the military because they are visible symbols of one's professional and personal accomplishments. Neither women nor men sought these small scraps of colored fabric and metal for their own sake, but they remained essential for career advancement. Women were painfully aware that the policies that "protected" them and reduced their exposure to danger would also necessarily limit their careers. When questions arose as to whether or not the recipients actually deserved this recognition, it served to reinvigorate the debate about whether women should participate at all. Women in the military found themselves frustrated. They abhorred the idea that they might be benefitting from some kind of "affirmative action" effort, and at the same time they also believed that the legitimacy of the awards given to men was rarely publically questioned.

It was not news to women in military aviation that they were treated differently from men. Most felt that change would occur, albeit slowly, if women continued to show excellent performance on the job. Like most men in military aviation, the women also believed that it was also a matter of having the right combination of mental toughness, determination, skill, and luck. By "luck," most women meant not having unwanted attention: sexual harassment, accusations of lesbianism, or too much press for simply doing her job. The latter was the most pernicious because it directly affected troop cohesion. It was hard to prove you were a team player if you were always being pulled out for a photo opportunity or media interview or if a "three-star" (a lieutenant general or vice admiral) reviewed your every promotion. When women tried to come together to discuss these problems, they received still further criticism.

Some women came to believe that only through collective action—from the inside—would it be possible to make real progress. This insight came from a previous generation of women military pilots, the WASP. Following the successful legislative battle to win veteran's recognition for the women who served in the Women's Airforce Service Pilots during World War II, the board of the

WASP decided it was vital to reach out to the new generation of women. In 1978, they voted to form a new organization for any woman who had ever served as a military pilot. The Women Military Pilots Association (WMPA) was incorporated in the Commonwealth of Massachusetts and Bernice "Bee" Haydu, who was then the president of the WASP, became the new group's first president. For the first four years, the WASP nurtured the group. In 1982, the Women Military Pilots Association's board of directors met with two active duty women who had been trying to form a similar group. The WASP happily turned over the reins, and Captain Barbara Brumme (now Garwood) became the first active duty president. In 1988 the WMPA changed its name to Women Military Aviators and expanded its membership to include navigators.[29]

At biennial conventions in Indianapolis (1983), San Antonio (1985), Colorado Springs (1987), Washington (1989), and Sacramento (1991), the women began to forge vital bonds across ranks and the services. The women made many eye-opening discoveries concerning which jobs were open to women (i.e., a job that was closed to women in the Navy might be open in the Air Force). The group exerted a powerful influence on its membership. No longer isolated, the women gained new perspectives and a willingness to take risks. Some of the most influential women in military aviation attribute their professional maturation and activism to this group. ·

Chief among them was Rosemary Mariner, arguably the most historically significant woman in American aviation since Amelia Earhart and Jacqueline Cochran. Mariner was different from most young girls in the 1950s and 1960s; from the time she was very small and throughout her childhood Mariner *knew* she wanted to be a pilot. Hindsight might suggest that this was her way of coming to know her father, an Air Force pilot killed in an aircraft accident when she was three, but her precociousness and the intensity with which she pursued the dream went well beyond simplistic psychological explanations. She read books about aviation and spent much of her free time watching the jets take off and land at Miramar Naval Air Station. She started flying lessons in high school, cleaning houses and washing airplanes at Gillispie and Lindbergh Fields to help support her quest. She earned her ticket at seventeen and headed off to Purdue University, the school that had hired Amelia Earhart to be an advisor to women students four decades earlier.[30]

Mariner was among the first to enter Purdue's new professional aviation degree program. Though her mother and the Catholic nuns who taught her in high school had all encouraged her ambitions to be a pilot, most in the aviation profession did not. Several representatives from airlines told Mariner during campus visits that they would not hire a woman pilot. In the fall of 1972, her mother sent her a news clipping that reported the Navy's decision to open pilot

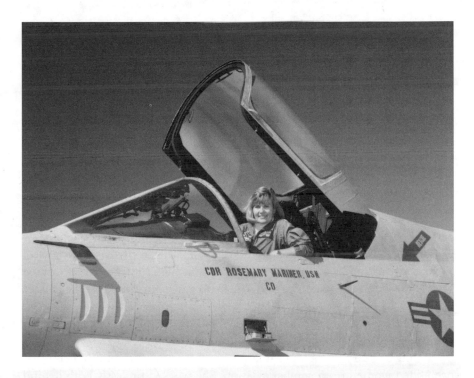

Rosemary Mariner has become one of the most influential figures in the recent history of women in military aviation. *Courtesy of Rosemary Mariner.*

training to women. Mariner immediately went to speak with the Navy recruiter on campus as well as her dean. Unbeknownst to Mariner at the time, the Navy had hoped to select a small group of eight women who were already commissioned officers. Unsuccessful in filling all eight slots in this manner, they decided to admit civilian women. Mariner was told she would be one of them if she was able to graduate by January. Mariner had been already pushing hard to finish her education as quickly as possible, and Purdue officials decided to help her "make history" and agreed to award Mariner her degree in December 1972. Two weeks later she was on her way to Newport, Rhode Island, to attend the Navy's Officer Candidate's School for women. In May 1973, she received her commission and immediately went to Pensacola, Florida, to begin her flight training.[31]

Mariner earned her wings and began her career as a Navy pilot. She found that though she shared the same passion for the Navy, the same ambitions and the same high standards as her male colleagues, her career path was much more constrained. "Put a wall in front of me and my reaction is to knock it down," is the way Mariner would describe her approach to her career. If grades had been the only criteria, Mariner would have been a jet pilot right from the start, she would have made regular sea-duty tours, and she would have accumulated the necessary assignments to become eligible for the highest Navy posts. Through the 1980s, Mariner would accumulate her share of firsts, including the first woman military pilot to fly a tactical jet (an A-4 Skyhawk) and the first woman to be an executive officer and then commanding officer of an operational air squadron (VAQ-34).[32]

Mariner was an exceptionally bold officer. Cerebral and an avid student of history, she also had an activist bent. As her career progressed, she found herself in the late 1980s reflecting on larger matters, such as the fundamental causes of gender discrimination. Mariner began reading and accumulating documents. She attended DACOWITS (Defense Advisory Committee on Women in the Services) meetings and went to meetings of the Women Military Pilots Association. "What were women's rights and responsibilities as citizens?" she mused. "Would the nation be stronger if its military was better integrated? If women were allowed to serve in combat?" Mariner became convinced that the answer was *yes*.

For Mariner, the Gulf War was a watershed event both personally and for women in the military. She, Kelly Hamilton, and Trish Beckman became leaders among military women pushing for an end to the laws and policies that prohibited women from combat aviation. She worked tirelessly both behind the scenes and in front of the camera. Although Mariner was still on active duty and therefore prohibited from lobbying Congress, she made sure the members knew the facts. She and the other leaders of the Women Military Aviators (formerly the Women Military Pilots Association) also made sure that other women in military aviation understood how laws were made and the stakes of this particular debate. Hers was a forceful presence, and by the time of her retirement in 1997 Mariner had become one of the nation's leading advocates for equal opportunity in the military. She continues to speak and write on this subject in addition to university teaching.[33]

On the civilian side, women airline pilots encountered many experiences similar to those of their counterparts in the military. Unlike the situation in the military, however, these women's participation was not forbidden by law (or policy), and while sexism and other forms of discrimination were very real, these women's accounts are decidedly upbeat. Airline deregulation in 1978 changed the way passengers traveled to their destinations. Instead of nonstop flights in lightly loaded craft, the new hub-and-spoke system funneled passengers from numerous regional locations into a small number of major terminals (hubs). Passengers did not favor the smaller commuter planes on which they

Trish Beckman was one of the Navy's first women navigators to qualify as a naval flight officer and attend test pilot school. Among her many achievements, she was the first woman to qualify as a crew member of the F-15. She is one of the leading advocates for women in military aviation and a major leader within the Women Military Aviators organization. *Courtesy of Patricia Beckman.*

were being forced to travel (although cheaper airfares mitigated some grumbling), but the change had significant implications for women airline pilots.

Seniority as much as prejudice could keep women out of the pilot ranks, but as regional airlines formed to shuttle passengers in the new fuel-efficient commuter aircraft, job opportunities opened for women.[34] Likewise, the rise of overnight package delivery services created similar opportunities for women who wanted to fly for companies such as Federal Express (today, FedEx), United Parcel Service, or Flying Tigers.

The experience of women employed by these new companies was often different. Lynn Rippelmeyer, reflecting on her experience at PEOPLExpress, noted that: "We're all the same age and most of the guys were hired after I was. I'm the senior person. I'm the captain. I'm in charge. Most of them, I'd say 90 percent of the men, have wives that work, so they're used to a professional woman and a professional woman's attitude, problems, and view on life. I'm not the foreign species that I was to a lot of those other guys [at other airlines]. Even the military men have dealt with women peers. So it's not like somebody changed the rules on them and they were angry about it as I think some were a few years ago."[35]

Patrice Clarke's is a good example of the typical career path followed by women in the 1980s. Clarke (now Clarke-Washington) was born and raised in Nassau, Bahamas, in a family of girls. Her mother encouraged her interest in becoming a pilot, a dream stimulated by frequent family trips by airplane to Miami. Clarke attended Embry-Riddle, one of the nation's top professional aviation colleges. After graduation, she returned to the Bahamas to fly for Trans Island Airways and Bahamasair. In 1988, UPS hired her as a flight engineer. When she earned her captain's stripes in 1994, Clarke became the first black female captain of a major airline. She had just married Ray Glenn Washington, a captain for American Airlines; so her promotion to the left seat made them the only black flying couple both serving as captains.[36]

Around the time she was promoted to captain, Clarke described herself as becoming more conscious of the effects of sexism and racism. In one news interview, she stated: "I never realized it was even an issue because I'd been flying in the Bahamas, where race was not the big deal it is here. But when UPS hired me, people started making me aware that I could be making history."[37] Clarke became active in the Organization of Black Airline Pilots. The group had a dual agenda of providing support for its members and outreach to encourage minorities to pursue an aviation career. It offered Clarke some perspective on the issue of race. She believed acceptance was a function of time as well as competent performance: "It takes time. Not that it's right, not that it's acceptable, but it's just the way it is." She went on to explain: "Most of the discrimination is extremely subtle. For the most part, I've never had anyone come to me and say, 'You are female and/or you are black; therefore, you can't do this. I'm not going to treat you well.' But based on my experience and the experiences of other people, I know that I was mistreated. Fortunately for me, I went on about my business and did what I wanted to do."[38]

Women often discovered that the strength to maintain this attitude of professionalism emanated from support groups. The group ISA+21, International Society of Women Airline Pilots, formed in 1978 when twenty-one women

United Parcel Service pilot Patrice Clarke gets ready for a flight. Clarke was hired by UPS in 1988. *Photo by Carolyn Russo, National Air and Space Museum, Smithsonian Institution.*

pilots met in Las Vegas and agreed on the need for a social and support organization. All of these women were members of pilots unions, and they did not want to compete with the union responsibility to represent their professional needs. What they wanted was a group to share stories with. Bonnie Tiburzi, the first woman pilot for American Airlines, included an entire chapter in her 1984 autobiography *Takeoff!* on the importance of this organization. "I was enchanted," she wrote, "I listened and talked as if in a dream, or as if having finally awakened." The most lasting and important impression of her first ISA meeting, held in 1979, was a "new sense of belonging."[39]

ISA was not a "professional" organization (its stated goal was to be a social organization), but its members had a strong sense of history. They kept records, beginning with a compilation of a master seniority list of women airline pilots. One new member, Lori Legat Griffith, would become an especially key figure. Griffith's interest in history led her to encourage ISA to support museums and writers doing projects on women in aviation. She formed a particularly fruitful collaboration with Henry Holden, an aviation writer who would become one of the nation's leading chroniclers of women in aviation. In 1991, Holden and Griffith published *Ladybirds: The Untold Story of Women Pilots in America*, a compilation of hundreds of biographies and descriptions of important organizations. Among other things, Griffith helped gather material on more than two dozen women airline pilots, making their book the first significant documentation of women in the airline pilot profession.[40]

The number of women with airline transport pilot ratings rose from 480 in 1980 to 2,082 in 1990. (Not every pilot with this rating has a job with the airlines, however.)[41] Scrutiny of the ISA Master Seniority List shows that a real boom in hiring started in 1983. This was due largely to the general improvement in the airline business and an increase in passenger air travel. However, law suits, court settlements, and affirmative action policies also had an important effect.

For example, United Airlines was required by a 1976 court settlement to increase substantially its efforts to recruit minorities and women as pilots. An *Atlanta Journal and Constitution* article in 1993 noted that United had the highest percentages of minority and women pilots (US Airways was second).[42] Gail Gorski was the first woman hired by United (January 8, 1978); of the forty-eight women hired by various U.S. airline companies in 1978, United hired the most: fourteen. But it would take another nine years for United to hire a woman of color. Shirley Tyus had been a United Airlines flight attendant since 1972. She earned a pilot's license in 1979 and worked part-time as a pilot for Wheeler Airlines, a black-owned company, but she was still a flight attendant. In 1987, United hired Tyus as a Boeing 727 flight engineer. At the time, it was thought she was the third black woman to become an airline pilot.[43]

It is important to note that the word "minority" is not synonymous with "black" or "African American." However, this characterization generally reflected the understanding in the industry during this period. Careful study of the records does not reveal whether or not women of any other racial or ethnic background were hired during this period. For all minority women, the barriers to entry were high. Prejudice was a major factor, but so too was economics. Learning to fly and accumulating enough hours to apply for an airline job was very expensive. Further, where you lived mattered. Flying lessons were offered at small or regional airports, often removed from minority population concentrations and rarely tied to any public transit system.

Once hired, regardless of race, few airlines made any formal efforts to integrate women pilots into their workforce. The seniority system ruled, leaving it up to women to figure out strategies of "assimilation." The most common meth-

ods involved cultivation of "father-daughter" or "student-teacher" type relationships. However, these techniques worked best if the individuals shared common racial and socio-economic backgrounds. The fact that the majority of
men joined the airlines after military service (an option only recently available
to women) was a big gap to bridge. Almost all women airline pilots in this
period make explicit reference to the need to demonstrate their technical proficiency in order to obtain the most basic collegial acceptance.

This was also true for most professional women pilots. Charlotte Larson,
the second woman pilot for the U.S. Forest Service, once received a letter of
tribute from another woman pilot: "I don't know you, but I think I owe my job
to you. The man who hired me was so impressed by your professionalism that
he was convinced a woman could do this job."[44] Larson flew fire-fighting as
well as aerial photography missions throughout the western part of the United
States. Likewise, Gayle Ranney, a bush pilot in Alaska, believes her greatest com-
pliment is that no one has refused to fly with her simply because she happens
to be a woman. When she was interviewed in 1981, there were about 400 female bush pilots in Alaska (out of 10,500), a job which required a certain brash-
ness and sense of adventure.[45]

As Larson's and Ranney's careers suggest, there were other careers for
women interested in aviation. Small businesses continue to employ women as
bush pilots, as agricultural aviation pilots, and in a host of jobs at small airports and fixed-base operations across the United States. Agricultural aviation
is an area where women are both pilots and educators. Many states have agricultural aviation organizations for women who are in, or affiliated with, the
profession. Several women helicopter pilots operate crop-dusting businesses.

An increasing number of women are following the example of Olive Ann
Beech, the premier woman entrepreneur in American aviation. Dr. Nydia
Meyers, president and chief stockholder of the Al Meyers Airport Corporation
in Tecumseh, Michigan, was an active pilot and a member of the Ninety-Nines,
the Aircraft Owners and Pilots Association, and the Experimental Aircraft Association. Dr. Meyers had an equally successful career in scientific and medical
research, publishing numerous papers and teaching college classes. But as co-
owner with her husband, Al Meyers, of a thriving airport in Tecumseh, she
played a major role as a general aviation advocate in the state of Michigan.[46]

More women in the 1980s were flight instructors than airport owners, however. Women could be found teaching at almost every airport in the United
States; they were sufficiently prevalent that their sex became less likely to be
commented on. An article about Morgan Greschel (now Reeb) of Virginia, one
of Janelle Aviation's two assistant flight instructors, highlighted her many accomplishments in general aviation. What the author saw as unusual about

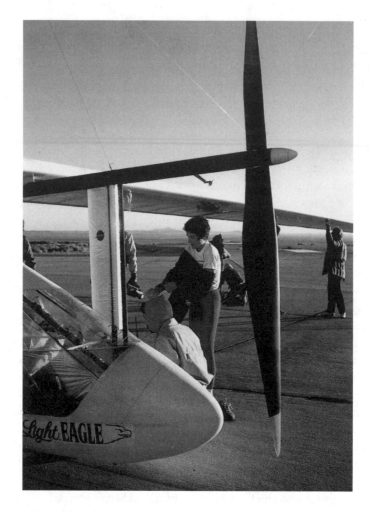

Lois McCallin prepares for her world record human-powered distance flight in January 1987 at NASA Dryden. *Author's collection.*

Greschel's accomplishments of two thousand flight hours, an FAA Gold Seal Instructor award, and a variety of flying ratings was not her sex but rather her youth. Greschel was only twenty-five.[47]

Although women were very active in general aviation, during this decade the number of women general aviation pilots diminished. For example, women held 26,006 student and 21,554 private pilot's licenses in 1980. Ten years later, those numbers were 15,007 and 17,301, respectively. The change was worrisome to many women in aviation, in part because the visibility of women had never been greater. Jeana Yeager made history and all the front pages in 1986 when she and Dick Rutan piloted the *Voyager* in the first nonstop round-the-world flight. Yeager was the first woman to receive American aviation's highest award, the Collier Trophy. Lois McCallin set records in 1987 as a test pilot for the MIT Daedalus Human-Powered Flight Project. Women built and exhibited aircraft shown at the Experimental Aircraft Association's annual summer Oshkosh Fly-In. One woman served on the ground crew of the Goodyear blimp *Columbia*.[48]

Women still flew competitively, although the popularity of air racing was diminishing. The All Women's International Air Race was still run, but for the Ninety-Nines the major event had become the Precision Flying Competition. In November 1981, Janet Green, president of the Ninety-Nines, signed the resolution that gave the Ninety-Nines sole responsibility for sponsorship, training, and organization of the U.S. Precision Flight Team, as well as management of the regional and national meets. In 1985 the Ninety-Nines hosted the sixth World Precision Flight Team Championship at Kissimmee, Florida.

Precision flying was not the only activity in which the Ninety-Nines were involved. They continued to support the National Intercollegiate Flying Association and undertake humanitarian projects, such as "Blood Flights," the delivery of donated blood from urban centers to rural communities. Perhaps their most important work related to aerospace education. Former international president Hazel Jones constantly advocated this effort, both internally and externally. Jones believed that an understanding of the past coupled with an awareness of new pioneers are the twin sources of inspiration for future success. In 1982 the Ninety-Nines joined the National Congress on Aerospace Education. The general belief was that aviation was vital to the economy. It was critical to encourage popular understanding as well as to encourage young people to consider aerospace careers. The Ninety-Nines wanted to ensure a strong advocacy for the enlarged participation of girls and women.[49]

It is not a coincidence that while the organization's membership was only about sixty-five hundred, many of the women who were active in positions of responsibility and power in the aviation world were also Ninety-Nines; examples include Dr. Dora Strother, manager of human factors engineering and cockpit arrangement at Bell Helicopter Textron; Carol Rayburn, manager of the FAA's General Aviation and Commercial Divisions; and Jean Ross Howard (now Howard-Phelan), director of Helicopter Activities, Aerospace Industries Association, and the Whirly-Girls executive director. Ninety-Nines tended to be women of action, ambition, and excellent stories. Because they took their inspiration from each other, they had great faith in the mentor model of encour-

Jean Tinsley earned her helicopter rating in 1965 and joined both the Whirly-Girls and the Ninety-Nines. She has served both organizations with distinction and achieved success in many flying competitions. As the directing NAA official for the XV-15 world record flights, she took the opportunity to become the first woman to pilot the Bell Helicopter Textron Tilt Rotor. *From the collection of Jean K. Tinsley; courtesy of Bell Helicopter Textron, Inc.*

aging other women to pursue aviation, and through this decade they showed great (if sometimes naive) determination.

However, fortitude and merit were not enough to guarantee women's advancement in the workforce. In the eighties, the phrases "glass ceiling" and "mommy track" entered the American vocabulary. The public debates about the place of women in American society were intense. Was it true that women managers were more expensive than men? Why so few female CEOs, even in fields where there were plenty of women in the pipeline? Women in aviation reflected the same range of opinions as the American public when it came to questions about whether mothers should work. However, most felt that if women chose to work then the glass ceiling was only likely to be shattered by proving competence and through careful networking. Analysts quickly sensed a more complicated reality; factors such as irrational gender discrimination had to be considered.[50]

Women who worked as flight attendants were different. Like the analysts, they understood that relying on oversimplified interpretations about the "working woman" would not yield meaningful change. But they had a different perspective on the problem. The women who led the various flight attendant unions had considerable executive power. When the largest union, the Association of Flight Attendants (representing approximately one-half of all flight attendants) decided to affiliate with the Airline Pilots Association in 1981, the decision proved to be hugely contentious. Up until that point, the flight attendant unions were managed by women. They feared a fast takeover by male executives and a fundamental change in the character of their organization. They feared the glass ceiling, not because it existed, but because they thought it would become a factor.

Anticipating that airline executives in the 1980s would ask employee groups to bear the brunt of cutbacks in this new era of deregulation, flight attendants perceived themselves as the most vulnerable of all the airline employee groups. To help minimize this, the flight attendants began to further redefine their job. For example, they sought to make safety be the emphasis in training school, particularly the handling of potentially catastrophic situations such as accidents or terrorist attacks. The flight attendant unions knew that the airlines wanted their passengers to be comfortable and have a sense of well-being. The earliest flight attendants had been nurses. Over time the airlines had adopted a strategy of distraction in order to soothe nervous flyers. In the 1980s flight attendants wanted to make sure that both the airlines and the traveling public understood that it was skill, not sex appeal, that qualified an individual to be a member of this profession. To that end, educational requirements increased, with some airlines beginning to require a college degree.[51]

The flight attendants' struggles during the decade did not make news headlines, however. What really caught the public's attention were images of teary-eyed children clutching flags and waving goodbye to Soldier Mom in the fall of 1990. The military had expected public outrage when confronted with the news of female prisoners of war or casualties; to the surprise of many there was virtually none. Americans had sat mesmerized in front of their televisions watching soldiers from the United States and its allies wage war against Iraq. The cameras captured Scuds and Smart Bombs, Pentagon briefings, amazingly detailed depictions of troop activities, and *women*. The participation of more than thirty-three thousand women in almost every aspect of Operation Desert Storm was one of the war's major stories.[52]

The "Mommy War" made excellent copy. Major Susan Alderson always thought it would be her husband who would go to war. He was an Army Ranger;

To further enhance the status of the flight attendant, in the 1980s United Airlines adopted a new uniform similar to the business attire of its customers. *From the Association of Flight Attendants Collection; courtesy of United Airlines.*

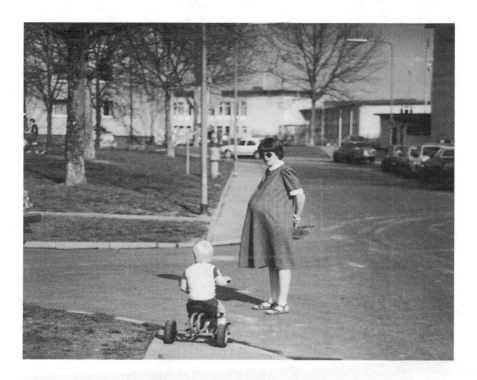

Connie Reeves graduated from the Army's helicopter flight school in 1980. She is shown here wearing a military maternity uniform. In an earlier era, the military discharged pregnant women, but in the 1980s two-career military families became increasingly common. *Courtesy of Connie L. Reeves.*

she was an Army nurse. In a *Boston Globe* article, Alderson expressed her surprise when an entirely different set of orders were issued: "Sure I am a modern woman, a professional, but I have to admit it came as a shock, a real, real role reversal. Here was Mommy going off to war. And there was Daddy packing her rucksack. Fred was so nervous he repacked it six times."[53]

The real story concerned the performance of the women. The Army had deployed twenty-six thousand women to the Gulf (the other branches of the services deployed far fewer: Air Force, thirty-eight hundred; Navy, twenty-five hundred; Marines, one thousand), making this conflict the first large-scale test of the All Volunteer Force. Were women the "weak link"? The nature of media coverage encouraged Americans to come to a new conclusion. Modern news coverage emphasized the individual; from the short "Merry Christmas, Mom and Dad!" clips that punctuated television coverage of sporting events to more detailed interviews on CNN and the major networks. Although women only

A Navy plane captain on the flight line. *Courtesy of the U.S. Defense Visual Information Center.*

comprised about 6 percent of the total troops deployed, they got nearly equal coverage. This fact would be critical to policy changes proposed after the war.[54]

For women pilots, the most common Gulf War experience would be flying support missions. Eva Rodriguez Koller's experience was typical for the Army. Koller had enlisted in the Army right out of high school in 1981. In addition to earning a bachelor's degree in professional aeronautics from Embry-Riddle, she also graduated from flight school. She was appointed a warrant officer in 1988 and started flying UH-1 Iroquois ("Huey") helicopters. In Desert Storm/Shield she flew VIPs and crews shooting historical film footage. Though most flights were administrative or logistical in nature, Koller logged nearly two hundred hours of "imminent danger and combat time" as a pilot-in-command and was awarded an Air Medal for service.[55]

Commander Lucy Young had served seven years active duty and another seven years in the Naval Reserve when the Navy gave her a twenty-four-day assignment to fly C-9Bs carrying passengers and cargo in the European/Middle East theater. The Gulf War was the largest airlift operation since the Berlin blockade, and even operating at full capacity the active duty command could not meet the demand. Not only were Guard and Reserve squadrons activated, but

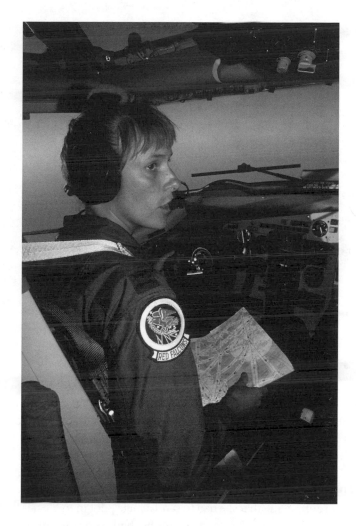

Captain Katarina Bentler pilots a KC-135 Stratotanker on a refueling mission during Operation Desert Shield. *Courtesy of the U.S. Defense Visual Information Center.*

for the first time in history the Civil Reserve Air Fleet as well. Young's missions were part of the "aluminum bridge" between the United States and the Saudi peninsula.

She flew two missions to Jedda, Saudi Arabia, in support of Desert Shield. The Naval Reservists flying these C-9 missions found themselves operating in an imperfect environment. They lacked training, such as chemical- and

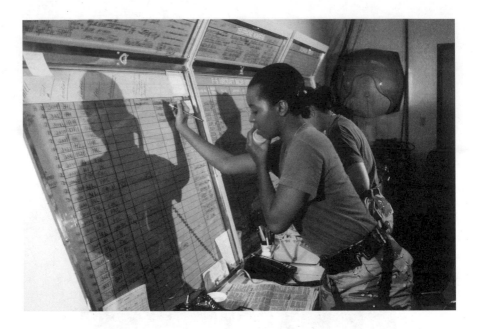

An airman updates a status board in an aircraft maintenance and control center during Operation Desert Shield. *Courtesy of the U.S. Defense Visual Information Center.*

biological-warfare training, and were unfamiliar with how to conduct combat-support missions. Young also encountered specific difficulties related to gender. Some things were more easily resolved. For example, when she landed, she discovered that the local naval air station did not have suitable facilities for women. She and the other women in her crew used the aircraft bathrooms instead. Young found it more annoying that she had to send a male pilot in to file her flight plan, but she shrugged it off. The hardest parts for her had been adjusting to the lack of contrast in the terrain and spotting a runway in the desert.[56]

Women served military aviation in other ways, including maintenance and aviation support, air traffic control, air defense artillery, and aeromedical evacuation. Iraqi soldiers discovered "Doc" Cornum, an Army flight surgeon, was a woman when they pulled off her helmet. The helicopter transporting Cornum was shot down on 27 February 1991 en route to rescuing another downed pilot. Cornum had two broken arms from the crash when she was taken prisoner. Upon her release, her mother said: "God, she's tough, she's tough. She could always do anything and she still will."[57]

Major Marie Rossi would not be as fortunate. Rossi died when the Chinook helicopter she was piloting crashed into a microwave tower on March 1,

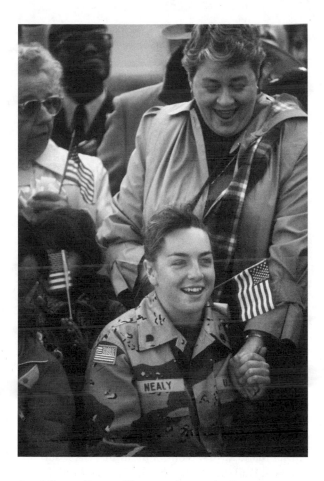

Specialist Melissa Rathbun-Nealy was the first woman to
be taken prisoner of war by Iraqi forces during Operation
Desert Storm. Her elation (and that of her mother) is
clearly apparent during this speech welcoming the POWs
home to the United States. *Courtesy of the U.S. Defense
Visual Information Center.*

1991, one day after the cease-fire. Rossi had been featured in a number of news
accounts, including a widely televised interview on CNN. She was a good pilot
and a capable soldier taking in stride the criticisms and challenges faced by
most women in military aviation. When she died, ordinary citizens as well as
her sister military pilots viewed her as a hero and admired her forthright con-
viction and willingness to die for her country. Rossi had stated in the CNN
interview: "I think if you talk to the women who are professionals in the mili-

Major Marie Rossi was one of the media "stars" during the Gulf War; she was also the first woman Army aviator to be killed while flying combat support missions in an active theater of war. Her funeral attracted national publicity and transformed Rossi into an important Gulf War figure. Advocates for women in the military saw her as a hero; opponents called her death an unnecessary tragedy. *Courtesy of the U.S. Defense Visual Information Center.*

tary, we see ourselves as soldiers. We don't really see it as man versus woman. What I am doing is no greater or less than the man who is flying next to me or in back of me."[58]

Yet there was a backlash against Rossi within a segment of the military because the media ignored the three men who died with her. Questions about her promotions and her leadership abilities surfaced and were quickly spread by those who did not want women in the military. Colorado Congresswoman Patricia Schroeder framed the debate this way: "By pretending they were protecting women from harm, all they were really protecting them from was promotions." Reacting to that observation, *New York Times* columnist Anna Quindlen added: "To become a Stormin' Norman, you have to have flown the bombing raids, led the troops through the jungles. Thousands of women who have chosen the service as their life's work face sanctioned job discrimination, a glass ceiling permitted by statute."[59]

And so the debate about the roles of men and women in American society was revived. The Gulf War was short-lived, but it was of great import to society. The military regained a degree of prestige and respect not experienced since the days before the Vietnam War. The popularity of George H.W. Bush was the highest experienced by any president to that date. The new vets reveled in their status. Supporters of women in the military took this to heart and proceeded to make the most of what would later be deemed "the most perfect legislative window of opportunity ever." By midsummer, Congress voted to repeal the laws that prohibited women from flying combat aircraft. It remains a stunning moment in the history of American women in aviation. Not only *could* women fly, but it seemed Americans thought they *should*.

Yet, it proved to be only a *moment* in history, for it became quickly apparent that this shift in attitudes toward women in combat, women in the workplace, women in aviation, had not gained nearly the momentum as the advocates had thought. For a brief period, some thought optimistically Colleen Nevius's dream of equality expressed in the chapter's opening epigraph had been nearing realization. There had been change, but the struggle persisted.

10

New World Order?

1992–2000

*Amy E. Foster and Deborah G. Douglas
with the assistance of Alan D. Meyer*

> No one's going to give me any grief.
>
> Lori Legat Griffith, US Airways pilot

In the 1990s women in aviation witnessed their greatest expansion of opportunities since World War II. From military to commercial aviation, from flying helicopters to Boeing 747s, from airport management to the Pentagon, the percentage of women (more than 20 percent) in the aviation workforce was larger than ever. Expanded professional opportunities created new arenas of participation for women as they pushed the gender envelope and continued a path of unprecedented achievement as fliers and on the ground. Nonetheless, the decade was also marked by equally prominent harassment and discrimination cases that checked the progress toward parity in employment and participation.

Liberals and conservatives resumed what was often a scalding hot national conversation about women's rights. This was somewhat unexpected, for while all expected the endless debates about women's reproductive rights to continue, no one could have predicted the explosive results of Supreme Court Justice Clarence Thomas's nomination hearings. Anita Hill's controversial testimony brought the subject of sexual harassment into the fore as it had never been in American politics. Angered by conservatives, liberal women's groups sent (or returned) forty female Democrats into public office during the November 1992 congressional elections and were central to the reelection defeat of President George H.W. Bush.[1] As politicians reassessed their responsibilities to women and popular media proclaimed 1992 "The Year of the Woman," many Americans asked for some resolution to questions of equality between the sexes. Women in aviation were often the focal point for this debate about gender.[2]

On July 31, 1991, the whole world changed for women in aviation. On that day, in response to the enormous enthusiasm over the military men and women in the Persian Gulf War, Congress passed the Kennedy-Roth Amendment. In doing so, it repealed the laws forbidding women from flying in combat and authorized the Air Force, Navy, and Marine Corps to make their own decisions about what positions should be open to women. In the course of this debate many discovered the fact that the prohibition against assigning women to combat posts in the Army was *not* a law, only a policy. This had not been widely understood until pointed out by activists in the 1980s. The Army resisted change, however, by insisting that Congressional intent was clear and that conformity across the services was imperative.[3]

Women aviators' excitement over the bill was short-lived, however, for while the House and Senate Conference Committee completed its reconciliation of the 1992 Defense Authorization Bill, an important concession was made to opponents of the Kennedy-Roth Amendment. A bipartisan presidential commission was established in order to advise the services as to whether or not they should allow women in combat.[4]

Legislators quickly determined that the post–Desert Storm affection for "our soldiers"—male or female—was too strong to risk voting against the combat exclusion repeal. It would have been unseemly to vote "against" the crisply attired military women who came to testify at congressional hearings. The commission was a sop to the right. Proponents of women in combat thought it was unnecessary but harmless. Opponents saw it as an opportunity to keep the discussion alive until the euphoric afterglow of the war had abated. Indeed, as soon as the president signed the law, Secretary of Defense Richard Cheney announced he would not permit women to be assigned to combat aircraft (and other combat occupations) until the commission issued its recommendations.[5]

The Presidential Commission on the Assignment of Women in the Armed Forces addressed several critical questions: Should the military initiate "gender-neutral" training? Should the armed services maintain their system of occupational physical requirements regardless of the sex of the candidate? Most importantly, should America's historic exclusion of women from direct combat roles be retained? In addressing these specific questions, the commission also confronted head-on the broader societal issues of equal opportunity, job discrimination, and sexual harassment. The main criteria for evaluating the new law was the nation's overall combat readiness, but the conservative membership quickly succeeded in imposing a narrow definition of this concept based

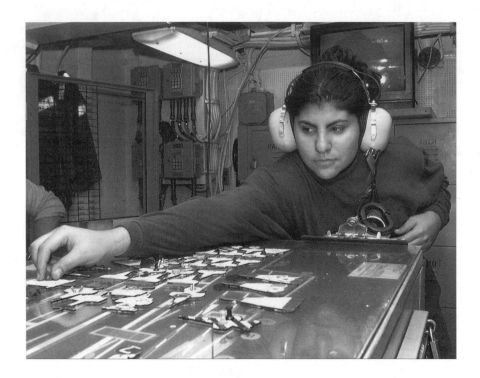

Airman Mirna Gonzales updates a flight deck status board while coordinating placement of aircraft during fueling operations on the flight deck of the USS *Nimitz* during Operation Southern Watch in support of UN sanctions against Iraq. *Courtesy of the U.S. Defense Visual Information Center.*

exclusively on the proposition that physical strength was the key factor (perhaps the *only* factor) in group cohesion and combat readiness.

Commission member and Army pilot Captain Mary Finch would later lament that the overt ideological agenda of some of the commission's membership "did not allow for objective assessment [of the present and future assignment of women.]"[6] The debates hinged on the question of "equal opportunity." For advocates there could be no compromise. For opponents, the greater good of national defense necessitated the placing of limits on women's participation in the military.

In the end, the commission concluded that allowing women to serve in limited combat situations was acceptable. If the military services deemed a woman able to perform a job or fulfill a duty, then she should be allowed to do it. That statement meant that women could be armed and serve in peacekeeping and ground support missions near the front line.[7]

Ironically, given the tone of the debate in Congress the previous year and the explicit repeal of the combat aviation laws, the panel recommended women pilots not be allowed to fly combat missions. It was a close 8–7 decision, but the official recommendation of the commission was the restoration of the sections of the U.S. legal code to their original wording before Congress modified them with the passage of the Kennedy-Roth Amendment. At the same time, the commission encouraged the Bush administration to support greater opportunity for women in military aviation to fly outside of combat.[8]

When it came out, the commission's report received little political or public support. The American public had expected a better clarification of what constituted combat and noncombat roles than what the commission provided. News accounts revealed the fiery debates within the commission. Elaine Donnelly, one of the conservative leaders on the commission, would later describe the experience this way: "DACOWITS was kindergarten; the Commission was like getting a Ph.D."[9]

The tension was palpable from practically the first page of the report. Far from a sober assessment, the Presidential Commission on the Assignment of Women in the Armed Forces delivered a bizarre set of vague and contradictory recommendations that encouraged the military to allow a woman to command a tank but not pilot a fighter airplane.[10] The lame-duck Bush administration distanced itself from the commission's report, which eventually landed on the desks of incoming President Bill Clinton and Secretary of Defense Les Aspin. It was up to the Clinton administration to set new American policy on women in combat.

Overwhelmed in the early days of the new administration by the furor over opening the military to gays and lesbians, Secretary of Defense Aspin did not immediately address the matter of women in combat. This turned out to be politically helpful to the administration, as some of the sting of "Don't Ask, Don't Tell" was mitigated by headlines announcing women would be able to fly combat aircraft. In the details of Aspin's policy issued in April 1993, it was clear that he had not strayed very far from the way things were before the passage of the Kennedy-Roth Act. Still, the military understood that the Clinton administration expected to see some visible changes in assignments.[11]

Quickly, plans were made to begin training women to fly a number of fighter aircraft, including the Navy's F-14 and the Air Force's F-15. Air Force Lieutenant Jeannie Flynn, an aerospace engineering major at the University of Texas–Austin (she later earned her master's at Stanford), graduated first in her pilot training class but was banned from the normal fighter pilot career path. She had started the flight instructor course when the policy changed. Suddenly she was reassigned to Luke Air Force Base and the 555th Fighter Squadron. Air Force Chief of Staff General Merrill McPeak was adamantly opposed to allow-

First Lieutenant Jeannie Flynn's career changed dramatically when the laws restricting women from flying combat aircraft were repealed. Flynn became the first woman F-15E fighter pilot. *Courtesy of the U.S. Defense Visual Information Center.*

ing women to fly in combat but stated bluntly: "The secretary of defense made the decision to open combat cockpits to women. We saluted smartly and we're doing this job in the traditional Air Force way. . . . On issues like this, I do what I'm told."[12] Flynn completed her training and reported to Seymour Johnson Air Force Base in Goldsboro, N.C., the first female fighter pilot in the U.S. Air Force.[13]

Since Flynn, a 1999 report indicated that the Air Force had trained seven more women to fly the F-15E. Eventually, some were tested on combat missions. For example, Cathy De La Garza, a member of the 71st Fighter Squadron based at Langley Air Force Base, flew approximately fifty missions in southern Iraq's "no-fly" zone.[14]

But despite the success stories, opponents, led by Elaine Donnelly and abetted by military men who despised the idea of women in the military, seized on a series of sex scandals and accidents involving women in the military to reignite public debate on the matter. The Tailhook scandal, in particular, fueled the flames. On September 11, 1991, the Tailhook Association, an organization of naval aviators who have "carrier-qualified," met at a Las Vegas hotel for its an-

Captain Sarah Deal, the first woman Marine Corps helicopter pilot, flies a Sea Stallion helicopter in the Kernel Blitz 1997 training exercise. *Courtesy of the U.S. Defense Visual Information Center.*

nual meeting. A number of male officers allegedly formed two lines and forced their female colleagues to "walk the gauntlet" while the men groped the women.[15]

Although the U.S. Navy did not formally recognize or support Tailhook, the annual Tailhook Convention was a major event. Many Americans looked to the Navy for explanations to why the leadership would ignore, or worse, condone its officers' behavior.[16] Eventually, 50 of the 140 male officers investigated received "administrative discipline" from the Navy; none were court-martialed. In the midst of the investigations into the allegations of sexual harassment at Tailhook, the Navy dedicated itself to saving face.[17] Top Navy officials responded positively to Congress's decision to lift restrictions on women in combat by opening up 50 percent more jobs to women. The death of pilot Kara Hultgreen three years later would cause public consternation over the possibility that in its effort to give women equal treatment and equal opportunities, the Navy might have sacrificed its standards and the female aviators' safety.[18]

Lieutenant Kara Hultgreen was the U.S. Navy's first woman to achieve full qualification as a fleet fighter pilot. On 25 October 1994, while trying to land her F-14 Tomcat on the deck of the aircraft carrier *Abraham Lincoln,* Hultgreen was killed when she tried to eject after a last-ditch effort to recover the airplane. She ejected just as her plane rolled over, propelling her directly into the Pacific Ocean.[19]

Much of the media coverage maligned Hultgreen as the U.S. Navy's token woman pilot, suggesting that she never would have qualified as a fighter pilot on her own merits. Roger Hedgecock, a San Diego radio talk show host, argued, "The Navy had pushed her through because it needed to get women in the pipeline to fly combat jets in the wake of the Tailhook scandal."[20] By and large, Hedgecock's and other media coverage sensationalized the Hultgreen accident. Opponents argued that the cause of the accident was "pilot error" and misguided social policies. Proponents rebutted with detailed reports that concluded the tragic accident was largely caused by a technical problem and that there was nothing wrong with the Navy's flight training program. The Navy's internal investigation found Hultgreen's accident stemmed from a malfunction in her aircraft's left engine, a problem that occurred at an extremely vulnerable moment as she approached the carrier for a landing. Critics of women in military aviation have argued that the official Mishap Investigation Report falsified information in the name of "political correctness." The sustained discussion of innuendoes and allegations has had an impact on the careers of several women and in 1996 triggered a major lawsuit against the Center for Military Readiness.[21]

The Hultgreen case raised the question of her competence as a qualified combat pilot, and thus women's competence in the cockpit generally, when it did not in any way merit that level of discussion. But in the American social and cultural milieu of the early 1990s, that sort of politicization was inevitable. On the bestseller list in 1992 and 1993 were two books that offered theories on essential differences between men and women: Deborah Tannen's *You Just Don't Understand* and John Gray's *Men Are From Mars, Women Are From Venus*. Many Americans thus viewed Hultgreen's accident as another reason why differences between men and women and their roles in society had to be discussed.[22]

Amidst the media melee over Lieutenant Hultgreen, it is easy to forget that seventeen other women were on board the USS *Abraham Lincoln* at that time. Loree Draude Hirschman arrived on the carrier the day her fellow pilot was killed. Most of the discussion around the first female fighter pilots surrounds their struggles to fit into their new environments. Hirschman attended the University of California–San Diego on a Navy ROTC scholarship. She majored in math, but her real goal was to be a Navy pilot. The *Lincoln* cruise was a first for her, but Hirschman (nicknamed "Rowdy"), in her opinion, thrived as the only woman in the ship's S-3B Viking antisubmarine warfare squadron. Her colleagues each describe this cruise differently, indicating that there is no single viewpoint that captures all Navy women pilots. Still all recognize that the Pacific-fleet *Lincoln* and the Atlantic-fleet USS *Dwight D. Eisenhower* deployments were milestones.[23]

Three years later, however, another case involving a female military aviator sparked a different sort of controversy and brought those concerns that had been expressed by the Presidential Commission on Women in the Armed Forces about sexual tensions endangering military cohesiveness back to the forefront. News broke in February 1997 that First Lieutenant Kelly Flinn, the U.S. Air Force's first bomber pilot, was facing a court-martial for behavior that threatened "good order and discipline." She had become romantically involved with the husband of an enlisted woman. Instead of fighting the charges brought against her, Flinn, who had been flying the U.S. military's proven behemoth, the B-52 Stratofortress, chose to resign from the service. The media made the Flinn case into a spectacle.[24] What became clear is that neither Flinn's affair nor Hultgreen's accident had much to say directly about the cause of women in combat. Both cases provided critics of women as military pilots with examples to use in their arguments that women's presence creates an internal threat to the military's mission. If the debate over women in the military had not been as heated as it was in the early 1990s, the civilian media services might not have even reported Flinn's story.[25]

While these incidents generated concern among some about women's roles in the military, such experiences were not the norm for most military women. However, just as opponents of women in combat exploited the negative, supporters turned a magnifying glass on women who brought tremendous strength and honor to their professions.[26] In particular, Eileen Collins, the first woman to command the space shuttle, has been singled out for exceptional recognition. Her life story is remarkable. Growing up in Elmira, New York, she saw the gliders take off and land at the Soaring Hall of Fame. She worked as a waitress during high school to earn money for flying lessons. Her academic career began at the local community college. Transferring to Syracuse University, Collins participated in Air Force ROTC and became the first woman to enter pilot training directly out of college. She served throughout the 1980s as a flight instructor in the T-38, the C-141, and the T-41 and as a mathematics instructor at the Air Force Academy. In 1990, while Collins was finishing her training at the Air Force test pilot school, NASA informed her of her selection for the astronaut corps. In February 1995, Collins became the first female shuttle pilot. To help celebrate her launch, Collins invited Jerrie Cobb and the surviving women who had participated in the Mercury astronaut tests at the Lovelace Clinic in the early 1960s. Not surprisingly, Collins's special guests attracted a lot of media attention. She was thrilled, as one of her professional goals was to increase the visibility of

Eileen Collins became the first woman to command the space shuttle in 1999. *Photo by Carolyn Russo, National Air and Space Museum, Smithsonian Institution.*

women's contributions to aviation. In 1999, Collins made headlines again when she became the first woman commander of a space mission.[27]

The success of military women aviators like Collins, Jeannie Flynn, and Loree Hirschman had a salutary effect on the opportunities for women piloting *any* kind of aircraft—military or civilian, professionally or just for fun. It was most significant for women commercial airline pilots, however. Military aviation had long been a typical career path for men who wanted to fly for the airlines. In the early 1990s, it was clear that this had now become a viable option for women as well. Over the course of the decade, the number of women commercial airline pilots increased by 26 percent, from 7,292 in 1990 to 9,214 in 1998. It should be noted that the recession of 1991–1992 did result in a large number of pilot furloughs.[28] "Last hired, first fired" remains airline employment policy, so not surprisingly the numbers of women pilots fluctuated wildly. Still, the opportunities were real and all the airlines made serious efforts to recruit women.

In 1993, the *Atlanta Constitution* ran an article surveying the state of women pilots in U.S. commercial aviation. Female pilots like Lori Griffith admitted, "There are still a few guys who will maybe say, 'Hey, honey, time for the checklist,'" and occasions when deplaning passengers look past her into the cockpit

Lucy Young was among the first women to follow the typical career path of men airline pilots: learn to fly in the military and then join the airlines. *Courtesy of Lucy B. Young.*

to "thank the captain." But all of the pilots interviewed exuded great pride in their achievements and virtually all felt that the level of discrimination in the industry had declined. "I have never encountered any discrimination," stated Griffith, adding, "No one's going to give me any grief."[29] The fact that women pilots such as Griffith were seemingly unaware of discrimination could be interpreted as a sign that most of their male colleagues and much of society have accepted women as professional aviators.[30]

By and large, the women acknowledged that real improvements had come in the way the aviation industry treated female pilots. Captain June Viviano, who flies Boeing 727s for FedEx, noted that after a nearly twenty-year career she "can walk through a concourse now and not have people look at me like I have two heads."[31] United Airlines First Officer Melissa Ward said that she felt more discrimination coming from her passengers than from her colleagues. She noted in 1998 that "They walk in (the plane), look in the cockpit and do a double take."[32]

The "double take" phenomenon was partly due to the fact that women remained such a small percentage of the total number of airline transport pi-

Dorothy Aiksnoras-Vallee was the first woman flight engineer hired by Republic Airlines in 1980. When women started to fly for the largest commercial airlines, one of the most popular places to have their picture taken was inside the engine cowling, the engine's power being a metaphor for women's ascendancy to the top of the pilot hierarchy. *Photo by Carolyn Russo, National Air and Space Museum, Smithsonian Institution.*

lots. In 1990, the Federal Aviation Administration estimated that 2,082 women held airline transport ratings, 1.9 percent of the total 107,732. Ten years later, the number of women had more than doubled to 4,411. Women now held 3.1 percent of the total 141,596 airline transport certificates. These numbers are minuscule, and not all who hold ratings are employed, which is why the odds of having a woman pilot on your commercial airline flight are so low. Yet, it is important to note that whereas there has been an overall decline in the number of women pilots, among those who fly airplanes for a living the numbers show steady growth.[33]

One key factor that contributed to the increased presence of women in aviation in the mid-1990s was the sudden upturn of the American economy. More people were flying and suddenly the airlines faced a serious pilot shortage. Military downsizing meant fewer people—male or female—were being trained as military pilots, a major source of pilots for commercial aviation. Fewer slots meant fewer trained pilots who would eventually leave the military and enter civilian aviation. The question for aviation managers became: where does one find a new pool of pilots? Women suddenly seemed an untapped source. But as the military had only recently granted women greater opportunities to train as pilots, the pool of licensed women pilots remained small. In the short term, any increase in the number of women would have to come via civilian training programs.

Greater access to training proved the key to opening up piloting to women. Much of the task was taken on by universities. In 1995, the School of Aviation Science at Western Michigan University received a $2.9 million grant from the W.K. Kellogg Foundation to pay for recruiting, scholarships, and support services for female and minority students. Joseph Dunlap, the school's director, understood that "many women and minority students don't have role models and can't envision themselves in these types of careers." Dunlap's codirector, Maureen Pettitt, explained, "It's not just the recruitment but the retention end of it. What normally happens both at a collegiate level, as well as the industry level, is that there are those spurts of recruiting women and minorities and then everybody pats themselves on the back and says, 'Oh, we did this good thing.'"[34] Programs like that at Western Michigan were designed with the goal of providing nontypical student pilot recruits with the resources essential for long-term success. Confirmation of WMU's initial success came in January 2001, when Delta Airlines announced a four-year, $1.65 million partnership with the school to train a minimum of twenty-four (and as many as forty) women and minority pilots.[35]

Despite an observable decrease in the resistance toward women as commercial pilots, there are still many men who remain skeptical. The rise of the Internet has seen an increase in the postings of "rants" in which the writer suggests women are incompetent and so different from men that they should not work together. Occasionally, the results of a legitimate scientific study get released that would seem to support the anti-women skeptics. The most significant example of this was a study conducted by the Johns Hopkins University School of Public Health on the role gender plays in pilot errors that cause civilian aircraft accidents.[36]

Researchers studied 431 accidents (287 men; 144 women) to see if gender was a useful indicator for understanding the causes of aviation crashes. (The data was originally collected for a larger study on the effect of aging and flight safety.) Their conclusions indicated that for all pilots "mishandling aircraft kinetics, poor decision making and inattention are the most common pilot errors."[37] They found that there were measurable differences between men and women, however. When a male pilot caused an accident, the cause could be any one of three: "mishandling," "flawed decision-making" (flying in poor conditions), or "inattention" (landing with landing gear in the up position). The pilot error most commonly made by female pilots was "mishandling" (such as the inability to recover from a stall).[38]

The results of the Hopkins study got unexpected attention when news media began to imply in their reports that women were less capable pilots. This was not the purpose of the study. But critics of women pilots overlooked the researchers' objectives, which had been to improve pilot training for all pilots. It was not news that women pilots had accidents. The study showed the accident rate was comparable. What surprised researchers had been the apparent gender differences associated with the causes of these accidents. The study was a small one and the conclusions vague and based on evidence collected for a different purpose. As a result, it has had little impact on human factors engineering research, regulation, or pilot training programs. The Hopkins case illustrates the fact that the practice of mischaracterizing results of legitimate investigations to serve a political (or other) cause became much more commonplace in the past decade.[39]

One aviation role where the presence of women has remained unquestioned is the flight attendant job. In January 2001, Frances Hall Craft, one of the original United Airlines stewardesses who helped found the Association of Flight Attendants predecessor, the Air Line Stewardesses Association, died. AFA founder Ada Brown Greenfield died soon thereafter, in March 2002. For the AFA, Craft's and Brown's deaths were vivid reminders that the factors prompting unionization in 1945 remained half a century later. As evidenced by lawsuits, some airlines still maintained discriminatory hiring practices, especially related to age and weight.[40]

The legal liability of airlines for luggage crammed into overhead bins, electronic hazards to navigational systems caused by the operation of laptop computers and handheld computer games, whistle-blower protection, "air rage," and terrorist attacks were among the new challenges that the unions addressed in this decade. However, the 1990s was mainly a period of constant activity for the union in response to the reorganization, expansion, and contraction of the airline industry. Flight attendants throughout the industry have parleyed their numbers into bargaining power. For example, in 2000 the Association of Flight Attendants represented more than fifty thousand employees at twenty-six different airlines. But even as of 2003, Delta Airlines' twenty thousand flight attendants were unrepresented by any union.[41] As the lowest-paid group among airline contract employees, unionization has provided flight attendants with some protection and benefits.[42]

Throughout the decade, flight attendants have offered their support for their fellow employees under contract, pilots and mechanics in particular. Most recently, Northwest Airlines flight attendants (Teamsters, Local Union 2000)

New US Airways flight attendants complete their training program in 1998. *From the Association of Flight Attendants Collection; courtesy of US Airways, Inc.*

put their own contract negotiations at risk (they had been working without an agreement for more than three years), crossed union lines, and lent support to Northwest mechanics who belonged to the Teamsters rival, Aircraft Mechanics Fraternal Association. The flight attendants joined the mechanics in informational picketing. In previous instances, return support for the flight attendants was less forthcoming (attributed to gender as much as power relations among the various unions), which will likely make such actions more rare.[43]

For those who wanted to work as mechanics, women struggled more for opportunities in the field with less public support. In the late 1980s, economic uncertainty had resulted in hundreds of layoffs. The aviation recession bottomed out in 1992 and a period of modest employment growth began. Women held maintenance positions but always in low numbers. By the end of the 1990s, women represented only about 1.5 percent of the workforce maintaining aircraft.[44]

In 1996, Robin Lamar, a mechanic for United Airlines, and Marcia

The Association of Flight Attendants team that worked to organize the flight attendants of Delta Airlines. Though 98 percent of those who voted were in favor of unionization, the effort failed. The law requires at least 50 percent plus 1 of all eligible voters to be pro-union. Only 30 percent of Delta flight attendants chose to vote. Supporters felt the election was influenced by the dramatic downturn in air travel after September 11. Opponents felt they got a better deal by remaining independent. *Courtesy of the Association of Flight Attendants.*

Buckingham, the first female spacecraft operator at NASA's Kennedy Space Center, sponsored an organizational meeting at the annual meeting of Women in Aviation, International for mechanics interested in establishing an organization to provide support and resources for women (and men) in the field. In January 1997, the board of directors for the newly formed Association for Women in Aviation Maintenance held its first meeting. Two years later, the group had 180 members. AWAM led efforts to encourage employers to consider more than a person's strength. Marcia Buckingham observed, "One thing the employers have found is that many times you need a small hand or body to fit into tight spaces—just as many times you need someone to lift a 90-pound box."[45]

In addition, AWAM was particularly interested in encouraging minority and low-income women to pursue aviation careers. They became one of the sponsors of the "Willa Brown Project," an effort that reached out to women in low-income housing projects and trained them for entry-level aviation maintenance positions.[46]

The mechanics followed a path similar to the one women air traffic controllers had taken a decade earlier. The Federal Aviation Administration felt a lot of external pressure to improve its percentages of women employees. With a possible annual salary upwards of $84,000, promotion of women as air traffic controllers offered promising opportunities.[47] By 1997, approximately thirty-three hundred women worked as air traffic controllers, filling about 15 percent of U.S. air traffic controller positions.[48]

The Professional Women Controllers (PWC) remained the sole organization for women controllers. Interestingly, over twenty years after its inception, the PWC continued to define its purpose exactly as it had in 1979: encourage women to enter the profession; promote professional and personal development; and provide support, education, and communication.[49] What changed over the decade were the issues. At annual conferences, PWC members discussed flextime, part-time, and job-sharing. Pregnancy policies and home schedules were big issues. At regional PWC meetings, courses in self-defense given by local police were offered.[50]

Women controllers faced challenges similar to those that women working in other industries faced. In 1997, for example, news of a serious sexual harassment scandal broke. A class action complaint was filed against the FAA for its failure to address complaints of sexual harassment adequately. Not surprisingly, as they had with Tailhook and other military scandals of the decade, the women's congressional caucus, led by Representative Pat Schroeder, insisted on holding hearings. A contrite administrator, Jane Garvey, testified before the House Aviation Subcommittee, and this led to an intensification of the "zero tolerance" policy.[51]

The American Institute of Aeronautics and Astronautics is the leading professional society for aerospace engineers, but if one types the word "women" into the search engine at the AIAA website, the response is *zero* hits. It is an unusual occurrence, because there has been a tremendous number of studies and public policy debates on the situation of women and minorities in engineering and science. In September 2000, the Congressional Commission on the Advancement of Women and Minorities in Science, Engineering and Technology Development released its final report: *Land of Plenty: Diversity as America's Competitive Edge in Science, Engineering and Technology.* The American Association of University Women has commissioned multiple studies on this subject, beginning with their landmark work: *How Schools Shortchange Girls,* published in 1992.[52]

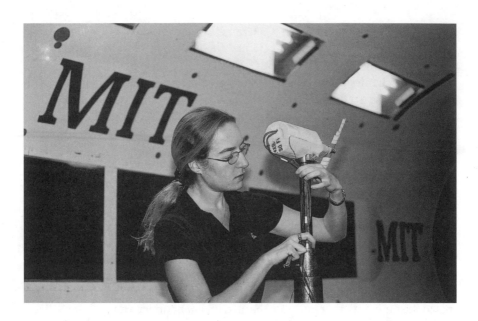

An Aero/Astro major at the Massachusetts Institute of Technology, Emily Craparo adjusts the wind tunnel model she designed, built, and tested for one of her engineering courses. *Author's collection.*

All of these studies point out that women comprise a very small number of engineers. For the 1999–2000 school year, the American Society for Engineering Education reported that only 20.8 percent of the 63,700 bachelor's degrees in engineering were awarded to women. Women received 246, or 20 percent, of the 1,230 bachelor's degrees awarded in aerospace engineering. The graduate statistics are as follows: there were 687 master's degrees in aerospace engineering awarded, 89 (13 percent) went to women; of the 208 doctoral degrees, 23 (11 percent) were awarded to women.[53] Women comprise a minuscule portion of engineering faculty. A 1999 survey by the National Research Council's Committee on Women in Science and Engineering recorded only 52 women teaching aerospace engineering.[54]

These facts have resulted in a deluge of special programs developed by both the public and private sector. It is notable that the National Science Foundation and the National Academy of Engineering have both initiated projects. The Society of Women Engineers (SWE) signed a Memorandum of Understanding in 2001 with the Girl Scouts, USA, to develop materials and activities to encourage the nation's 2.8 million Girl Scouts to consider engineering as a career. In particular, SWE members will begin an extensive mentoring effort.[55]

In 1992, Purdue University hired Gary M. Eiff to join the faculty of the Aviation Technology Department. Eiff was known for his earlier studies of women in aviation technology, and while Purdue had gained considerable recognition in the 1930s for hiring Amelia Earhart as a consultant to encourage female college students, the department wanted to do more. Eiff and his wife, Mary Ann (who became an aircraft technician instructor for the department), were absolutely committed to this idea. Their research confirmed the importance of mentoring, and they soon became known around the department. Founding board members of Women in Aviation, International, they quickly established an active student chapter at Purdue.[56]

Affirmative action, when well conceived, is very effective. The Massachusetts Institute of Technology has nearly full parity in its undergraduate population because of a twenty-year effort. In the early 1980s, the admissions office and members of the faculty conducted an extensive study of the performance of male and female students. Close scrutiny was made of their scores on the Scholastic Aptitude Test. Though women did score lower on the SATs (and consequently were admitted in significantly smaller numbers), they outperformed the men once enrolled. Nearly two decades of monitoring continues to bear this fact out. As a result, MIT began to adjust the SAT scores of women applicants with the effect of both increasing the number of women and improving the quality of the student body.[57]

Women aerospace engineers work in every imaginable setting. From small, family-owned firms to large companies, such as Boeing and General Electric. They work on everything from computer reservation systems to hang gliders to supersonic transports. For example, Christine Darden, a Ph.D. in aerospace engineering and one of the most senior black female engineers, works for NASA. She has had many different assignments over her career, but while working at the NASA Langley Research Center in Hampton, Virginia, Darden was part of the 1990s atempt to revive efforts to design a commercial supersonic aircraft. Her particular contribution was in the area that had dogged the first SST program in the 1960s: noise. The challenge she and her colleagues faced was to figure out how to eliminate the sonic boom that is both annoying and damaging to the environment. Though the program was cancelled at the end of the decade, Darden's research is of use to many, including the military.[58]

The fact that Darden has found success at NASA is important not only because she is a woman, but also because she is black. While women generally have struggled throughout this period for freer opportunities in aviation, minority women have faced even greater resistance to their participation than white women. In the 1990s, all of the women's aviation organizations began to demonstrate concerns and speak openly about the lack of diversity of their

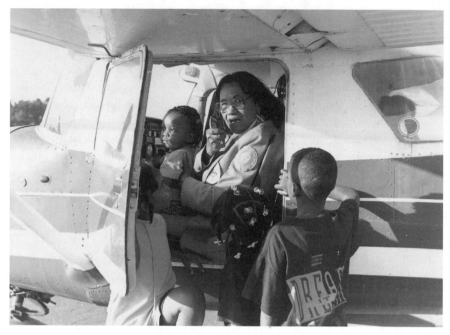

Ida Van Smith learned to fly in 1967 when she was fifty years old. She immediately started a flying club to encourage minority children to pursue interests in aviation. Smith remains one of the most important aviation educators of the past two decades. *Photo by Carolyn Russo, National Air and Space Museum, Smithsonian Institution.*

membership. That aviation had long been dominated by white Americans was nothing new. What was new was the fact that many felt it was important to take actions that would increase the opportunities for minority women.

The Black History Month phenomenon has had a salutary effect in that at least the names of some minority women have become well known. For example, in 1995 the U.S. Postal Service issued a stamp in honor of pioneer aviator Bessie Coleman, the first black to earn a pilot's license. Special events such as the 1992 shuttle flight of NASA mission specialist Mae Jemison stimulated still more attention. Yet the fact remains that minority women in aviation are few in number and largely invisible. Consider the fact that despite the crush of media and political attention when the Cuban military shot down two aircraft operated by Brothers to the Rescue (Hermanos al Rescate) in 1996, few Americans knew that one of the organization's founders (and pilots), Mayte Greco, was a woman.[59]

In 1990, Marcelite Harris became the first black woman to be promoted to

In 1993, Ensign Matice Wright became the Navy's first black woman naval flight officer. *Courtesy of the U.S. Defense Visual Information Center.*

the rank of general in the U.S. Air Force. Harris was a pioneer throughout her military career, but especially in the field of aircraft maintenance. The military, especially the Army, likes to point out the fact that it is better integrated than the rest of American society. In 1993, for example, when black women made up 12 percent of the female population, they accounted for 30 percent of Army women. But minority women in the military are disproportionately clustered in administrative and support occupations, not prestige specialties, such as aviation. In fact, it was not until Matice Wright's 1993 assignment that the Navy had a single black female flight officer.[60]

In 1992 NASA administrator Daniel Goldin declared that the agency was too "pale, male and stale." He was a forceful agent for change, as the number of women in middle and senior management positions has grown from 5 to 18 percent over the decade. Minority employment has risen from 15 to 21 percent. Still, among scientists and engineers, the agency's most important employee group, the figures are relatively static, hovering between 15 and 17 percent

Raytheon Aircraft technicians work on the fabrication of aircraft made from composite materials. *Courtesy of Raytheon Aircraft.*

women and 15 and 18 percent minorities. However, in the mid-1990s most NASA civil servants participated in diversity training workshops intended to improve the work environment as well as recruitment.[61]

The gains elsewhere for women in senior leadership positions have not been as dramatic, but there have been many noteworthy appointments. In 1992, Martin Marietta named Gwendolyn King its first female board member. In 1993, Congress approved President Clinton's nomination of Sheila Widnall as the first female secretary of the Air Force. That same year, Carol Hallett accepted the position of president of the Air Transport Association. Jane Garvey took over as the FAA administrator in 1997. In June 2001, Colleen Barrett became president and chief operations officer of Southwest Airlines. Despite the visibility of women in the high-tech sector, such as Carly Fiorina, chief executive officer of Hewlett-Packard, no woman since Olive Ann Beech has served as CEO of a major aerospace firm.

The Boeing Company, one of the industry's leaders in aircraft production

Patty Wagstaff is one of the nation's top aerobatic pilots, having won both national and international competitions. *Courtesy of Patty Wagstaff Airshows.*

and the United States' largest exporter, worked hard in the mid 1990s to invite women employees into the fold. In general, only high-profile employees, such as Boeing's senior vice president (chief people and administration officer, and office of the chairman), Laurette T. Koellner, or Ellen Smith, president of Pratt & Whitney's power systems unit, get much media attention. A much larger percentage of the women workers serve in capacities such as assemblers (modern Rosie the Riveters). The total number of women employed by the aerospace industry in 1990 was approximately 209,300. By 2000 that number had shrunk to about 126,300, yet the percentage of women employees was almost unchanged (23.3 percent in 1990 and 22.9 percent in 2000). Except for occasional images in corporate annual reports, there are virtually no news accounts of these women.[62]

For the majority of women who seek opportunities in aviation, their goals are not to fly fighter jets or work for the largest aircraft company in the world. They just want to fly. In 2000, the number of women students and private pilots totaled 25,389, representing over two-thirds of all licensed women pilots. They all share a love for flying, a love encouraged and inspired by others like them in general aviation.[63]

Jean Ross Howard Phelan (center) was inducted into the Women in Aviation International Pioneer Hall of Fame in 1995, celebrating the founder of the Whirly-Girls' lifetime of achievement. *Author's collection.*

For example, two real heroes for this community are Julie Clark and Patty Wagstaff, regulars at air shows around the nation. Since 1987, Patty Wagstaff has been the top-ranked female competitor. She is a three-time U.S. national aerobatic champion, a six-time member of the U. S. Aerobatic Team, and an International Aerobatic Club champion. In 1994, the Smithsonian Institution's National Air and Space Museum put Wagstaff's airplane, the Goodrich Extra 260, on display, and in 1995 she received the air show industry's highest honor, the "Sword of Excellence."[64]

The Ninety-Nines and the Whirly-Girls continue to be the most significant organizations encouraging and supporting women in general aviation. Yet, the 1990s saw an interesting shift. Sociologist Robert Putnam called it "Bowling Alone" and noted that Americans were less likely to join older, established civic, social, religious, or recreational organizations.[65] Thus, it is not surprising that the entity that really grabbed the attention of women in aviation during this decade was the commercial enterprise "Women Fly." Ball caps with those

For all the campaigns proposed and led by adults, few have had as much success getting today's youth interested in aviation as the effort of Vicki Van Meter. Van Meter got interested in learning to fly at a very young age, and in the summer of 1994 she flew (with an adult instructor) from Augusta, Maine, to Glasgow, Scotland, when she was twelve years old. *Photo by Carolyn Russo, National Air and Space Museum, Smithsonian Institution.*

words stitched on them became hot items. The owners showed a flare for marketing, tapping their customers' interest in history and political action. Their "Jerrie Cobb" T-shirt included a postcard that petitioned NASA to "let Jerrie fly in space." The effort garnered the attention of CNN and CBS's *60 Minutes,* as well as NASA, however, Cobb was not afforded the opportunity extended to Ohio senator (and former astronaut) John Glenn.[66]

The Women in Aviation conference each March has become the single most significant event and now attracts more than three thousand attendees annually. The conference awards more than a half million dollars in scholarship money (mostly for flight training). There is a tension at this conference that seeks to both segregate and integrate women in aviation. Peggy Baty Chabrian, the charismatic and entrepreneurial founder and organizer of this event (and the Women in Aviation, International organization), is constantly reframing this observation by stating that the conference is a celebration with the objectives of community and education. "Each one, reach one" has been her mantra for years, but "one" is not gender-neutral. This is a campaign to get more women and girls interested and involved in aviation.[67]

The airplane may not be able to distinguish the sex of a pilot (or engineer, air traffic controller, flight attendant, or assembler), but human beings *can* and *do*. Human ideas about gendered roles have long limited the careers that women can pursue because it was thought that women's participation would compromise a particular set of values (i.e., caring for one's husband, children, and home; providing stability; and sacrifice of personal ambitions for the good of the family). Even in the 1990s it was not uncommon to hear working women criticized as unfit mothers. The concern extended beyond the question of equal opportunity in the workplace, however. The real issue was gender. If women were to design, build, construct, maintain, and fly airplanes in the same numbers as men, how would the American definitions of femininity and masculinity be changed? How would that affect our understanding of the rights and responsibilities of citizenship?[68]

There are many Americans who still do not believe women *should* be in aviation. Their reaction to the changes of the past half century have ranged from benign acceptance to hostile, even violent, outbursts. The peculiarities of the news business in the last decade have often elevated petty battles of "He said/She said" to unprecedented (and often unseemly) levels. Social scientists do not know the causes of the extraordinary numbers of sexual harassment cases in the past decade. Is it better reporting? Or a sense among women that their complaints will be listened to? Was there an actual increase in the number of incidents? Are the experiences of women in aviation a reflection of the norm or are they the victims of targeted violence? We simply do not know the answers to these questions.

American men are just as challenged. Men who "allow" their wives and daughters to take such jobs are accused of transforming the United States into a "nation of sissies" and compromising national defense.[69] Such charges are absurd considered from the perspective of history. "Values" and "standards" are not immutable, static truths. They are constantly evolving concepts that reflect the circumstances human beings find themselves in. The relevant historical issue for women in aviation during this decade is that the Cold War ended and federal funding for the "military-industrial-university" complex shrank precipitously. There was a power vacuum created by the "new world order" and Americans—men and women—have been forced to respond.[70]

One hundred and fifty years ago, the word "technology" was invented. One hundred years ago, Orville and Wilbur Wright flew a modest assemblage of wood and fabric a few hundred feet. It was around that time that the meaning of the word "technology" narrowed. We stopped calling things like sewing needles or cooking "technologies" even when we knew them to be so. The new definition of technology did include things like airplanes and engineering. Historians who study this period tell us that this is the point when Americans linked ideas about technology and masculinity together. This fact makes the study of women in aviation particularly useful because it helps us understand men *and* women.[71]

In World War II, Americans learned that women *could* fly airplanes. There are biological differences between men and women, but in the pursuit of atmospheric flight, biology is not destiny. The persistent question has been "*should* they?" The fact that this question is still being asked suggests that the link between masculinity and technology is still strong. It also helps us to begin to explore the question of "invisibility."

This book documents the life experiences of hundreds of thousands of American women—hundreds of millions if you count the number of women who fly as commercial airline passengers. Yet if someone is pressed to identify a single woman in aviation, only Amelia Earhart's name will get mentioned. Where are the others? American women have both shaped and been shaped by aviation. Their pictures appear in magazines and newspapers. They write papers and books. They are featured in documentaries and films. There are now websites documenting the smallest minutia. So *why* are women in aviation "invisible"? When Americans can admit that they *know* the answer to that question, it will be time for the historians to write a new book. In the meantime, look up . . . the sky reveals clear signs of change.

Epilogue

May 2003

> It was a sortie with all the challenges we train for, except the threat of enemy aircraft. Just another day in the office with a view.
>
> "Kirby," USAF, a female F-16 pilot
> serving in Operation Iraqi Freedom

Chicks. "Killer Chicks." "Dixie Chicks." Thanks to the news media, that word has been on my mind the past few weeks. We are living in dramatic times, dangerous times, and it is now commonplace to hear quoted: "We sleep safe in our beds because rough men stand ready in the night to visit violence on those who would do us harm." The words are attributed to the British author George Orwell, who was equally dismayed by historical events of his own times. I've noted that American politicians and civic leaders are careful these days to extend their gratitude to both men and women in the armed services, but it is the breezy discourse of journalists that most fascinates me.

With a call sign like "Killer Chick," it is hard to imagine the reporters not being drawn to interview U.S. Air Force Captain Kim Campbell. Flying with the 332nd Air Expeditionary Wing, Campbell's A-10 "Warthog" jet sustained heavy fire over Baghdad in early April. Pretty quickly she realized that the hydraulic systems had been damaged, but she could still control the aircraft manually. With the support of her squadron commander, Lieutenant Colonel Richard Turner, Campbell made it safely back to Kuwait. It was not the first time she had experienced enemy fire; during patrol missions of Iraq's "no-fly" zone last year, Campbell had been shot at. But the bullet holes riddling her aircraft attracted reporters who were fascinated to see how the new women fighter pilots would hold up in a real war.

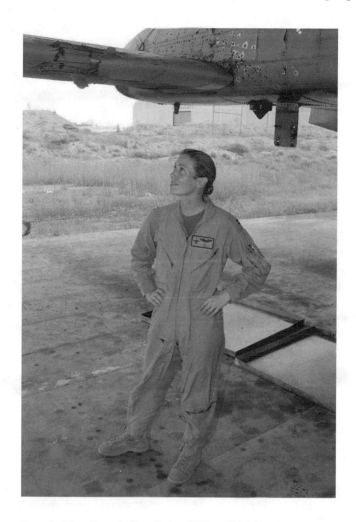

Captain Kim Campbell, call sign "Killer Chick," inspects some of the battle damage sustained by her A-10 "Warthog" jet during Operation Iraqi Freedom on April 7, 2003. *Courtesy of U.S. Air Force.*

I, too, have been interested in the roles played by women military aviators in Afghanistan, Iraq, and trouble spots elsewhere around the globe. It has been a decade since the laws were changed allowing the assignment of women to certain combat aviation jobs. There have been lots of "firsts," but military service during peacetime is different. The Center for Military Readiness has been ferocious in its insistence that women degrade the nation's capacity to fight

"Ladies' Night over Afghanistan" is how the Air Force described the all-woman crew that flew a KC-135 air refueling mission over Afghanistan as part of Operation Enduring Freedom on January 21, 2003. *Courtesy of U.S. Air Force. Photo by Captain Elizabeth Ortiz.*

and win wars. There are plenty of active duty and retired military personnel who hold this belief, too. I wondered if the start of Operation Iraqi Freedom might temper the shrillness of that criticism. It should be noted that both conservatives and liberals demonstrate a willingness to exploit and sensationalize a story to serve a cause, but I have been curious to see if battle experience would alter the debate.

It would seem not. There has been considerable commentary, but little has been based on rigorous inquiry. Consider the story of Private First Class Jessica Lynch. Lynch was a prisoner of war, held hostage in an Iraqi hospital. Special Forces troops launched a dramatic rescue of Lynch that made headlines everywhere. The opinion pieces followed shortly declaring American equanimity toward Lynch's capture a sign of progress or an abasement of the nation's values. Then came a spectacular piece of muckraking journalism by the BBC charging that the story was largely (albeit brilliantly) contrived to suit the political

Captain Jennifer Wilson became the first woman to pilot the B-2 Spirit bomber in combat on April 1, 2003. *Courtesy of U.S. Air Force. Photo by Technical Sergeant Richard Freeland.*

objectives of the Bush administration. It is reasonable to predict still more controversy associated with this particular story, not to mention the entire war. What is much harder to predict is what the impact of this war will have on American women in aviation.

Historians are not reliable fortune tellers, and we are not immune to the problem of being caught up in the experience of our times. Our sensibilities as citizens can sometimes collide with our professional ambitions of objectivity. It will hardly be a surprise to the reader to know that I am enthralled with the story of women in aviation. "So there I was . . ." begins one email message forwarded to me last month. Immediately I am drawn into "Kirby's" account of a SAM (surface-to-air missile) suppression mission. The female F-16 fighter pilot employs all the bravado, acronyms, and military slang that so easily seduce Americans. I admire the stories of courage and skill. I like it when a woman overcomes the odds against her. Readers of this book will recognize that the women military aviators in Iraq have much in common with the WASP who ferried military airplanes during World War II. I suspect they will have a grand time together getting to know each other and doing some hangar-flying at the next Women in Aviation conference. I know that I will be eager to listen.

This book is about something more than a compilation of good stories, however. Which brings me back to "chicks." When I was researching the first edition of this book in the mid-1980s, the word "chick" was anathema to most women. But times change. So now we have "Killer Chicks" and "Dixie Chicks," "Chick Flicks" and "Chick Magnets," "Chick Tracts" and "www.ask-a-chick.com." In the past two decades, the word has been transformed so completely as to be embraced, even celebrated by women.

It is always remarkable when you realize that the society you live in has the capacity to completely reverse its values, to accept experience and set aside old ideas. For the past half century, American women in aviation have been busy flying (or participating in activities related to flight), but they have also been transforming our society. Few appreciate this fact, because on the whole these women are preoccupied with the fact that their numbers remain so small. Even though they are optimistic that things can be changed, there remains a sense of failure that underlies the seemingly endless quest for the perfect strategy to encourage larger numbers of women to participate in the aviation community.

Outside this world, constitutional law scholars and conservative political activists alike believe these women have accomplished something revolutionary. They have become important bellwethers of political, legal, and social change. It is unlikely that in the near future the "National Defense Authorization Act for Fiscal Years 1992 and 1993" will be talked about by ordinary citizens the way they include Title IX, *Roe v Wade,* or the Civil Rights Act of 1964 in conversation. What sharp observers have recognized is that the repeal of the combat exclusion laws marked a very significant turning point in the definition of American citizenship. Throughout U.S. history, men and women had very different obligations as citizens, most notably with regard to the obligation to defend the nation. That changed this past decade, although recent headlines about sexual harassment and abuse at the U.S. Air Force Academy, for example, remind us that although the law changed, the work of changing minds and hearts is still unfinished.

Some are frightened by the change that necessarily means women will be intentionally placed in harm's way. Equality is the most fundamental truth asserted by the Declaration of Independence, which is why the legal scholars have been so interested in "Killer Chick" and her band of sisters in arms. "Just another day in the office with a view," writes "Kirby" in pilot-speak that denies the upside-down nature of war. Yet, for the first time, Americans having gotten a good look at women and men fulfilling the common obligations as citizens—together—might use bolder language. The director of the Women's Army Corps, Oveta Culp Hobby, told young women at the start of World War II that they had a "debt and a date." "A debt to democracy and a date with destiny."[1] Never has it seemed clearer than in recent weeks the fact that American women in aviation have fulfilled that obligation. It is not just another day; it is an extraordinary moment in history. *Ad inexplorata*; toward the unknown.

Appendices

Statistics for American Women and Flight

Appendix 1
Women Pilots, 1940–1945, 1960–2000

Year	Student	Private	Commercial	Airline Transport	Nonpilot	Total Women	Total Men & Women	% of Women
1940	311	476	86	—	na	902	31,264	2.9
1941	202	1,803	113	—	na	2,145	63,113	3.4
1942	—	3,009	184	—	na	3,206	100,787	3.2
1943	—	3,739	373	—	na	4,112	124,050	3.3
1944	—	4,211	618	—	na	4,829	132,435	3.6
1945	—	4,166	956	—	na	5,112	141,280	3.6
1960	5,748	3,425	738	25	2,080	9,966	348,062	2.9
1961	5,875	3,554	733	26	2,084	10,246	352,860	2.9
1962	5,939	3,683	728	27	2,116	10,512	365,971	2.9
1963	6,755	4,004	813	51	2,142	11,757	378,700	3.1
1964	8,179	5,218	1,047	55	2,235	14,627	431,041	3.4
1965	10,106	6,147	1,137	40	2,280	17,555	479,770	3.7
1966	11,424	7,319	1,317	61	2,376	20,265	548,757	3.7
1967	13,173	8,775	1,479	57	2,477	23,659	617,931	3.8
1968	16,243	10,164	1,691	71	2,707	28,401	691,695	4.1
1969	16,055	11,174	1,824	76	2,912	29,415	720,028	4.1
1970	15,787	11,409	1,897	79	3,078	29,472	732,729	4.0
1971	16,417	12,332	2,032	88	3,413	31,216	741,009	4.2

1972	17,053	13,391	2,196	101	3,594	33,001	750,869	4.4
1973	18,593	13,232	2,083	95	3,074	34,356	714,607	4.8
1974	19,298	14,465	2,596	116	3,471	36,943	733,728	5.0
1975	19,600	14,952	2,733	137	3,809	37,934	728,187	5.2
1976	22,254	15,838	2,857	160	4,252	41,643	744,246	5.6
1977	25,705	17,702	3,090	193	3,672	47,294	783,932	6.0
1978	26,354	19,267	3,306	270	3,984	49,874	798,833	6.2
1979	26,714	20,275	3,618	361	4,350	51,733	814,667	6.4
1980	26,006	21,554	3,993	480	4,779	52,902	827,071	6.4
1981	22,591	19,602	4,101	584	5,201	47,721	764,182	6.2
1982	19,958	19,388	4,257	749	5,697	45,305	733,255	6.2
1983	18,696	18,801	4,281	884	6,151	43,648	718,004	6.1
1984	19,435	18,616	4,232	1,032	6,591	44,339	722,376	6.1
1985	19,058	17,974	4,185	1,184	6,017	43,483	709,540	6.1
1986	18,899	17,532	4,176	1,334	6,502	43,082	709,118	6.1
1987	18,367	17,349	4,208	1,538	7,101	42,578	699,653	6.1
1988	17,529	17,544	4,410	1,745	7,842	42,299	694,016	6.1
1989	17,637	16,988	4,760	1,898	10,683	42,366	700,010	6.1
1990	15,007	17,301	5,210	2,082	9,557	40,515	702,659	5.8
1991	14,501	17,514	5,652	2,308	10,324	40,931	692,095	5.9
1992	13,921	17,276	5,918	2,530	11,514	40,620	682,959	5.9
1993	12,788	16,997	5,981	2,738	12,363	39,460	665,069	5.9
1994	12,061	17,196	6,000	2,924	13,026	39,157	654,088	6.0

Note: Information about women pilots was not collected for 1946–1959. The total number of women's certificates in some years does not equal the sum of the preceeding columns because some certificates issued by the government have not been included in this table or because some women held more than one certificate. Dash = information not available; na = not applicable.

Appendix 1: Women Pilots, 1940–1945, 1960–2000 (cont'd)

Year	Student	Private	Commercial	Airline Transport	Nonpilot	Total Women	Total Men & Women	% of Women
1995	12,710	15,398	5,694	3,134	15,120	38,032	639,184	6.0
1996	11,632	14,868	5,495	3,346	13,909	36,433	622,261	5.9
1997	11,217	14,257	5,392	3,572	14,562	35,531	616,342	5.8
1998	11,289	14,152	5,366	3,848	15,380	35,762	618,298	5.8
1999	11,191	15,171	5,720	4,126	15,662	37,373	635,472	5.9
2000	10,809	14,554	5,807	4,411	16,552	36,757	625,581	5.9

Sources:

1940–1945: Aeronautical Chamber of Commerce of America, *Aircraft Yearbook, 1940–1946.*

1960–1969: U.S. Department of Transportation, *U.S. Civil Airmen Statistics*, June 1971. Nonpilot certificates include mechanics, parachute riggers, dispatchers, control tower operators, and ground instructors.

1970–1979: U.S. Department of Transportation, *U.S. Civil Airmen Statistics*, 1979–1985/86. Nonpilot certificates include mechanics, parachute riggers, ground instructors, dispatchers, and control tower operators.

1980–1985: U.S. Department of Transportation, *U.S. Civil Airmen Statistics*, 1985/86. Total pilot certificates include student, private, commercial, airline transport, helicopter only, glider only, and lighter-than-air only categories. Nonpilot certificates include mechanics, parachute riggers, ground instructors, dispatchers, flight engineers, and flight navigators.

1985–2000: U.S. Department of Transportation, *U.S. Civil Airmen Statistics*. Prior to 1995 pilots were categorized as private, commercial, or airline transport based on their airplane certificate. In 1995, these pilots were categorized based on their highest certificate. For example, if a pilot held a private certificate and a commercial helicopter certificate, prior to 1995 the pilot would have been categorized as private; 1995 and after as commercial. The FAA began issuing a "recreational" certificate in 1990. This category is included in the total but does not have a separate column entry.

Appendix 2

Women Military Pilots, 1985–2000

Pilots	Commissioned			Warrant			Total		
	Men	Women	% Women	Men	Women	% Women	Men	Women	% Women
2001	25,234	1,009	3.84	4,360	123	2.74	29,594	1,132	3.68
2000	25,324	960	3.65	4,423	111	2.45	29,747	1,071	3.48
1999	26,183	885	3.27	4,586	112	2.38	30,769	997	3.14
1998	27,355	841	2.98	4,728	109	2.25	32,083	950	2.88
1997	28,526	803	2.74	5,022	118	2.30	33,548	921	2.67
1996	29,429	748	2.48	5,295	106	1.96	34,724	854	2.40
1995	30,234	717	2.32	5,371	90	1.65	35,605	807	2.22
1994	31,051	673	2.12	6,078	84	1.36	37,129	757	2.00
1993	29,915	632	2.07	6,393	81	1.25	36,308	713	1.93
1992	31,852	642	1.98	6,360	79	1.23	38,212	721	1.85
1991	34,239	708	2.03	6,624	82	1.22	40,863	790	1.90
1990	35,983	699	1.91	6,519	80	1.21	42,502	779	1.80
1989	37,406	683	1.79	6,339	78	1.22	43,745	761	1.71
1988	38,282	700	1.80	6,148	64	1.03	44,430	764	1.69
1987	30,425	574	1.85	6,203	61	0.97	36,628	635	1.70
1986	31,192	564	1.78	6,404	66	1.02	37,596	630	1.65
1985	31,406	531	1.66	6,559	67	1.01	37,965	598	1.55
Total	524,036	12,369	2.31	97,412	1,511	1.53	621,448	13,880	2.18

Appendix 2: Women Military Pilots, 1985–2000 (cont'd)

		Commissioned			Warrant			Total		
		Men	Women	% Women	Men	Women	% Women	Men	Women	% Women
Crew	2001	8,361	304	3.51	19	0	0.00	8,380	304	3.50
	2000	8,279	260	3.04	19	0	0.00	8,298	260	3.04
	1999	8,432	231	2.67	19	0	0.00	8,451	231	2.66
	1998	8,746	210	2.34	18	0	0.00	8,764	210	2.34
	1997	8,865	190	2.10	18	0	0.00	8,883	190	2.09
	1996	9,118	165	1.78	18	0	0.00	9,136	165	1.77
	1995	9,603	167	1.71	20	0	0.00	9,623	167	1.71
	1994	10,560	177	1.65	21	0	0.00	10,581	177	1.65
	1993	9,484	163	1.69	22	0	0.00	9,506	163	1.69
	1992	10,605	166	1.54	24	0	0.00	10,629	166	1.54
	1991	11,438	175	1.51	26	0	0.00	11,464	175	1.50
	1990	11,974	178	1.46	29	0	0.00	12,003	178	1.46
	1989	12,132	172	1.40	30	0	0.00	12,162	172	1.39
	1988	12,248	167	1.35	32	0	0.00	12,280	167	1.34
	1987	6,775	100	1.45	37	0	0.00	6,812	100	1.45
	1986	7,156	106	1.46	40	0	0.00	7,196	106	1.45
	1985	7,316	115	1.55	35	0	0.00	7,351	115	1.54
Total		161,092	3,046	1.86	427	0	0.00	161,519	3,046	1.85

	Commissioned			Warrant			Total		
	Men	Women	% Women	Men	Women	% Women	Men	Women	% Women
2001	33,595	1,313	3.76	4,379	123	2.73	37,974	1,436	3.64
2000	33,603	1,220	3.50	4,442	111	2.44	38,045	1,331	3.38
1999	34,615	1,116	3.12	4,605	112	2.37	39,220	1,228	3.04
1998	36,101	1,051	2.83	4,746	109	2.25	40,847	1,160	2.76
1997	37,391	993	2.59	5,040	118	2.29	42,431	1,111	2.55
1996	38,547	913	2.31	5,313	106	1.96	43,860	1,019	2.27
1995	39,837	884	2.17	5,391	90	1.64	45,228	974	2.11
1994	41,611	850	2.00	6,099	84	1.36	47,710	934	1.92
1993	39,399	795	1.98	6,415	81	1.25	45,814	876	1.88
1992	42,457	808	1.87	6,384	79	1.22	48,841	887	1.78
1991	45,677	883	1.90	6,650	82	1.22	52,327	965	1.81
1990	47,957	877	1.80	6,548	80	1.21	54,505	957	1.73
1989	49,538	855	1.70	6,369	78	1.21	55,907	933	1.64
1988	50,530	867	1.69	6,180	64	1.02	56,710	931	1.62
1987	37,200	674	1.78	6,240	61	0.97	43,440	735	1.66
1986	38,348	670	1.72	6,444	66	1.01	44,792	736	1.62
1985	38,722	646	1.64	6,594	67	1.01	45,316	713	1.55
Total	685,128	15,415	2.20	97,839	1,511	1.52	782,967	16,926	2.12

Source: U.S. Defense Manpower Data Center, "U.S. Military Pilots by Gender, 1985–2001."

Appendix 3

Women Airline Pilots and Navigators, 1983–2000 (in thousands, age 16 and over)

Year	Total	Women	Percent
1983	69	1	1.4
1984	75	2	2.7
1985	77	2	2.6
1986	79	1	1.3
1987	78	2	2.6
1988	88	3	3.4
1989	109	4	3.7
1990	114	6	5.3
1991	100	3	3.0
1992	96	2	2.1
1993	101	4	4.0
1994	104	3	2.9
1995	114	4	3.5
1996	114	2	1.8
1997	120	1	0.8
1998	113	4	3.5
1999	143	4	2.8
2000	129	5	3.9

Source: Department of Labor, Bureau of Labor Statistics, Current Population Survey, "Employed Persons by Detailed Occupation and Sex, 1983–2000 Annual Averages."

Appendix 4

*Women Air Traffic Controllers, 1983–2000
(in thousands, age 16 and over)*

Year	Total	Women	Percent
1983	29	7	24.1
1984	28	4	14.3
1985	34	5	14.7
1986	34	7	20.6
1987	32	8	25.0
1988	30	5	16.7
1989	35	8	22.9
1990	36	12	33.3
1991	34	11	32.4
1992	23	4	17.4
1993	25	5	20.0
1994	24	4	16.7
1995	30	3	10.0
1996	32	7	21.9
1997	36	2	5.6
1998	26	6	23.1
1999	24	5	20.8
2000	23	3	13.0

Source: Department of Labor, Bureau of Labor Statistics, Current Population Survey, "Employed Persons by Detailed Occupation and Sex, 1983–2000 Annual Averages."

Appendix 5

Women Aviation Industry Workers during World War II

Month/Year	Total	Women	Percent
Jan. 1942	460,356	23,137	5.0
Feb.	501,753	30,218	6.0
Mar.	538,060	38,455	7.1
Apr.	572,616	48,009	8.4
May	611,272	60,350	9.9
June	653,033	77,135	11.8
July	695,359	95,482	13.7
Aug.	753,425	119,967	15.9
Sept.	796,954	153,301	19.2
Oct.	852,862	196,665	23.1
Nov.	910,932	237,002	26.0
Dec.	970,359	280,497	28.9
Jan. 1943	1,027,914	321,788	31.3
Feb.	1,072,573	351,752	32.8
Mar.	1,106,664	370,635	33.5
Apr.	1,139,018	387,092	34.0
May	1,166,555	402,385	34.5
June	1,203,479	421,548	35.0
July	1,233,385	435,468	35.3
Aug.	1,257,427	449,938	35.8
Sept.	1,290,181	468,169	36.3
Oct.	1,311,765	479,923	36.6
Nov.	1,326,345	486,073	36.6
Dec.	1,310,799	472,519	36.0

Month/Year	Total	Women	Percent
Jan. 1944	1,307,953	466,292	35.7
Feb.	1,295,791	461,074	35.6
Mar.	1,267,657	454,412	35.8
Apr.	1,247,182	448,066	35.9
May	1,227,724	445,725	36.3
June	1,197,974	439,503	36.7
July	1,180,866	435,608	36.9
Aug.	1,139,919	419,216	36.8
Sept.	1,095,198	398,418	36.4
Oct.	1,062,900	386,466	36.4
Nov.	1,050,320	379,822	36.2
Dec.	1,045,635	375,520	35.9
Jan. 1945	1,058,236	376,804	35.6
Feb.	1,053,089	372,719	35.5
Mar.	1,031,363	364,141	35.4
Apr.	996,356	349,446	35.1
May	920,441	316,032	34.4

NB: Employment in Airframe, Engine, and Propeller Plants (Prime Contractors) during World War II (January 1942 to May 1945)

Source: Department of Labor, Bureau of Labor Statistics, "Wartime Development of the Aircraft Industry," *Bulletin* 800, Nov. 20, 1944, pp. 4, 8. (Brought up to date by Department of Labor, Bureau of Labor Statistics, Division of Construction and Public Employment.) Reprinted in Aircraft Industries Association of America, *Aviation Facts and Figures, 1945,* ed. Rudolf Mooley (New York: McGraw-Hill, 1945).

Appendix 6

Women Aircraft Industry Workers, 1947–1961 (in thousands of workers)

Month/Year	Total	Women	Percent
Oct. 1947	241.5	28.5	11.8
Sept. 1949	266.4	33.3	12.5
Dec. 1949	260.0	32.5	12.5
Mar. 1950	259.2	31.1	12.0
June 1950	262.5	31.5	12.0
Sept. 1950	291.9	36.2	12.4
Dec. 1950	345.6	47.0	13.6
Mar. 1951	407.3	61.1	15.0
June 1951	458.6	77.5	16.9
Sept. 1951	500.6	88.6	17.7
Dec. 1951	562.7	104.1	18.5
Mar. 1952	600.5	111.1	18.5
June 1952	634.6	117.4	18.5
Sept. 1952	655.0	117.9	18.0
Dec. 1952	711.5	130.2	18.3
Mar. 1953	735.0	130.1	17.7
June 1953	729.4	131.3	18.0
Sept. 1953	757.9	133.4	17.6
June 1954	804.1	136.7	17.0
Sept. 1954	797.0	132.3	16.6

Month/Year	Total	Women	Percent
Oct. 1955	754.1	118.4	15.7
Oct. 1956	867.9	135.4	15.6
Oct. 1957	847.2	134.7	15.9
Oct. 1958	762.8	112.9	14.8
Oct. 1959	717.2	108.3	15.1
Oct. 1960	655.6	100.3	15.3
Oct. 1961	678.8	99.1	14.6

Sources:

1947–1953: Aircraft Industries Association of America, *Aviation Facts and Figures, 1953,*
ed. Rudolf Mooley and Thomas J. Cawley (Washington: Lincoln Press, 1954), p. 61,
Table 3-17 derived from: Bureau of the Census, "Census of Manufactures, 1947,
Aircraft and Parts," p. 3 and Bureau of Labor Statistics, "Employment and Payrolls"
(Monthly).

1954: Aircraft Industries Association of America, *Aviation Facts and Figures, 1955,* comp.
Rudolf Mooley and Thomas J. Cawley, ed. Ben. S. Lee (Washington: Lincoln Press,
1955), p. 22, "Women Employees in the Aircraft Industry, 1942 To Date" derived
from: Department of Commerce, Bureau of the Census, "Census of Manufactures
1947"; Department of Labor, Bureau of Labor Statistics, "Employment and Earnings"
(Monthly) (Formerly "Employment and Payrolls"); Department of Labor, Bureau of
Labor Statistics, "Revised Series—Employment" and "Wartime Development of the
Aircraft Industry," *Bulletin* 800.

Appendix 7

Women Aerospace Industry Workers,
1959–2000 (in thousands, not seasonally
adjusted, annual average)

Year	Total	Women	Percent
1959	694.2	103.8	15.0
1960	604.8	90.2	14.9
1961	587.3	86.1	14.7
1962	615.0	89.3	14.5
1963	615.7	85.6	13.9
1964	583.1	77.8	13.3
1965	601.3	80.2	13.3
1966	725.6	104.0	14.3
1967	803.0	123.1	15.3
1968	820.7	124.5	15.2
1969	774.8	115.5	14.9
1970	644.1	91.8	14.3
1971	509.0	70.5	13.9
1972	481.3	69.0	14.3
1973	510.1	77.2	15.1
1974	524.1	82.2	15.7
1975	499.4	79.4	15.9
1976	473.2	75.1	15.9
1977	467.3	76.6	16.4
1978	511.1	88.8	17.4
1979	592.5	109.0	18.4
1980	633.1	115.5	18.2
1981	626.4	119.5	19.1
1982	584.0	112.5	19.3

Year	Total	Women	Percent
1983	561.6	108.8	19.4
1984	574.9	114.7	20.0
1985	616.2	126.1	20.5
1986	655.8	138.3	21.1
1987	678.0	145.0	21.4
1988	683.5	147.5	21.6
1989	711.0	157.4	22.1
1990	712.3	161.1	22.6
1991	669.2	150.0	22.4
1992	611.7	135.1	22.1
1993	542.0	116.0	21.4
1994	481.5	100.9	21.0
1995	450.5	93.3	20.7
1996	458.1	95.7	20.9
1997	500.6	107.4	21.5
1998	525.1	115.3	21.9
1999	496.3	109.6	22.1
2000	464.1	105.0	22.6

NB: This table does not include employment figures for the "Guided Missiles, Space Vehicles and Parts" (SIC 376) segment of the aerospace industry.

Source: U.S. Department of Labor, Bureau of Labor Statistics, "National Employment, Hours, and Earnings, Aircraft and Parts Industry, SIC 372." Data extracted from *Bureau of Labor Statistics Data* online, http://data.bls.gov.

Appendix 8

Women Aerospace Engineers, 1983–2002 (in thousands, age 16 and over)

Year	Total	Women	Percent
1983	80	6	7.5
1984	80	3	3.8
1985	95	4	4.2
1986	93	7	7.5
1987	104	8	7.7
1988	115	7	6.1
1989	112	4	3.6
1990	110	8	7.3
1991	102	9	8.8
1992	88	6	6.8
1993	82	6	7.3
1994	75	11	14.7
1995	78	4	5.1
1996	80	4	5.0
1997	87	4	4.6
1998	86	7	8.1
1999	79	9	11.4
2000	78	8	10.3

Source: Department of Labor, Bureau of Labor Statistics, Current Population Survey, "Employed Persons by Detailed Occupation and Sex, 1983–2000 Annual Averages."

Notes

Introduction

1. Douglas, *United States Women in Aviation, 1940–1985*, 1.

2. There are numerous books and articles of varying quality documenting the pre-1940 history of American women in aviation. In addition to the Smithsonian Institution series, readers should also consult the many excellent biographies. One of the best accounts remains Amelia Earhart's book, *The Fun of It*, published in 1932. The two most important scholarly works are Susan Ware's *Still Missing: Amelia Earhart and the Search for Modern Feminism* and Joseph Corn's essay "Making Flying 'Thinkable': Women Pilots and the Selling of Aviation" in his book *The Winged Gospel: America's Romance with Aviation.*

3. Rich, *The Magnificent Moisants*, 159 quotes "Why a Woman Can Run an Airship Better Than a Man," *Mobile (Ala.) Register*, 3 September 1911; Oakes, *United States Women in Aviation through World War I*, 2 quotes "Why a Woman Can Run an Airship Better Than a Man," *Mobile (Ala.) Register*, 3 September 1911.

4. Oakes, *United States Women in Aviation through World War I*, 17–19.

5. Moolman, *Women Aloft*, 18.

6. Rich, *Amelia Earhart: A Biography*, 53–71; Backus, *Letters from Amelia*, 65–73. See also Ware, *Still Missing*.

7. Ware, *Still Missing*, 62 quotes Thaden, *High, Wide and Frightened*, 258.

8. Jessen, *The Powder Puff Derby of 1929*, 199.

9. Earhart, *The Fun of It*, 144.

10. Nielsen, *From Sky Girl to Flight Attendant*, 7–13.

11. Kerfoot, *Propeller Annie*, 43.

12. Ibid., 58.

13. Corn, *The Winged Gospel*, 76.

14. Ibid., 81 quotes J.C. Johnson, "Betsy Ross Goes Modern," *Cincinnati Enquirer*, 11 June 1933.

15. Ibid, 85.

16. Cochran, letter.

1. Students and Teachers, Clubs and Colleges: Women in Civilian Aviation Organizations

Epigraph: From unidentified contemporary newspaper clipping.

1. Rickman, *The Originals,* 153–55.

2. Fort, "At the Twilight's Last Gleaming," 19.

3. Ibid.

4. Link Trainers were special training units manufactured by the Link Company; they were used to teach pilots how to fly exclusively by instruments. The trainers simulated the cockpit, as well as all the physical sensations of flight. Instructors created the flight conditions, monitored their students' flights, and taught the skills needed to navigate. It was a rigorous occupation that required the ability to pilot an aircraft. Women who worked as instructors "knew" how to fly military aircraft, even if they never had the opportunity to pilot a real vehicle.

5. Ninety-Nines, *The History of the Ninety-Nines, Inc.,* 10.

6. Arthur, "Airways to Earning," 34–35.

7. Ninety Nines, *The History of the Ninety-Nines, Inc.,* 23; "Babies, Just Babies," n.p.

8. Planck, *Women with Wings,* 248; Arthur, "Now You Can Learn to Fly," 321, 336; Arthur, "Wings for the Working Girl," 41.

9. Opal Kunz was also a founder of the Betsy Ross Corps, which was started in 1931. It was a well-trained women's paramilitary air corps dedicated to the sole purpose of national defense, through humanitarian relief work. (Ninety-Nines, *The History of the Ninety-Nines, Inc.,* 11.)

10. Arthur, "Now You Can Learn to Fly," 320–21, 336.

11. Ibid., 336.

12. The original goal of the WFA was to provide a "trained, disciplined corps of women to replace men behind the air lines in a national emergency." (Arthur, "Now You Can Learn to Fly," 336.) A member of the Washington, D.C., chapter was quoted as saying: "Every member of the Chapter is eager to serve in the Women's Auxiliary Ferry Service and the Group hopes to help as many students as possible accumulate flying time to qualify for this service." ("D.C. Women Flyer's Chapter," n.p.)

13. Arthur, "Wings for the Working Girl," 136; Arthur, "Now You Can Learn to Fly," 336.

14. Wixson, "Air Ferrying Service," n.p.

15. Laura Brown, "Flier or No," 8; Logan, "Women Volunteers," n.p.

16. Shoemaker, "Air Schooling for Milady," 39–40, 42, 112; Planck, *Women with Wings,* 225.

17. Pisano, "A Brief History," 21–25, 27; Planck, *Women with Wings,* 139–43.

18. Arthur, "Airways to Earnings," 55.

19. Planck, *Women with Wings,* 140. The CAA paid a standard fee of $290 for each student to the flight operators and a lump sum of $200 to each institution giving the ground school course. ("The Civilian Pilot Training Program," 4.) Rough estimates of actual expenses based on figures supplied by the CAA indicate that the costs were $390 per student in fiscal 1940 and $640 per student in fiscal 1941 (the fiscal year ran from 1 July to 30 June). (U.S. Civil Aeronautics Authority, *Wartime History of the Civil Aeronautics Administration,* 23.)

20. Howard, interview.

21. Planck, *Women with Wings,* 150–51.

22. Ibid., 150.

23. Strickland, *The Putt-Putt Air Force,* 56.

24. Tubbs, letter.

25. "Women Instructors Graduated," 239; Slack, "Tennessee's Airwomen," 47.

26. Oakes, *United States Women in Aviation: 1930–1939,* 9.

27. CAA administrator C.I. Stanton stated: "It is my opinion that since women have always excelled in instructing and have done most of the teaching of our nation, this should be their natural function in aviation. Our problem is to give the 1,000,000 boys who will graduate into the draft each year, flight training. I believe we should train at least 200,000 of them each year. To do that, we shall need at least 5,000 women instructors." (Slack, "Tennessee's Airwomen," 46.)

28. Ibid., 128.

29. Ibid.; Knapp, *New Wings for Women,* 166.

30. "Women Instructors Graduated," 239; Chapelle, *Girls at Work in Aviation,* 44.

31. Planck, *Women with Wings,* 154–55.

32. Bates, "Lady with Wings," 55.

33. Chapelle, *Girls at Work in Aviation,* 40.

34. Mary Steele Ross, *American Women in Uniform,* 49–51; Nichols, *Wings for Life,* 267–78.

35. They included C.R. Smith, president of American Airlines; William Patterson, president of United Airlines; Jack Frye, president of TWA; Eddie Rickenbacker, president of Eastern Airlines; C.V Whitney, chairman of the board of Pan American Airways; and Walter and Olive Ann Beech, owners of Beechcraft.

36. "Now a Civil Air Patrol," 44.

37. Mary Steele Ross, *American Women in Uniform,* 20.

38. Reiss, "Ground Pilot," 122, 126; Charles P. May, *Women in Aeronautics,* 165.

39. Reiss, "Ground Pilot," 122, 126.

40. Chapelle, *Needed,* 22.

41. "Lieut. Willa Brown," n.p.; Charles P. May, *Women in Aeronautics,* 165.

42. Chapelle, *Needed,* 19.

43. Knapp, *New Wings for Women,* 35. Initially these scholarships, which were offered at the Massachusetts Institute of Technology, New York University, California Institute of Technology, University of Chicago, and the University of California at Los Angeles, were available only to men, but in March 1942 women were included in the program.

44. Knapp, *New Wings for Women,* 35–38, 43. An interesting side note is that the CAA asked Tonkin to conduct a recruiting tour to interest women in applying. She was not very successful, and upon returning to Washington she commented: "Women usually consider calculus and physics rather dry and colorless subjects and shy away from them in college. So I found few with such training plus a private pilot's license." (Ibid., 38.)

45. Edward J. Gardner, "Help Wanted!" 48, 128.

46. Oakes, *United States Women in Aviation: 1930–1939,* 9; Noyes, "Air Marking—Reversed," 107; "The Reminiscences of Blanche Noyes," n.p.

47. Glen Gilbert, *Air Traffic Control,* 11. After the war, many military-trained women would transfer their skills to the CAA.

2. Coffee, Grease, Blueprints, and Rivets: Women at Work in the Aviation Industry

Epigraph: "Demand Growing," 102, 112.

1. Planck, *Women with Wings,* 196–97; Chapelle, *Girls at Work in Aviation,* 198, 201.

2. Nielsen, *From Sky Girl to Flight Attendant: Women and the Making of a Union,* 37.

3. Ibid., xvii.

4. Ibid.

5. "Coffee, Tea or Customer Service Managers?" D5.

6. Planck, *Women with Wings,* 197; Knapp, *New Wings for Women,* 76–77.

7. Nielsen, *From Sky Girl to Flight Attendant: Women and the Making of a Union,* 17.

8. Knapp, *New Wings for Women,* 73, 80.

9. Nielsen, *From Sky Girl to Flight Attendant: Women and the Making of a Union,* 24.

10. Ibid., 15, 25; Aircraft Industries Association of America, *Aviation Facts and Figures, 1945,* 28 [quotes U.S. Department of Labor, Bureau of Labor Statistics, "Wartime Development of the Aircraft Industry," *Bulletin* 800, 20 November 1944, 20]; Planck, *Women with Wings,* 195.

11. Nielsen, *From Sky Girl to Flight Attendant: Women and the Making of a Union,* 23. Banger, *The Transportation Industries, 1889–1946,* 266 [quotes Civil Aeronautics Administration, *Statistical Handbook of Civil Aviation,* 1948 issue].

12. It was the "no-marriage" rule that absolutely distinguished flight attendants from women in other wartime professions. During World War II, for the first time married women outnumbered single women in the workforce. In particular Karen Anderson noted that (1) wives of servicemen were three times more likely to work than those women whose husbands were at home, and (2) women over thirty-five or between the ages of fourteen and twenty-five composed most of the female workforce. (Anderson, *Wartime Women,* 4–5.)

13. This observation was expressed by John R. Hill, Santa Barbara, California, 7 March 1981. (Nielsen, *From Sky Girl to Flight Attendant: Women and the Making of a Union,* 30.)

14. Chapelle, *Girls at Work in Aviation,* 196–97.

15. Planck, *Women with Wings,* 191.

16. Hays, "The WAMS," 38–39, 168; Chapelle, *Girls at Work in Aviation,* 79.

17. "The Month" (December 1942), 10–11. One hundred ninety-one women were assigned to the famous Clipper ships.

18. "Fleet—'Feminine Army,'" 27.

19. "Transatlantic—'Respect for Women,'" 15. It is interesting that the article emphasized Betty Travis's background in automobile engine repair and the fact that she could "throw a baseball like a man." There was an implied connection made by the article in highlighting these traditionally masculine pursuits.

20. "Transatlantic—'The Women,'" 12–13.

21. Chapelle, *Girls at Work in Aviation,* 181–84. Women served in other non–production line positions, such as administrative assistants, personnel officers, statistical assistants, and secretaries. See "The Girls Everyone Likes," 6–7, 21, and "The Forgotten Woman," 6–7, 21, for further information on the experiences of women in these occupations.

22. Eaves, "Wanted," 133.

23. Rossiter, *Women Scientists in America,* 91, 173, 226, 389; Hacker, "Mathematization of Engineering," 45–46; Eaves, "Wanted," 158.

24. *Women in Aircraft Engineering,* 3, 5–7, 11.

25. Ibid., 5–7; Erler, letter; *Women in Aircraft Engineering,* 7.

26. Ahnstrom, "Look . . . Women," 31; Chapelle, *Girls at Work in Aviation,* 153–54.

27. Ahnstrom, "Look . . . Women," 66.

28. Chapelle, *Girls at Work in Aviation,* 154; Chapelle, *Needed,* 169. See also Bix, "'Engineeresses' Invade Campus."

29. Hacker, "Mathematization of Engineering," 48–49; Baker, *Wanted,* 45; Monroe, "Women Artists Are Different," 4.

30. Planck, *Women with Wings,* 219–20.

31. Knapp, *New Wings for Women,* 169–79; Chapelle, *Girls at Work in Aviation,* 151–53.

32. Knapp, *New Wings for Women,* 179.

33. Eaves, "Wanted," 159.

34. Bender, telephone interview.

35. "Hellcat Teasers," 123.

36. Roberts, "You Can't Keep Them Down," 91; Knapp, *New Wings for Women,* 11–12; "Hellcat Teasers," 123.

37. Roberts, "You Can't Keep Them Down," 91.

38. Ibid.

39. Bright, *The Jet Makers,* 2–3; Jablonski, *America in the Air War,* 18.

40. Jablonski, *America in the Air War,* 28.

41. Aircraft Industries Association of America, *Aviation Facts and Figures, 1945,* 20–21, 24, 35 [pp. 20–21 quotes Department of Labor, Bureau of Labor Statistics, "Wartime Development of the Aircraft Industry," *Bulletin 800,* Nov. 20, 1944, 5; p. 24 quotes the same Department of Labor, Bureau of Statistics, *Bulletin 800,* 8].

42. "Women Are Welcome," 22.

43. Aircraft Industries Association, *Aviation Facts and Figures, 1945,* 20–21, 24 [see note 41, this chapter, for quoted sources].

44. Anderson, *Wartime Women,* 36–40.

45. "Demand Growing," 112.

46. "The Gals Come Through," 7.

47. Ibid., 12.

48. Anthony J. Smith, "Menstruation and Industrial Efficiency," 1–5.

49. Neville, "Education Alone," 89.

50. Ibid. For a contrasting account, read Chapelle, *Girls at Work in Aviation,* 90.

51. "Demand Growing," 112; Baker, *Wanted,* 72; "The Gals Come Through," 7; "It's Up to the Women," 6. It is important to note that this idea is somewhat misleading. Labor history indicates that many women, including some married women with families, were in the workplace during the 1930s. Nearly 25 percent of the adult female population (21.2 million females over age fourteen) were gainfully employed during the decade prior to the war (according to the "General Report of Occupations," *Fifteenth Census of the United States 1930,* vol. 5, 272). Proportionally twice as many black women as white women were in the workforce. The basic fact was that most working-class and many middle-class men "were not paid enough to support their families according to the American standard of living." Thus it is clear that the trend of increasing numbers of women in the workplace, though small and strongly resisted by married white women, was well established prior to the war. (Wandersee, *Women's Work,* 1.)

52. "Alaska," 19.

53. Common in the aircraft-production plants during World War II was the following story. It was often used by recruiters as a parable to illustrate the importance of attitude and patriotism.

"Three girls were inspectors of valve spring washers in an airplane engine factory. They worked side by side, each doing exactly the same job as the others. A visitor passing through the factory asked one of them what she was doing.

"She smiled and said, 'I'm making eighty-five cents an hour,' and went back to her work.

"The visitor asked the second one what she was doing.

"'I'm inspecting valve spring washers for bomber engines,' she said seriously.

"When the visitor repeated his question to the third girl, she looked up happily, without letting her fingers miss a motion.

"'I'm helping to win the war, sir,' she said." (Chapelle, *Needed*, 149–50.)

54. Baker, *Wanted*, 11.

55. Ibid., 191.

56. Thorburn and Thorburn, *No Tumult, No Shouting*, 66.

57. Bowman, *Slacks and Callouses*, 165. The swing shift ran from 4:30 P.M. to 1:00 A.M. and paid an additional 8 cents per hour.

58. Ibid., 168.

59. Chapelle's books, including *Needed: Women in Aviation* (1942) and *Girls at Work in Aviation* (1943), along with similar ones by other authors were part of a carefully orchestrated propaganda program designed to convince women that working in aircraft factories was both fitting and proper. They were written for teenage girls and contain many mini biographies of women as well as specific instructions on how to enter the field. (Ostroff, *Fire in the Wind*, 77; Bernardin, *Women in the Work Force*, 31.)

60. Chapelle, *Girls at Work in Aviation*, 7.

61. Bernardin, *Women in the Work Force*, 31; Baker, *Wanted*, 23; Planck, *Women with Wings*, 209–10.

62. "The Gals Come Through," 7. Retooling the factories for wartime production marked a dramatic change for the manufacturers. The U.S. government enlisted the aid of automobile manufacturers to help aircraft companies change from a "job shop" system to line production. (Bright, *The Jet Makers*, 4.) It is interesting that the two new factors—women and production line techniques, just as with the case of women and absenteeism—are linked together.

63. "It's Up to the Women," 7.

64. Despite claims to the contrary, women did earn less. It was during this period that the National War Labor Board (NWLB) created two important policies to counter the problems of pay discrimination. Title II of Executive Order 9250 was a Wage and Salary Stabilization Policy, which promoted wage adjustments for the "correction of maladjustments or inequalities, the elimination of substandards of living and the correction of gross inequities." The second policy was General Order No. 16, which stated "that wages for women could be increased without approval of the NWLB to 'equalize the wage or salary rate paid to females with rates paid to males for comparable quality and quantity of work on the same or similar operations.'" (Beatty and Beatty, "Job Evaluation and Discrimination," 211; Aircraft

Industries Association, *Aviation Facts and Figures, 1945,* 30 [quotes Department of Labor, Bureau of Labor Statistics, "Hourly Earnings in Aircraft Engine Plants, August, 1943," Serial No. 81632, pp. 5, 6; also cites Department of Labor, Bureau of Labor Statistics, "Wages in Aircraft Propeller Industry, October 1942," Serial 81526, 8]).

65. Corn, *The Winged Gospel,* particularly chapter 3 and pages 126–27; Baker, *Wanted,* 173; Chapelle, *Needed,* 215.

66. "Madame Mechanic," 136.

67. Anderson, *Wartime Women,* 7–8.

3. Daughters of Minerva: Military Women in Aviation

Epigraph: Unidentified newspaper clipping of a weekly column, "Just Folks," by Edgar Guest.

1. De Pauw, "Women in Combat," 210; see also Holm, *Women in the Military,* 3–15.

2. Hancock, *Lady in the Navy,* 22–23.

3. Thaden, *High, Wide and Frightened,* 229–54.

4. Holm, *Women in the Military,* 18–20; Keil, *Those Wonderful Women,* 100; U.S. Congress, House, Select Subcommittee of the Committee on Veterans' Affairs, *To Provide Recognition,* 50–51.

5. Jacqueline Cochran's September 1939 record was 305.926 mph for 100 km, Burbank to San Francisco in a Seversky. (Planck, *Women with Wings,* 318.)

6. Craven and Cate, *The Army Air Forces,* 528; Backus, *Letters From Amelia,* 149, 171. In a column published 1 September 1942, Eleanor Roosevelt described America's female pilots as "a weapon waiting to be used" (quoted in Strother, "Statement before the Committee on Veterans' Affairs," in U.S. Congress, House, Select Subcommittee of the Committee on Veterans' Affairs, *To Provide Recognition,* 286).

7. Cochran and Odlum, *The Stars at Noon,* 6.

8. Ibid., 40.

9. The record was from Burbank, California, to Cleveland, Ohio, 2,042 miles in 8 hours, 10 minutes, and 31 seconds. (Cochran and Odlum, *The Stars at Noon,* 65).

10. Craven and Cate, *The Army Air Forces,* 528 [quotes USAF Historical Studies, No. 55: "Women Pilots with the AAF, 1941 1944," 2–3, and H.H. Arnold, *Global Mission* (New York, 1940), 311].

11. Keil, *Those Wonderful Women,* 48.

12. Margaret C. Love, interview; Douglas, "Wasps of War," 46–49; Photograph and caption in *College Humor and Sense* (August 1932), 32. Air marking involved painting large markings (in all the major American cities) that were visible from an aircraft as a navigational aid to pilots. Love's responsibility was for the East Coast region, New York State in particular. (Knapp, *New Wings for Women,* 52.)

13. Love to Harry Kelliher, 14 December 1937; Knapp, *New Wings for Women,* 52–53; Oakes, *United States Women in Aviation; 1930–1939,* 62.

14. Harry Bruno to J.M. Gwinn, Jr., 25 October 1937; Love to Harry Kelliher, 14 December 1937.

15. "Women Ferry Pilots," 1; Knapp, *New Wings for Women,* 55–56.

16. Love to Lt. Colonel Robert Olds, 21 May 1940.

17. Treadwell, *The Women's Army Corps*, 15 [quotes memo, Capt. Williston B. Palmer for G-1, 2 October 1939, sub: Women with the Army (Emergency), G-1/15839].

18. Ibid., 16.

19. Moolman, *Women Aloft*, 141–43.

20. Cochran and Odlum, *The Stars at Noon*, 98–107.

21. Ibid., 107.

22. Ibid., 98–107; Keil, *Those Wonderful Women*, 50–51, 97–100.

23. Bradbrooke, "Atta Girls!" 35, 44; Bowater, "Air Transport Auxiliary Service," 172–73.

24. Bradbrooke, "Atta Girls!" 73.

25. Ibid., 44; Moolman, *Women Aloft* , 143.

26. Treadwell, *The Women's Army Corps*, 19–20, 23.

27. Bandel, *The WAC Program*, 4 [quotes letter from General Headquarters, Air Force, to Chief of Air Corps, ACC 324.5 AWS (Women), dated 27 December 1941]. The Army Air Corps became the Army Air Forces on 20 June 1941; however, many individuals continued to refer to it as the Army Air Corps throughout the war.

28. Bandel, *The WAC Program*, 15.

29. Craven and Cate, *The Army Air Forces*, 510; Bandel, *The WAC Program*, 9.

30. Bandel, *The WAC Program*, 13, note.

31. Craven and Cate, *The Army Air Forces*, 508.

32. By contrast, the WAVES did not accept any black women during its first three years. (Treadwell, *The Women's Army Corps*, 58.) Neither did the Marine Corps Women's Reserve (MCWR), nor the Coast Guard's women's corps (SPARs), although there was no explicit legislation preventing their doing so. (MacGregor, *Integration of the Armed Forces, 1940–1965*, 74.)

33. Treadwell, *The Women's Army Corps*, 58–59, 596.

34. The War Department restricted service by Japanese-American women until late in the war, when it wanted to recruit them (from relocation centers) to translate captured Japanese war documents. Virtually no one signed up, partly due to Japanese cultural opposition to working women, but primarily because of the Japanese-Americans' profound anger at the U.S. government for their wartime experience. (Treadwell, *The Women's Army Corps*, 589.)

35. Hancock, *Lady in the Navy*, 50–51.

36. Ibid., 51–52.

37. Brecht, "Long May She WAVE," 70, 78–79.

38. Hancock, *Lady in the Navy*, 53–56.

39. Ibid., 61.

40. Ibid., 62–63.

41. "WAVES," 15.

42. Hancock, *Lady in the Navy*, 271, 275–76.

43. Holm, *Women in the Military*, 64–65.

44. Wirtschafter, interview.

45. The one exception to this rule was Joy Bright Hancock. Because her job entailed extensive traveling between the various aviation schools of the Training Division in order to supervise the arrangements for the WAVES, she received official permission to fly Navy airplanes. One magazine article about her noted that "there are no soreheads among the men in the cockpits—for she talks their language." It is not clear, however, whether she was the

pilot of these aircraft or simply a pilot who was permitted to occasionally sit at the controls. (Brecht, "Long May She WAVE," 79.)

46. "WAVES," 13.

47. "Rulers of the Air," 68.

48. Hancock, "The Waves," 249.

49. The MCWR program had been authorized 30 July 1942, and like the WAVES it had a World War I precedent, as women had served as Marine (F). (Holm, *Women in the Military,* 33, 65; "Women Marines," 18.

50. "Women Marines," 18.

51. Holm, *Women in the Military,* 32–33.

52. Legislation permitting women to serve outside the continental United States was passed in September 1944; Hancock, *Lady in the Navy,* 209–13, 269–70.

53. Craven and Cate, *The Army Air Forces,* 512, 528.

54. Keil, *Those Wonderful Women,* 101, 103.

55. Crane, "The Women with Silver Wings," 8; La Farge, *The Eagle in the Egg,* 60–61.

56. Keil, *Those Wonderful Women,* 105.

57. Ibid.; Margaret C. Love, interview.

58. Cochran and Odlum, *The Stars at Noon,* 118.

59. Ibid., 117–18.

60. "Mrs. Love of the WAFS," 46, 51; Keil, *Those Wonderful Women,* 107; La Farge, *The Eagle in the Egg,* 131.

4. Nieces of Uncle Sam: The Women's Airforce Service Pilots

Epigraph: Women's Airforce Service Pilots, Class 44-W-10, *WASP "Songbook,"* N.p.

1. Teague, "Memorandum on Miss Jacqueline Cochran."

2. Ibid.

3. Knowles, memorandum.

4. Carter, "The Ladies Join the Air Forces," 96.

5. Ibid., 88.

6. Fort, "At the Twilight's Last Gleaming," 19.

7. Crane, "The Women with Silver Wings," 10; Gillies, interview; Bohn, interview; Margaret C. Love, interview.

8. Selby, "The Fifinellas," 76. There were three Soviet Air Force regiments composed of women pilots. These women not only flew for their country's war effort but also were actually engaged in combat. (Myles, *Night Witches.*) Information about these women was limited, so Cochran's statement, while not entirely accurate, did reflect the fact that the United States was the only country which established a major training program to teach women to fly military aircraft, although it was never possible for such a woman to "enlist" without some previous flight experience.

9. Cochran, "Final Report," 6–10. Given the assumption that military flying was quite different from general aviation and the establishment's fear that women might not be capable of mastering these unique skills, the reasons for the flight time requirement were twofold. First, it was believed that a significant number of flying hours demonstrated a woman's genuine commitment to aviation, and further, it suggested that she possessed the requisite

capabilities, such as mechanical aptitude and general knowledge of aeronautics. The second reason was Cochran's desire to have an outstanding "success to failure" ratio in her first classes. Using experienced pilots in the early phases of the program ensured a high level of achievement. Later, as the women proved themselves, the requirement was lowered.

10. Weisfeld, "The Role of the Women Airforce Service Pilots," 13; Cochran and Odlum, *The Stars at Noon,* 127. Black men were at least admitted into training programs and would eventually comprise four squadrons, the 99th, 100th, 301st, and 302nd.

11. Cochran and Odlum, *The Stars at Noon,* 127–28; Hull, Scott, and Smith, *All the Women Are White,* 21. On the surface it would appear that class discrimination was the least pernicious. Of the women who were accepted, it is clear that they came from a variety of socio-economic backgrounds. The cost of learning to fly and of keeping one's rating current was formidable, especially during the Great Depression of the 1930s. Close scrutiny reveals that many of the poorer women who joined the WASP had been able to fly because they lived at home and did not bear the full cost-of-living expenses.

12. Cochran and Odlum, *The Stars at Noon,* 127–28.

13. If candidates failed or left the program, they had to pay for their trip home. (Strother, "The W.A.S.P. Training Program," 299–301.)

14. Strother, "The W.A.S.P. Training Program," 299–301; Tanner, "We Also Served," 16.

15. Felker, interview. It should be noted that Felker's opinion does *not* apply to most WASP.

16. Cochran, "Final Report," cover letter.

17. Weisfeld, "The Role of the Women Airforce Service Pilots," 20–21; Felker, interview.

18. Cochran, "Final Report," 33.

19. "The Reminiscences of Jacqueline Cochran," quoted by permission from the Oral History Research Office, Columbia, University.

20. Weisfeld, "The Role of the Women Airforce Service Pilots," 24, 27 [quotes interview with S.R. Constance Howerton, 43-W-4].

21. Ibid., 28–29; Cochran and Odlum, *The Stars at Noon,* 126–27.

22. Carl has written an excellent autobiography recounting the details of her unique experience as a military test pilot. See Carl, *A WASP among Eagles.*

23. Cochran, "Final Report," 28; Weisfeld, "The Role of the Women Airforce Service Pilots," 30–31; Pateman, interview.

24. Cochran prevailed on this issue despite major protests from the quartermaster general of the Army. Her work succeeded in overturning several regulations concerning uniforms for civilians as well as an advisory from the air judge advocate that upheld the policy against issuing any uniform to nonmilitary personnel. An exception was authorized by the comptroller general, provided that the uniform was limited to outer garments and remained government property. (Risch, *A Wardrobe for the Women of the Army,* 147–48; Cochran and Odlum, *Stars at Noon,* 123–24.)

25. "Unnecessary and Undesirable?" 66.

26. Tunner, memorandum.

27. Keil, *Those Wonderful Women,* 268.

28. Cochran and Odlum, *The Stars at Noon,* 121; "Battle of the Sexes," 71.

29. Treadwell, *The Women's Army Corps,* 784.

30. Knowles, memorandum; U.S. Congress, House, Select Subcommittee of the Committee on Veterans' Affairs, *To Provide Recognition,* 204–23.

31. Cochran, "Final Report"; Gen. H.H. Arnold, memorandum.

32. Poole, "Requiem for the Wasp," 55.

33. By 1944, sixty-five hundred nurses were assigned to the AAF, six thousand at AAF station hospitals, five hundred as flight nurses. Flight nurses served on aircraft in the evacuation of the wounded throughout the world. Nursing was the only established and accepted female branch in the military prior to World War II, but flight nursing was a new occupation. The nurses received special training and had to pass the flight surgeon's physical examination. (Craven and Cate, *The Army Air Forces*, 537.)

34. Arnold, "Address to Last W.A.S.P. Graduate Class."

35. See Heilbrun, *Reinventing Womanhood*, for a discussion of this concept.

Part II: Should Women Fly?

Epigraphs: Congress, House, Representative Barbara Kennelley Congratulating the Committee on Armed Services, p. H2907; U.S. Presidential Commission, *Report to the President*, 118.

5. Demobilization and the Postwar Transition: 1945–1949

Epigraph: *99s Newsletter* (15 April 1948): 8.

1. "Home by Christmas," 68–69.

2. "Women and Wrenches."

3. Aircraft Industries Association of America, *Aviation Facts and Figures, 1955*, 17–27; U.S. Department of Commerce, Bureau of Labor Statistics, *Historical Statistics of the U.S.: Colonial Times to 1970*, Series D 29-41, 131.

4. Aircraft Industries Association of America, *Aviation Facts and Figures, 1953*, 61 [quotes Bureau of the Census, *Census of Manufactures, 1947*, "Aircraft and Parts," 3]; Bright, *The Jet Makers*, 11–13.

5. Aircraft Industries Association of America, *Aviation Facts and Figures, 1953*, 61 [quotes Bureau of Labor Statistics, "Employment and Payrolls," (Monthly)].

6. Gillies, interview.

7. McDaniel, *The History of Beech*, 13, 19–20, 26–27, 100, 106; Charles P. May, *Women in Aeronautics*, 182–83.

8. "Air-Minded Miss," 23.

9. Elizabeth Gardner, interview.

10. Pateman, interview.

11. "Ex-WASPs Ferrying Surplus War Training Planes," 1.

12. Bohn, interview; Bohn, "Personal Data Record."

13. Bright, *The Jet Makers*, 77–79.

14. Nielsen, *From Sky Girl to Flight Attendant: Women and the Making of a Union*, 30–32. This account is derived from Nielsen's excellent monograph (especially chapter 2) on the history of flight attendant unionization.

15. "So You Want to Be a Hostess," 6.

16. "Braniff Topnotchers," 10.

17. Nielsen, *From Sky Girl to Flight Attendant: Women and the Making of a Union*, 32–35, 37, 40.

18. Ibid., 41, 44–45, 48–49.

19. Merryfield, "Five Hours to Solo," 20.

20. Ibid.

21. Dallimore, "Ceiling Unlimited," 2.

22. Lempke, "President's Column," 1; The Ninety-Nines conducted an informal survey during 1945 which indicated that nationally flight time in a Cub trainer was averaging about $7 an hour for solo time and $10 for dual instruction. ("Ex-WASPs Ferrying Surplus War Training Planes," 1.)

23. *99s Newsletter* (15 November 1945): 1; (15 April 1946): 1; (15 August 1946): 1.

24. *99s Newsletter* (15 March 1947): 3; Ninety-Nines, *The History of the Ninety-Nines, Inc.*, 32.

25. *99s Newsletter* (15 April 1948): 1.

26. Ninety-Nines, *The History of the Ninety-Nines, Inc.*, 77–79.

27. Noyes, "Again Women Fliers," 8. Betty Skelton, a champion aerobatic pilot who made her debut in the first All-Women Air Show in 1947, had this advice for women pilots: "Be a lady." A contemporary account noted that Skelton "doesn't see any point to slopping about an airport in overalls" and that her standard flying luggage always included "an evening dress, a hat, and some nifty slack suits." (Fuller, "Betty Skelton Flies an Airshow," 76.)

28. Downey, "Future Flyers," 16–17.

29. "Skymarker," 115; White, "The Sky's Their Limit," 328.

30. Holm, *Women in the Military*, 103.

31. "Wave Power in Aviation," 15.

32. Treadwell, *The Women's Army Corps*, 739–42, 747–48; Holm, *Women in the Military*, 114.

33. Holm, *Women in the Military*, 113.

34. Hancock, *Lady in the Navy*, 236.

35. "Waves Have Good Record," 16; "Waves Join Reserves," 23; "Air Ambulances Fly Men to Hospitals," 20.

36. MacGregor, *Integration of the Armed Forces*, 248, 267 [p. 267 quotes letter, A. Philip Randolph to General C.B. Cates, 8 March 1949, and letter, CMC to Randolph, 10 March 1949, AW828].

37. Holm, *Women in the Military*, 130, 132.

38. Ibid., 135–47; Rasmussen, interview.

6. "The Feminine Mystique" and Aviation: The 1950s

Epigraph: American Airlines publication, ca. 1950.

1. Crist, "Operation Polar," 8.

2. Ibid.

3. Kraft, "Flying in the Face of Age," 30; Vetterlein, "Newfoundland to Ireland, Non-Stop," 18; Buck, "The Most Unforgettable Character," 115; Hart, "She Flew the Atlantic," 76.

4. Buck, "The Most Unforgettable Character," 117.

5. "Miss Cochran Holds Most Jet Records," 26; "Cochran Sets Sights," 18. Women were not allowed to fly USAF aircraft. Cochran was no exception to this rule. She arranged to be hired by aircraft companies that manufactured military aircraft. In the case of this record, Cochran flew an airplane owned by the Canadian government. The USAF did not place any

restrictions on the pilots employed by companies or other governments, which explains how it was possible for Cochran to make this flight.

6. Cochran and Odlum, *The Stars at Noon,* 221–43.

7. Holm, *Women in the Military,* 141–44.

8. Geraldine May, letter.

9. Holm, *Women in the Military,* 148–57.

10. "Air Force Executive," 13. The underlying issue was American attitudes toward homosexuality. The World War II fears that women who served in the military would become masculinized and/or lesbians were fully extant in the postwar period. Although many lesbians did (and continue to) participate in the military, homosexuality remains a bar to service.

11. "Wolfe, "Women and the Nation's Security," 13; Thruelsen, "Flying WAF," 28–29, 137.

12. "The Glamour Corps," 99, 149.

13. "Woman Fills Many Roles at Sheppard," 19.

14. "Women in Aviation," 6.

15. "Gals Try Their Hands," 33.

16. "The Lady Is Also a Wave," 24.

17. Holm, *Women in the Military,* 152–53.

18. "Navy Flight Nurses Care for Wounded," 19–20.

19. "DACOWITS History Update," 1–22.

20. "A Record of DACOWITS," 1–2.

21. Peggy Phillips, "Readin', Writin', and RPM's," 21, 48.

22. "Top-Flight Scholar," 55.

23. Burnham, "U.S. Ladies in the Air," 32, 37. There was an assumption that women might not take the CAP as seriously as men. Note comments such as Burnham's following: "Even when doing a man's job, Harriet enjoys her woman's prerogative—first to get a steaming cup of hot coffee" (p. 33).

24. Burnham, "The Defense Department's First Lady of Flight," 15.

25. "Lady Flier Completes 10-Day Tour," 29; Nichols, *Wings for Life,* 250–82, 309.

26. Brick, *Powder Puff Derby,* 36.

27. Ibid., 6.

28. Ibid., 6–7; Brick, "Million Dollar Race," 46–47, 74, 76.

29. "TAR," 44. There was a contest rule after 1952 requiring all contestants to wear dresses or suits. Slacks or shorts were not permitted. "This regulation stems from the same desire for serious recognition that has led the TAR participants to shun the title 'Powder Puff Derby,' which was originally applied to their big race." (Wolfe, "Women's Air Race," 50.)

30. Brick, *Powder Puff Derby,* 20.

31. Ibid., 28.

32. In 1959, *Newsweek* described the AWTAR as follows: "This is the way of women—or at least 100 American women—in the aviation age. Once each year, they shed their household duties, climb into tiny aircraft and with unladylike abandon, race from one coast of the U. S. to the other. They zoom in and out of obscure airports, scream at attendants to fill up their gas tanks, and roar through treacherous rainstorms. Since this annual female aerial madness began in 1947, it has become known as the Powder Puff Derby." The description was erroneous and overblown, but it also betrayed a certain lack of seriousness on the part

of the editorial staff and revealed something of the underlying attitude toward women in aviation. ("Powderpuff Derby," 88.)

33. Eddleman, *Cows on the Runway,* 172.

34. Ingells, "Their Eggbeaters Aren't in the Kitchen," 7.

35. Dougherty, letter; Charles P. May, *Women in Aeronautics,* 208.

36. Aerospace Industries Association of America, *Aviation Facts and Figures, 1959,* 75.

37. Ibid., 73.

38. "Unlimited Opportunities for Women," 9.

39. "Designing Women," 13. Out of twenty-one hundred engineering students at the University of Washington in Seattle (right next to Boeing), only ten were women.

40. Ibid.

41. Aerospace Industries Association of America, *Aerospace Facts and Figures, 1961,* 83 [quotes Department of Labor, Bureau of Labor Statistics, "Employment and Earnings"].

42. Aerospace Industries Association of America, *Aviation Facts and Figures, 1959,* 77; U.S. Department of Commerce, *Historical Statistics of the United States: Colonial Times to 1970, Part 1,* 298.

43. Flynn, "Ladies with the Last Word," 17. Also see Ida F. Davis, "The Lady Finally Hacked It!" 16–17.

44. "Topside Aviation Club," 32.

45. "First All-Women's A & E Mechanics Course," 1.

46. Chase, *Skirts Aloft,* 79–81.

47. Nielsen, *From Sky Girl to Flight Attendant: Women and the Making of a Union,* 61; Nielsen, "From 'Sky Girl' to Flight Attendant: A Proud Union Legacy," 6.

48. Nielsen, "From 'Sky Girl' to Flight Attendant: A Proud Union Legacy," 6.

49. Wilson, "Salute to the Ninety-Nines," 22.

7. The Impact of the Women's Rights Movement: The 1960s

Epigraph: Title VII, PL 88-352 (Civil Rights Act of 1964).

1. "The Reminiscences of Ruth Nichols," 43.

2. Weitekamp, "The Right Stuff, The Wrong Sex," 155–57. For information on the Lovelace Foundation, see chapter 2, "'This Buck Rogers Nonsense': Aviation and Aerospace Medicine."

3. Cobb and Riecker, *Woman into Space,* 129–35.

4. Weitekamp, "The Right Stuff, The Wrong Sex," 211–12.

5. Ibid., 241–43, 271–75.

6. Ibid., 242–53.

7. "Follow Up on the News," 33; "The U.S. Team," 32–33.

8. Cochran, "Women in the Space Age."

9. Cochran, letter.

10. Dryden, letter, 26 April 1962; Dryden, letter, 30 July 1962.

11. Swenson et al., *This New Ocean,* 159–65; Hansen, *Spaceflight Revolution,* 40–41.

12. Webb, letter; Lyndon B. Johnson, letter; Werne, "For and About Women," 9–10; Cochran, letter.

13. Luce, "But Some People," 31.

14. The Civil Rights Act also made discrimination on the basis of race, color, religion, and national origin illegal. For further discussion see Beatty and Beatty, "Job Evaluation and Discrimination," 212–13.

15. Friedan, *The Feminine Mystique,* 367.

16. Enloe, *Does Khaki Become You?* 188–90.

17. Fitzroy, *Career Guidance for Women,* 16–17, 124, 142. This percentage represents a change, albeit small, from the beginning of the time period covered by the present study. In 1938 there were less than a dozen women in all fields of engineering, according to statistics compiled by Margaret Rossiter. (Rossiter, *Women Scientists in America: Struggles and Strategies to 1940,* 136.)

18. Fitzroy, interview.

19. Parrish, *Women in Engineering,* 5.

20. Dietrich, "The Pilot Is a Lady," 50.

21. Ibid., 105.

22. Horowitz, "Aviation Careers," 51.

23. Demarest, "Just a Little Squeeze, Please," 44.

24. Parke, "The Feminine Case," 28.

25. Horowitz, "For Men Only?" 30–33.

26. Nielsen, *From Sky Girl to Flight Attendant: Women and the Making of a Union,* 81 [quotes Kelly Rueck, "A Time of Change," *Flightlog,* June 1973, 2, 3, 6].

27. Saunders, *So You Want to be an Airline Stewardess,* 11, 164; Nielsen, *From Sky Girl to Flight Attendant: Women and the Making of a Union,* 83.

28. Nielsen, *From Sky Girl to Flight Attendant: Women and the Making of a Union,* 85–86.

29. Friedan, *The Feminine Mystique,* 372.

30. Nielsen, *From Sky Girl to Flight Attendant: Women and the Making of a Union,* 89–90.

31. Ibid., 90.

32. U.S. Department of Transportation, FAA, *U.S. Civil Airman Statistics, 1960–1969.*

33. Merriam [Smith], "I Flew Around the World Alone," 77. [This article was signed "Joan Merriam," but all her awards and honors refer to her as "Joan Merriam Smith."]

34. James Gilbert, "The Loser," 80–84; "Shades of Amelia," 20–21.

35. Pellegreno, "I Completed Amelia Earhart's Flight," 48; Ninety-Nines, *The History of the Ninety-Nines, Inc.,* 40.

36. Buegeleisen, "Confessions of a Powderpuffer," 62.

37. Tully, "Those Whirly-Girls," 1.

38. U.S. Department of Transportation, FAA, *History of the Women's Advisory Committee on Aviation,* 1967, 1–2.

39. Buegeleisen, "Skirts Flying," 32; "Traffic Pattern," 19–20; Howard, interview.

40. Holm, *Women in the Military,* 183.

41. Ibid., 177, 184.

42. Ibid., 202.

43. "VF-126's Historical First," 2.

44. "Wave Solos in T-34 Mentor," 33.

45. Morris, "Service Women Get Shot," 34; "Another Wave 'First' Cited," 37.

46. Johnson, *Black Women in the Armed Forces,* 23, 33.

47. Holm, *Women in the Military,* 205, 210, 223, 227; Pateman, interview.

48. Callander, "Why Can't a Woman Be a Military Pilot?" 13.

49. Ibid.

50. Buegeleisen, "Skirts Flying," 24.

8. Women with "The Right Stuff": The 1970s

Epigraph: U.S. Congress, House, Select Subcommittee of the Committee on Veterans' Affairs, *To Provide Recognition,* 277.

1. Aerospace Industries Association of America, "Employment of Women in Aerospace," memoranda from 22 October 1979 and 14 April 1980; International Society of Women Airline Pilots Master Seniority List, January 1989.

2. The term "light" refers to the weight and size of the end product. Manufactured goods are usually described as being either "light" or "heavy," "durable" or "nondurable." Sometimes the industry that provides such a product is also labeled "light" or "heavy." Light industries such as textiles, garments, food processing, or electronics traditionally have had higher concentrations of women in their labor force. The perceived inability of women to meet certain physical standards in conjunction with the stereotypes about women's ability to excel (such as dexterity or the ability to endure tedium and repetition) work to channel women into these particular areas of employment.

3. Bruer, "Women in Science," 3 [quotes National Research Council, *Climbing the Academic Ladder II* (Washington, D.C., National Academy of Sciences, 1983)]; Fitzroy, *Career Guidance,* 16.

4. Ruina, *Women in Science and Technology,* 13, 21.

5. Howard, "A Salute to Women in Aerospace," 2–3.

6. "First Lady of Aviation," 10.

7. Cardozo, "Athley Gamber," 22.

8. Elizabeth Simpson Smith, *Breakthrough,* 150.

9. "Air-Traffic Controllers," 64. From 1977 to 1980 the total number of controllers remained nearly constant, while the presence of women rose from 4.2 percent to 5.3 percent (U.S. Department of Transportation, *FAA Statistical Handbook.*)

10. Howard, "A Salute to Women in Aerospace," 4. In the Department of Transportation there were 14,864 engineers in 1973; 72 (or 0.5 percent) were women. For comparison, both the military and NASA employed similar numbers of women engineers. NASA had 110 (0.8 percent) of 14,193; the Air Force, 144 (0.9 percent) of 15,245; the Navy, 386 (1 percent) of 39,363; the Army, 475 (1.4 percent) of 33,025. All other women engineers employed by the federal government were outside of the aerospace field. (Fitzroy, *Career Guidance,* 131.)

11. For ten months in 1934 and 1935, Helen Richey worked as a copilot for Central Airlines. (Oakes, *United States Women in Aviation: 1930–1939,* 13.) Also see: "Women in the Airline Cockpit," 95; Elizabeth Simpson Smith, *Breakthrough,* 150.

12. Schweider, "Emily Howell," 55.

13. Kanner, "Women Airline Pilots," 33, 35.

14. Schweider, "Emily Howell," 55.

15. Kanner, "Women Airline Pilots," 37.

16. Ibid.

17. Burgen, "Winging It at 25,000 Feet," 58, 60.

18. U.S. Department of Transportation, FAA, Office of Aviation Policy, *Women in Aviation and Space,* 13.

19. U.S. Department of Transportation, FAA, Office of Aviation Policy, *Flight Attendants,* 5.

20. Nielsen, *From Sky Girl to Flight Attendant: Women and the Making of a Union,* 113–14, 131–32.

21. Ibid., 115.

22. Ibid., 120–21; Nielsen, "From 'Sky Girl' to Flight Attendant: A Proud Union Legacy," 6.

23. Holm, *Women in the Military,* 246–50; "Skirts for Twenty Percent," 16.

24. Holm, *Women in the Military,* 250, 313.

25. Collins, "From Plane Captains to Pilots," 9, 12.

26. "Young, Successful, and First," 53.

27. Shipman, "The Female Naval Aviator," 84.

28. Collins, "From Plane Captains to Pilots," 13–14.

29. Ibid., 16; Farrell, ". . . and Navy Women Today," 28.

30. Collins, "From Plane Captains to Pilots," 17–18.

31. "Army's 1st Female Pilot," 43.

32. Streeter and Hamilton, "Womanpower in Dungarees," 22.

33. Ibid.

34. Collins, "From Plane Captains to Pilots," 15. Not until 1979 were there any black women pilots in the military, when Second Lieutenant Marcella A. Hayes graduated from the Army aviation school. ("Air Force Graduates," 46.)

35. "Distaff Pilots?," 3; "Women Pilots," 47.

36. "Test Pilot School," 26.

37. "Women Soon to Train," 2.

38. Famiglietti, "Female Flier Plans Shaping Up," 4.

39. "Six Women to Enter Navy Training," 22.

40. Famiglietti, "Planes Listed for Women Pilots," 11.

41. Famiglietti, "Women Named to Undergo UPT," 30.

42. Terry Arnold, "Baptizing the New Breed," 5.

43. Farrell, ". . . and Navy Women Today," 28; "Young, Successful, and First," 53, 134.

44. Terry Arnold, "Baptizing the New Breed," 6–7.

45. Eaker, "Combat Duty for Women," 17; Jenkins, "WAVES Established Women," 1.

46. U.S. Department of Transportation, FAA, Office of Aviation Policy, *Women in Aviation and Space,* 8.

47. Stiehm, *Bring Me Men and Women,* 18–20.

48. Holm, *Women in the Military,* 309–10.

49. "Brief History on WASP Struggle," 3–4.

50. Keil, *Those Wonderful Women,* 311, 315–16.

51. Ibid., 313.

52. U.S. Department of Transportation, FAA, *Civil Airmen Statistics 1970–1980.* See also Appendix 1, "Women Pilots, 1940–1945, 1960–2000."

53. Novello and Youssef, "Psycho-Social Studies in General Aviation: II," 631, 633.

54. Phinzy, "Mary, Mary Quite Contrary," 80. Gaffaney was later awarded the Lady Hay

Drummond-Hay, Jessie R. Chamberlin Memorial Trophy by the Women's International Association of Aeronautics. (Ninety-Nines, *The History of the Ninety-Nines, Inc.*, 45.)

55. Howard, "The Whirly-Girls—Flying Ambassadors," 22.

56. Ninety-Nines, *The History of the Ninety-Nines, Inc.*, 45.

57. Gasnell, "The Last Powder Puff," 8.

58. Zirker, "Moline, Illinois, July 9," 105–6.

59. The Ninety-Nines encountered a problem in trying to serve the woman pilot who was working full time. Unable to attend meetings in the middle of the day, these women felt different from the "flying housewife," and a small split in the organization began to develop. Although flying still bonded these women together, their life experiences were quite different. The Ninety-Nines' solution, in keeping with its grassroots orientation, has been simply to assist in the formation of new chapters. Thus in metropolitan regions it is not uncommon to find two or three chapters, each with its own distinct personality, each addressing the needs of its membership.

9. Captains of Industry, Airlines, and the Military: 1980–1992

Epigraph: Christman, "Navy's First Female Test Pilot," 26.

1. Flowers, *Women in Aviation and Space,* ii, 20.

2. Woo, "TRW to Donate $1 Million for Math, Science School," B3; "Our Past, Present, and Future," 2; Oakes, *United States Women in Aviation through World War I*; Brooks-Pazmany, *United States Women in Aviation, 1919–1929*; Oakes, *United States Women in Aviation: 1930–1939*; Douglas, *United States Women in Aviation, 1940–1985.*

3. Department of Labor, Bureau of Labor Statistics, "National Employment, Hours and Earnings," Series 372 and 376.

4. *Jane's All the World's Aircraft, 1990–1991,* 21; Aerospace Industries Association of America, *Aerospace Facts and Figures, 1984–85,* 6–7.

5. Revkin, "Hundreds Wait Hours," Part 2, page 10; Wiener, "New Aid Programs for Firms, Workers," 51.

6. Adelson, "Women Still Finding Bias in Engineering," D6.

7. Fowler, "Careers—Optimism on Women Engineers," D17.

8. Holden, "Featured Women: Nelda Lee"; "Ann R. Karagozian Homepage," http://www.seas.ucla.edu/~ark/.

9. "It's Women's Week," 1; Fitzroy, interview; Adelson, "Women Still Finding Bias in Engineering," D6.

10. Adelson, "Women Still Finding Bias in Engineering," D6.

11. Ibid.

12. Henderson, "Airport Panel to Try Voluntary Affirmative Action Policy," B5.

13. There are numerous biographical accounts of NASA's women astronauts. NASA publications and websites (http://www.nasa.gov) are the best source of factual information. See the bibliography for additional recommendations.

14. *Aerospace Facts and Figures, 1983–84,* "Passenger Statistics—U.S. Air Carrier Scheduled Service, Domestic and International Operations, 1968–1982," [Source: Civil Aeronautics Board, Information Management Division, 92.]

15. Strickland, "PATCO Demands," 133; Pels, "The Pressures of PATCO."

16. The issue of "prejudice" against women on the part of the FAA is complicated. Demographics suggested discrimination, but the FAA lost a contradictory case in 1981. In 1976 Richard Sevigny, a white man and a former Navy air traffic controller, accused the FAA of hiring less qualified applicants who were women or members of minority groups. In March 1981, the Equal Employment Opportunity Commission upheld a previous ruling by a hearing officer in favor of Sevigny. The EEOC ordered the FAA to appoint Sevigny as an air traffic controller and pay him wages (plus interest and lawyer's fees) retroactive to his 1976 job application. Many felt that the case was part of the Reagan administration's efforts to mitigate or eliminate affirmative action. "Panel Backs White Air Controller in 1976 Job Discrimination Case," 46.

17. Washburn, "Professional Women Controllers," 14.

18. *Katz v. Dole,* 790 F.2d 251, 253–54 (4th Cir 1983); Smith, "Court Says Ex-Air Controller Was Victim of Sexual Harassment," C1; Mansfield, "The Rough Landing of Deborah Katz," B1. In addition to *Katz v. Dole,* other important cases concerning sexual harassment include *Faragher v. City of Boca Raton* and *Ford Motor Company v EEOC.*

19. Blume, "Mt. SAC May Be Ok'd to Certify Air Controllers," J1.

20. Holm, *Women in the Military,* rev. ed., 381–85.

21. Ibid., 384–87.

22. U.S. Defense Manpower Data Center, "U.S. Military Pilots by Gender, 1985–2001." Contact DMDC (http://www.dmdc.osd.mil) for more information.

23. Holden and Griffith, *Ladybirds,* 120–21.

24. Ibid.

25. Parisi, "Women See Gain as Pilots," Sec. 11, p. 12.

26. There are dozens of articles, books, and reports on this subject. In this period, two path-breaking works appeared: Jean Bethke Elshtain's *Women and War* and Cynthia Enloe's *Does Khaki Become You?* These books offered a broad synthesis of masculinity and femininity as defined by war and the military and would exert tremendous influence on intellectuals and scholars of military doctrine. Stiehm made this observation during her commentary at the "Women in the Military: International Perspectives" conference, sponsored by the Women's Research and Education Institute, 30 April 1992, in Washington, D.C.

27. Moore, "Open Doors Don't Yield Equality," A1; Holm, *Women in the Military,* rev. ed., 426.

28. Jehl, "2 U.S. Women Pilots Came under Heavy Panama Fire," A5.

29. Haydu, "How We Got Our Start," n.p.

30. Zamichow, "Navy Pilot Blazes Trail for Other Women Fliers to Follow," B1.

31. Ibid.

32. "Her Most Impossible Mission Yet," B6; Russell, "Womanpower in Naval Aviation: 20 Years of Progress," 19.

33. Francke, *Ground Zero: The Gender Wars in the Military,* 234.

34. Promotion for airline pilots is based on the date of hire. New pilots begin as flight engineers, move up to first officer (copilot), and then to captain (pilot). Each type of aircraft and each type of route is also "ranked," meaning that a pilot could be a captain for "lesser" aircraft on one type of route (e.g., a 737 flying New York to Boston) but only have enough

seniority to be a flight engineer or first officer on a 747 flying a transatlantic route. Women pilots in the 1980s who worked for the older carriers often commented that it would take a long time before they could attain the coveted "left seat" position of captain.

35. Rippelmeyer, interview.

36. Kurson, "Women Take Wing," 6; Podmolik, "Pioneering Black Woman Pilot Takes Career Firsts in Stride," 37.

37. Kurson, "Women Take Wing," 6.

38. Russo, *Women and Flight*, 51.

`39. Tiburzi, *Takeoff!*, 254, 260.

40. Holden and Griffith, *Ladybirds*.

41. U.S. Department of Transportation, FAA, *U.S. Civil Airmen Statistics, 1985/86*; U.S. Department of Transportation, FAA, Aviation Policy and Plans, *U.S. Civil Airmen Statistics for 2000*, "Table 7-1: Estimated Active Women Airmen Certificates Held, December 31, 1987–1996." This publication is available online. Table 7-1 can be found at: http://www.api.faa.gov/handbook96/sh7-196.pdf.

42. Thurston, "Blacks Still Rare in the Cockpit," F1.

43. Elder, "Flight Attendant to Pilot's Seat," District Weekly Section, 1; O'Hanlon, "Pilot Urges Girls, Minorities," B5.

44. "Sky High About Her Job," 1.

45. Milton, "Gayle Ranney," 96, 99, 100.

46. Meyers, letter, 11 June 1985; Meyers, letter, 23 July 1985.

47. "Meet Your Instructors," 2.

48. Yeager and Rutan, *Voyager;* Dorsey, *The Fullness of Wings*, 165–68; Nelson, "Women in Hang Gliding," 16; de Man, "She's Magnificent in Her Flying Machine," 36.

49. "Hazel Henson McKendrick Jones," 14; "Sixty and Counting—60th Anniversary Commemorative Collection, 1929–1989," http://www.ninety-nines.org/sixty.html.

50. See Morrison, *Breaking the Glass Ceiling,* and Schwartz, "Management Women." It is interesting to note that several new organizations were established at this time. In 1985, Women in Aerospace was founded for professional women in the aerospace field, including journalists and congressional staff members. In 1988 the International Aviation Women's Association (IAWA) was formed for women holding senior positions in airline, airport, finance, insurance, law, manufacturing, and government. The Technical Women's Organization (TWO) was recognized by the FAA in 1988. TWO served women in technical positions at the FAA's airway facilities.

51. "Coffee, Tea or Customer Service Managers?" D5.

52. There are numerous accounts of the Gulf War, although no substantive scholarly treatment has been published. Official government accounts include U.S. Department of Defense, *Conduct of the Persian Gulf War: Final Report to Congress,* and the unclassified version of the *Gulf War Air Power Survey* published as a USAF White Paper titled *Reaching Globally, Reaching Powerfully: The United States Air Force in the Gulf War.* It should be noted that both accounts have been criticized. For official information about women, see: U.S. General Accounting Office, *Women in the Military: Deployment in the Persian Gulf War: Report to the Secretary of Defense,* and U.S. Department of Defense, Office of the Secretary of Defense, *Utilization of American Military Women in Operations Desert Shield and Desert Storm: August 2, 1990 to April 11, 1991.* There are two doctoral dissertations on this subject: Brill,

"Women in the Gulf War Call-Up," and Jones, "United States Foreign Policy and Promotion of American Democratic Values Abroad: Women Warriors in the Arabian Peninsula." One of the best collections of fact sheets, news articles, and legislative debates is "Women in the U.S. Armed Services: The War in the Persian Gulf," compiled by Carolyn Becraft for the Women's Research and Education Institute in 1991.

53. Nickerson, "Combat Barrier Blurs," 1.

54. Moore, "Women on the Battlefield," A1.

55. Koller, letter to author, December 1, 1993.

56. Danielson, "Reserve C-9s Support the Gulf War," 89–90; Young, memorandum to author, 1993.

57. Holm, *Women in the Military*, rev. ed., 459; See also Cornum and Copeland, *She Went to War.*

58. Sullivan, "Army Pilot's Death Stuns Her New Jersey Neighbors," B1; Dart, "Taps at Arlington for Woman Pilot," A7.

59. Quindlen, "Women Warriors," Sec. 4, p. 19.

10. New World Order? 1992–2000

Epigraph: Quoted in Thurston, "Women Pilots on Course," A1.

1. For the 1992 Congressional election results, see: "New in the United States Senate," B6; and "Results of Contests for the U.S. House, District by District," B18-B19.

2. For more on 1992 as "The Year of the Woman" from a political perspective, see Cook, Wilcox, and Thomas, eds., *The Year of the Woman*; and Hill and Jordan, eds., *Race, Gender, and Power in America.*

3. Title 10 of the U.S. Code, Section 8549, stated that all female members of the Air Force, save medical and dental personnel and chaplains, may not be assigned to aircraft engaged in combat missions. Title 10, U.S. Code 6015, prohibited the assignment of Navy and Marine women to vessels or aircraft used in combat. Under certain circumstances, they were permitted a temporary duty assignment on a noncombat vessel, only if that vessel was not intended for combat. Navy and Marine women could be assigned to hospital ships and transports. The modification of these laws allowed women to fly combat aircraft and permitted their permanent assignment on combat vessels as part of an air wing or element assigned to that ship. See U.S. Congress, House, *National Defense Authorization Act for Fiscal Years 1992 and 1993.* In addition, the Women's Research and Education Institute (WREI) prepared two fact sheets that further illuminate the intricacies behind the restructuring of these laws. See Becraft, *Women in the U.S. Armed Services: The War in the Persian Gulf;* and Becraft, *Women in the Military: 1980–1990.*

4. One of the best summaries of the debate over women in combat is found in Holm, *Women in the Military*, rev. ed., 473–510. For examples directly related to Operation Desert Storm, see Julie Johnson, "The New Top Guns," 31; Kantrowitz, Clift, and Barry, "The Right to Fight," 22–23; and Hackworth, "War and the Second Sex," 24–28.

5. Holm, *Women in the Military*, rev. ed. 473–510. See also Horowitz, "The Feminist Assault on the Military," 46–49; "The Week," 10–12; and Barry and Thomas, "At War over Women," 48–49.

6. U.S. Presidential Commission, *Report to the President,* 106; Francke, *Ground Zero: The Gender Wars in the Military,* 241–60.

7. For further discussion of the discrete issues involving women in the military, such as whether sex should be a factor in involuntary assignment decisions, whether fitness, wellness, and basic training standards should be gender-neutral, and how to define both general and specific combat roles for women, see U.S. Presidential Commission, *Report to the President,* 3–14. See also Devilbiss, "To Fight, to Defend, and to Preserve the Peace: The Evolution of the U.S. Military and the Role of Women within It," in *It's Our Military, Too!* ed. Stiehm, 195–202; and De Groot, "Do Women Make Better Peacekeepers?" 9.

8. For the wording of the official recommendation along with dissenting arguments for including women in combat aviation, see U.S. Presidential Commission, *Report to the President,* 28–29 and 80–89.

9. Editorial, *Washington Post,* A22; Elaine Donnelly to Deborah G. Douglas, telephone interview, 11 March 2002. Donnelly had been active in the Reagan presidential campaign. Fearful that changing laws (such as the Equal Rights Amendment) might mean her daughters would be drafted, she was very interested in getting involved in the issue of military policy on women. For her campaign work she was rewarded with an appointment to the Defense Advisory Committee on Women in the Services in 1984–1986. After serving on the U.S. Presidential Commission, she founded The Center for Military Readiness in 1993. It is the most significant organization (and Donnelly the most significant national figure) representing the interests of individuals opposed to the expansion of women's military opportunities that might affect troop readiness. According to a "spotlight" article in *Human Events,* the organization "has been working to expose and counter [the Clinton administration's] agenda." More information about the CMR can be found in "The Center for Military Readiness," *Human Events,* 17; and on the CMR's homepage.

10. U.S. Presidential Commission, *Report to the President,* 22–29.

11. To see the policy's impact on the number of jobs open to women in the Armed Services, see the statistics compiled by the Office of Chief of Naval Operations and published in Becraft, *Women in the Military.*

12. Dempsey, "First Female Combat Pilot to Fly out of N.C. Base," 1A, 11A.

13. Lieutenant Shannon Workman became the Navy's first combat-qualified pilot in May 1993. She reported to Prowler Squadron VAQ-130 in December and in November 1994 set sail on the first integrated deployment of the USS *Eisenhower.* See Bowman, "Flying into the History Books: The Navy's First Female Combat Pilot," 1B, 3B.

14. McMichael, "Just Doing Her Job," A1.

15. "Wall of Silence," I34.

16. Elaine Donnelly argued that while Tailhook 1991 was a scandal, the Navy's attempt to cover up the Tailhook incident was the real scandal. See "The Tailhook Scandals," 59–62. Conservatives were not the only critics of the Navy's behavior. See also the following articles: Cary et al., "What's Wrong with the Navy?" 22–29, and "Inside the Tailhook Affair," 26–27; along with Bruce B. Auster's interview with Admiral Frank Kelso, Chief of Naval Operations, "It's Not Boys Will Be Boys," 28.

17. For discussion of the Navy's reaction to Tailhook, see Kammer, "Recovering from a Tailspin," 48–50; and Auster, "The Navy Sets a Different Course," 49–50.

18. Two books in particular address the Tailhook scandal: McMichael, *The Mother of All Hooks,* and Zimmerman, *Tailspin: Women at War in the Wake of Tailhook.* Unlike Zimmerman, McMichael argues that the Navy's push of unqualified women through training caused Hultgreen's accident. See McMichael, 336.

19. "Death of an Aviator," 22.

20. Spears, *Call Sign Revlon,* 274–75.

21. On February 28, 1995, the Navy released the findings (including a video) of its investigation into the cause of Hultgreen's accident. The report found that Hultgreen and her radar intercept officer, Lieutenant Matthew Klemish—he only received minor injuries when he bailed out—were both fully qualified to perform their jobs. The Navy News Service quoted Vice Admiral Robert Spane, Commander, Naval Air Force, U.S. Pacific Fleet: "All too often we forget how narrow the margin of safety is in naval carrier aviation. This pilot did her best to keep this aircraft flying under conditions that were all but impossible." The official conclusion then was "mechanical error" (see "Investigation Findings on F-14 Accident Released," available online). What has sustained the debate is the fact that the internal Mishap Investigation Report (MIR) stated that she overcorrected during landing, causing an engine to stall (see Howard and Peyser, "The Death That Won't Die," 6). In 1996 *Lohrenz v. Donnelly and the Center for Military Readiness* was filed in U.S. District Court for the District of Columbia. The case was dismissed on August 16, 2002, although an appeal has been filed with U.S. District Court of Appeals for the District of Columbia.

22. Tannen, *You Just Don't Understand,* and Gray, *Men Are From Mars, Women Are From Venus.* Other relevant works in this period include Faludi, *Backlash: The Undeclared War Against American Women,* and Bly, *Iron John: A Book About Men.*

23. Hirschman and Hirschman, *She's Just Another Navy Pilot.* When the *Ike* deployed in October 1994 in support of Operations Southern Watch and Deny Flight, it was the first time women were deployed as crew members of a U.S. Navy combatant.

24. Flinn, *Proud to Be.* Information about Flinn's resignation can be found in Sciolino, "Pilot Facing Adultery Charge Agrees to a General Discharge," A1. Not only did Kelly Flinn receive considerable negative press, but also the first female secretary of the Air Force, Sheila Widnall, found her decisions about the case under careful scrutiny. See Hohler, "Pilot's Case Has Air Force Chief in Hot Seat," A3.

25. Citation searches for Flinn in newspapers and on the Internet locate thousands of hits and at least several hundred articles. In a tense political climate, conservatives were eager to publicize the perceived "failures" of the Clinton administration. Normally, such cases do not receive extreme media attention.

26. For example, see Russo, *Women and Flight.*

27. Information about Eileen Collins can be found in Briggs, *Women in Space;* "Eileen Collins: First Woman Shuttle Commander," available online; or via NASA's "Astronaut Biography" website.

28. These numbers were compiled from data available through the U.S. Department of Labor, Bureau of Labor Statistics online database, "Current Population Survey." This website allows users to select factors like sex and occupation. The data compiled for this chapter and found in table format in Appendix 1 covers 1940 to 1945, then 1960 to 2000.

29. Quoted in Thurston, "Women Pilots on Course," A1.

30. Lori Griffith coauthored (and is featured in) two books with Henry M. Holden: *Ladybirds: The Untold Story of Women Pilots in America* (1992) and *Ladybirds II: The Continuing Story of American Women in Aviation* (1993).

31. Quoted in Branch, "Careers of Women in Aviation Taking Off," B1.

32. Ibid.

33. U.S. Department of Transportation, FAA, Aviation Policy and Plans, *U.S. Civil Airmen Statistics for 2000*, "Table 1: Estimated Active Airmen Certificates Held, December 31, 1991–2000," "Table 2: Estimated Active Women Airmen Certificates Held, December 31, 1991–2000," "Table 7-1: Estimated Active Airmen Certificates Held, December 31, 1987–1996," and "Table 7-2: Estimated Active Women Airmen Certificates Held, December 31, 1987–1996." This publication is available online. Tables 1 and 2 can be found at: http://api.hq.faa.gov/CivilAir/DocList.asp?ID=33. Tables 7-1 and 7-2 can be found at: http://www.api.faa.gov/handbook96/sh7-196.pdf.

34. "WMU Program Aims to Put More Women in Pilot's Seat," B7.

35. "Program to Boost Number of Female, Minority Pilots" [press release]; "Delta Partnership Impacts Future U.S. Flight Crews" [press release]; "Delta and WMU Announce Scholarship Recipients" [press release].

36. The original research report (Baker et al., "Characteristics of General Aviation Crashes Involving Mature Male and Female Pilots") was published in *Aviation, Space, and Environmental Medicine* in 2001. For media analysis of the study, see Payne, "Gender Gap in the Air Study," available online.

37. See Baker et al., "Characteristics of General Aviation Crashes," 447.

38. Ibid., 450. The breakdown is as follows: mishandling: m = 138, w = 116; flawed decision: m = 82, w = 27; inattention: m = 91, w = 27.

39. While this study may influence training methods and licensing standards in the future, none of the major organizations reporting information on aviation accidents—in particular, the FAA and the National Transportation Safety Board (NTSB)—include statistics on the sex of the pilot at fault. For accident statistics, see U.S. Department of Transportation, FAA, Aviation Policy and Plans, *Statistical Handbook of Aviation*, available online; and the NTSB "Accident Database & Synopses" webpage at: http://www.ntsb.gov/ntsb/query.asp.

40. Examples of flight attendants struggling to overcome discriminatory policies in this era are Gearan, "Flight Attendants Win Court Fight with United Airlines," available online; Oldham, "AMR Will Pay to Settle EEOC Suit," 2D; Seligman, "Fat Chances," 155–56; and "Employer Weight Restrictions," 77–78.

41. See the Association of Flight Attendants homepage. Many articles about conflicts between flight attendants and the airlines were printed during this decade. A few examples include: Maxon, "American, Union Reach Agreement," 1A; Schlangenstein, "Frontier Flight Attendants to Vote on Union," C2; Ho, "Flight Attendants Call for Action," available online; and "No Raise for United Flight Attendants," C11. Also of interest is Kolm's dissertation, "Women's Labor Aloft: A Cultural History of Airline Flight Attendants in the United States, 1930–1978."

42. The Office of Human Resources for the Department of Transportation reported that in 1994 beginning flight attendants earned $12,700 and senior flight attendants made up to only $40,000 annually. The wage statistics for 1994 can be found in U.S. Department of Transportation, Department of Human Resources Management, "Flight Attendants," avail-

able online. More positive statistics for the year 2000 (starting salaries of $18,090 and senior salaries of $83,630) are available in U.S. Department of Labor, Bureau of Labor Statistics, "Flight Attendants," *Occupational Outlook Handbook,* also available online.

43. For coverage of the Northwest Flight Attendant contract negotiations, see for example: Kennedy, "NWA Flight Attendants Defy Union, Help AMFA," 1D. The NWA flight attendants did not achieve an agreement until 2000, but the final contract dramatically increased pension rates and base pay, as well as provided full health insurance benefits for domestic partners.

44. U.S. Department of Transportation, FAA, Aviation Policy and Plans, *U.S. Civil Airmen Statistics for 2000,* "Table 1: Estimated Active Airmen Certificates Held December 31, 1991–2000," and "Table 2: Estimated Active Women Airmen Certificates Held, December 31, 1991–2000." This publication is available online at: http://api.hq.faa.gov/CivilAir/DocList.asp?ID=33. In 2000, the FAA reported that there were 5,047 female mechanics out of a total of 344,434 certified mechanics.

45. Hedden, "AWAM Helps Recruit Women for Aviation Maintenance Jobs," in "Women in Aerospace," S12.

46. Ibid., S12.

47. Salary figures for air traffic controllers are available in the U.S. Department of Labor, Bureau of Labor Statistics, *National Compensation Survey*; Jacobs, ed., *Handbook of U.S. Labor Statistics*; and Department of Transportation, FAA, "Careers in Aviation," available online.

48. The FAA reported these numbers to the House Aviation Subcommittee during an investigation into allegations that the FAA failed to adequately address some of their female controllers' complaints of sexual harassment. See U.S. Congress, House Subcommittee on Transportation and Infrastructure, *Allegations of Sexual Harassment at the Federal Aviation Administration.*

49. See the Professional Women Controllers homepage.

50. Dettmer, "Professional Women Controllers: Striving for Safety, Cooperation," 3–4.

51. Despite the public exposure surrounding this investigation in late 1997, women controllers apparently saw little improvement. In June 1998, a number of female controllers filed a formal lawsuit against the FAA. See Woodyard and Rosato, "Female Air Traffic Controllers File Harassment Suit," 2B.

52. The American Institute of Aeronautics and Astronautics (AIAA) does not currently incorporate any demographic information on its website. For the findings of the Congressional Commission created by Public Law 105-255, see U.S. Congress, Commission on the Advancement of Women and Minorities in Science, Engineering and Technology Development, *Land of Plenty: Diversity as America's Competitive Edge in Science, Engineering and Technology.* In 1991 the American Association of University Women (AAUW) commissioned a national poll on girls. The data and executive summary were published that year. See American Association of University Women, *Shortchanging Girls, Shortchanging America.* Analysis and policy recommendations, published one year later, launched a national discussion of gender bias in education. See American Association of University Women, and the Wellesley College Center for Research on Women, *How Schools Shortchange Girls: A Study of Major Findings on Girls and Education: The AAUW Report.*

53. American Society for Engineering Education, *Profiles of Engineering and Engineer-*

ing Technology Colleges, 2000 Edition, 9–10, 16, 18. Portions of this publication are available online.

54. National Research Council, Division of Policy and Global Affairs, Committee on Women in Science and Engineering, "Female Engineering Faculty at U.S. Institutions: A Data Profile," Washington, D.C.: National Academy Press, 1999, 11, Table 1-2: "Race/Ethnicity of Female Engineering Faculty at U.S. Institutions, by Field of Highest Degree," available online.

55. While the National Science Foundation focuses most of its energies on the sciences, in 1997 it formed POWRE (Professional Opportunities for Women in Research and Education), which offered $1 million in funding for engineering. For annual reports on POWRE program activities starting with Fiscal Year 1997, see U.S. National Science Foundation, *POWRE.* More information on both the National Academy of Engineering and the Society of Women Engineers is available online.

56. See Eiff et al., *Eliminating Sexual Bias in Aviation Occupations;* and Rodriguez, "A Descriptive Study of Females Preparing for a Nontraditional Career in Aviation."

57. Elizabeth Johnson, "College Women's Performance in a Math-Science Curriculum: A Case Study," 74–77; Kaplan, "MIT Will Increase Women on Campus," 19, 25.

58. "Christine Mann Darden—Biography," press release, NASA Langley Research Center, 9 July 1999.

59. Russo, *Women and Flight,* 71.

60. "Brig. Gen. Marcelite J. Harris: The Air Force's First Black Female General," 62, 64, 66; and Moore, "From Underrepresentation to Overrepresentation: African American Women," in *It's Our Military, Too!* ed. Stiehm, 129–33.

61. These statistics are derived from a series of tables collected by NASA and made available online under the heading "Historical Information about the NASA Workforce." In particular, data comes from tables grouped under the topic heading "Diversity Profile." The relevant tables are: "Percent of Women Executives, FY 1989 to FY 1999"; "Percent of Minority Executives, FY 1989 to FY 1999"; "Percent of Minorities by Occupation and Installation, FY 1999 and FY 1998"; "Percent of Minorities by Occupation and Installation, FY 1997 and FY 1996"; "Percent of Minorities by Occupation and Installation, FY 1995 and FY 1994"; "Percent of Women by Occupation and Installation, FY 1999 and FY 1998"; "Percent of Women by Occupation and Installation, FY 1997 and FY 1996"; and "Percent of Women by Occupation and Installation, FY 1995 and FY 1994."

62. Statistical information is derived from the Bureau of Labor Statistics (BLS) online database, "National Employment, Hours and Earning." These numbers reflect the combined "non-seasonally adjusted" figures from SIC 372 "Aircraft and Parts" and SIC 376 "Guided Missiles, Space Vehicles and Parts" categories. See "Get Detailed Statistics" at the Bureau's website for specific instructions. "Boeing's CEO Moves Three to the Office of Chairman," *Boston Globe* (12 March 2002), D8; "Ellen Smith named President, Pratt & Whitney Power Systems; Jean Colpin named Vice President, Commercial Engine Programs," available as an online article. Regarding the coverage of women in the aerospace industry, for example: Pratt & Whitney received the Department of Labor's Opportunity 2000 award for the advancement of women and minorities in the workforce, yet no announcement can be found in the company's online archives of press releases.

63. U.S. Department of Transportation, FAA, Aviation Policy and Plans, *U.S. Civil Air-*

men Statistics for 2000, "Table 1: Estimated Active Airmen Certificates Held December 31, 1991–2000"; and "Table 2: Estimated Active Women Airmen Certificates Held, December 31, 1991–2000." This publication is available online at: http://api.hq.faa.gov/CivilAir/DocList.asp?ID=33. In 2000, the FAA reported that there were 36,757 women (5.9 percent) with active pilot certificates (all categories) out of a total of 625,581.

64. For more information on Patty Wagstaff, see Wagstaff and Cooper, *Fire and Air: A Life on the Edge.*

65. Putnam, *Bowling Alone: The Collapse and Revival of American Community,* 25–26, 277–84.

66. The founders of the Women Fly project were frustrated by the dearth of educational information for and about women in aviation at the Experimental Aircraft Association's 1989 Oshkosh Fly-In. They established the Women Fly project in 1990 with the philosophy to "generate awareness for women's achievements in aviation." See the organization's homepage for more information.

67. The single best source for information on Women in Aviation, International (WAI) is the organization's homepage.

68. For a discussion of women's obligations of citizenship, see Kerber, *No Constitutional Right to Be Ladies.*

69. "What's the Matter with Rick?" 3.

70. This concept is particularly well illustrated by John Keegan in *A History of Warfare.* Keegan's subject is "warfare," not "gender," but the points he makes about "warfare tradition" are especially apropos in light of the current debate on women in combat. It should be noted that Keegan believes there is a distinct warrior class that functions in parallel with but nonetheless distinct from civil society.

71. Oldenziel, *Making Technology Masculine: Men, Women, and Modern Machines in America.*

Epilogue

1. "Remarks by Mrs. Hobby, Dir WAAC, to Students at WAAC Tng Cen.," WDBPR Press Release. 23 Jul 92, revised copy. quoted in Treadwell, *The Women's Army Corps,* p. 66. Also available online: http://www.army.mil/cmh-pg/books/wwii/Wac/ch03.htm.

Glossary of Abbreviations

AIAA	American Institute of Aeronautics and Astronautics
AAF	Army Air Forces
AAFTD	Army Air Forces Flying Training Detachment
AATC	Alabama Aviation and Technical College
AF	Air Force (United States)
AFA	Association of Flight Attendants
Air WAC	Member of the Women's Army Corp (WAC) serving with the Army Air Forces (AAF)
ALPA	Air Line Pilot's Association
ALSA	Air Line Stewardess Association
ALSSA	Air Line Stewards and Stewardesses Association
ATA	Air Transport Auxiliary (Great Britain)
ATC	Air Transport Command
ATO	Air Transport Officers
AWAM	Association for Women in Aviation Maintenance
AWS	Aircraft Warning Service
AWTAR	All-Woman Transcontinental Air Race
AWVS	American Women's Voluntary Services
BuAer	Bureau of Aeronautics, United States Navy
CAA	Civil Aeronautics Administration (Civil Aeronautics Authority prior to 1940)

CAP	Civil Air Patrol
CNN	Cable News Network
CO	Commanding Officer
CPTP	Civilian Pilot Training Program
DACOWITS	Defense Advisory Committee on Women in the Services
FAA	Federal Aviation Agency, 1958–1967; Federal Aviation Administration, 1967–present
FAI	Federation Aeronautique Internationale
ISA+21	International Society of Women Airline Pilots
IUFA	Independent Union of Flight Attendants
MCWR	Marine Corps Women's Reserve (United States)
MOS	Military Occupational Specialty
NAA	National Aeronautic Association
NASA	National Aeronautics and Space Administration
NASM	National Air and Space Museum, Smithsonian Institution
NATO	North Atlantic Treaty Organization
NIFA	National Intercollegiate Flying Association
99s	Ninety-Nines, Inc., International Women Pilots Association
NOW	National Organization for Women
NWLB	National War Labor Board
PATCO	Professional Air Traffic Controllers Organization
PWC	Professional Women Controllers
RAF	Royal Air Force
ROTC	Reserve Officer Training Corps
SPAR	Semper Paratus—Always Ready (U.S. Coast Guard motto and the name given to the women's corps of the Coast Guard during World War II)
SWE	Society of Women Engineers
TWU	Transport Workers Union
USA	United States Army
USAF	United States Air Force

USMC	United States Marine Corps
USN	United States Navy
VA	Veterans Administration
WAAC	Women's Army Auxiliary Corps
WAC	Women's Army Corps
WACOA	Women's Advisory Committee on Aviation
WAF	Women in the Air Force
WAFS	Women's Auxiliary Ferry Squadron
WAMS	Women Apprentice Mechanics
WASP	Women's Airforce Service Pilots
WAVES	Women Accepted for Voluntary Emergency Service (Initially it was "Women Appointed . . ." until it was recognized that only officers were appointed, and the term was changed to "Accepted.")
WFA	Women Flyers of America
WFTD	Women's Flying Training Detachment
WMA	Women Military Aviators
WMPA	Women Military Pilots Association
WNAA	Women's National Aeronautical Association
WREI	Women's Research and Education Institute
WTS	War Training Service

Bibliography

Alan D. Meyer

Like the first edition, this book is an introductory survey. It highlights events and individuals, but its main goal is to explore critical questions and issues surrounding American women's involvement in aviation from 1940 to the present.

The decade since this book was originally published has witnessed increased interest in this subject. Recent articles, books, documentaries, and websites enhance our understanding of women's contributions to all aspects of aviation. The bulk of these works explore the Women's Airforce Service Pilots (WASP) of WWII and the recent debates concerning women in the military, including women pilots of combat aircraft. This progress is heartening, but much remains to be done on other topics.

This bibliography serves two purposes. First, it lists all sources used in creating this book. Second, it is a guide for readers who wish to learn more about specific topics. There are several additional bibliographies that researchers should consult: Dorothy Niekamp's two comprehensive bibliographies, *Annotated Bibliography of Women in Aviation* (1980) and *Women and Flight, 1978–1989: An Annotated Bibliography* (1990), both published in Oklahoma City by the Ninety-Nines; and the WPA's bibliography (U.S. Works Progress Administration [Work Projects Administration], *Bibliography of Aeronautics*, New York, 1936–1940 [50 volumes, including one on women aviators]), which gives an overview of the period before 1940.

This bibliography includes all of the works in the first edition plus more than two hundred new citations. These are arranged under seven categories:

Books
Periodicals and Published Articles
Archival and Unpublished Materials
Master's Theses and Ph.D. Dissertations
Government Documents
Multi-Media and Web
General Reading

The last, General Reading, highlights a number of books intended for a popular audience. While it includes works written specifically for juveniles, all are good introductions to the subject and many can be found at the local library. The Multi-Media and Web category is representative rather than comprehensive, and is only a starting point. Web users should note that new websites appear (and sometimes disappear) on a regular basis, and while online resources can be very useful, not all sites exercise the same level of editorial oversight and fact-checking as published periodicals and books. Many articles and government publications used in chapters 9 and 10 are also available online, but because they were cited for specific facts these sources are listed under their traditional categories instead of under Multi-Media and Web.

Finally, the research materials (including the oral history interviews) used for the first edition are now part of the archival collections of the Archives Division of the National Air and Space Museum at the Smithsonian Institution in Washington, D.C. Researchers interested in consulting this material should contact the NASM Archives Division and request: Accession Number 1995-0062 "United States Women in Aviation, 1940–1985" and Accession Number 1990-0062 "United States Women in Aviation, 1940–1985 Photographs." Research materials acquired since 1990 are identified as being located in the author's files. It is anticipated that following publication of this edition, these records will be donated to the National Air and Space Museum.

Books

Aircraft Industries Association of America. *The Aircraft Year Book for 1946.* New York: Lanciar Publications, 1946.

American Association of University Women. *Shortchanging Girls, Shortchanging America: A Call to Action: AAUW Initiative for Educational Equity.* Washington, D.C.: AAUW, 1991.

American Association of University Women and the Wellesley College Center for Research on Women. *How Schools Shortchange Girls: A Study of Major Findings on Girls and Education: The AAUW Report.* Washington, D.C.: AAUW Educational Foundation and the National Education Association, 1992.

American Society for Engineering Education. *Profiles of Engineering and Engineering Technology Colleges, 2000 Edition.* Washington, D.C.: American Society for Engineering Education, 2000. Portions of this publication are also available online at http://www.asee.org/colleges/part1.PDF.

Anderson, Karen. *Wartime Women: Sex Roles, Family Relations, and the Status of Women.* Westport, Conn.: Greenwood Press, 1981.

Arnold, Henry ["Hap"] Harley. *Global Mission.* New York: Harper, 1949 [see especially 311, 358–59, 522].

Aviation Facts and Figures [later, *Aerospace Facts and Figures*]. Aircraft Industries Association of America compiled issues of this title for 1945, 1953, and 1955–1958, various publishers. This title did not become an annual publication until 1955. After 1958, it was compiled by Aerospace Industries Association of America, and beginning in 1961 volumes were issued as *Aerospace Facts and Figures,* various publishers.

Backus, Jean L. *Letters From Amelia: An Intimate Portrait of Amelia Earhart.* Boston: Beacon Press, 1982.

Baker, Laura Nelson. *Wanted: Women in War Industry: The Complete Guide to a War Factory Job.* Introduction by Elinore M. Herrick. New York: Dutton, 1943.

Banger, Harold. *The Transportation Industries, 1889–1946: A Study of Output, Employment, and Productivity.* New York: National Bureau of Economic Research, 1951.

Beatty, Richard W., and James R. Beatty. "Job Evaluation and Discrimination: Legal, Economic, and Measurement Perspectives on Comparable Worth and Women's Pay." In *Women in the Work Force,* ed. H. John Bernardin, 205–34. New York: Praeger, 1982.

Becraft, Carolyn. *Women in the Military: 1980–1990.* Washington, D.C.: Women's Research and Education Institute, 1990.

———. *Women in the U.S. Armed Services: The War in the Persian Gulf.* Washington, D.C.: Women's Research and Education Institute, 1991.

Bell, Elizabeth S. *Sisters of the Wind: Voices of Early Women Aviators.* Pasadena: Trilogy Books, 1994.

Bell, Susan E. "PMS and the Medicalization of Menopause: A Sociological Perspective." In *The Premenstrual Syndrome: Legal and Ethical Implications,* ed. B. Ginsburg and B.F. Carter, 151–72. New York: Plenum Press, 1987.

Bernardin, H. John, ed. *Women in the Work Force.* New York: Praeger, 1982.

Binkin, Martin. *America's Volunteer Military: Progress and Prospects.* (Studies in Defense Policy.) Washington, D.C.: The Brookings Institution, 1984.

Binkin, Martin, and Shirley J. Bach. *Women in the Military.* (Studies in Defense Policy.) Washington, D.C.: The Brookings Institution, 1977.

Bly, Robert. *Iron John: A Book About Men.* New York: Vintage Books, 1992.

Bowman, Constance. *Slacks and Callouses.* New York: Longmans, Green, 1944. [Reprinted in 1999 with a new introduction, a different spelling for the title, and under the author's married name: Reid, Constance. *Slacks and Calluses: Our Summer in a Bomber Factory.* Washington, D.C.: Smithsonian Institution Press, 1999.]

Bradley, La Verne. "Women in Uniform." In *Insignia and Decorations of the U.S. Armed Forces,* rev. ed., 159–60, 185–98. Washington, D.C.: National Geographic Society, 1944.

Bragg, Janet Harmon, and Marjorie M. Kriz. *Soaring Above Setbacks: The Autobiography of Janet Harmon Bragg, African American Aviator.* Washington, D.C.: Smithsonian Institution Press, 1996.

Brick, Kay, ed. *Powder Puff Derby: The Record, 1947–1977.* Fallbrook, Calif.: AWTAR, 1985.

Bright, Charles D. *The Jet Makers: The Aerospace Industry from 1945 to 1972.* Lawrence, Kans.: The Regents Press of Kansas, 1978.

Brooks-Pazmany, Kathleen L. *United States Women in Aviation, 1919–1929.* (Smithsonian Studies in Air and Space, 5.) Washington, D.C.: Smithsonian Institution Press, 1983.

Carl, Ann B. *A WASP among Eagles: A Woman Military Test Pilot in World War II.* Washington, D.C.: Smithsonian Institution Press, 1999.

Chapelle, Georgette L. [pseud. Dickey Meyer]. *Girls at Work in Aviation.* New York: Doubleday, Doran, 1943.

———. *Needed—Women in Aviation.* New York: Robert M. McBride, 1942.

Chase, Lucille. *Skirts Aloft.* Chicago: Louis Mariano, 1959.

Churchill, Jan. *On Wings to War: Teresa James, Aviator.* Manhattan, Kans.: Sunflower Univ. Press, 1992.

Cobb, Jerrie, and Jane Riecker. *Woman into Space: The Jerrie Cobb Story.* Englewood Cliffs, N.J.: Prentice-Hall, 1963.

Cochran, Jacqueline, and Floyd Odlum. *The Stars at Noon.* Boston: Little, Brown, 1954.

Cole, Jean Hascall. *Women Pilots of World War II.* Salt Lake City: Univ. of Utah Press, 1992.

Cook, Elizabeth Adell, Clyde Wilcox, and Sue Thomas, eds. *The Year of the Woman: Myths and Realities.* Boulder: Westview Press, 1993.

Corn, Joseph J. *The Winged Gospel: America's Romance with Aviation, 1900–1950.* New York: Oxford Univ. Press, 1983.

Cornum, Rhonda, and Peter Copeland. *She Went to War: The Rhonda Cornum Story.* Novato, Calif.: Presidio Press, 1992.

Craven, Wesley Frank, and James Lea Cate, eds. *The Army Air Forces in World War II.* (Services Around the World, 7.) Chicago: Univ. of Chicago Press, 1958. [See especially Section 5, "Women in the AAF," by Kathleen Williams Boom.]

Crouch, Tom D. *The Eagle Aloft: Two Centuries of the Balloon in America.* Washington, D.C.: Smithsonian Institution Press, 1983.

Delaney, Janice, Mary Jane Lupton, and Emily Toth. *The Curse: A Cultural History of Menstruation.* New York: Dutton, 1976.

Devilbiss, M.C. "To Fight, to Defend, and to Preserve the Peace: The Evolution of the U.S. Military and the Role of Women within It." In *It's Our Military, Too! Women and the U.S. Military,* ed. Judith Hicks Stiehm, 195–202. Philadelphia: Temple Univ. Press, 1996.

"Distinctive Indications of Women in Armed Forces." In *Insignia and Decorations of the U.S. Armed Forces,* rev. ed., 134–36. Washington, D.C.: National Geographic Society, 1944.

Dorsey, Gary. *The Fullness of Wings: The Making of a New Daedalus.* New York: Viking, 1990.

Earhart, Amelia. *The Fun of It,* 3rd printing. Chicago: Academy Chicago Publishers, 1984. [Reprint of edition published by Harcourt Brace in 1932.]

Eddleman, Jo. *Cows on the Runway,* 2nd ed. New Bern, N.C.: Owen G. Dune, 1984.

Eiff, Gary, with the assistance of Charles Rodriguez, Mary Ann Eiff, and William Milton. *Eliminating Sexual Bias in Aviation Occupations.* Carbondale: School of Technical Careers, Southern Illinois University at Carbondale, 1986

Elshtain, Jean Bethke. *Women and War.* New York: Basic Books, Inc., 1987.

Enloe, Cynthia. *Does Khaki Become You?: The Militarisation of Women's Lives.* Boston: South End Press, 1983.

Faludi, Susan. *Backlash: The Undeclared War Against American Women.* New York: Crown, 1991.

Fitzroy, Nancy D., ed. *Career Guidance for Women Entering Engineering.* N.p.: Society of Women Engineers, 1973.

Flinn, Kelly. *Proud to Be.* New York: Random House, 1997.

Francke, Linda Bird. *Ground Zero: The Gender Wars in the Military.* New York: Simon and Schuster, 1997.

Friedan, Betty. *The Feminine Mystique,* rev. ed. New York: Norton, 1963. New York: Dell Publishing, 1974.

Gilbert, Glen. *Air Traffic Control: The Uncrowded Sky.* Washington, D.C.: Smithsonian Institution Press, 1973.

Gluck, Sherna Berger. *Rosie the Riveter Revisited: Women, the War, and Social Change.* Boston: Twayne Publishers, 1987.

Gray, John. *Men Are From Mars, Women Are From Venus: A Practical Guide for Improving Communication and Getting What You Want in Your Relationships.* New York: Harper Trade, 1992.

Hacker, Sally L. "Mathematization of Engineering: Limits on Women and the Field." In *Machina Ex Dea: Feminist Perspectives on Technology,* ed. Joan Rothschild, 38–58. (Athene Series.) New York: Pergamon Press, 1984.

Hancock, Joy Bright. *Lady in the Navy; A Personal Reminiscence.* Annapolis: Naval Institute Press, 1972.

Harris, Grace McAdams. *West to the Sunrise.* Ames: Iowa State Univ. Press, 1980.

Hawkins, Regina Trice. *Hazel Jane Raines, Pioneer Lady of Flight.* Macon, Ga.: Mercer Univ. Press, 1996.

Heilbrun, Carolyn G. *Reinventing Womanhood.* New York: Norton, 1979.

Hertog, Susan. *Anne Morrow Lindbergh: Her Life.* New York: Nan A. Talese, 1999.

Hess, Fjeril. *WACs at Work: The Story of the "Three B's" of the AAF.* New York: Macmillan, 1945.

Hill, Anita, and Emma Coleman Jordan, eds. *Race, Gender, and Power in America: The Legacy of the Hill-Thomas Hearings.* New York: Oxford Univ. Press, 1995.

Hirschman, Loree Draude, and Dave Hirschman. *She's Just Another Navy Pilot: An Aviator's Sea Journal.* Annapolis: Naval Institute Press, 2000.

Hodgman, Ann, and Rudy Djabbaroff. *Skystars: The History of Women in Aviation.* New York: Atheneum, 1981.

Hodgson, Marion Stegeman. *Winning My Wings: A Woman Airforce Service Pilot in World War II.* Annapolis: Naval Institute Press, 1996.

Holm, Jeanne. *Women in the Military: An Unfinished Revolution.* Novato, Calif.: Presidio Press, 1982 [see also rev. ed., 1992].

Howard, Jean Ross. *All About Helicopters.* New York: Sports Car Press, 1969.

Hull, Gloria T., Patricia Bell Scott, and Barbara Smith. *All the Women Are White, All the Blacks Are Men, But Some of Us Are Brave: Black Women's Studies.* Old Westbury, N.Y.: Feminist Press, 1982.

Jablonski, Edward. *America in the Air War.* (The Time-Life Epic of Flight Series.) Alexandria, Va.: Time-Life Books, 1982.

Jacobs, Eva E., ed. *Handbook of U.S. Labor Statistics: Employment, Earnings, Prices, Productivity, and Other Labor Data,* 1st through 4th eds. Lanham, Md.: Bernan Press, 1997–2001.

Jane's All the World's Aircraft, 1990–1991. London: Jane's Defence Data, 1990.

Jaros, Dean. *Heroes Without Legacy: American Airwomen, 1912–1944.* Niwot, Colo.: Univ. of Colorado Press, 1993.

Jessen, Gene Nora. *The Powder Puff Derby of 1929: The First All Women's Transcontinental Air Race.* Naperville, Ill.: Sourcebooks, 2002.

Johnson, Jesse J., ed. *Black Women in the Armed Forces, 1942–1974: A Pictorial History.* Hampton, Va.: Jesse J. Johnson and the Hampton Institute, 1974.

Keegan, John. *A History of Warfare.* New York: Knopf, 1993.

Keil, Sally Van Wagenen. *Those Wonderful Women in Their Flying Machines: The Unknown Heroines of World War II.* New York: Rawson, Wade Publishers, 1979.

Kerber, Linda K. *No Constitutional Right to Be Ladies: Women and the Obligations of Citizenship.* New York: Hill and Wang, 1998.

Kerfoot, Glenn. *Propeller Annie: The Story of Helen Richey, The Real First Lady of the Airlines.* Lexington, Ky.: Kentucky Aviation History Roundtable, 1988.

Kessler, Lauren. *The Happy Bottom Riding Club: The Life and Times of Pancho Barnes.* New York: Random House, 2000.

Knapp, Sally. *New Wings for Women.* New York: Thomas Y. Crowell, 1946.

La Farge, Oliver. *The Eagle in the Egg.* Boston: Houghton Mifflin, 1949.

Lomax, Judy. *Women of the Air.* London: John Murry, 1986; New York: Dodd, Mead, 1987.

MacGregor, Morris J., Jr. *Integration of the Armed Forces, 1940–1965.* (Defense Studies Series.) Washington, D.C.: Center of Military History, United States Army, 1981.

May, Charles P. *Women in Aeronautics.* New York: Thomas Nelson and Sons, 1962.

McDaniel, William H. *The History of Beech.* Wichita, Kans.: McCormick-Armstrong, 1982.

McMichael, William H. *The Mother of All Hooks: The Story of the U.S. Navy's Tailhook Scandal.* New Brunswick, N.J.: Transaction Publishers, 1997.

Mead, Cary Hoge. *Wings Over the World: The Life of George Jackson Mead.* Wauwatosa, Wisc.: Swannet Press, 1971.

Merryman, Molly. *Clipped Wings: The Rise and Fall of the Women Airforce Service Pilots (WASPs) of World War II.* New York: New York Univ. Press, 1998.

Miller, Ronald, and David Sawers. *The Technical Development of Modern Aviation.* London: Routledge and Kegan Paul, 1968.

Moolman, Valerie. *Women Aloft* (The Time-Life Epic of Flight Series.) Alexandria, Va.: Time-Life Books, 1981.

Moore, Brenda L. "From Underrepresentation to Overrepresentation: African American Women." In *It's Our Military, Too! Women and the U.S. Military,* ed. Judith Hicks Stiehm, 115–35. Philadelphia: Temple Univ. Press, 1996.

Morrison, Ann M., et al. *Breaking the Glass Ceiling: Can Women Reach the Top of America's Largest Corporations?* Reading, Mass.: Addison-Wesley, 1992.

National Research Council, Division of Policy and Global Affairs, Committee on Women in Science and Engineering. "Female Engineering Faculty at U.S. Institutions: A Data Profile." Washington, D.C.: National Academy Press, 1999. Also available online at http://www.nap.edu/openbook/0309060923/html/R1.html.

Nichols, Ruth. *Wings for Life.* New York: J.B. Lippincott, 1957.

Niekamp, Dorothy Rinehart. *Annotated Bibliography of Women in Aviation.* Oklahoma City: Amelia Earhart Memorial Scholarship Fund, the Amelia Earhart Research Scholar Program, the Ninety-Nines, 1980.

———. *Women and Flight, 1978–1989: An Annotated Bibliography.* Oklahoma City: Ninety-Nines, 1990.

Nielsen, Georgia Panter. *From Sky Girl to Flight Attendant: Women and the Making of a Union.* Introduction by Alice H. Cook. Ithaca, N.Y.: ILR Press/New York State School of Industrial and Labor Relations, Cornell University, 1982.

Ninety-Nines. *The History of the Ninety-Nines, Inc.* Oklahoma City: Ninety-Nines, 1979.

Oakes, Claudia M. *United States Women in Aviation: 1930–1939.* (Smithsonian Studies in Air and Space, 6.) Washington, D.C.: Smithsonian Institution Press, 1985.

————. *United States Women in Aviation through World War I*. (Smithsonian Studies in Air and Space, 2.) Washington, D.C.: Smithsonian Institution Press, 1978.

Oldenziel, Ruth. *Making Technology Masculine: Men, Women, and Modern Machines in America, 1870–1945*. Amsterdam: Amsterdam Univ. Press, 1999.

Ostroff, Roberta. *Fire in the Wind: The Life of Dickey Chapelle*. New York: Ballantine Books, 1992.

Pacey, Arnold. *The Culture of Technology*, 2nd printing. Cambridge, Mass.: MIT Press, 1984.

Pateman, Yvonne C. *Women Who Dared: American Female Test Pilots, Flight-test Engineers and Astronauts, 1912–1996*. U.S.: Nohrstar Publishing, 1997.

Patterson, Elois. *Memoirs of the Late Bessie Coleman, Aviatrix Pioneer of the Negro People in Aviation*. N.p.: Elois Patterson, 1969.

Pisano, Dominick A. *To Fill the Sky with Pilots: The Civilian Pilot Training Program, 1939–1946*. Washington, D.C.: Smithsonian Institution Press, 2001 [reprint of edition published by the University of Illinois Press in 1993].

Planck, Charles E. *Women with Wings*. New York: Harper and Brothers, 1942.

Putnam, Robert D. *Bowling Alone: The Collapse and Revival of American Community*. New York: Simon and Schuster, 2000.

Rae, John B. *Climb to Greatness: The American Aircraft Industry, 1920–1960*. Cambridge, Mass.: MIT Press, 1968.

Reid, Constance [Bowman]. *Slacks and Calluses: Our Summer in a Bomber Factory*. Washington, D.C.: Smithsonian Institution Press, 1999 [originally published as Bowman, Constance. *Slacks and Callouses*. New York: Longmans, Green, 1944].

Rich, Doris L. *Amelia Earhart: A Biography*. Washington, D.C.: Smithsonian Institution Press, 1989.

————. *The Magnificent Moisants: Champions of Early Flight*. Washington: Smithsonian Institution Press, 1998.

————. *Queen Bess: Daredevil Aviator*. Washington, D.C.: Smithsonian Institution Press, 1993.

Rickman, Sarah Byrn. *The Originals: The Women's Auxiliary Ferrying Squadron of World War II*. Sarasota, Fla.: Disc-Us Books, 2001.

Risch, Erna. *A Wardrobe for the Women of the Army*. Washington, D.C.: Office of the Quartermaster General, 1945.

Rogan, Helen. *Mixed Company: Women in the Modern Army*. New York: G.P. Putnam's Sons, 1981.

Ross, Mary Steele. *American Women in Uniform*. Garden City, N.Y.: Garden City Publishing, 1943. [Reprinted in Petersen, George, compiler. *American Women at War in World War II*, vol. 1, *Clothing, Insignia and Equipment of the U.S. Army WACs and Nurses, American Red Cross, USO, AWVS, Civil Defense and Related Wartime Woman's Organizations*. Springfield, Va.: George Petersen, n.d.]

Rossiter, Margaret W. *Women Scientists in America: Before Affirmative Action, 1940–1972*. Baltimore: Johns Hopkins Univ. Press, 1995.

————. *Women Scientists in America: Struggles and Strategies to 1940*. Baltimore: Johns Hopkins Univ. Press, 1982.

Ruina, Edith. *Women in Science and Technology: A Report on the Workshop on Women in Science and Technology*. Cambridge, Mass.: MIT Press, 1973.

Russo, Carolyn. *Women and Flight: Portraits of Contemporary Women Pilots.* Washington, D.C.: National Air and Space Museum, Smithsonian Institution; Boston: Bulfinch Press, 1997.

Saunders, Keith. *So You Want to Be An Airline Stewardess.* New York: Arco, 1967.

Spears, Sally. *Call Sign Revlon: The Life and Death of Navy Fighter Pilot Kara Hultgreen.* Annapolis: Naval Institute Press, 1998.

Stiehm, Judith Hicks. *Bring Me Men and Women: Mandated Change at the U.S. Air Force Academy.* Berkeley: Univ. of California Press, 1981.

———, ed. *It's Our Military, Too! Women and the U.S. Military.* Philadelphia: Temple Univ. Press, 1996.

Tannen, Deborah. *You Just Don't Understand: Women and Men in Conversation.* New York: Morrow, William, 1990.

Thaden, Louise. *High, Wide and Frightened.* New York: Stackpole Sons, 1938.

Thorburn, Lois, and Don Thorburn. *No Tumult, No Shouting: The Story of the PBY.* New York: Henry Holt and Co., 1945.

Tiburzi, Bonnie. *Takeoff! The Story of America's First Woman Pilot for a Major Airline.* New York: Crown Publishers, 1984.

Treadwell, Mattie E. *The Women's Army Corps in the United States Army in World War II— Special Studies.* Washington, D.C.: Department of the Army, Office of the Chief of Military History, 1954.

Trippe, Betty Stettinius. *Pan Am's First Lady: The Diary of Betty Stettinius Trippe.* Edited by R.E.G. Davies. McLean, Va.: Paladwr Press, 1996.

Vecsey, George, and George C. Dade. *Getting off the Ground: The Pioneers of Aviation Speak for Themselves.* New York: Dutton, 1979.

Wagstaff, Patty, and Ann L. Cooper. *Fire and Air: A Life on the Edge.* Chicago: Chicago Review Press, 1997.

Wandersee, Winifred D. *Women's Work and Family Values, 1920–1940.* Cambridge, Mass.: Harvard Univ. Press, 1981.

Ware, Susan. *Still Missing: Amelia Earhart and the Search for Modern Feminism.* New York: Norton, 1993.

Welch, Rosanne. *Encyclopedia of Women in Aviation and Space.* Santa Barbara: ABC-CLIO, 1998.

Whyte, Edna Gardner, and Ann L. Cooper. *Rising Above It: An Autobiography.* New York: Orion Books, 1991.

Wolfe, Tom. *The Right Stuff.* New York: Bantam Books, 1980. [Originally published by Farrar, Straus and Giraux, 1979.]

Wolko, Howard S. *In the Cause of Flight: Technologists of Aeronautics and Astronautics.* (Smithsonian Studies in Air and Space, 4.) Washington, D.C.: Smithsonian Institution Press, 1981.

Women in the Allied Forces. Brussels: Public Information Advisor, International Military Staff, NATO, 1982. [Part of Aspects of NATO.]

Yeager, Chuck, and Leo Janos. *Yeager.* Toronto: Bantam Books, 1985.

Yeager, Jeana, and Dick Rutan with Phil Patton. *Voyager.* New York: Knopf, 1987.

Zimmerman, Jean. *Tailspin: Women at War in the Wake of Tailhook.* New York: Doubleday, 1995.

Periodicals and Published Articles

Adelson, Andrea. "Women Still Finding Bias in Engineering." *New York Times* (9 March 1988): D6.

Ahnstrom, Doris N. "Look . . . Women." *Skyways* 2 (September 1943): 30, 32, 66.

"Air Ambulances Fly Men to Hospitals." *Naval Aviation News* (August 1946): 20–21.

"Air Force Executive." *National Business Woman* 36 (June 1957): 12–14.

"Air Force Graduates First Black Woman Pilot." *Ebony* (January 1983): 46.

"Air-minded Miss." *Flying* 40 (May 1947): 22–23.

"Air-Traffic Controllers." *Working Woman* 4 (February 1979): 63–64.

"Alaska—Thumbs Up." *New Horizons* 13 (April 1943): 19.

"The Alleged Weaker Sex." *Independent Woman* 19 (October 1940): 316.

"America's Interesting People: 4-M, Arlene Davis." *American Magazine* 129 (February 1940): 67.

"Another Wave 'First' Cited." *Naval Aviation News* (July 1967): 37.

"Army's 1st Female Pilot Wins Helicopter Wings." *Army* 24 (July 1974): 43.

Arnold, Terry. "Baptizing the New Breed." *Airman* 21 (October 1977): 2–7.

"Around the World in 33 Days." *Air Pictorial* 28 (August 1966): 297.

Arthur, Julietta K. "Airways to Earning." *Independent Woman* 19 (February 1940): 34–35, 55–56.

———. "Now You Can Learn to Fly." *Independent Woman* 19 (October 1940): 320–21, 336.

———. "Wings for the Working Girl." *Flying* 31 (December 1942): 41–42, 136–37.

Ash, Mae, and Jerome Beatty. "I Let My Daughter Fly." *American Magazine* 130 (September 1940): 32–33, 131–33.

Auster, Bruce B. "It's Not Boys Will Be Boys. The Times Have Changed." *U.S. News and World Report* 113 (13 July 1992): 28.

———. "The Navy Sets a Different Course." *U.S. News and World Report* 114 (3 May 1993): 49–50.

"Babies, Just Babies." *Flying Time* (9 March 1940).

Bach, Richard. "An Airplane for Bette." *Flying* 84 (April 1969): 32–33.

———. "The Invisible 99s." *Flying* 77 (August 1965): 39–41.

Bacon, Marion. "Aviatrix in Blue." *Airman* 16 (January 1972): 31–32.

Bailey, Mildred C. "Army Women and a Decade of Progress." *Army* 24 (October 1974): 85–91.

Baker, Susan P., Margaret W. Lamb, Jurek G. Grabowski, George Rebok, and Guohua Li. "Characteristics of General Aviation Crashes Involving Mature Male and Female Pilots." *Aviation, Space, and Environmental Medicine* 72 (May 2001): 447–52.

Barnard, Richard C. "Jackie Cochran: Famed Pilot Says Women Shouldn't Fight." *The Times Magazine* (supplement to the *Air Force Times*) 38 (23 January 1978): 18, 20.

Barry, John, and Evan Thomas. "At War over Women." *Newsweek* 129 (12 May 1997): 48–49.

Bates, Stephen. "Lady with Wings." *Popular Aviation* (May 1940): 55–56, 88.

"Battle of the Sexes." *Time* 43 (8 May 1944): 68, 71.

Baxter, Gordon. "The Bax Seat: The T-Shirt 206." *Flying* 103 (December 1978): 112.

———. "Cochran." *Flying* 101 (September 1977): 178.

Bix, Amy Sue. "'Engineeresses' Invade Campus: Four Decades of Debate over Technical Education." *IEEE Technology and Society Magazine* (spring 2000): 20–26.

Black, Thomas H. "Pros' Nest, I've Got It." *Flying* 102 (May 1978): 22.

Blackmore, Orra Heald. "This Is How It Began." *Skylady* 2 (March–April 1946): 27.

"Blonde First." *New Horizons* 13 (November 1942): 15.

Blume, Howard. "Mt. SAC May Be Ok'd to Certify Air Controllers." *Los Angeles Times* (13 October 1991): J1.

"Board to Tap Women in July." *Air Force Times* 36 (19 January 1976): 10.

"Boeing's CEO Moves Three to the Office of Chairman." *Boston Globe* (12 March 2002): D8.

Bowater, Eric V. "Air Transport Auxiliary Service." *Flying and Popular Aviation* 31 (September 1942): 172–73, 260.

Bowman, Tom. "Flying into the History Books: The Navy's First Female Combat Pilot." *Baltimore Sun* (2 October 1994): 1B, 3B.

Boyne, Walter, J. "Blame It on Women." *AOPA Pilot* (October 1984): 98–100.

Bradbrooke, Joan. "Atta Girls! American Girls Join the ATA to Ferry Britain's Fighters." *Skyways* 2 (January 1943): 34–35, 44–45, 73.

Branch, John. "Careers of Women in Aviation Taking Off." *Colorado Springs Gazette-Telegraph* (14 March 1998): B1.

"Braniff Topnotchers." *Skylady* 2 (May–June 1946): 10–11.

Brecht, Raymond C. "Long May She WAVE." *Skyways* 2 (April 1943): 19, 70, 78–79.

Brick, Kay. "Million Dollar Race." *Flying* 64 (June 1959): 46–47, 74, 76.

"Brief History on WASP Struggle for Militarization!" *WASP Newsletter* 13 (December 1976): 3–4.

"Brig. Gen. Marcelite J. Harris: The Air Force's First Black Female General." *Ebony* 48 (December 1992): 62, 64, 66.

Brown, Betty. "Women Fliers Are Active in War Effort." *Cleveland Plain Dealer* (19 July 1943).

Brown, Gwilym S. "With a Huff and a Puff." *Sports Illustrated* 39 (30 July 1973): 50.

Brown, Laura. "Flier or No, Girl Can Fill a Vital War Role." *New York World-Telegram* (23 January 1943): 8.

Bruce, Jeannette. "Fly Away on Ladies' Day." *Sports Illustrated* 35 (19 July 1971): 44, 47.

Bruer, John T. "Women in Science: Toward Equitable Participation." *Science, Technology and Human Values* 9 (summer 1984): 3–7.

Buck, Robert N. "The Most Unforgettable Character I've Met." *Reader's Digest* 70 (August 1957): 114–18.

Buegeleisen, Sally. "Abbott's Rib." *Flying* 77 (August 1965): 35–37, 98, 100, 102, 104, 106, 108.

———. "Confessions of a Powderpuffer." *Flying* 81 (December 1967): 58–63.

———. "Skirts Flying." *Flying* 78 (February 1966): 24. Also other columns of the same title in subsequent issues of *Flying:* vol. 78 (March 1966): 32, (April 1966): 30, (May 1966): 24, 25; vol. 79 (July 1966): 28, (September 1966): 22, 138; vol. 80 (January 1967): 74, (March 1967): 101, (April 1967): 16, (June 1967): 28; vol. 81 (October 1967): 22, (November 1967): 26, (December 1967): 24.

Burdette, Liz. "Making It in the Military." *99 News* 11 (June 1984): 17–19.

Burgen, Michele. "Winging It at 25,000 Feet." *Ebony* 33 (August 1978): 58–60, 62.

Burnham, Frank. "The Defense Department's First Lady of Flight." *U.S. Lady* 2 (spring 1958): 14–15.

————. "U.S. Ladies in the Air." *U.S. Lady* 1 (April 1956): 32–37.

Callander, Bruce. "Why Can't a Woman Be a Military Pilot?" *Air Force Times* 27 (9 August 1967): 13.

————. "Women in the Military: An Ongoing Revolution." *Air Force Times* (20 December 1982): 8.

Cardozo, Yvette. "Athley Gamber: Flying High in Aircraft Sales and Service." *Working Woman* 5 (January 1980): 20–22.

Carter, Rowland. "The Ladies Join the Air Forces." *Flying* 31 (December 1942): 67, 88, 96.

Cary, Peter, Bruce B. Auster, Douglas Pasternak, Joseph L. Galloway, Mary Lord, and Mike Tharp. "Inside the Tailhook Affair." *U.S. News and World Report* 113 (13 July 1992): 26–27.

————. "What's Wrong with the Navy?" *U.S. News and World Report* 113 (13 July 1992): 22–29.

"The Center for Military Readiness." *Human Events* 50 (14 October 1994): 17.

Chirchman, Deborah. "Flying Them or Fixing Them She Loves Planes." *Chronicle-Telegram* (9 September 1984).

Christman, Timothy J. "Navy's First Female Test Pilot." *Naval Aviation News* (November–December 1985): 24–26.

Chun, Victor K. "The Origin of the WASPs." *American Aviation Historical Society Journal* 14 (winter 1969): 259–62.

"The Civilian Pilot Training Program." *Civil Aeronautics Journal* 1 (1 January 1940): 3–4.

Cochran, Jacqueline. "A Woman's Views on Aviation." *Consolidator* (December 1940): 29, 98.

"Cochran Sets Sights on 700 mph Record." *Aviation Week* 58 (18 May 1953): 18.

"Coffee, Tea or Customer Service Managers?" *Washington Post* (31 January 1986): D5.

Collins, Helen F. "Fifinella and Friends." *Naval Aviation News* (July 1977): 21–23.

————. "From Plane Captains to Pilots: Women in Naval Aviation." *Naval Aviation News* (July 1977): 8–18.

Conant, Jennet, et al. "Women in Combat?" *Newsweek* (11 November 1985): 36–38.

"Coup for Cochran." *Newsweek* 22 (19 July 1943): 40–41.

Covey, Ralph F. "'Equal Rights, Equal Risks.'" *U.S. Naval Institute Proceedings* 112 (January 1986): 16, 19.

"Crafts Shop Fills Idle Hours." *Naval Aviation News* (February 1946): 23.

Crandell, Susan. "Karen Coyle: Speaking on Our Behalf." *Flying* 104 (April 1979): 97.

Crane, Mardo. "The Women with Silver Wings." *99 News* 5 (special issue, 1978): 8–13.

Crist, Judith. "Operation Polar." *Senior Scholastic* 63 (16 September 1953): 8.

Crook, Bette. "Pilot? Who, Me?" *Flying* 62 (February 1958): 40–41, 88–89.

Cubbedge, Robert. "Vicki Frankovich: Toe-to-Toe with Carl Icahn." *Airport Press* 7 (November 1985): 19.

Dallimore, Gladys. "Ceiling Unlimited. . . ." *Skylady* 1 (March–April 1945): 2.

"Dangers to Female Pilots to Be Checked on Planes." *Air Force Times* 37 (21 March 1977): 2.

Danielson, M.W. "Reserve C-9s Support the Gulf War." *U.S. Naval Institute Proceedings* (January 1992): 89–90.

Dart, Bob. "Taps at Arlington for Woman Pilot; One of Six U.S. Females Killed in Gulf War Buried with Honors." *Atlanta Journal-Constitution* (12 March 1991): A7.

Davis, Ida F. "The Lady Finally Hacked It!" *Flying* 61 (August 1957): 36–37, 90–91.

"D.C. Women Flyer's [*sic*] Chapter Marks Second Anniversary." *Washington (D.C.) Star* (18 March 1943). WFA Collection, scrapbook, NASM Archives, Washington, D.C.

Dean, Paul. "Women in Flight, Women in Space." *Monterey (Calif.) Herald Weekend Magazine* (2 March 1986): 13–14.

"Death of an Aviator." *New York Times* (5 November 1994): 22.

Deerman, Ruth. "The Winners." *Flying* 55 (November 1955): 29, 46–47.

De Groot, Gerard J. "Do Women Make Better Peacekeepers?" *Christian Science Monitor* 91 (7 July 1999): 9.

Delfmo, Adriano G. "The Expanding Role of Airline Women." *Mainliner* (January 1972): 14–16.

de Man, Elaine. "She's Magnificent in Her Flying Machine." *Women's Sports* 4 (March 1982): 36–37.

"Demand Growing for Women in Aircraft Industry." *Civil Aeronautics Journal* 3 (15 April 1942): 102, 112.

Demarest, Pat. "Just a Little Squeeze, Please." *Flying* 77 (August 1965): 43–45.

Dempsey, Crystal. "First Female Combat Pilot to Fly out of N.C. Base." *Charlotte Observer* (17 February 1994): 1A, 11A.

De Pauw, Linda Grant. "Women in Combat: The Revolutionary War Experience." *Armed Forces and Society* 7 (winter 1981): 209–26.

"Designing Women." *Boeing Magazine* 25 (February 1955): 12–13.

Dettmer, Barbara J. "Professional Women Controllers: Striving for Safety, Cooperation." *Women in Aviation* (March–April 1991): 3–4.

Dietrich, Jan. "The Pilot Is a Lady." *Flying* 70 (February 1962): 50–51, 103–5.

"Distaff Pilots? Why Not, Laird Asks." *Air Force Times* 32 (12 April 1972): 3.

Douglas, Deborah G. "WASPS of War." *Aviation History* 2 (May 1992): 46–53.

Downey, Peggy. "Future Flyers." *Skylady* 2 (January–February 1946): 16–17.

Dunn, D.B. "Waves Serve at Intelligence Data Center." *Naval Aviation News* (July 1967): 10–11.

Eaker, Ira C. "Combat Duty for Women." *Air Force Times* 38 (10 April 1978): 17–18.

Eaves, Elsie. "Wanted: Women Engineers." *Independent Woman* 21 (May 1942): 132–33, 158–59.

Ebbert, Jean. "Should Women Serve at Sea?" *The Navy Times Magazine* (1 August 1983): 16–20.

Edgerly, Beatrice. "Weather All the Way." *Flying* 53 (October 1953): 32, 57.

Editorial. *Washington Post* (7 November 1992): A22

Ehrlich, Elizabeth. "Is the Mommy Track a Blessing—Or a Betrayal." *Business Week* (15 May 1989): 98.

———. "The Mommy Track." *Business Week* (20 March 1989): 126.

"Eileen Collins: First Woman Shuttle Commander." Available online through the Aviation Archives Women in Aviation website at http://www.womeninaviation.com/eileen.html [not to be confused with the Women in Aviation Resource Center: http://www.women-in-aviation.com].

Elder, Charles. "Flight Attendant to Pilot's Seat; Shirley Tyus Broke a Lot of Barriers to Fly." *Washington Post* (9 March 1989): J1.

"Ellen Smith named President, Pratt & Whitney Power Systems; Jean Colpin named Vice President, Commercial Engine Programs." United Technologies Corporation, Pratt & Whitney press release (22 December 2000). Available as an online article at http://www.pratt-whitney.com/unique/html/releases/1222a.html.

"Employer Weight Restrictions." *Monthly Labor Review* 121 (March 1998): 77–78.

Eskind, Amy. "A Post-Gulf Memorial Day, 1991: Arms and the Woman; In the War, Did Combat Laws Save Women From Death, or Promotion?" *Washington Post* (26 May 1991): D3.

Evans, Ernestine. "The Sky's No Limit." *Independent Woman* 21 (November 1942): 326–28, 346.

"Exchanges Start Taking Orders for Women's Greens in March." *Navy Times* (13 January 1986): 33.

"Ex-WASPs Ferrying Surplus War Training Planes." *99 Newsletter* (15 April 1945): 1.

Famiglietti, Len. "Female Flier Plans Shaping Up." *Air Force Times* 36 (10 December 1975): 4.

———. "Planes Listed for Women Pilots." *Air Force Times* 36 (12 April 1976): 11.

———. "20 Women Officers to Train as Pilots." *Air Force Times* 36 (12 January 1976): 22.

———. "Women Named to Undergo UPT." *Air Force Times* 37 (2 August 1976): 30.

Farrell, Vicki A. ". . . and Navy Women Today." *Naval Aviation News* (July 1972): 28.

Feinsilber, Pamela. "Sky Queen." *Women's Sports* 4 (April 1982): 12–16.

Feldman, Joan. "Airline Deregulation Is Working." *Air and Space* 1 (June–July 1986): 56–59.

"Feminine Fliers." *Newsweek* 18 (1 December 1941): 45.

"First All-Women's A & E Mechanics Course." *The Woman Flyer* 12 (April 1951): 1.

"First Female Navigators Will Graduate Oct. 12." *Air Force Times* 38 (26 September 1977): 3.

"First Female to Leave Bows out of Pilot School." *Air Force Times* 37 (20 June 1977): 8.

"First Lady of Aviation." *National Aeronautics* (December 1980): 8–10.

"First Lady Sonic Flier Takes Tour at Chanute." *Air Force Times* 18 (7 September 1957): 38.

"First Woman Designated Naval Aviation Dies in Plane Crash." *Naval Aviation News* (October 1982): 48.

Fisher, Susan. "Downed Chopper Pilot Remembered." *(Burlington, Iowa) Hawk Eye* (13 October 1985).

"Fleet—'Feminine Army.'" *New Horizons* 13 (June 1943): 26–27.

"Flight Nurses." *Naval Aviation News* (1 May 1945): 11–13.

Flynn, George. "Ladies with the Last Word." *The Bee-Hive* 34 (spring 1959): 16–17.

"Follow Up on the News." *New York Times* (26 June 1983): 33.

Forbes, K.J. Trefusis. "Women's Auxiliary Air Force." *Flying and Popular Aviation* 31 (September 1942): 127–29, 254.

"The Forgotten Woman." *Ryan Flying Reporter* 8 (2 December 1944): 6–7, 21.

Fort, Cornelia. "At the Twilight's Last Gleaming." *Woman's Home Companion* 70 (July 1943): 19.

"Four Stripes and Female." *Flight International* 126 (17 November 1984): 1315–1323.

"Four Top Service Women Tell It Their Way: Brig. Gen. Jeanne M. Holm, Director of Women in the Air Force." *Air Force Times Family Magazine* 32 (5 April 1972): 9, 11, 17.

Fowler, Elizabeth M. "Careers—Optimism on Women Engineers." *New York Times* (21 July 1987): D17.

Fraze, Jim. "Her Wings in Space Was Cary's Dream." *Washington Times* (9 June 1983).

Fuller, Curtis. "Betty Skelton Flies an Airshow." *Flying* 44 (February 1949): 36–37, 76–77.

"The Gals Come Through." *Ryan Flying Reporter* 5 (26 March 1943): 7, 12.

"Gals Try Their Hands at Men's Jobs." *Naval Aviation News* (February 1954): 33.

Gardner, Edward J. "Help Wanted!" *Flying* 31 (November 1942): 48, 128.

Gasnell, Mariana. "The Last Powder Puff." *Newsweek* 88 (2 August 1976): 8, 10.

Gearan, Anne. "Flight Attendants Win Court Fight with United Airlines." *Associated Press* (5

March 2001). Available online through the Associated Press Archive at http://ap.pqarchiver.com.

Gibbons, Sheila. "Reaching for Stars." *Military Lifestyle* 18 (February 1986): 14–15, 33, 69–70.

Gilbert, James. "The Loser." *Flying* 77 (August 1965): 80–84.

Giles, John A. "Women's Air Force." *Flying* 45 (July 1949): 28–29, 58.

Gillespie, Judy. "Operation Earhart." *Us* (20 June 1983): 28, 32.

Gilliam, Dorothy. "An Unfulfilled Dream." *Washington Post* (2 October 1986): C3.

"Girl Pilots: Air Force Trains Them at Avenger Field in Texas." *Life* 15 (19 July 1943): 73–81.

"The Girls Everyone Likes." *Ryan Flying Reporter* 5 (5 March 1943): 6–7, 21.

"The Glamour Corps." *Flying* 48 (May 1951): 98–99, 149.

Glines, C.V. "The One-Year Challenge." *Professional Pilot* 20 (July 1986): 12.

Gordon, Natalie. "Our Gracious Ladies." *Boston Traveler* (24 March 1943 and 17 April 1943). WFA Collection, scrapbook, NASM Archives, Washington, D.C.

Hackworth, David H. "War and the Second Sex." *Newsweek* 118 (5 August 1991): 24–28.

Haesloop, Betty. "Flight of the Honey Bees." *Flying* 74 (February 1964): 48–49, 94–95.

Hager, Alice Rogers. "Mercy Takes Wings." *Skyways* 2 (September 1943): 18–19, 58, 60–62.

———. "Women as Service Pilots: WASP's on the Wing Lug the Targets to Sharpen Shooting of Anti-Aircraft Command." *Skyways* 3 (February 1944): 28, 67–68.

Halliday, E.M. "WAACS—The Corps Completes Its First Year Working Hard at Men's Army Jobs." *Yank* 1 (4 June 1943): 6–7.

Hancock, Joy Bright. "The Waves." *Flying* 32 (February 1943): 182–83, 247, 249, 254.

Hart, Marion. "She Flew the Atlantic." *Holiday* 19 (May 1956): 76–77, 79–83, 126, 128–31.

Hays, Idell D. "The WAMS." *Flying* 32 (June 1943): 38–39, 168.

"Hazel Henson McKendrick Jones." *Ninety-Nine News* 17 (January–February 1991): 14.

Hebert, Joe. "Elizabeth Dole: Top Person in U.S. Aviation." *Airport Press* 7 (November 1985): 18.

Hedden, Carol. "AWAM Helps Recruit Women for Aviation Maintenance Jobs." In "Women in Aerospace" [advertiser-sponsored supplement]. *Aviation Week and Space Technology* 151 (16 August 1999): S12–S13.

"Hellcat Teasers." *American Magazine* 137 (March 1944): 123.

Henderson, Nell. "Airport Panel to Try Voluntary Affirmative Action Policy." *Washington Post* (11 July 1989): B5.

"Her Most Impossible Mission Yet." *Los Angeles Times* (June 26, 1990): B6.

Hixson, R.M. "Equal Rights, Equal Risks." *U.S. Naval Institute Proceedings* 111 (September 1985): 36–41.

Ho, David. "Flight Attendants Call for Action on 'Air Rage.'" *Associated Press* (6 July 2001). Available online through the Associated Press Archive at http://ap.pqarchiver.com.

Ho, Rodney. "Pilot Inspires Others to Follow Her Lead." *Atlanta Journal-Constitution* (25 January 1995): D3.

Hohler, Bob. "Pilot's Case Has Air Force Chief in Hot Seat." *Boston Globe* (22 May 1997): A3.

Holden, Henry. "Featured Women: Nelda Lee." Women in Aviation Resource Center. Np: Black Hawk Publishers, 2001. available online at http://women-in-aviation.com/cgi-bin/links/detail.cgi?ID=340.

———. "The Mercury 13." *Private Pilot* 36 (November 2001): 64–67.

"Home by Christmas." *Time* 44 (16 October 1944): 68–69.

Horowitz, David. "The Feminist Assault on the Military." *National Review* 44 (5 October 1992): 46–49.

Horowitz, Milton W. "Aviation Careers." *Flying* 79 (September 1966): 42–47, 51.

———. "For Men Only?" *Flying* 77 (August 1965): 30–33.

Howard, Jean Ross. "A Salute to Women in Aerospace." Originally published in *Aerospace: Official Publication of the Aerospace Industries Association*. Seen only as a reprint by: U.S. Department of Transportation, FAA, Office of General Aviation, Aviation Education, GA-300-113, [1975].

———. "Don't Be Afraid, Charlie!" *Rotor & Wing* (October 1967): 20–27.

———. "The Whirly-Girls—Flying Ambassadors." *National Aeronautics* (fall 1973): 20–27.

———. "The Whirly-Girls: International Flying Ambassadors." *ICAO Bulletin* (December 1975): 17–19.

———. "The Whirly-Girls—No Longer an Exclusive Club." *Vertiflight* (May–June 1984): 104–7.

Howard, Lucy, and Marc Peyser. "The Death That Won't Die." *Newsweek* 125 (27 March 1995): 6.

"IFIS and LITIS." *BuAer News* 197 (15 July 1943): 19–20.

Ingells, Douglas J. "Their Eggbeaters Aren't in the Kitchen." *Pegasus* 25 (April 1956): 7–11.

"Interesting People on the American Scene: Ladybirds—Women Fliers of America." *American Magazine* 131 (May 1941): 86–87.

"Interesting People on the American Scene: Skylarker—Helen Montgomery." *American Magazine* 130 (November 1940): 85.

"Investigation Findings on F-14 Accident Released." *Navy News Service* (28 February 1995): available online at http://www.chinfo.navy.mil/navpalib/news/navnews/nns95/nns95010.txt.

"It's up to the Women." *Ryan Flying Reporter* 4 (11 December 1942): 6–7, 11.

"It's Women's Week; Five Are Honored." *Orbiter* 26 (5 March 1986): 1, 3.

Jehl, Douglas. "2 U.S. Women Pilots Came under Heavy Panama Fire." *Los Angeles Times* (9 February 1990): A5.

Jenkins, Lynn. "WAVES Established Women as Part of Navy." *Air Scoop* 34 (26 July 1985): 1.

Johnson, Ann R. "The WASP of World War II." *Aerospace Historian* 17 (summer–fall 1970): 76–82.

Johnson, Elizabeth S. "College Women's Performance in a Math-Science Curriculum: A Case Study." *College & University* 68 (spring–summer 1993): 74–77.

Johnson, Julie. "The New Top Guns: In the Wake of Desert Storm, the Senate Clears Women Pilots for Combat." *Time* 138 (12 August 1991): 31.

Johnson, Tom. "Women in the Air." *Flying* 70 (February 1962): 104.

Jolidon, Laurence. "Females on the Front Lines: No Easy Task." *USA Today* (13 December 1990): 5A.

Kammer, Jack. "Recovering from a Tailspin." *Reason* 23 (January 1994): 48–50.

Kanner, Bernice. "Women Airline Pilots: Come Fly with Them!" *Working Woman* 3 (April 1978): 33–37, 85.

Kantrowitz, Barbara, with Eleanor Clift and John Barry. "The Right to Fight." *Newsweek* 118 (5 August 1991): 22–23.

Kaplan, Karen. "MIT Will Increase Women on Campus." *The Tech* (19 October 1991): 19, 25.

Keevers, Robert J., et al. "'Equal Rights, Equal Risks.'" *U.S. Naval Institute Proceedings* 111 (November 1985): 106, 108, 109.

Kennedy, Tony. "NWA Flight Attendants Defy Union, Help AMFA: Aiding Mechanics Flouts AFL-CIO." *Minneapolis Star Tribune* (30 March 2001): 1D.

Killion, Sandra A. "TAR Coming Up." *Flying* 60 (May 1957): 40, 76–77.

Knight, Sherry. "The Whirly Girls—Pioneering Women Helicopter Pilots." *Helicopter Update* 1 (summer 1986): 16.

Kosier, Edwin J. "Women in the Air Force . . . Yesterday, Today and Tomorrow, The Story of the WAF." *Aerospace Historian* 15 (summer 1968): 18–23.

Kraft, Virginia. "Flying in the Face of Age." *Sports Illustrated* 42 (13 January 1975): 28–31.

Kurson, Bob. "Women Take Wing." *Chicago Sun-Times* (14 March 1999): 6.

Kvaka, Margaret. "Ladies' Day at the Races." *Flying* 87 (August 1970): 62–63.

"Kwajalein Offers Cordial Welcome." *Naval Aviation News* (April 1954): 28.

"Lady Aeronaut at Toro." *Naval Aviation News* (September 1956): 32.

"Lady Flier Completes 10-Day Tour." *Air Force Times* 18 (10 August 1957): 29.

"The Lady Is Also a Wave." *Naval Aviation News* (July 1956): 24.

Larson, Mark. "Best in the Wild Blue Yonder." *Neighbors* (16 February 1984): 3, 9.

Lawson, Charlie. "Women in Aviation." *Hartford Woman* 2 (July 1983): 6–7, 12–13.

Lempke, Jeannette. "President's Column." *99s Newsletter* (15 January 1946): 1.

"Letters." *Naval Aviation News* (15 October 1943): 32.

"Letter to the Editor." *Naval Aviation News* (15 June 1945).

"Lieut. Willa Brown, Aviatrix-Maker of Pilots." *Philadelphia Tribune* (26 February 1944).

"Lineup for Cleveland Air Races." *Aviation Week* 49 (23 August 1948): 14.

Link, Marilyn. "Lady's Day in the Comanche 400." *Flying* 75 (September 1964): 49–51.

Luce, Clare Boothe. "But Some People Simply Never Get the Message." *Life* 54 (28 June 1963): 31.

"MA-9 Pilot Counters Skeptics on Sightings of Small Objects." *Aviation Week and Space Technology* 79 (1 July 1963): 31.

"Madame Mechanic." *Flying* 43 (February 1944): 58–59, 132, 136.

Mansfield, Stephanie. "The Rough Landing of Deborah Katz: A Case of Sexual Harassment at the Radar Screen." *Washington Post* (10 June 1983): B1.

"A Man-Sized Job." *Naval Aviation News* (May 1973): 23.

Masee, Kate. "Women in War Work." *Chicago Tribune* (28 April 1943).

Maxon, Terry. "American, Union Reach Agreement." *Dallas Morning News* (1 July 2001): 2D.

McDonnell, James A. "Belated Benefits for AAF's Women Pilots." *Air Force Magazine* 60 (April 1977): 76–77.

McMichael, William H. "Just Doing Her Job: The Timing Was Right When She Decided to Fly." *Newport News Daily Press* (15 March 1999): A1.

Merriam [Smith], Joan. "I Flew Around the World Alone." *Saturday Evening Post* 237 (25 July–1 August 1964): 77–83.

Merryfield, Mary. "Five Hours to Solo." *Woman's Home Companion* 72 (March 1945): 20, 60.

"Military Flight Nurses Eligible for New Award." *CAF Dispatch* 10 (March–April 1985): 31.

Milton, Barbara. "Gayle Ranney: Bush Pilot." *Working Woman* 6 (November 1981): 96–100.

"Miss Cochran Holds Most Jet Records." *Aviation Week* 58 (22 June 1953): 26.

Mohler, Stanley. "Sport Pilot Medicine." *Sport Aviation* 35 (May 1986): 61.

Monroe, Keith. "Women Artists Are Different." *Ryan Flying Reporter* 8 (11 August 1944): 4–5.

"The Month." *New Horizons* 13 (December 1942): 9–12.

"The Month—Distaff Service." *New Horizons* 13 (March 1943): 9.

Moore, Molly. "Open Doors Don't Yield Equality; 'Combat' Ban Symbolizes Limits to Female Advancement in Services." *Washington Post* (September 24, 1989): A1.

———. "Women on the Battlefield; Gulf War Role Helps Bring Shift in Attitude." *Washington Post* (16 June 1991): A1.

Morris, W.J. "Service Women Get Shot." *Naval Aviation News* (January 1960): 34.

"Mrs. Love of the WAFS." *Newsweek* 20 (21 September 1942): 46, 51.

"Mrs. Victory." *New Horizons* 13 (February 1943): 20.

Muhlfeld, Edward D. "Lady AWTAR Comes of Age." *Flying* 80 (June 1967): 98–100.

"N99NJ, Cleared as Filed, Except. . . ." *99 News* 10 (April 1983): 10–13.

"Navy Flight Nurses Care for Wounded." *Naval Aviation News* (August 1951): 19–23.

"Navy Gets Female Fliers in '75." *Air Force Times* 33 (22 November 1975): 6.

"The Navy Takes to the Air Waves." *Yank* 2 (27 August 1943): 16.

Nelson, Lynda. "Women in Hang Gliding." *Hang Gliding* 16 (February 1986): 16.

Neville, Leslie E. "Education Alone Will Reduce Absenteeism." *Aviation* 42 (March 1943): 89.

Newcomb, Harold. "Cochran's Convent." *Airman* 21 (May 1977): 16–22.

"New in the United States Senate." *New York Times* (6 November 1992): B6 (late edition).

"News Names—'Suffragette Glory.'" *New Horizons* 13 (June 1943): 19–20.

"News Names—'13 for 10.'" *New Horizons* 13 (June 1943): 20.

Nickerson, Colin. "Combat Barrier Blurs for Women on the Front Line; Crisis in the Middle East." *Boston Globe* (13 November 1990): 1.

Nielsen, Georgia Panter. "From 'Sky Girl' to Flight Attendant: A Proud Union Legacy." *Union Update* (April 1980): 4–6.

"Nineteenth Woman for UPT." *Air Force Times* 37 (23 August 1976): 2.

99 Newsletter (15 November 1945): 1.

99s Newsletter (15 April 1946): 1; (15 August 1946): 1; (15 March 1947): 3; (15 April 1948): 1, 8.

Noble, Barbara Presley. "A Feminist and the Art of Persuasion." *New York Times* (28 March 1993): Sec. 3, p. 29.

"No Raise for United Flight Attendants." *New York Times* (16 May 2001): C11.

Novello, Joseph R., and Zakhour I. Youssef. "Psycho-Social Studies in General Aviation," Part I, "Personality Profile of Male Pilots," and Part II, "Personality Profile of Female Pilots." *Aerospace Medicine* 45 (February 1974): 185–88; (June 1974): 630–33.

"Now a Civil Air Patrol." *Independent Woman* 21 (January 1942): 44.

Noyes, Blanche. "Again Women Fliers Cover Themselves with a Cloak of Glory." *99s Newsletter* (15 June 1948): 7–8.

———. "Air Marking—Reversed." *Flying and Popular Aviation* 31 (July 1942): 107.

Nye, Sandy. "Up Front with Judy." *Naval Aviation News* (July 1977): 18–20.

O'Hanlon, Ann. "Pilot Urges Girls, Minorities to Spread Their Wings." *Washington Post* (19 April 1996): B5.

Oldham, Charlene. "AMR Will Pay to Settle EEOC Suit." *Dallas Morning News* (2 August 2000): 2D.

O'Malley, Patricia. "Women with Wings." *Scholastic* 42 (19–24 April 1943): 23–24.

"Open Combat Roles to Military Women." *USA Today* (20 August 1990), Lexis-Nexis, http://web.lexis-nexis.com.

Orr, Verne. "Finishing the Firsts." *Air Force Magazine* (February 1985): 85–89.

Ostlere, Hilary. "The Plane and the Single Girl." *Flying* 84 (February 1969): 74–75.

"Our Past, Present, and Future." *The IWASM Quarterly*. 1 (1987): [2].

"Panel Backs White Air Controller in 1976 Job Discrimination Case." *New York Times* (15 March 1981): 46.

Parisi, Albert J. "Women See Gain as Pilots." *New York Times* (22 May 1983): Sec. 11, p. 12.

Parke, Robert B. "The Feminine Case." *Flying* 77 (August 1965): 28.

Payne, Paul. "Gender Gap in the Air Study: Male Pilots Crash Due to Inattention; Females, Mishandling." *Associated Press* (19 May 2001). Available online through the Associated Press Archive at http://ap.pqarchiver.com.

Pellegreno, Ann Holtgren. "I Completed Amelia Earhart's Flight." *McCall's* 95 (November 1967): 48, 50, 52, 54, 56.

Pels, Rebecca. "The Pressures of PATCO: Strikes and Stress in the 1980s." *Essays in History* 37 (1995): http://etext.virginia.edu/journals/EH/EH37/Pels.html.

Phillips, Don. "House Panel Criticizes Low Number of Black Airline Pilots." *St. Petersburg Times* (1 August 1988): 3A.

Phillips, Peggy. "Readin', Writin', and RPM's." *Flying* 53 (October 1953): 20–21, 48.

Phinzy, Coles. "Mary, Mary Quite Contrary." *Sports Illustrated* 38 (12 March 1973): 76–80, 82, 84, 89, 92.

Podmolik, Mary Ellen. "Pioneering Black Woman Pilot Takes Career Firsts in Stride." *Chicago Sun-Times* (25 June 1995): 37.

Poole, Barbara E. "Requiem for the Wasp." *Flying* 35 (December 1944): 55–56, 146, 148.

"Powderpuff Derby." *Newsweek* 54 (20 July 1959): 88.

Quindlen, Anna. "Women Warriors." *New York Times* (3 February 1991): Sec. 4, p. 19.

Radford, Arthur W. "CPT and the Navy." *Flying* 32 (January 1943): 20–21, 132.

Reiss, George R. "Ground Pilot." *Flying* 35 (July 1944): 43, 122, 126.

"Results of Contests for the U.S. House, District by District." *New York Times* (6 November 1992): B18–B19 (late ed.). .

Revkin, Andrew C. "Hundreds Wait Hours for 15-Second Shot at a Lockheed Job." *Los Angeles Times* (23 November 1986): Part 2, p. 10.

Richards, Paul. "The Flying Grandmother." *Aviation Space* (winter 1985): 35.

Robb, Izetta Winter. "Reflections on the WAVES." *Naval Aviation News* (July 1967): 6–9.

———. "The WAVES in Retrospect." *Naval Aviation News* (July 1972): 26–29.

Roberts, Margot. "You Can't Keep Them Down." *Woman's Home Companion* 71 (June 1944): 19, 91.

Roosevelt, Eleanor. "Flying Is Fun." *Collier's* 103 (22 April 1943): 15, 88–89.

Ross, Gloria D. "Sisters of the Sky." *Airman* 29 (March 1985): 16–20.

Ross, Paul. "Sweet Explosion in the Air." *Sports Illustrated* 19 (July 1963): 16–17.

"Rulers of the Air." *Time* 41 (21 June 1943): 67–68.

Russell, Sandy. "High Flying Ladies." *Naval Aviation News* (February 1981): 7–15.

———. "Womanpower in Naval Aviation: 20 Years of Progress." *Naval Aviation News* (September–October 1992): 12–19.

"Saved from Official Fate." *Time* 43 (3 April 1944): 63–64.

Schachter, Jim. "Aerospace Firms Target of GAO Discrimination Investigation." *Los Angeles Times* (28 January 1988): Part 4, p. 1.

Schafer, Susanne M. "Services under Fire for Keeping Women out of Combat Jobs." *Los Angeles Times* (22 April 1990): A2.

Schlangenstein, Mary. "Frontier Flight Attendants to Vote on Union." *Denver Post* (4 March 2000): C2.

Schwartz, Felice N. "Management Women and the New Facts of Life." *Harvard Business Review* (January/February 1989): 68.

Schweider, Sara. "Emily Howell: The Airlines' First Lady." *Flying* 93 (November 1973): 50, 55, 96.

Sciolino, Elaine. "Pilot Facing Adultery Charge Agrees to a General Discharge." *New York Times* (23 May 1997): A1 (late ed.).

Selby, Barbara. "The Fifinellas." *Flying* 33 (July 1943): 76, 78, 166–67.

Seligman, Daniel. "Fat Chances." *Fortune* 123 (20 May 1991): 155–56.

"Shades of Amelia." *Newsweek* 63 (30 March 1964): 20–21.

Shamburger, Page. "Nuts to Fashion." *Flying* 79 (October 1966): 88.

Sheffield, Dick. "They Call Her 'Jug' . . ." *Airman* 17 (August 1973): 34–36.

Shipman, Richard P. "The Female Naval Aviator: A Free Ride?" *U.S. Naval Institute Proceedings* 101 (September 1975): 84.

Shoemaker, Arlene. "Air Schooling for Milady." *Flying* 37 (November 1945): 39–42, 112.

"Sixty and Counting—60th Anniversary Commemorative Collection 1929–1989," http://www.ninety-nines.org/sixty.html.

"Six Women to Enter Navy Training." *Air Force Times* 37 (6 December 1976): 22.

"Six Women Will Get UNT." *Air Force Times* 36 (2 February 1976): 10.

"Skirts for Twenty Percent." *Armed Forces Journal* 110 (September 1972): 16–17.

"Sky High About Her Job." *USDA [News]* 40 (22 April 1981): 1–2.

"Skymarker." *The American Magazine* 146 (July 1948): 115.

Slack, Gene. "Tennessee's Airwomen." *Flying* 32 (May 1943): 46, 47, 128, 130, 132.

Smith, Anthony J. "Menstruation and Industrial Efficiency, I: Absenteeism and Activity Level." *Journal of Applied Psychology* 34 (February 1950): 1–5.

Smith, Philip. "Court Says Ex-Air Controller Was Victim of Sexual Harassment; Slurs Aimed at Women at Leesburg Center." *Washington Post* (3 June 1983): C1.

Smith, Stella. "Lynn Rippelmeyer. People Express' Lady Ace." *Airport Press* 7 (November 1985): 17.

Sobol, Louis. "New York Cavalcade—'Mid-Week Potpourri.'" *New York Journal American* (15 July 1942): 17.

"So, You Want to Be a Hostess." *Skylady* 1 (March–April 1945): 6–7.

"'The Stars at Noon' Book Review." *Air Pictorial and Air Reserve Gazette* 17 (November 1955): 356.

Stone, Andrea. "Servicewomen Again Are in Close to the Action." *USA Today* (17 August 1990); Lexis-Nexis, http://web.lexis-nexis.com.

Story, John. "Meet the First Woman OOD on a Carrier." *Campus* (1981): 24–25.

Strade, Lynn. "Behind the Stick." *Skylady* 2 (July–August 1946): 18.

Streeter, Tom, and Bill Hamilton. "Womanpower in Dungarees." *Naval Aviation News* (February 1974): 22–23.

Strickland, Louis W., Jr. "PATCO Demands." *Aviation Week and Space Technology* (21 September 1981): 133.

Stromberg, Amy. "Whirly Girls at the Mayflower All Abuzz over 30th Anniversary." *Washington Times* (29 April 1985).

Strother, Dora Dougherty. "The W.A.S.P. Training Program." *American Aviation Historical Society Journal* 19 (winter 1974): 298–306.

Stroud, Patricia. "Women in Aviation." *Flight* 66 (20 August 1954): 245–47.

Stuart, John. "The WASP." *Flying* 34 (January 1944): 73–74, 148, 163.

Sturm, Ted R. "Heiress of the Airways." *Airman* 18 (October 1974): 8–11.

Sullivan, Joseph F. "Army Pilot's Death Stuns Her New Jersey Neighbors." *New York Times* (7 March 1991): B1.

"The Tailhook Scandals." *National Review* 46 (7 March 1994): 59–62.

Tanner, Doris Brinker. *Cornelia Fort.* N.p.: self-published, 1980. [Seen only as reprints from the *Tennessee Historical Quarterly* 40 (winter 1981) and 41 (spring 1982).]

———. "We Also Served." *American History Illustrated* 20 (November 1985): 12–21, 47–49.

"TAR." *Flying* 56 (May 1955): 44, 58.

"Test of Women in Space Ends by 12 AF Nurses." *Aerospace Medicine* 44 (November 1973): 1317.

"Test Pilot School Graduates a Woman." *Air Force Times* 35 (9 July 1975): 26.

"They Do Their Bit." *Independent Woman* 21 (March 1942): 68, 89.

Thruelsen, Richard. "Flying WAF." *Saturday Evening Post* 225 (25 April 1953): 28–29, 136–38, 140, 142.

Thurston, Scott. "Blacks Still Rare in the Cockpit but Aviators Try to Show Youths a Career Option." *Atlanta Journal-Constitution* (20 August 1993): F1.

———. "Women Pilots on Course: Airline Industry Accepting Them Slowly but Steadily." *Atlanta Journal-Constitution* (13 May 1993): A1.

Tibbets, Paul W., and James P. McDonell, Jr. "With a Little Help from a Friend . . . The B-29 Stretches Its Wings." *CAF Dispatch* 10 (July–August 1985): 24–28.

"Tinker Ladies Keep 'em Flying." *Grit* (13 July 1969): 17.

"Top-Flight Scholar." *The American Magazine* 159 (March 1955): 55.

"Topside Aviation Club in Washington Unites Leading Women in Air Industry." *Air Force Times* 20 (26 December 1959): 32.

"To Serve on Vocational Advisory Committee." *Independent Woman* 25 (February 1946): 64.

"Traffic Pattern—News and Views: 'Whispering Women.'" *Flying* 77 (August 1965): 19–20.

"Transatlantic—'Lady Lindys.'" *New Horizons* 13 (August–September–October 1943): 21.

"Transatlantic—'Respect for Women.'" *New Horizons* 12 (April 1942): 14–15.

"Transatlantic—'The Women.'" *New Horizons* 12 (February 1942): 12–13.

"Transpacific—'West Coast Invasion.'" *New Horizons* 12 (March 1942): 22.

"Transport—'Traffic at War.'" *New Horizons* 12 (August 1942): 23–27.

"Transport—'Women at War.'" *New Horizons* 12 (July 1942): 26–27.

Tully, Barbara Witchell. "Those Whirly-Girls." *AOPA Pilot.* [Seen only as reprint from April 1962 issue, pages 1–3.]

"Unlimited Opportunities for Women in Aviation Engineering." *U.S. Air Services* 40 (April 1955): 9.

"Unnecessary and Undesirable?" *Time* 43 (29 May 1944): 66.

"UPT Test Program for Women to Continue; 9 More Sought." *Air Force Times* 37 (18 July 1977): 2.

"The U.S. Team Is Still Warming up the Bench." *Life* 54 (28 June 1963): 32–33.

Vetterlein, Wayne. "Newfoundland to Ireland, Non-Stop." *Flying* 54 (January 1954): 18–19, 48, 52.

"VF-126's Historical First: WAVE Joins Fighter Squadron." *Naval Aviation News* (May 1967): 2.

"WAAF." *Naval Aviation News* (15 September 1943): 18.

"The Wafs Take Over." *Ryan Flying Reporter* 6 (30 July 1943): 21.

"Wall of Silence Slows Navy in Inquiry into Convention." *New York Times* (14 June 1992): I34 (late ed.).

Washburn, Pat K. "Professional Women Controllers." *99 News* 10 (April 1983): 14.

"WASP Days Recounted." *Air Force Times* 28 (12 June 1968): 29.

Watson, Emily. "A Lady's Flying Post." *The Bee-Hive* 33 (summer 1958): 25–27.

"Wave 'Air Boots' in Reserve." *Naval Aviation News* (April 1950): 26–27.

"Wave Goes to Nato Air Agency." *Naval Aviation News* (July 1959): 24.

"Wave Gunnery Instructors." *Naval Aviation News* (15 April 1944): 8.

"Wave Power in Aviation." *Naval Aviation News* (October 1946): 13–15.

"Wave Reunion at Willow Grove." *Naval Aviation News* (February 1948): 25.

"The WAVES." *Flying* 35 (October 1944): 158–59, 322.

"WAVES." *Naval Aviation News* (1 June 1943): 13–18.

"Waves Become Flight Orderlies." *Naval Aviation News* (15 January 1945): 18.

"Waves Have Good Record in Transport Duties." *Naval Aviation News* (June 1948): 16.

"Waves Join Reserves." *Naval Aviation News* (April 1946): 23.

"Waves Observe Third Birthday." *Naval Aviation News* (1 August 1945): 13.

"Wave Solos in T-34 Mentor." *Naval Aviation News* (May 1966): 33.

"Waves Study for Jobs on Link Program." *Naval Aviation News* (1 August 1944): 14.

"Waves to Teach Gunnery." *Naval Aviation News* (1 January 1944): 7.

Webb, James. "Women Can't Fight." *Washingtonian* 15 (November 1979): 144–48, 273, 275, 278, 280, 283.

"The Week." *National Review* 44 (30 November 1992): 10–12.

Werne, Jo. "For and about Women—Jerrie Cobb." *Miami Herald* (5 April 1965): 9–10.

"What's the Matter with Rick?" *Human Events* 53 (30 May 1997): 3.

Whitaker, Betty. "Women in Ag-viation." *World of Agricultural Aviation* 9 (July 1982): 38.

White, Ruth Baker. "The Sky's Their Limit." *Independent Woman* 28 (November 1949): 326–28.

Wiener, Caryn Eve. "New Aid Programs for Firms, Workers." *Newsday* 26 (26 May 1988): 51.

Wilson, Gill Robb. "Powder for the Powder Puff." *Flying* 74 (January 1964): 20.

———. "Salute to the Ninety-Nines." *Flying* 65 (August 1959): 22.

Winchester, James H. "Leading Ladies." *Flying* 68 (January 1961): 54–55, 87–88.

"WMU Program Aims to Put More Women in Pilot's Seat." *Detroit News* (26 April 1995): B7.

Wolfe, Betty Ryan. "Women and the Nation's Security." *Flying* 50 (May 1952): 12–13, 48.

———. "Women's Air Race." *Flying* 51 (July 1952): 30–31, 50.

"Woman Fills Many Roles at Sheppard." *Air Force Times* 18 (7 September 1957): 19.

"'A Woman's Place' in VP-30." *Naval Aviation News* (May 1967): 29.

"'Women Are Welcome'—in Aviation." *Education for Victory* 1 (1 June 1943): 22–23.

"Women in Aviation Volunteer Essential Services." *Naval Aviation News* (July 1952): 6.

"Women Increasingly Becoming Airline Pilots." *Aviation Week and Space Technology* 108 (1 May 1978): 31.

"Women in Marine Corps." *Naval Aviation News* (15 February 1944): 1–3.

"Women Instructors Graduated." *Aviation* 42 (April 1943): 239, 241.

"Women in the Airline Cockpit." *Exxon Air World* 30, no. 4 (1978): 95.

"Women Learn Welding as New Plant Classes on Ryan Methods Commence." *Ryan Flying Reporter* 4 (9 October 1942): 9.

"Women Marines." *Naval Aviation News* (1 October 1943): 18.

"Women Pilots: Still No Combat." *Air Force Times* 36 (10 December 1975): 47.

"Women Soon to Train as Noncombat Pilots." *Air Force Times* 36 (26 November 1975): 2.

Woodyard, Chris, and Donna Rosato. "Female Air Traffic Controllers File Harassment Suit." *USA Today* (11 June 1998): B2.

"WRENS Play Leading Role in Air Arm, Keeping Its Planes Flying." *Naval Aviation News* (15 January 1944): 18.

"Yank Truck: Bad Landings Reduced through Quonset Plan." *Naval Aviation News* (15 November 1944): 31.

Yoffe, Emily. "Roxi's Moxie: The Pluck of a Pilot." *Washington Post Magazine* (27 January 1985): 4–5, 8, 11.

"You Can't Keep up with These Joneses." *American Magazine* 124 (December 1942): 88–89.

Young, Sharon B. "Need to Define Women's Sea Duty Clearly." *Navy Times* (13 January 1986): 32–33.

"Young, Successful, and First; Naval Aviator Lt. (j.g.) Barbara Allen." *Saturday Evening Post* 246 (October 1974): 53, 134.

Zamichow, Nora. "Navy Pilot Blazes Trail for Other Women Fliers to Follow." *Los Angeles Times* (25 June 1990): B1.

Zirker, Lorette. "Moline, Illinois, July 9." *Flying* 91 (October 1972): 105–6.

Archival and Unpublished Materials

Aerospace Industries Association of America. "Employment of Women in Aerospace." Statistical Series from 22 October 1979 to present. On file in A.I.A.'s Economic Data Service Library, Washington, D.C.

"Ann Devers Joins NBAA Staff as Manager, Educational Programs." National Business Aircraft Association press release, 22 September 1985.

Arnold, General H.H. Memorandum to General Giles on WASP after demobilization, 5 October 1944. Nancy H. Love Papers, National Air and Space Museum (NASM) Archives, Washington, D.C.

Bandel, Betty. *The WAC Program in the Army Air Forces.* Washington, D.C.: Military Personnel Division, Assistant Chief of Air Staff-1, Army Air Forces Headquarters, 1945.

Bender, Rose Marie "Bonnie" C. Telephone interview, November 1985.

Bohn, Delphine [WAFS]. Interview, Washington, D.C., 23 January 1986.

———. "Personal Data Record." Autobiographical memorandum sent to author, 5 May 1986. Copy in author's files.

Bruno, Harry. Letter to J.M. Gwinn, Jr., 25 October 1937. Nancy H. Love Papers, NASM Archives, Washington, D.C.

"Christine Mann Darden—Biography." National Aeronautics and Space Administration (NASA) press release, 9 July 1999.

Cochran, Jacqueline. "Final Report on Women Pilot Program." Memorandum to Commanding General, Army Air Forces [1945]. Women Air Force Service Pilots, organization file, NASM Library, Washington, D.C.

————. Letter to Jerrie Cobb, 23 March 1962. Jerrie Cobb file, NASA History Office, Washington, D.C.

————. "Women in the Space Age." Speech made to Zonta Club of Cleveland, Ohio, 28 November 1962. Copy in Jackie Cochran file, NASA History Office, Washington, D.C.

"DACOWITS History Update." Memorandum, 1981. DACOWITS. Copy in author's files.

Davis, Dorothy H. "A Wasp's Eye-View of Pioneer Days at Chico State University." Unpublished article, received by D.G.D., 4 May 1985.

"Delta and WMU Announce Scholarship Recipients." Western Michigan University News press release, 6 June 2001.

"Delta Partnership Impacts Future U.S. Flight Crews." Western Michigan University News press release, 18 January 2001.

Dole, Elizabeth Hanford. "Remarks Prepared for Delivery by Secretary of Transportation Elizabeth Hanford Dole, Dedication of U.S. Coast Guard Reserve Training Center, October 25, 1985, Yorktown, Virginia." U.S. Department of Transportation press release, 25 October 1985.

Donnelly, Elaine. Telephone interview, 11 March 2002. Notes in author's files.

Dougherty, Dora J. Letter to Jean Ross Howard, 6 July 1959. Membership files, Whirly-Girls, Inc., International Women Helicopter Pilots, Alexandria, Va.

Dryden, Hugh L. Letter to Jacqueline Cochran, 26 April 1962. Jackie Cochran file, NASA History Office, Washington, D.C.

————. Letter to Jacqueline Cochran, 30 July 1962. Jackie Cochran file, NASA History Office, Washington, D.C.

Erler, R.J., Jr. Letter to Ann McFarland, 8 February 1944. Copy in NASM 1995-0062, "United States Women in Aviation, 1940–1985," NASM Archives.

Felker, Phyllis Tobias "Toby" [WASP]. Interview, Washington, D.C., 28 June 1985. Tape in NASM 1995-0062.

Fitzroy, Nancy D. [heat-transfer engineer; President, American Society of Mechanical Engineers]. Interview, Washington, D.C., 15 January 1986. Notes in NASM 1995-0062.

Gardner, Elizabeth [WASP]. Interview, Washington, D.C., 18 April 1986. Notes only in NASM 1995-0062.

Gillies, Betty Huyler. Interview, Baltimore, Md., 28 July 1985. Notes only in NASM 1995-0062.

Haydu, Bernice. "How We Got Our Start." Email to D.G.D., 10 August 2002. Copy in author's files.

"History of the Defense Advisory Committee on Women in the Services." Memorandum, 1971. DACOWITS, Washington, D.C. Copy in author's files.

Hodel, Emilia. "S.F. to Have Chapter of Women Flyers." *San Francisco News* (1 December 1942). WFA Collection, scrap book, NASM Archives, Washington, D.C.

Howard, Jean Ross [Executive Director, Whirly-Girls, International Women Helicopter Pilots]. Interview, Washington, D.C., 13 November 1985. Tape in NASM 1995-0062.

———. "Whirly-Girls Newsletter" (December 1984). Records of the Whirly-Girls are deposited at the Texas Woman's University, Blagg-Huey Library, Woman's Collection. MSS664.

"Jacqueline Cochran." Oral history interview conducted by the staff of the Dwight D. Eisenhower Library, 23 April 1969, 28 February 1970, and 1–2 May 1973. Copy in Oral History Research Office, Columbia University, New York.

"Jacqueline Cochran." U.S. Air Force Academy Oral History Interview, #44, 11–12 March 1976. Copy in Oral History Research Office, Columbia University, New York.

Johnson, Lyndon B. Letter to Jerrie Cobb, 17 March 1964. Jerrie Cobb file, NASA History Office, Washington, D.C.

"Julie Clark and the T-34 Mentor." In *NAS Point Mugu 1985 Airshow Souvenir Program*, p. 37. Copy in NASM 1995-0062.

Knowles, Miles H. Memorandum on Senate investigation, to Julius H. Amberg, 29 July 1943. Henry H. Arnold Papers, Library of Congress.

Koller, Eva Rodriguez. Letter to D.G.D., 1 December 1993. Copy in author's files.

Logan, Alice. "Women Volunteers." *Brooklyn (New York) Eagle* (1 February 1943). WFA Collection, scrapbook, NASM Archives, Washington, D.C.

Love, Margaret C. [daughter of Nancy Harkness Love]. Interview, Middleberg, Va., 22 June 1985. Tape in NASM 1995-0062.

Love, Nancy H. Letter to Harry Kelliher, 14 December 1937. Nancy H. Love Papers, NASM Archives, Washington, D.C.

———. Letter to Lt. Colonel Robert Olds, 21 May 1940. Nancy H. Love Papers, NASM Archives, Washington, D.C.

May, Lt. Colonel Geraldine [WAF Director]. Letter to Yvonne C. Pateman, 28 October 1986. Copy in NASM 1995-0062.

McLeod, Mike. "And Bottom." *Pensacola News-Journal.* N.d.: 10, 20. Copy in NASM 1995-0062.

"Meet Your Instructors." *Flying with Janelle Aviation* 3 (April 1986): 2. Copy in NASM 1995-0062.

Meyer, Alan D. "A New Air Age of Women? AOPA's 'Pinch-Hitter Course,' Masculinity, and Private Aviation in Post-WWII America." Paper presented at the annual meeting of the Society for the History of Technology, San Jose, Calif., October 2001. Copy in author's files.

Meyers, Nydia. Letter to D.G.D., 11 June 1985. Copy in NASM 1995-0062.

Nottke, Robert and Joann. "The Family that Flies Together . . ." In *NAS Point Mugu 1985 Airshow Souvenir Program*, p. 35. Copy in NASM 1995-0062.

Parrish, John, B. ed. *Women in Engineering—as Told by Women Engineers,* "Report No. 1: My Career as a Heat Transfer Engineer," by Nancy D. Fitzroy. N.p., n.d. Copy in author's files.

Pateman, Lt. Colonel Yvonne G. "Pat," USAF (Ret.) [WASP]. Interview, Washington, D.C., 26 September 1985. Tape in NASM 1995-0062.

———. "The WASP." Speech at final banquet, Ninety-Nines International Convention, Baltimore, Md., 27 July 1985. Notes in NASM 1995-0062.

"Pre-Aviation Classes Open to Both Sexes." *New York Journal American* (17 January 1943). WFA Collection, scrapbook, NASM Archives, Washington, D.C.

"Program to Boost Number of Female, Minority Pilots." Western Michigan University News press release, 9 January 2001.

Rassmussen, Janet [WAC, Army Air Forces]. Interview, Washington, D.C., 29 May 1985. Tape in NASM 1995-0062.

"A Record of DACOWITS Objectives and Accomplishments." Memorandum, 1983. Margaret Merrick Schefllin/DACOWITS Collection, NASM Archives, Washington, D.C.

"The Reminiscences of Blanche Noyes." Aviation Project, vol. 1, part 3, 1960. Oral History Research Office, Columbia University, New York.

"The Reminiscences of Jacqueline Cochran." Aviation Project, vol. 6, part 3, 1961. Oral History Research Office, Columbia University, New York. [NB: The author was granted permission to quote from this interview. If you wish to cite or quote material derived from this interview, you must write the Columbia Oral History Research Office.]

"The Reminiscences of Ruth Nichols." Aviation Project, vol. 3, part 4, 1960. Oral History Research Office, Columbia University, New York.

Rippelmeyer, Lynn [Pilot, PEOPLExpress]. Interview, Washington, D.C., 17 May 1985. Tape in NASM 1995-0062.

Samuelson, Nancy B. "Equality in the Cockpit????? A Brief History of Women in Aviation." Unpublished paper for Armed Forces Staff College, Norfolk, Va., 9 May 1977.

Teague, Capt. James I. "Memorandum on Miss Jacqueline Cochran" to Col. William H. Tunner, 22 September 1942. Nancy H. Love Papers, NASM, Washington, D.C.

Tubbs, Gertrude S. Letter to Claudia M. Oakes, 3 January 1982. Copy in author's files.

Tunner, William H. "Memorandum on Information for Congressional Inquiry" to Commanding General, Air Transport Command, 10 April 1944. Nancy H. Love Papers, NASM, Washington, D.C.

U.S. Department of Defense. "Air Force Officer Fields with Limitations on Females." [1984]. [Mimeographed.] Copy in NASM 1995-0062.

———. "Major U.S. Military Installations Where Women in the Services Are Stationed." June 1979. [Mimeographed.] Copy in NASM 1995-0062.

The WASP Collection. Blagg-Huey Library, Texas Woman's University, Denton, Texas.

W.A.S.P. *Women Airforce Service Pilots, WWII, 1982 Roster.* N.p.: Womens Airforce Service Pilots, 1982. Copy in author's files. Also available in the WASP Collection at Texas Woman's University, Blagg-Huey Library.

Webb, James. Letter to Jerrie Cobb, 5 April 1963. Jerrie Cobb file, NASA History Office, Washington, D.C.

West, Verna. "World Precision Flying Championships." 25 September 1985. Unpublished history, copy in NASM 1995-0062.

"Whirly-Girls Elect 1985 International Officers." Whirly-Girls press release, 14 February 1985. Records of the Whirly-Girls are deposited at the Texas Woman's University, Blagg-Huey Library, Woman's Collection. MSS664.

Wirtschafter, Captain Irene N., USN (Ret.). Interview, Baltimore, Md., 27 July 1985. Notes only in NASM 1995-0062.

Wixson, Gertrude. "Air Ferrying Service Endorsed by WFA." *New York Journal American* (8 November 1942). WFA Collection, scrapbook, NASM Archives, Washington, D.C.

"Women and Wrenches" [pamphlet]. New York: Batten, Barton, Durshine and Osburn, 1944. Copy in NASM 1995-0062.

"Women Ferry Pilots." Background information memorandum, 1 December 1944. Nancy H. Love Papers, NASM, Washington, D.C.

Women in Aircraft Engineering. N.p.: Chance Vought Aircraft, [1943]. Copy in NASM 1995-0062.

Women's Airforce Service Pilots, Class 44-W-10, compilers. WASP *"Songbook."* N.p. Copy in author's files.

Women's Equity Action League. "Recruitment Statistics and Policies Pertaining to Women in the Active Armed Services." In *WEAL Facts,* February 1984. Copy in NASM 1995-0062. Also available from the Women's Research and Education Institute.

Young, Lucy. "Desert Shield/Storm Experiences." Autobiographical memorandum sent to D.G.D., 1992. Copy in author's files.

Master's Theses and Ph.D. Dissertations

Atkinson, Joseph Donahue, Jr. "The National Aeronautics and Space Administration Astronaut Recruiting and Selection Process, 1959–1978: An Administrative History (NASA)." D.P.A. [Doctorate of Public Affairs] diss., University of Colorado at Denver Graduate School of Public Affairs, 1983.

Brill, Esther Levine. "Women in the Gulf War Call-Up." Ph.D. diss., New York University, 1997.

Jones, Dawn E. "United States Foreign Policy and Promotion of American Democratic Values Abroad: Women Warriors in the Arabian Peninsula." Master's of Science thesis, Troy State University, 1992.

Kolm, Suzanne Lee. "Women's Labor Aloft: A Cultural History of Airline Flight Attendants in the United States, 1930–1978." Ph.D. diss., Brown University, 1995.

Luedtke, Jacqueline R. "Maximizing Participation of Women in Collegiate Aviation Education (Nontraditional Careers)." Ed.D. diss., Oklahoma State University, 1993.

McGill, Jeannie M. "Women in the Military: Implications for Social Work Practice." Master of Social Work project thesis, California State University, Sacramento, 1985.

Pennington, Reina. "Women and Military Aviation in the Second World War: A Comparative Study of the United States of America and USSR, 1941–1945." Ph.D. diss., University of South Carolina, 2000.

Rodriguez, Charles L. "A Descriptive Study of Females Preparing for a Nontraditional Career in Aviation." Master's of Science thesis, Southern Illinois University at Carbondale, 1986.

Stewart-Smith, Natalie J. "The Women Airforce Service Pilots (WASP) of World War II: Perspectives on the Work of America's First Military Women Aviators." Master's thesis, Washington State University, 1981.

Weisfeld, Ellen Kay. "The Role of the Women Airforce Service Pilots in World War II." Master of Arts thesis, Villanova University, 1982.

Weitekamp, Margaret Ann. "The Right Stuff, The Wrong Sex: The Science, Culture, and Politics of the Lovelace Woman in Space Program, 1959–1963." Ph.D. diss., Cornell University, 2001.

Government Documents

Arnold, Henry H., "Address to Last W.A.S.P. Graduate Class," 1944, Attachment to "Statement by Dora Dougherty Strother before the Committee on Veterans' Affairs, House of Representatives, 95th Congress, 1st Session, In support of HR3321, Introduced by Congresswoman Lindy Boggs, 20 September 1977," pp. 321-322, reprinted in U.S. Congress, House, Select Subcommittee of the Committee on Veterans' Affairs, "*To Provide Recognition to the Women's Air Force Service Pilots....*"

Flowers, Sandra H., and Michael H. Abbott. *Women in Aviation and Space.* [Washington, D.C.]: U.S. Department of Transportation, Federal Aviation Administration; Ozark, Ala.: Alabama Aviation and Technical College, 1995.

Hansen, James R. *Spaceflight Revolution: NASA Langley Research Center from Sputnik to Apollo.* NASA SP-4308. Washington, D.C.: National Aeronautics and Space Administration, 1995.

Howard, Jean Ross. "A Salute to Women in Aerospace." *Aerospace* (fall 1979). Reprinted by Aviation Education, Department of Transportation, FAA, Office of General Aviation, GA-300-113.

Kriz, Marjorie, and Neal Callahan. "When Women Joined the Helmet and Goggles Set." *FAA World* (January 1980). [Seen only as reprint.]

National Aeronautics and Space Administration. "Astronaut Biographies." Available online at http://www.jsc.nasa.gov/Bios/.

———. "Historical Information about the NASA Workforce." Available online at http//www.hq.nasa.gov/office/codef/workforce/one.html.

National Transportation Safety Board. "Accident Synopses." This searchable database of more than forty-six thousand aviation accidents is available online through the National Transportation Safety Board homepage at http://www.ntsb.gov/aviation/aviation.htm.

Pisano, Dominick A. "A Brief History of the Civilian Pilot Training Program, 1939–1944." In *National Air and Space Museum 1986 Research Report,* 21–41.

Strickland, Patricia. *The Putt-Putt Air Force: The Story of the Civilian Pilot Training Program and War Training Service, 1939–1944.* Washington, D.C.: U.S. Department of Transportation, Federal Aviation Administration, Aviation Education Staff, n.d.

Swenson, Loyd S., Jr., James M. Grimwood, and Charles C. Alexander. *This New Ocean: A History of Project Mercury.* NASA SP-4201. Washington, D.C.: National Aeronautics and Space Administration, NASA History Office, Office of Policy and Plans, 1998.

U.S. Civil Aeronautics Authority. *Wartime History of the Civil Aeronautics Administration.* Washington, D.C.: Government Printing Office, [1945].

U.S. Congress, Commission on the Advancement of Women and Minorities in Science, Engineering and Technology Development (CAWMSET). *Land of Plenty: Diversity as America's Competitive Edge in Science, Engineering and Technology.* Arlington: CAWMSET, National Science Foundation, 2000.

U.S. Congress, House. *National Defense Authorization Act for Fiscal Years 1992 and 1993: Conference Report to Accompany H.R.. 2100.* 102nd Congress, 1st session, 13 November 1991. Washington, D.C.: Government Printing Office, 1991.

U.S. Congress, House, Committee on the Civil Service. *Concerning Inquiries Made of Certain Proposals for the Expansion and Change in Civil Service Status of the WASPS.* H. Resolution 16, 78th Congress, 2nd session, 1944. House Report No. 1600.

U.S. Congress, House, Committee on Transportation and Infrastructure Subcommittee on Aviation. *Allegations of Sexual Harassment at the Federal Aviation Administration: Hearing Before the Subcommittee on Aviation of the Committee on Transportation and Infrastructure, House of Representatives.* 105th Congress, 1st session, 23 October 1997. Washington, D.C.: Government Printing Office, 1998.

U.S. Congress, House, Select Subcommittee of the Committee on Veterans' Affairs. *To Provide Recognition to the Women's Air Force Service Pilots for Their Service during World War II by Deeming Such Service to Have Been Active Duty in the Armed Forces of the United States for Purposes of Laws Administered by the Veterans' Administration.* 95th Congress, 1st session, 20 September 1977. Washington, D.C.: U.S. Government Printing Office, 1977.

U.S. Congress, House, Subcommittee on Transportation and Infrastructure. *Allegations of Sexual Harassment at the Federal Aviation Administration.* 105th Congress, 1st session, 23 October 1997.

U.S. Defense Manpower Data Center. "U.S. Military Pilots by Gender, 1985–2001." 2001. For information about this data, contact DMDC, http://www.dmdc.osd.mil.

U.S. Department of Commerce. *Historical Statistics of the United States: Colonial Times to 1970.* Washington, D.C.: Government Printing Office, 1975.

U.S. Department of Defense. *Conduct of the Persian Gulf War: Final Report to Congress.* Washington: D.C.: Government Printing Office, 1992.

U.S. Department of Defense, Office of the Secretary of Defense. *Utilization of American Military Women in Operations Desert Shield and Desert Storm: August 2, 1990 to April 11, 1991.* Washington, D.C.: Office of the Secretary of Defense, 1991.

U.S. Department of Labor, Bureau of Labor Statistics. "Current Population Survey." Available online through the Bureau of Labor Statistics homepage at http://www.bls.gov.

———. "Flight Attendants." In *Occupational Outlook Handbook.* Available online at http://stats.bls.gov/oco/ocos171.htm.

———. *National Compensation Survey: Occupational Wages in the United States, 1999.* Washington, D.C.: U.S. Department of Labor, Bureau of Labor Statistics, 2001.

———. "National Employment, Hours and Earnings." Available online through the Bureau of Labor Statistics homepage at http://www.bls.gov.

U.S. Department of the Air Force. *Reaching Globally, Reaching Powerfully: The United States Air Force in the Gulf War.* Washington, D.C.: Department of the Air Force, 1991.

U.S. Department of the Air Force, History Office, Air Force Flight Test Center, Edwards Air Force Base, California. *Pancho Barnes—An Original: 1901–1975.* March 1982.

U.S. Department of Transportation, Department of Human Resources Management. "Flight Attendants" [wage statistics for flight attendants, with links to other occupations]. Available online at http://dothr.ost.dot.gov/careers/flight.htm.

U.S. Department of Transportation, FAA. "Careers in Aviation." Available online at http://www.faa.gov/education/documents/salary.doc.

———. *FAA Statistical Handbook of Aviation, Calendar Year 1980.* Washington, D.C.: Government Printing Office, 1981. Recent editions, starting with 1994, are also available online. See the entry in this section for U.S. Department of Transportation, FAA, Aviation Policies and Plans, "APO Publications."

————. *History of the Women's Advisory Committee on Aviation,* 1967.

————. *U.S. Civil Airmen Statistics.* Washington, D.C.: Government Printing Office, 1960–present. Recent editions, starting with 1995, are also available online. See the entry in this section for U.S. Department of Transportation, FAA, Aviation Policies and Plans, "APO Publications."

————, Aviation Policies and Plans. "APO Publications." Available online at http://www.api.faa.gov/apo_home.asp. [This is the FAA Aviation Policies and Plans (APO) homepage: click on the "APO Publications" and "Statistical Publications" headings to access recent editions of FAA publications on aircraft and pilot statistics, including *Civil Airmen Statistics* and the *Statistical Handbook of Aviation.*]

————, Office of Aviation Policy. *Flight Attendants,* by Walter Zaharevitz. (Aviation Careers Series.) Washington, D.C.: Government Printing Office, 1980.

————, Office of Aviation Policy. *Women in Aviation and Space,* by Chris Buethe. Washington, D.C.: Government Printing Office, 1980.

————, Women's Advisory Committee on Aviation. "Biographical Information." 1 July 1967.

U.S. Federal Aviation Administration, Office of Civil Rights, External Program Division. *The Employment of Minority Group Members and Women in the Airline Industry: A Report on Government Contractors.* [Washington, D.C.]: FAA Office of Civil Rights, External Program Division, 1976 and 1977.

————, Internal Program Division. *Status of Equal Employment Opportunity Program/Federal Aviation Administration.* Washington, D.C.: FAA Office of Civil Rights, Internal Program Division, 1970–present.

U.S. General Accounting Office. *Women in the Military: Deployment in the Persian Gulf War: Report to the Secretary of Defense.* Washington, D.C.: General Accounting Office, 1993.

U.S. National Science Foundation. *POWRE: Professional Opportunities for Women in Research and Education: FY __ Program Activities Report.* Arlington: National Science Foundation: 1998– [published annually beginning with fiscal year 1997]. Also available online at http://www.nsf.gov/home/crssprgm/powre/press.htm.

————. *Women and Minorities in Science and Engineering,* January 1982.

U.S. Presidential Commission on the Assignment of Women in the Armed Forces. *Report to the President, November 15, 1992.* Washington, D.C.: Government Printing Office, 1992.

U.S. Works Progress Administration [Work Projects Administration]. *Bibliography of Aeronautics,* 50 vols. [including one on women in aviation]. New York: Institute of the Aeronautical Sciences, 1936–1940.

Multi-Media and Web

American Institute of Aeronautics and Astronautics homepage. Online at http://www.aiaa.org. When this bibliography was updated, the AIAA still did not include any demographic information on its webpage, making it impossible to determine the level of women's participation in this professional society for aerospace engineers.

"Ann R. Karagozian Homepage." Curriculum vita and biographical information, University of California–Los Angeles. Copies can be found at: http://www.seas.ucla.edu/~ark/.

Association of Flight Attendants homepage. Online at http://www.afanet.org.

Center for Military Readiness homepage. Online at http://www.cmrlink.org. The CMR represents the interests of individuals opposed to the expansion of women's military opportunities that might affect troop readiness.

Federal Aviation Administration homepage. Online at http://www.faa.gov.

Fly Girls, written, produced, and directed by Laurel Ladevich for the PBS television series *The American Experience,* 56 min., Boston: WGBH Educational Foundation, 1999, videocassette.

The Life and Times of Rosie the Riveter, produced and directed by Connie Field, 65 min., Los Angeles: Direct Cinema, 1987, videocassette.

National Academy of Engineering homepage. Online at http://www.nae.edu. Follow the links from the homepage to "Programs," then "Celebration of Women in Engineering." Also available at http://www.nae.edu/nae/cwe/cwemain.nsf.

National Aeronautics and Space Administration homepage. Online at http://www.nasa.gov. The NASA homepage provides a direct link to NASA's webpage about women in aerospace, "There's Space in My Life," and includes a search option that leads to NASA's "Women Related Links" page at http://oeop.larc.nasa.gov/fwp/wom-links.html.

Ninety-Nines, Inc., homepage. Online at www.ninety-nines.org/index.html.

Professional Women Controllers homepage. Online at http://www.pwcinc.org.

Silver Wings and Santiago Blue, produced by Katharine King and Nelson Adams, directed by Nelson Adams, 60 min., Alexandria, Va.: PBS Video, 1980, videocassette.

Smithsonian Institution, National Air and Space Museum homepage. Online at http://www.nasm.edu.

Society of Women Engineers homepage. Online at http://www.swe.org.

Women Fly homepage. Online at http://www.womenfly.com.

Women in Aviation, International homepage. Online at http://www.wiai.org.

Women-in-Aviation Resource Center homepage. Online at www.women-in-aviation.com.

General Reading

Boase, Wendy. *The Sky's the Limit: Women Pioneers in Aviation.* New York: Macmillian, 1979.

Briggs, Carole S. *Women in Space.* Minneapolis: Lerner, 1998.

Cadogan, Mary. *Women with Wings: Female Flyers in Fact and Fiction.* London: Macmillan, 1992.

Cottam, Kazimiera Janina, ed. and trans. *Women in Air War: The Eastern Front of World War II.* New York: Legas, 1997.

Haynsworth, Leslie, and David Toomey. *Amelia Earhart's Daughters: The Wild and Glorious Story of American Women Aviators from World War II to the Dawn of the Space Age.* New York: Morrow, 1998.

Holden, Henry M. *Hovering: The History of the Whirly-Girls, International Women Helicopter Pilots.* Mt. Freedom, N.J.: Black Hawk, 1994.

Holden, Henry M., and Lori Griffith. *Ladybirds: The Untold Story of Women Pilots in America.* Freedom, N.J.: Black Hawk, 1991.

———. *Ladybirds II: The Continuing Story of American Women in Aviation.* Mt. Freedom, N.J.: Black Hawk, 1993.

Myles, Bruce. *Night Witches: The Untold Story of Soviet Women in Combat.* London: Granada Publishing, Panther Books, 1983.

Nathan, Amy. *Yankee Doodle Gals: Women Pilots of World War II*. Washington, D.C.: National Geographic Society, 2001.

Noggle, Anne. *A Dance with Death: Soviet Airwomen in World War II*. College Station: Texas A&M Univ. Press, 1994.

————. *For God, Country, and the Thrill of It: Women Airforce Service Pilots in World War II*. College Station: Texas A&M Univ. Press, 1990.

Roberts, Marjorie H. *Wingtip to Wingtip: 8 WASPs, Women's Airforce Service Pilots of World War II*. Arlington Heights, Ill.: Aviatrix, 2000.

Simbeck, Rob. *Daughter of the Air: The Brief Soaring Life of Cornelia Fort*. New York: Atlantic Monthly Press, 1999.

Smith, Elizabeth Simpson. *Breakthrough: Women in Aviation*. New York: Walker, 1981.

Van Meter, Vicki, and Dan Gutman. *Taking Flight: My Story*. New York: Viking, 1995.

Verges, Marianne. *On Silver Wings: The Women Airforce Service Pilots of World War II, 1942–1944*. New York: Ballantine Books, 1991.

Williams, Vera S. *WASPs: Women Airforce Service Pilots of World War II*. Osceola, Wisc.: Motorbooks International, 1994.

Index

Note: Page references for photographs are printed in italics.